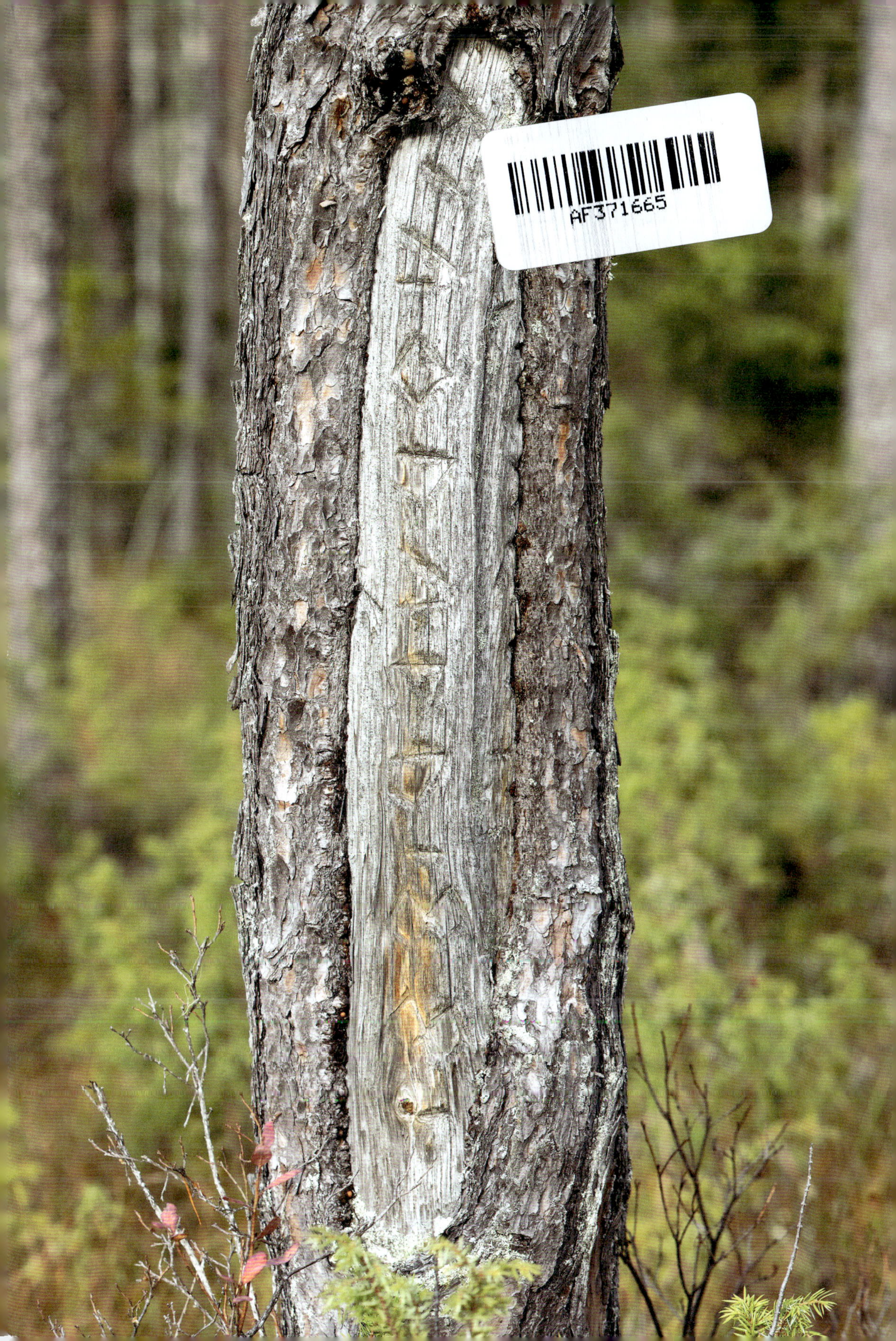
AF371665

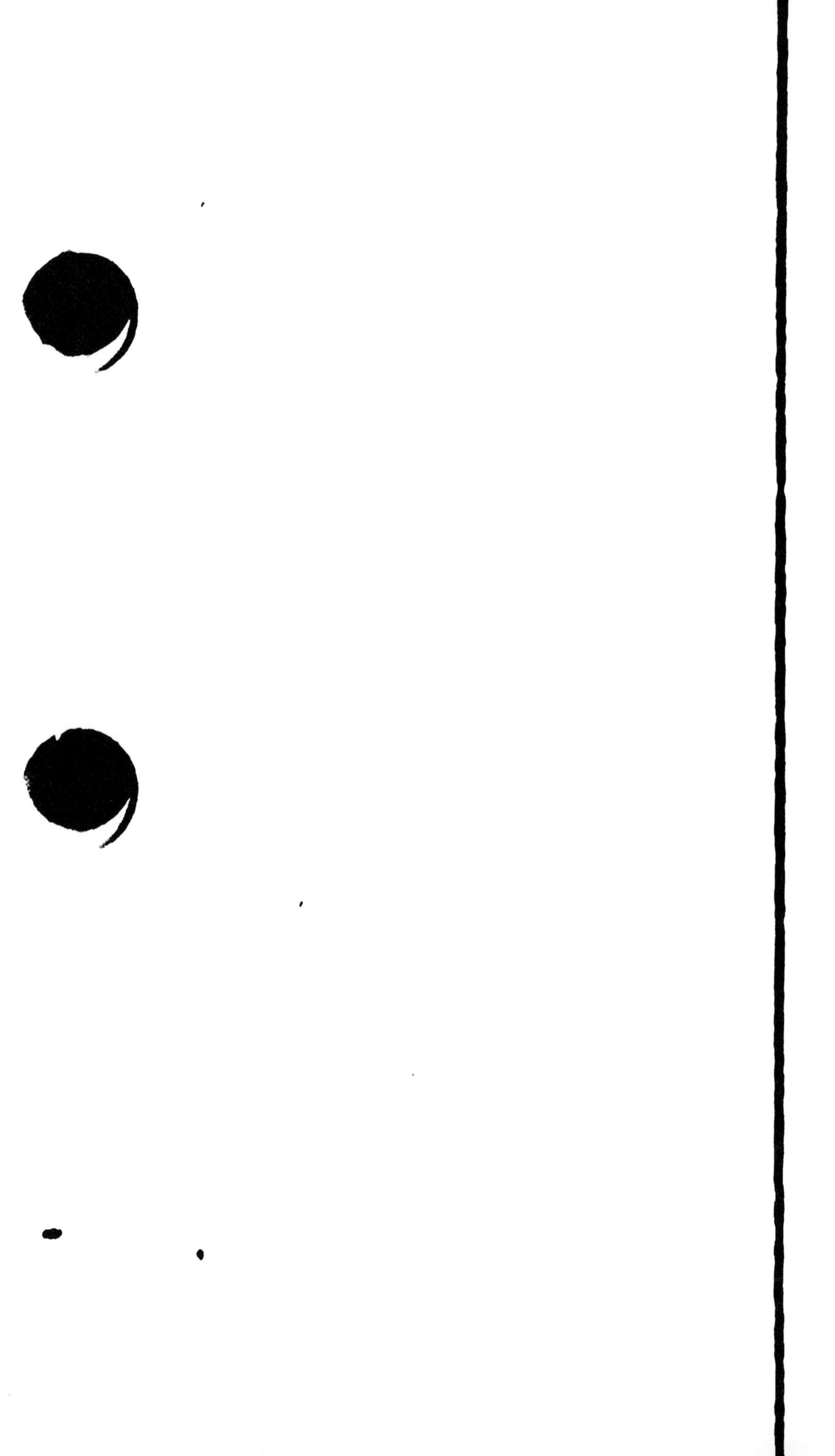

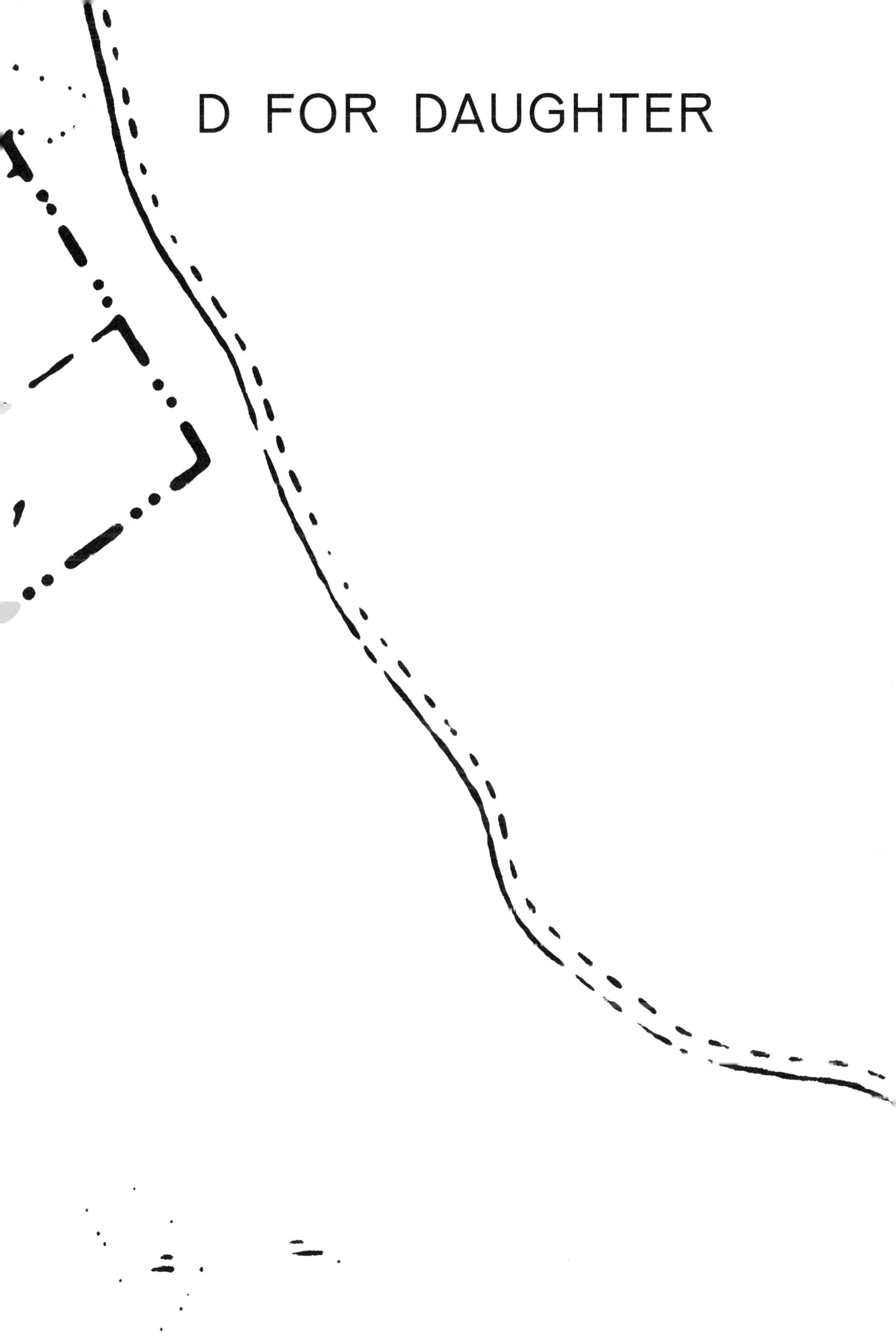

D FOR DAUGHTER

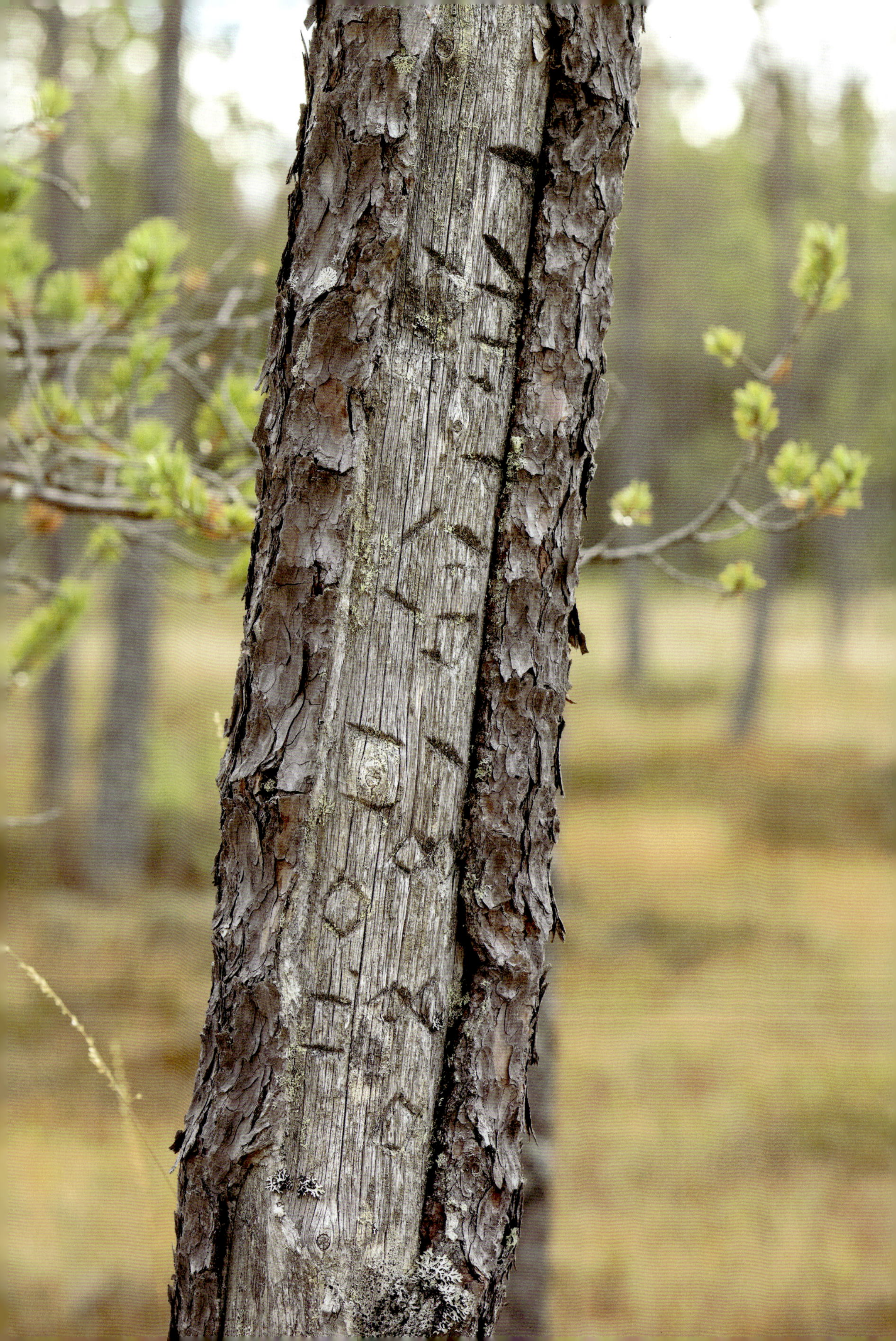

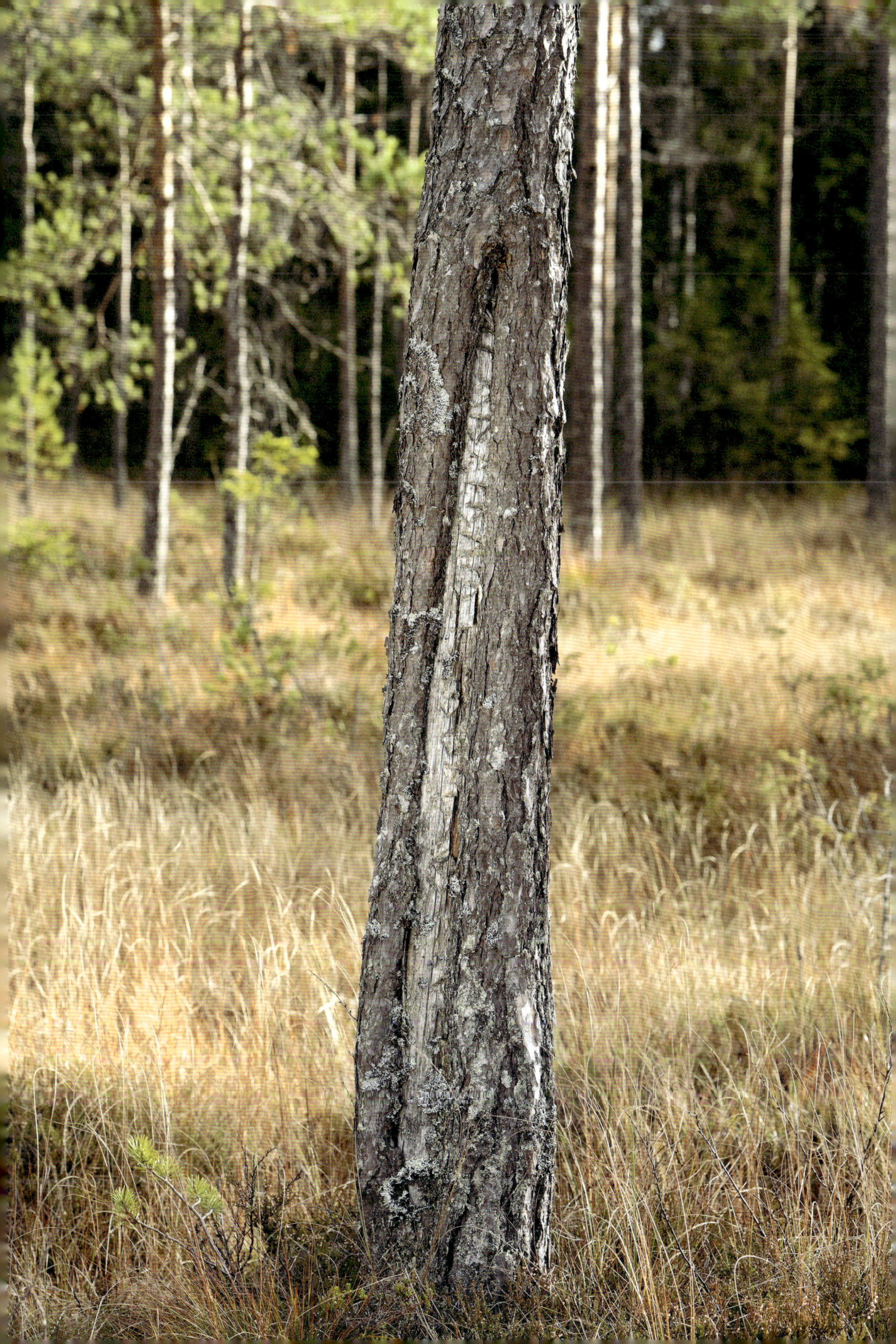

a headscarf

the backbone of a cow

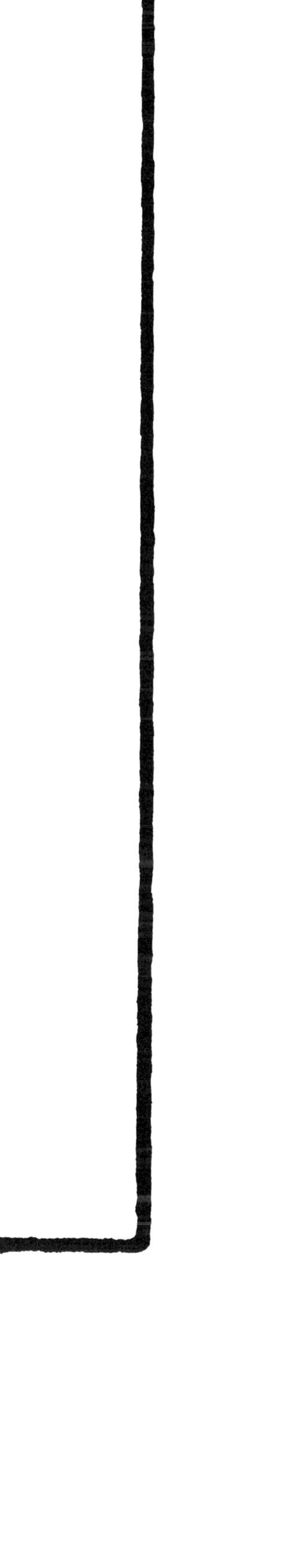

pepparkakkuburk

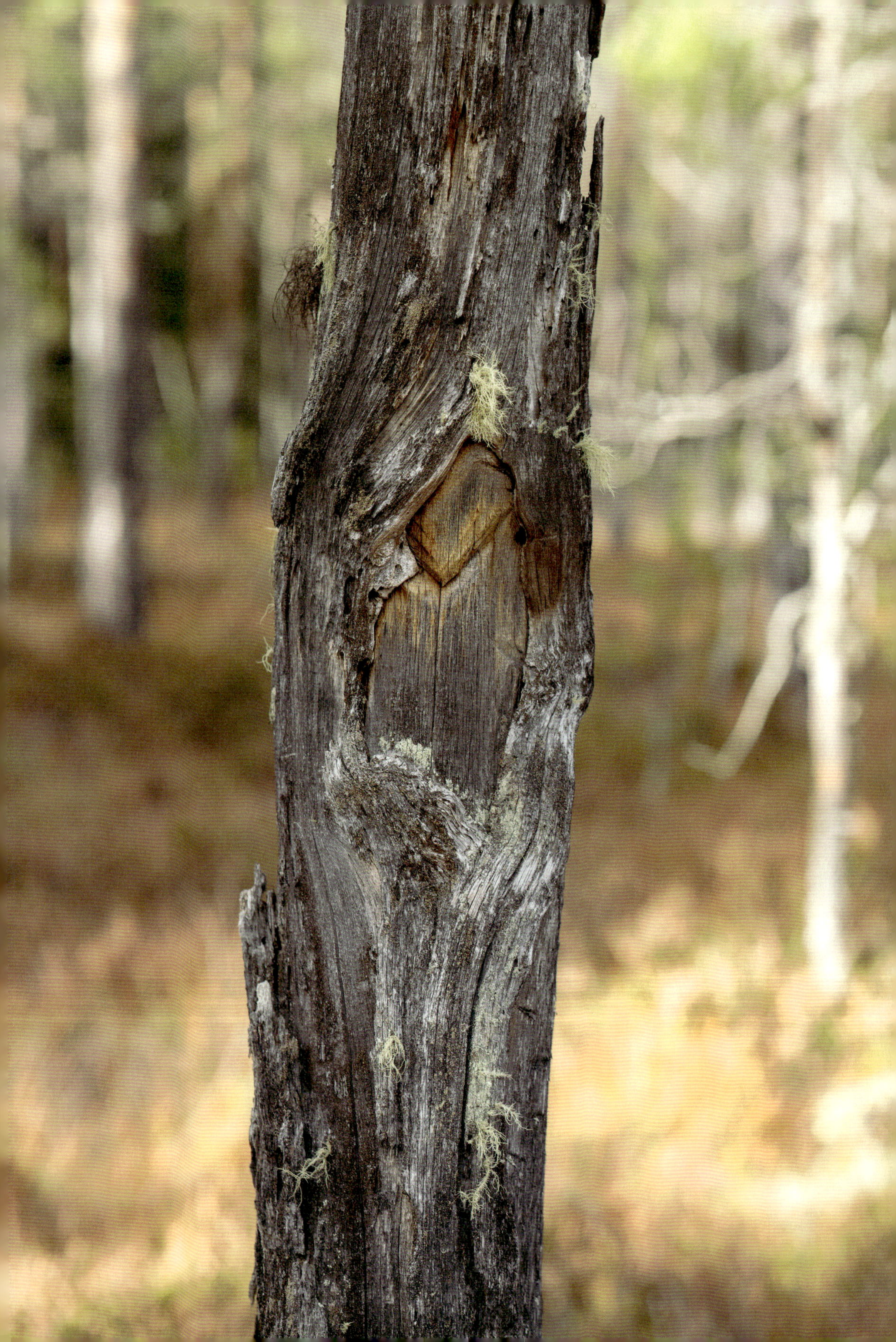

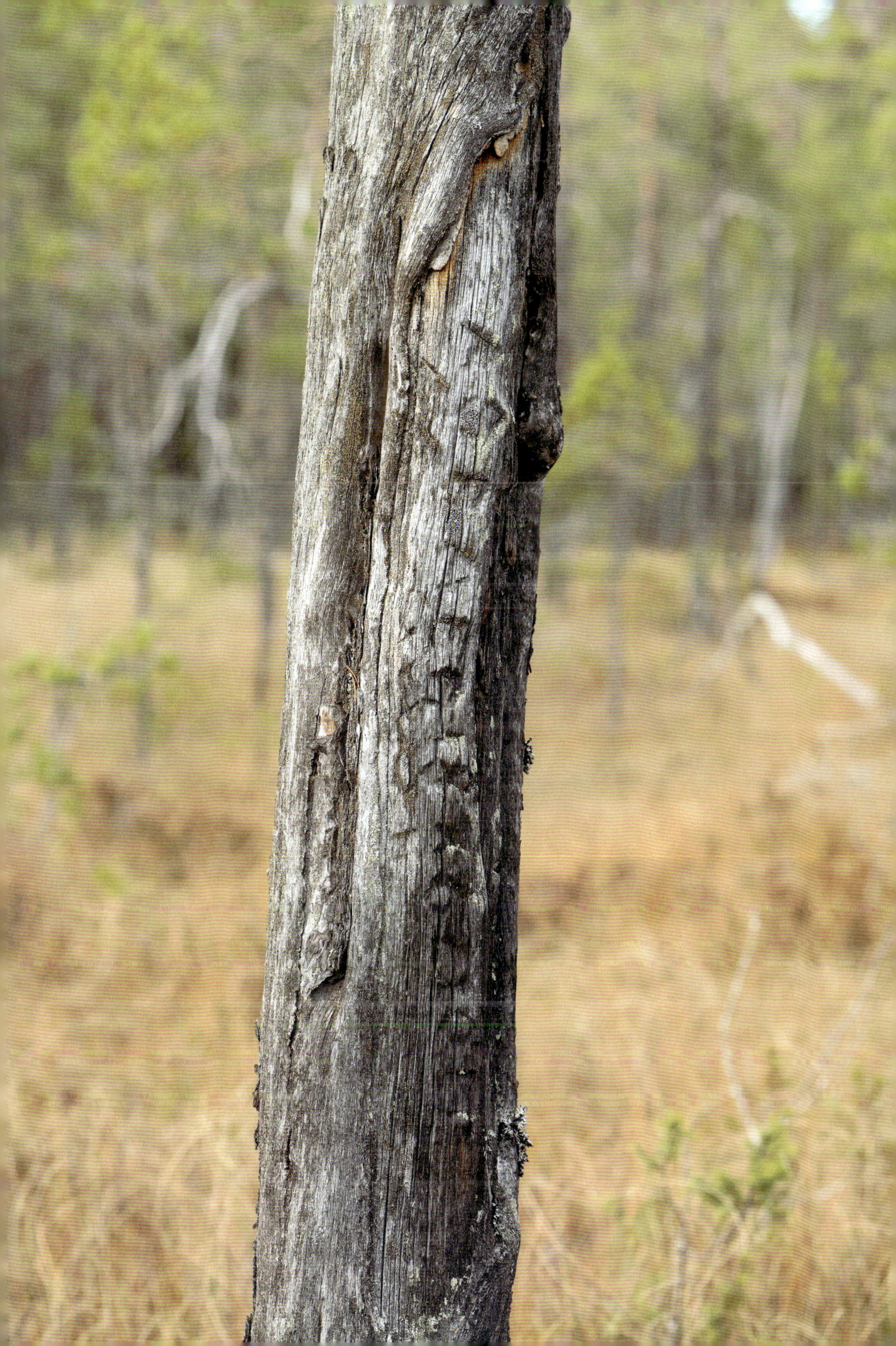

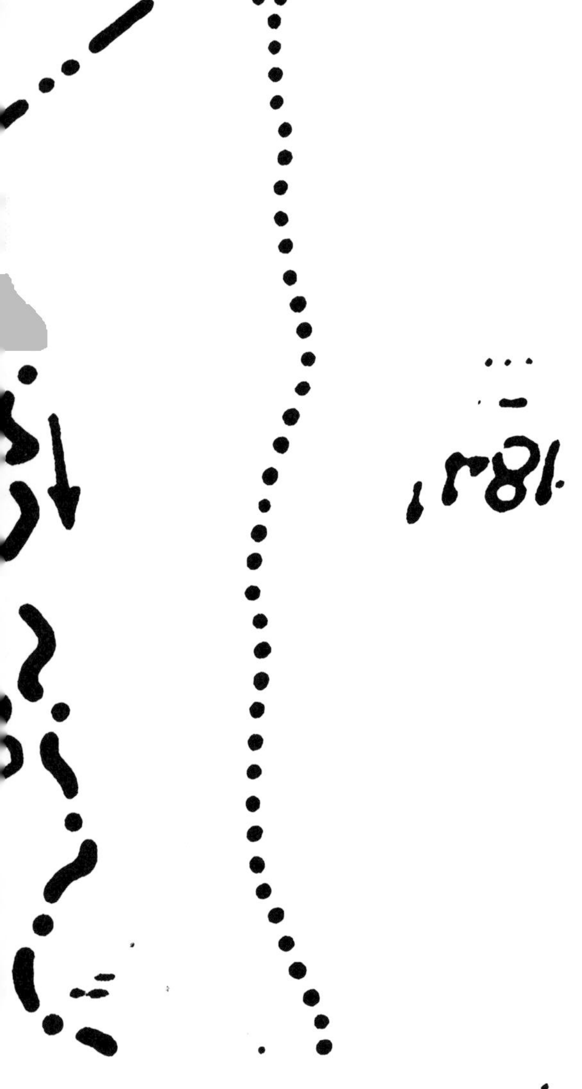

my mom said
they say they brought the cows over the lake on a raft

A KARTVERK

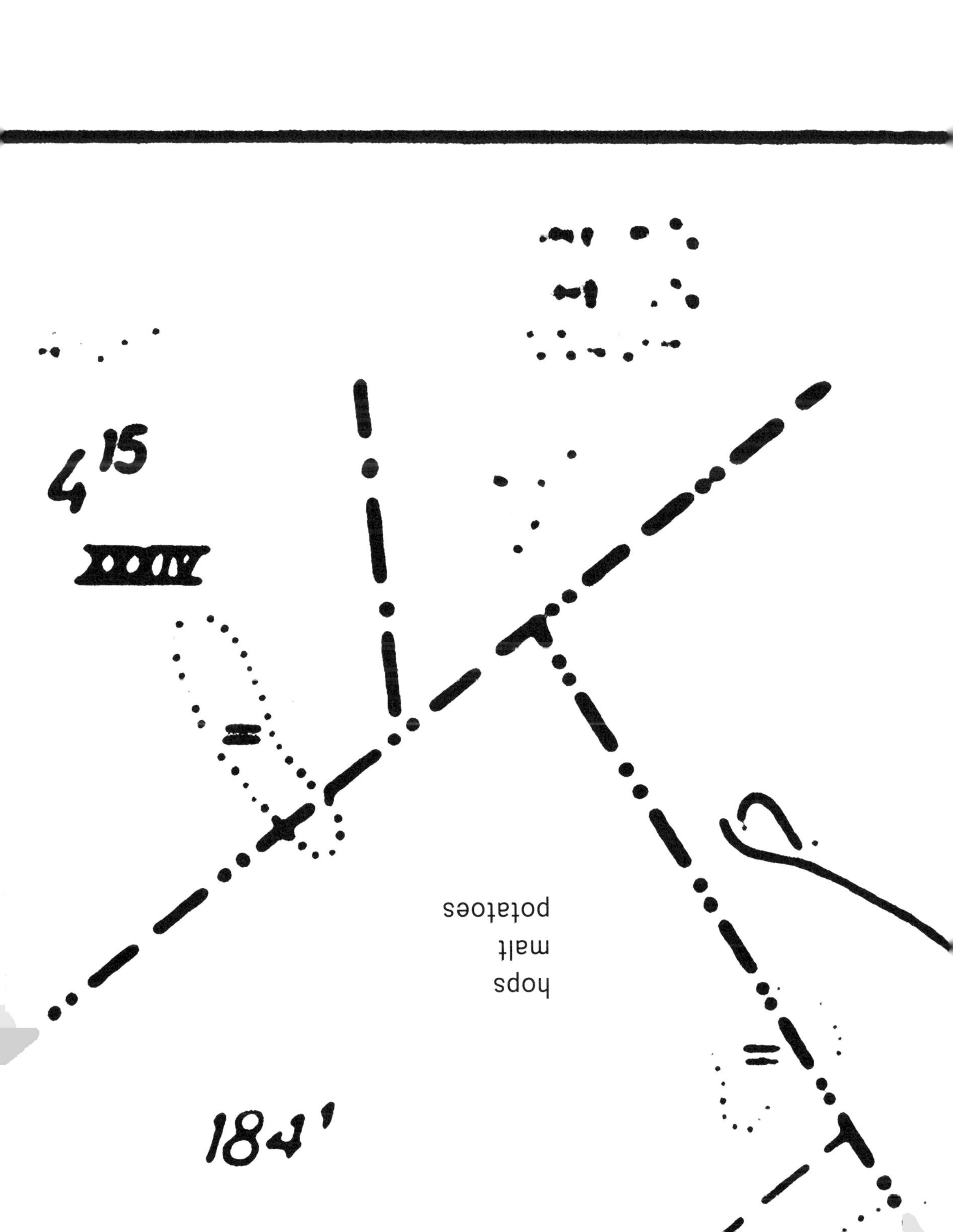

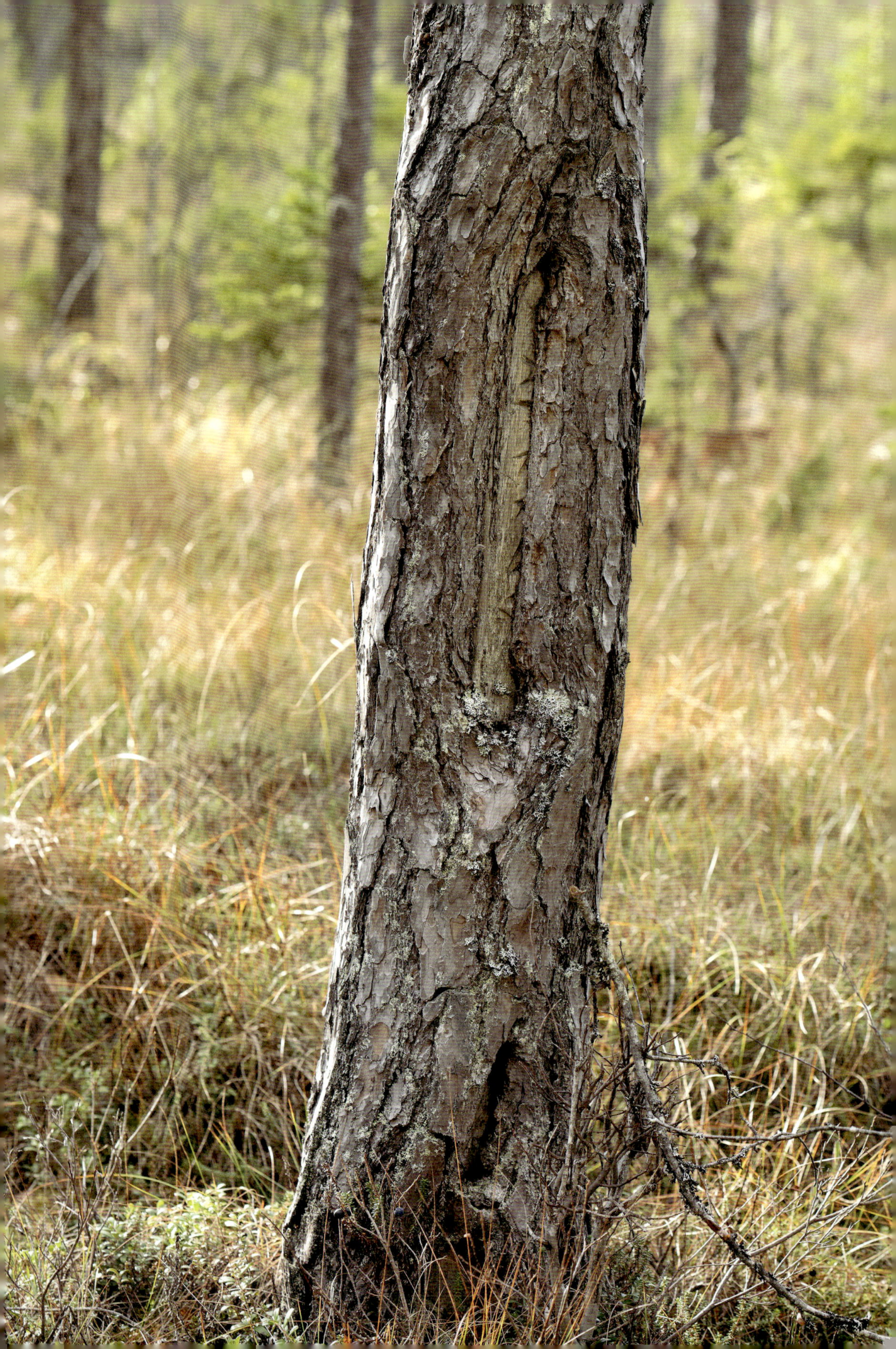

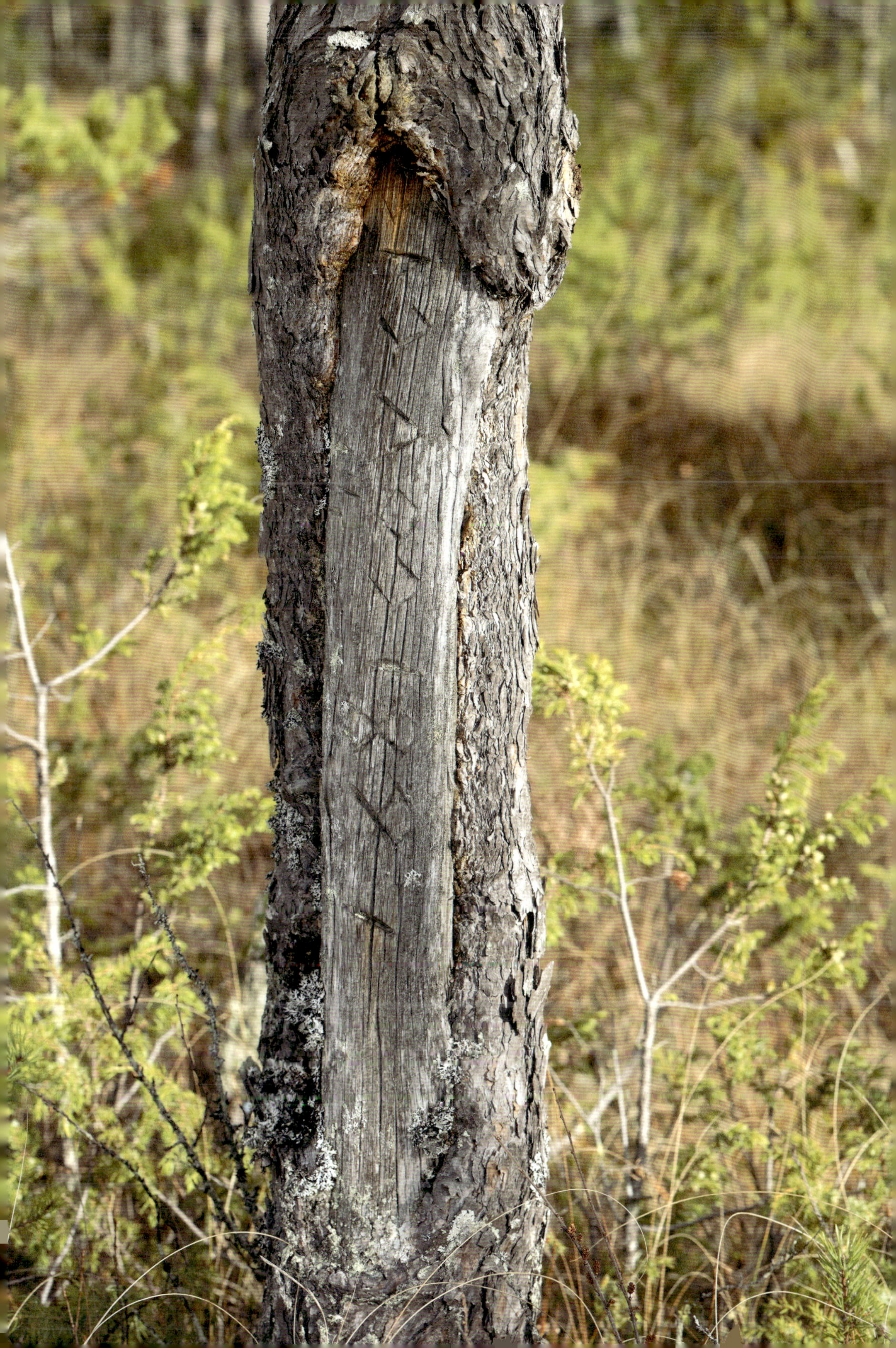

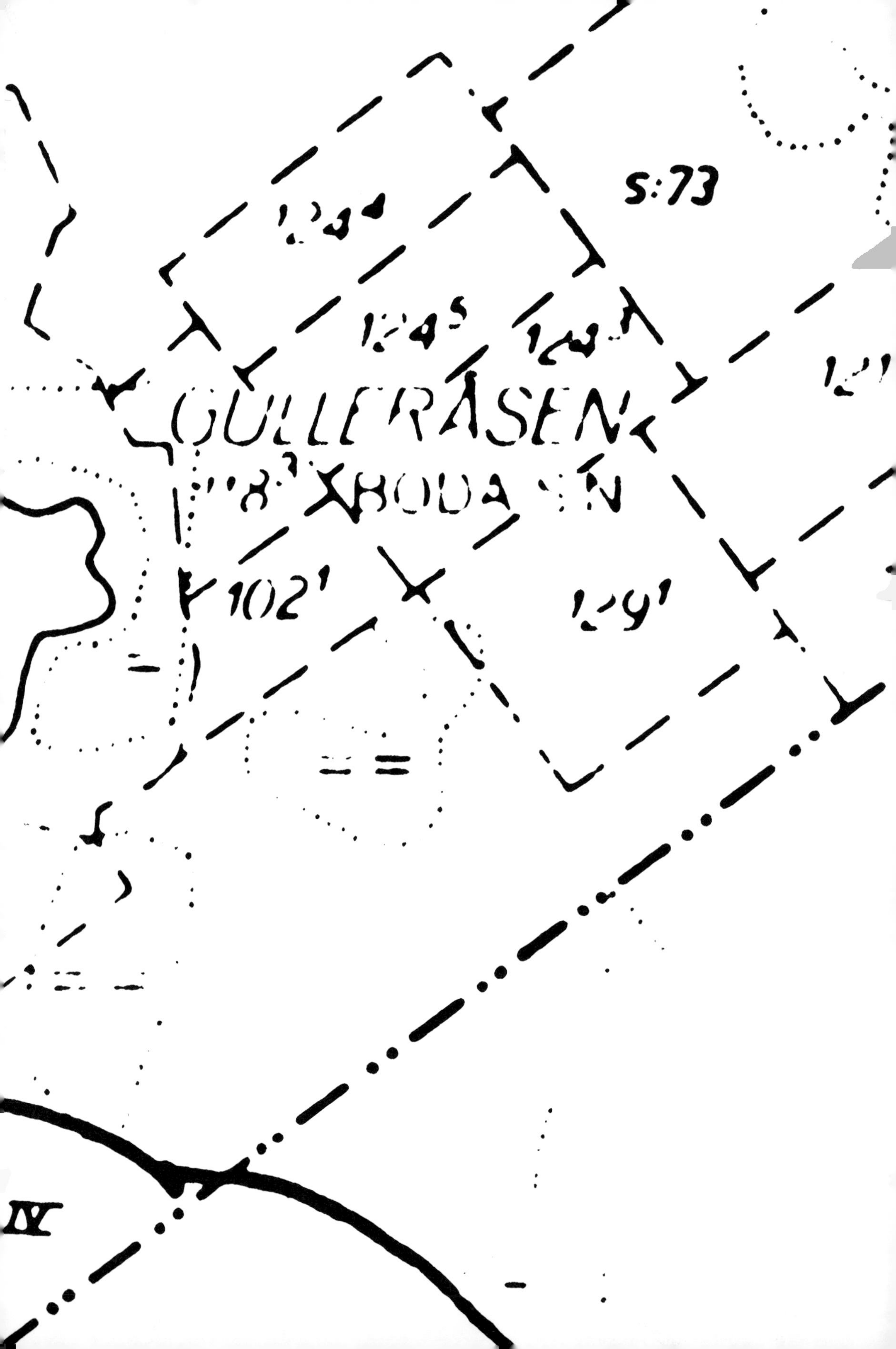
S:73
GULLERÅSEN
102'
IV

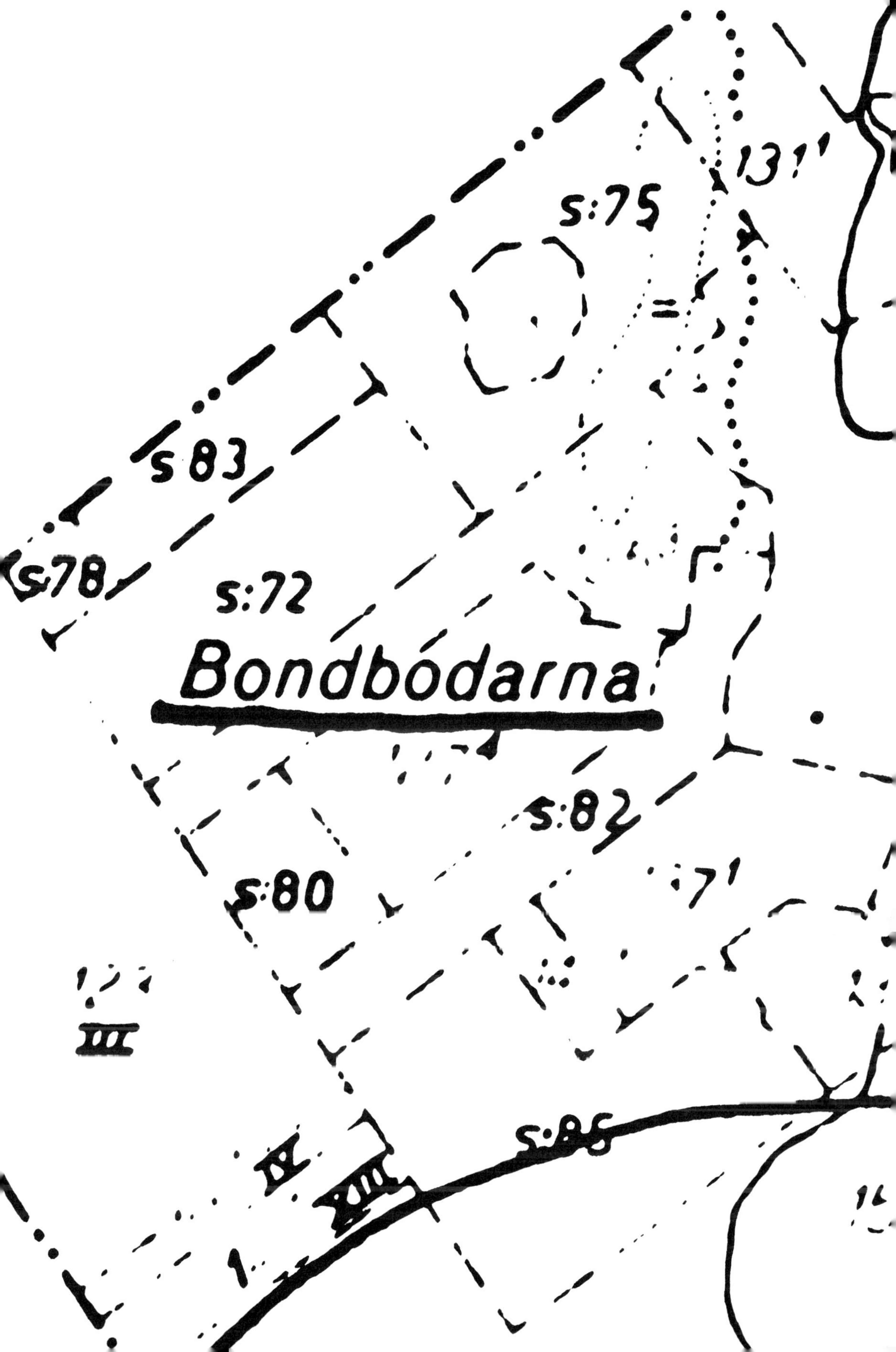

s:75
13"
s:83
s:78
s:72
Bondbodarna
s:82
s:80
s:71
III
IV
s:85

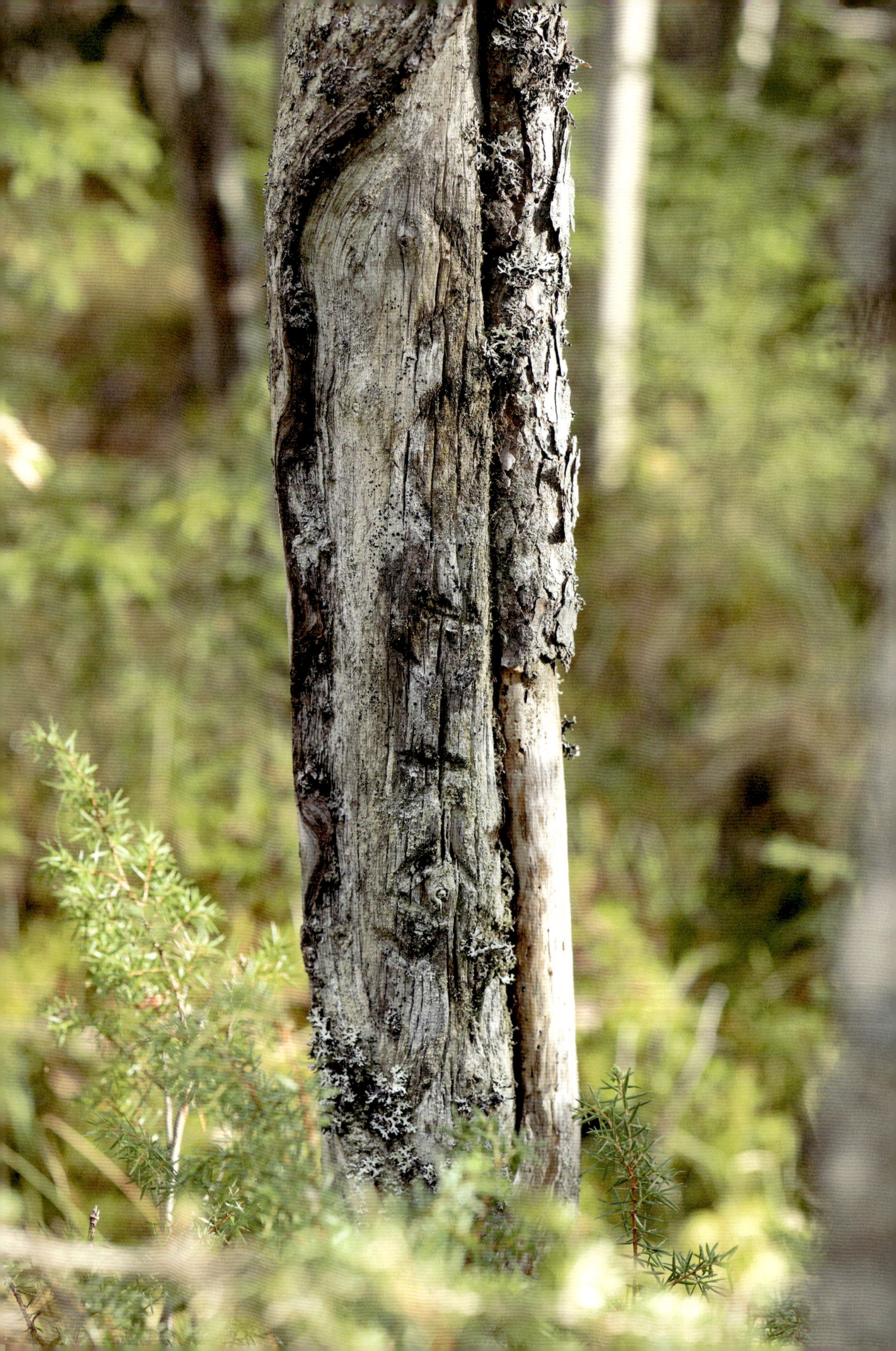

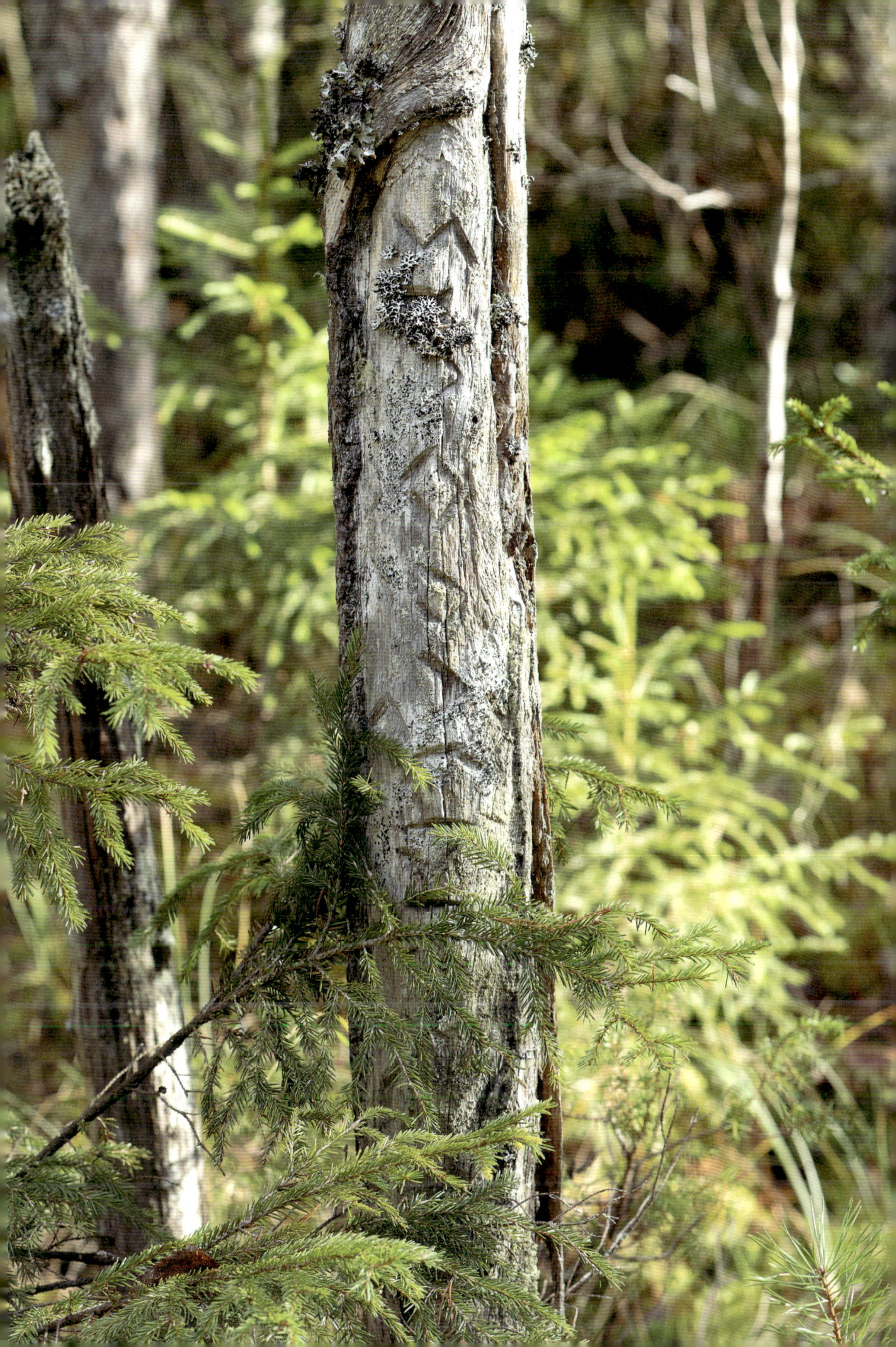

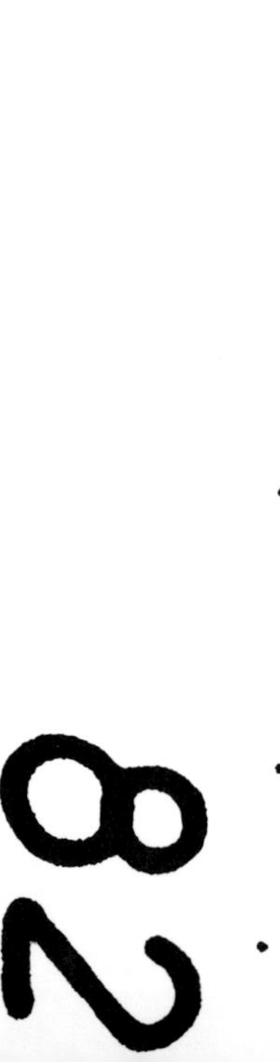

X HOS I X
MMD BOD

AOD KAD 77

F ⁵g

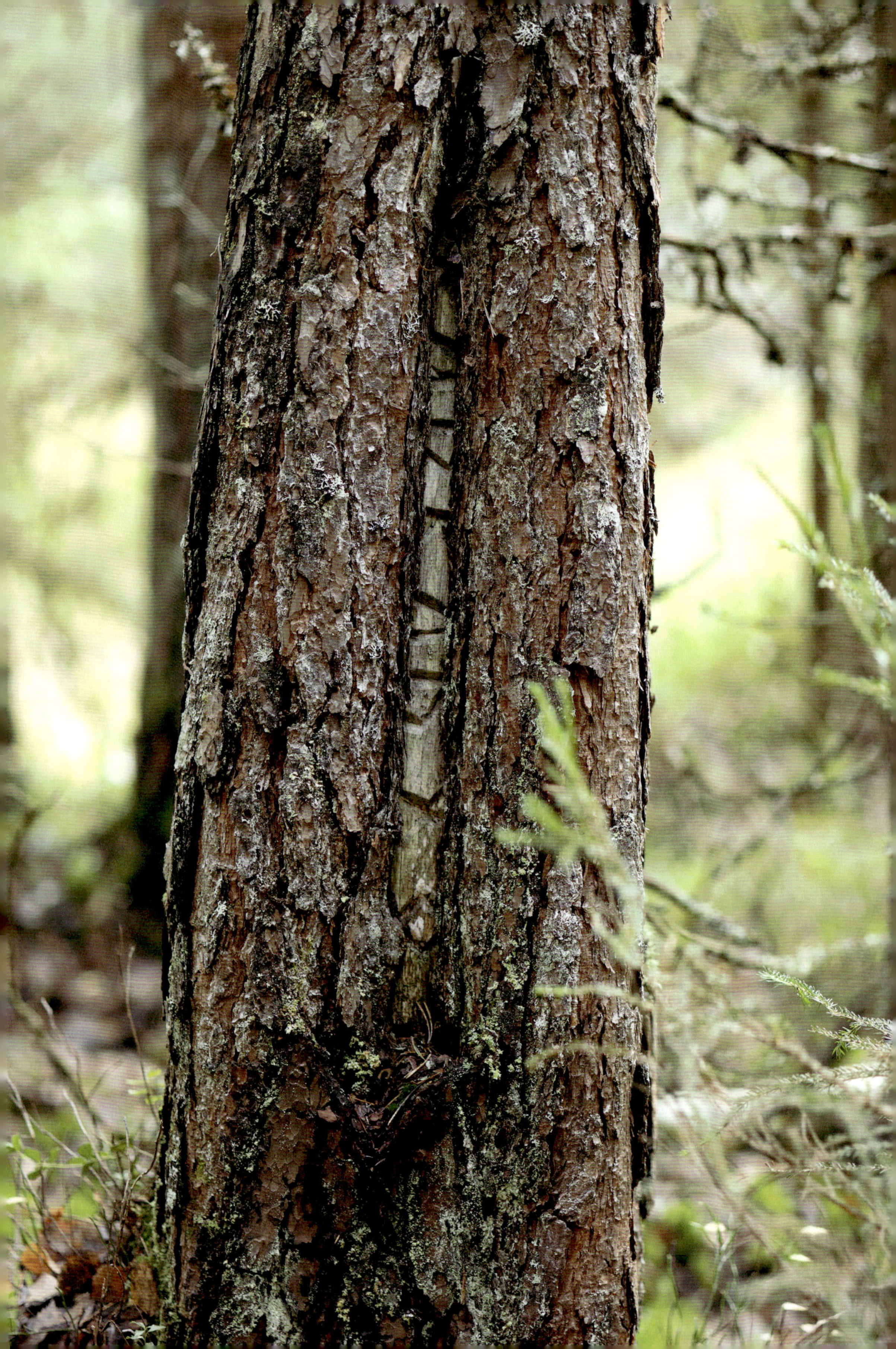

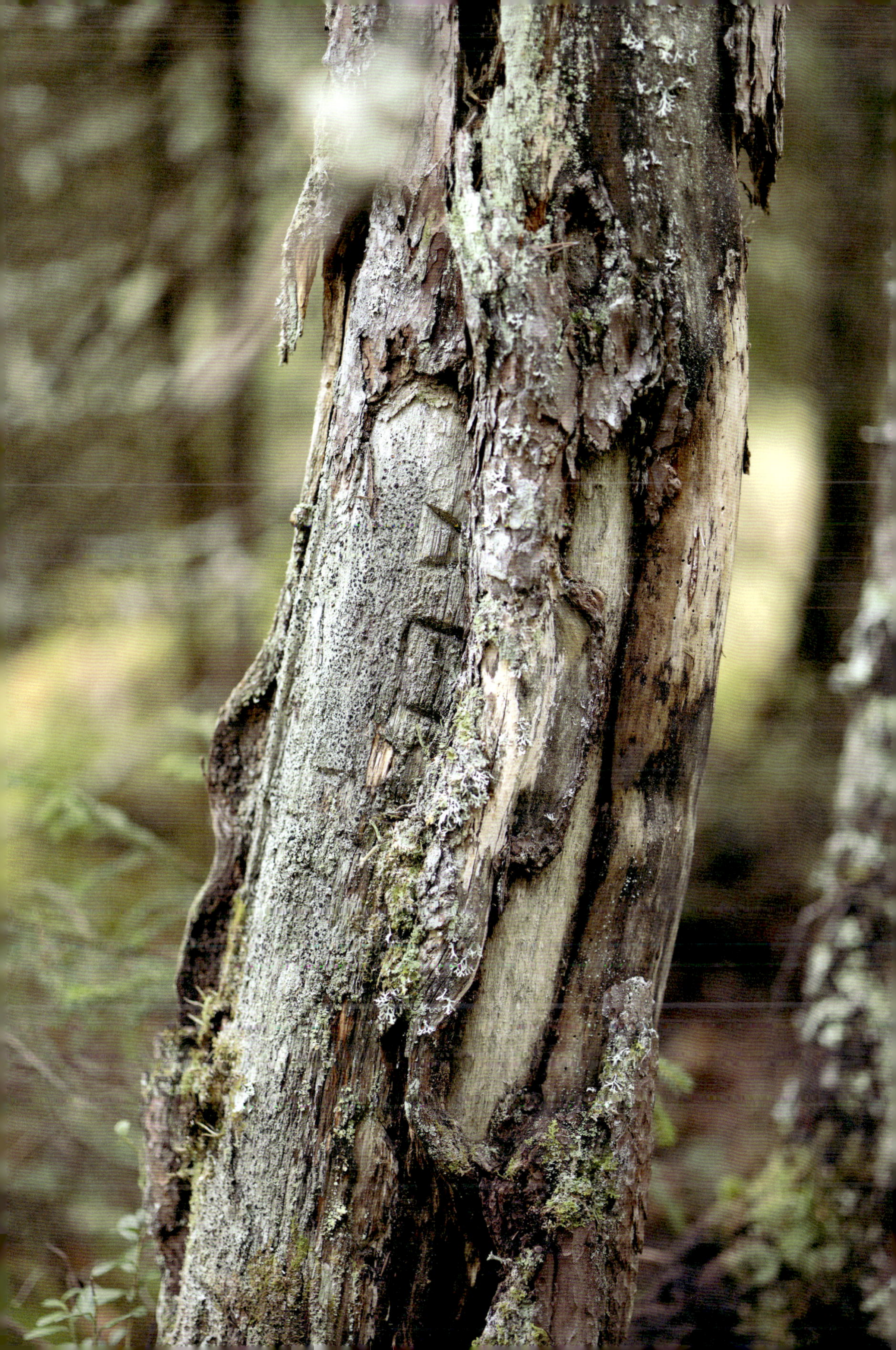

BÄCK 1,2

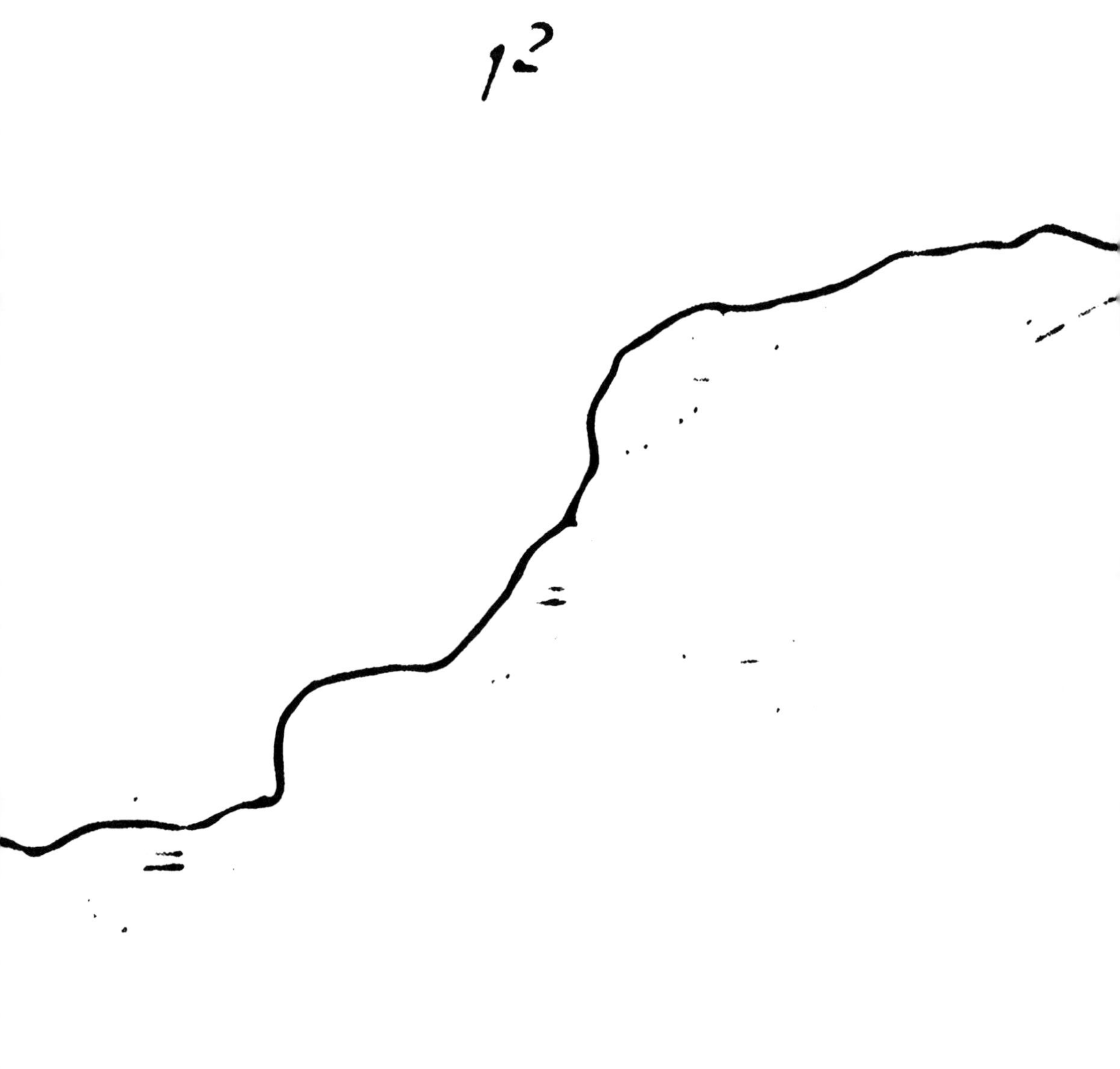

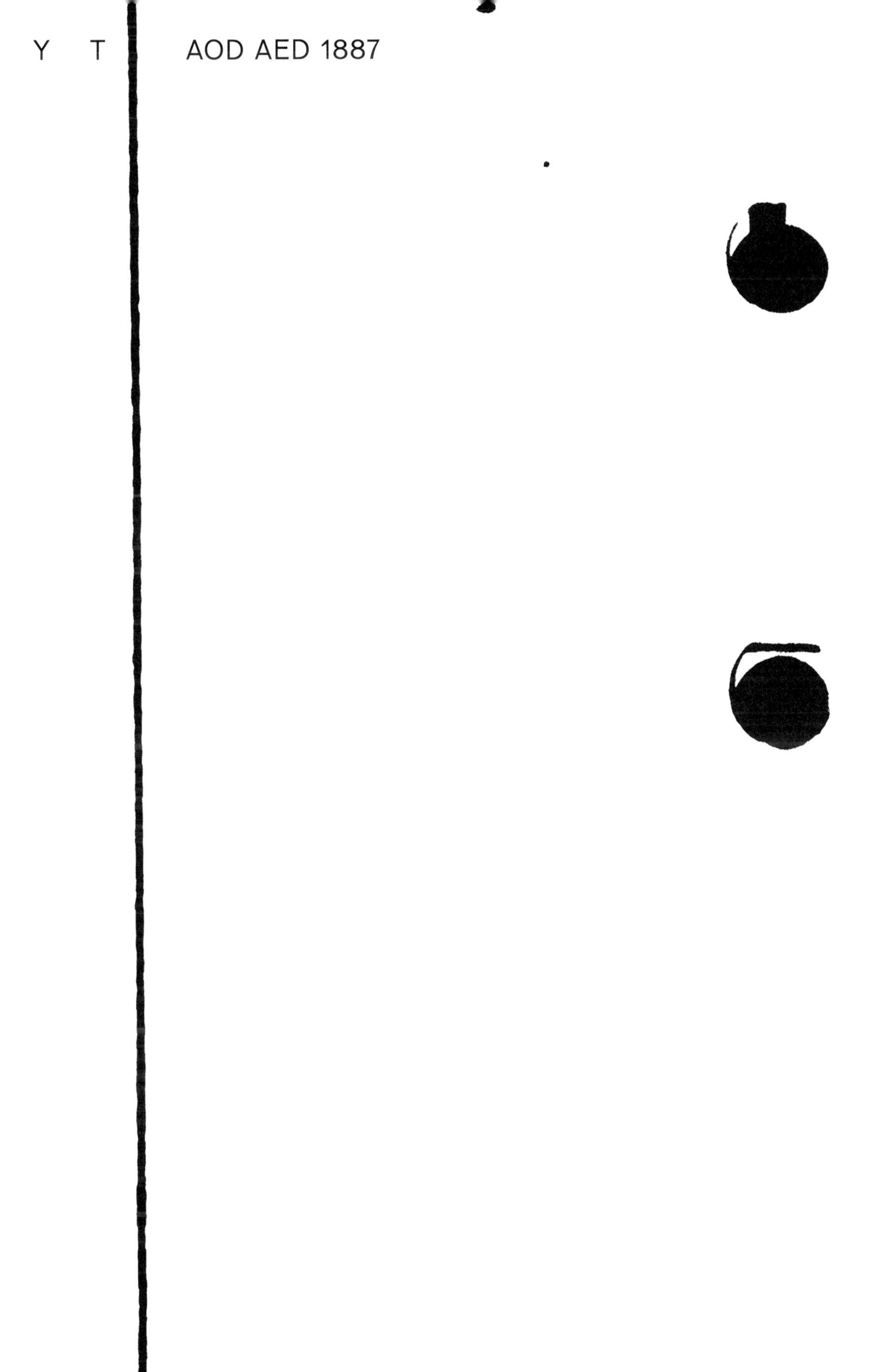
Y   T   AOD AED 1887
Y   T   AOD AED 1887

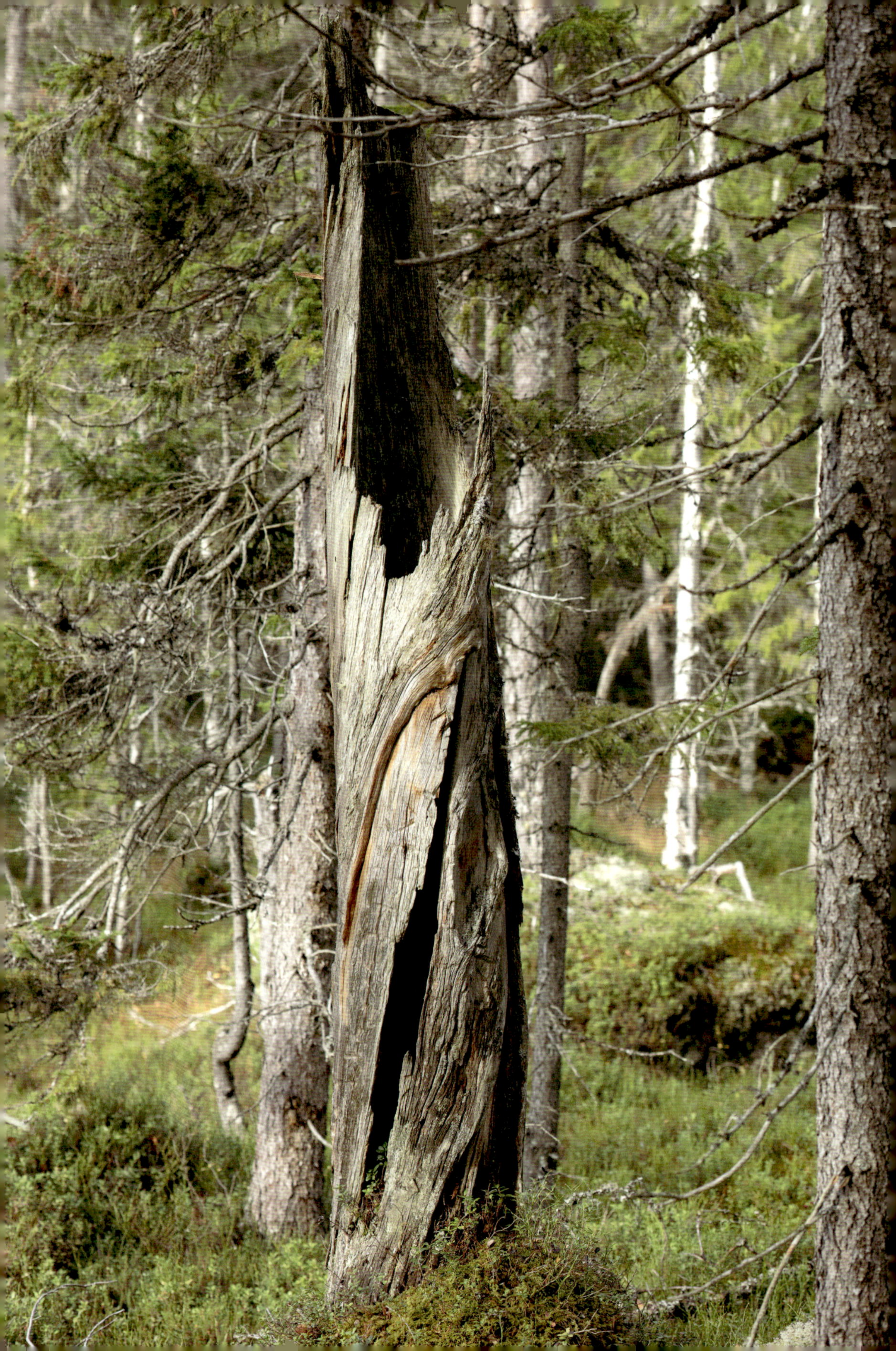

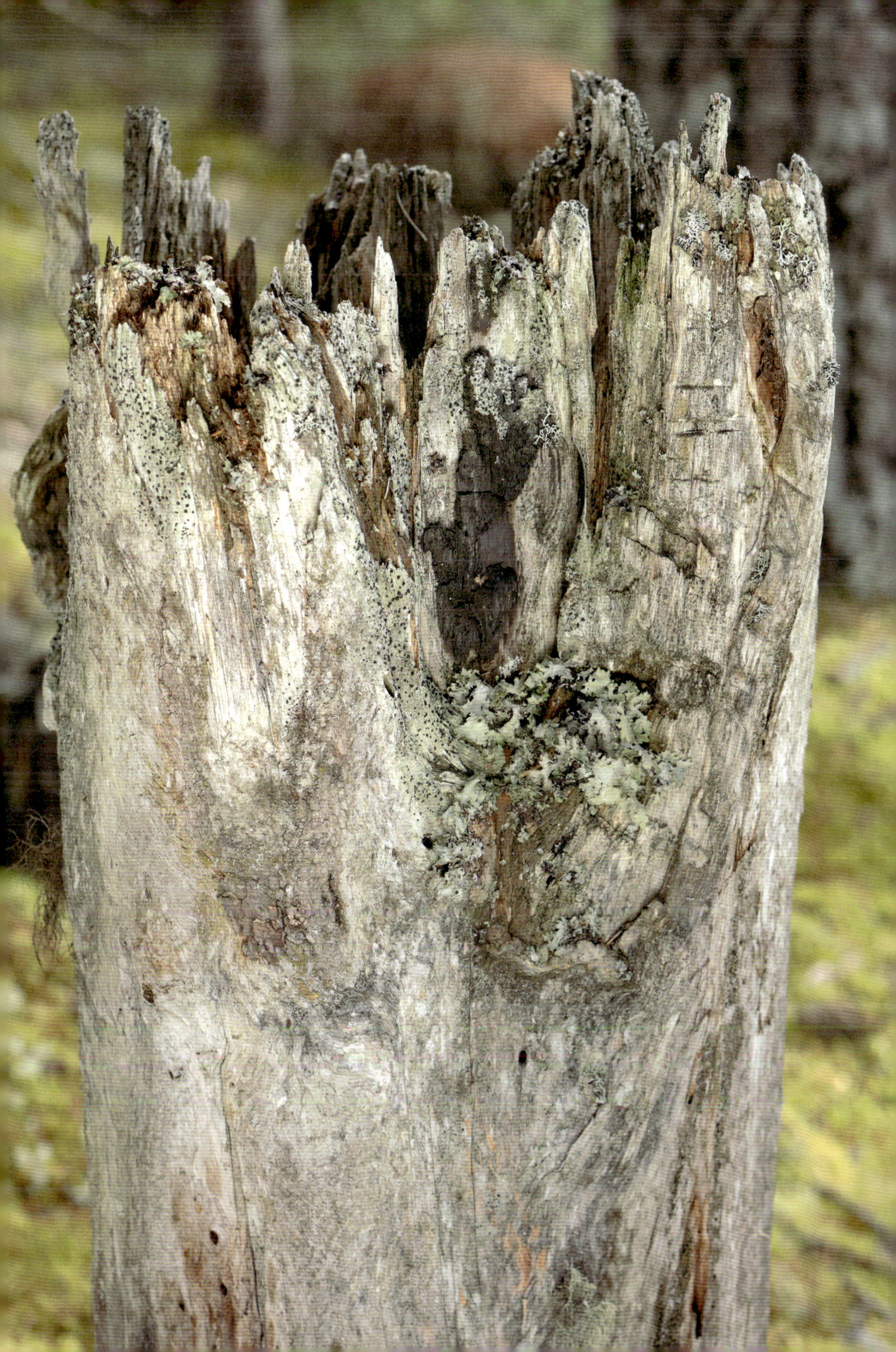

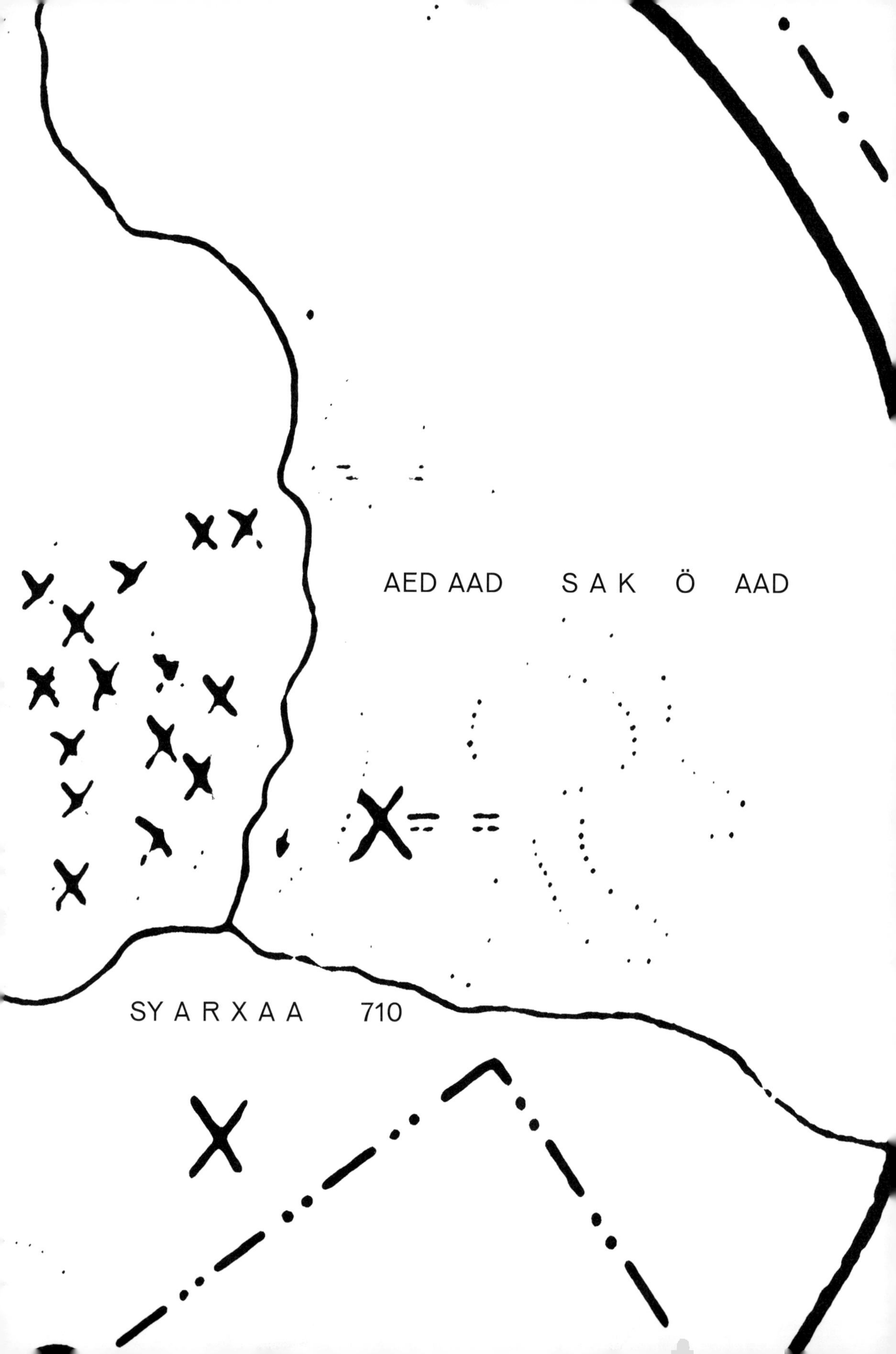

AED AAD   S A K Ö AAD
SYARXAA   710

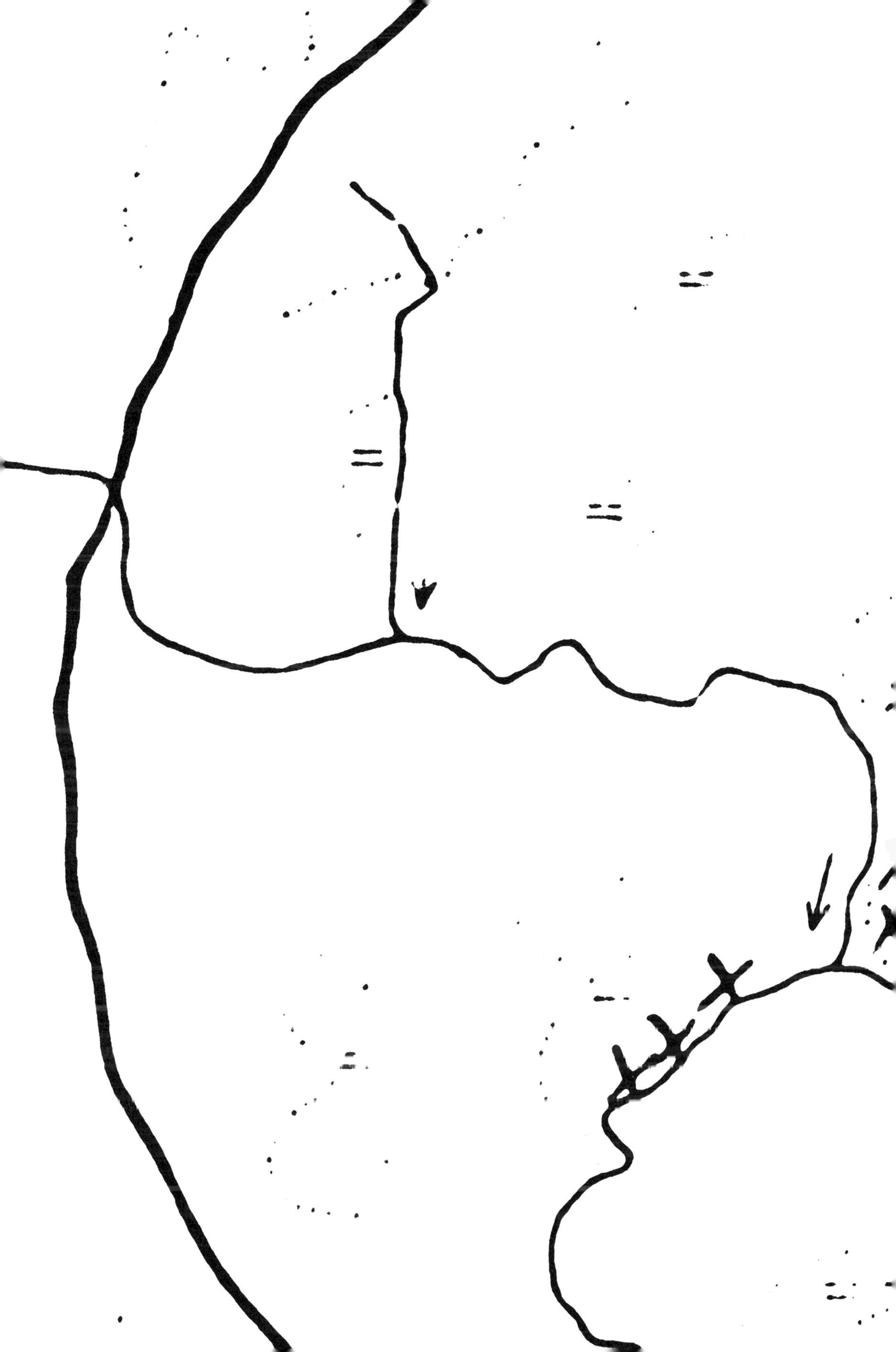

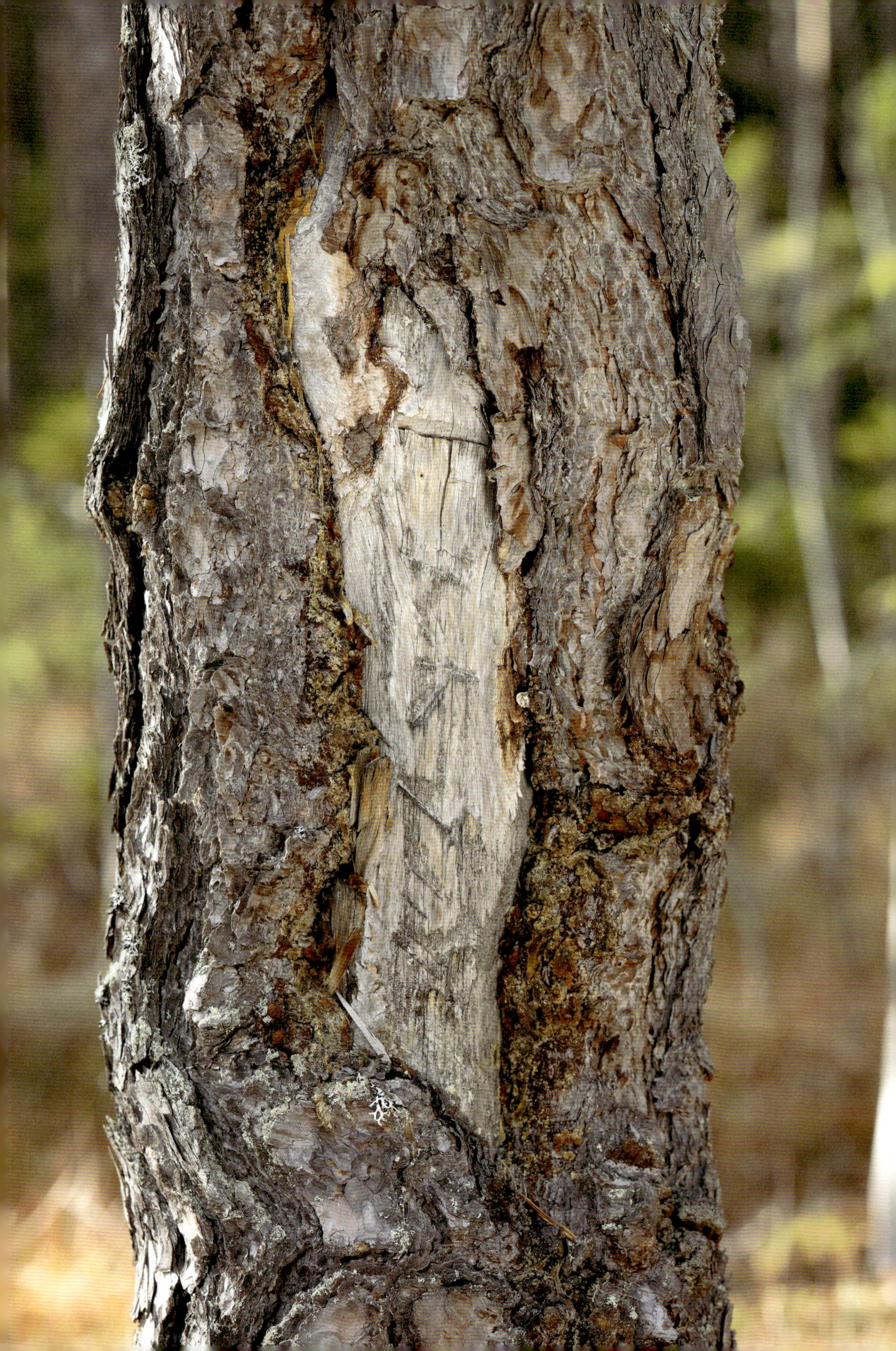

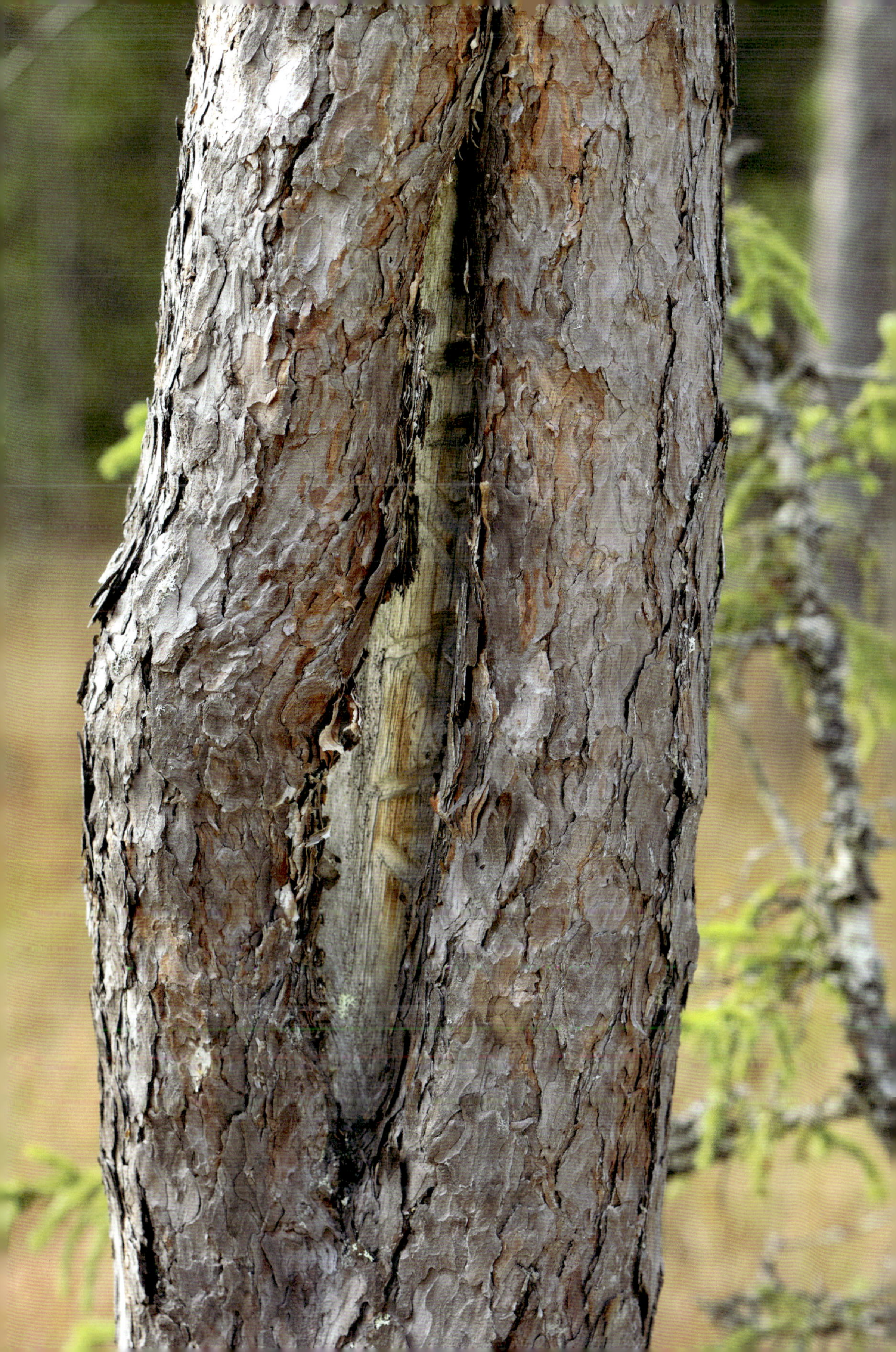

while the men work in the village, anna is carving in the forest
   i imagine her holding the axe in her left hand and a stone
in her right

with the stone, she taps the butt of the axe so that the blade
pokes its way through the soft fibers of the pine   around her,
seven cows are grazing

in their stomachs, grass turns to butter

OBJEKT 1

yr S Bondbodarna 1

äck 1:2 m f1

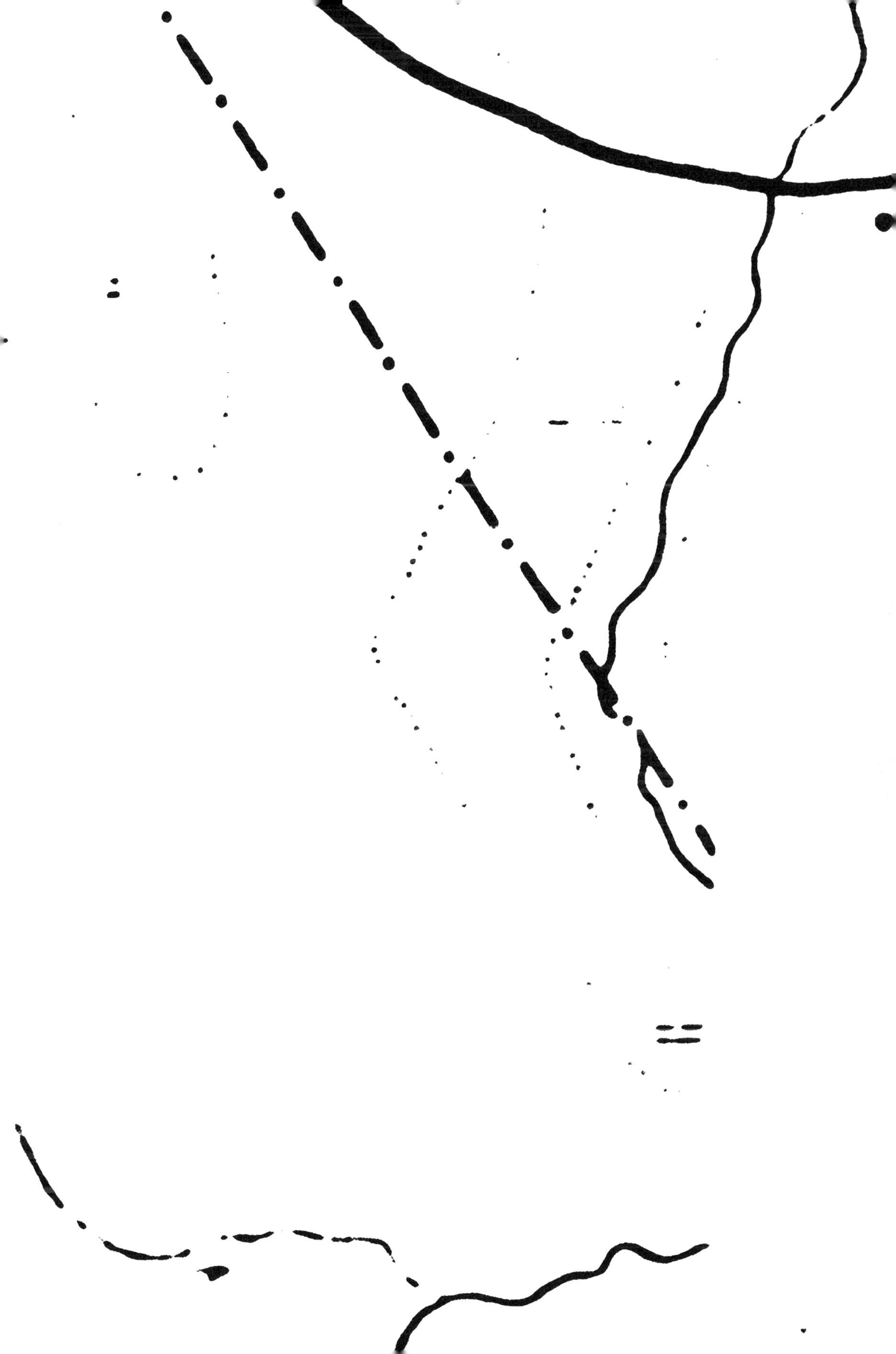

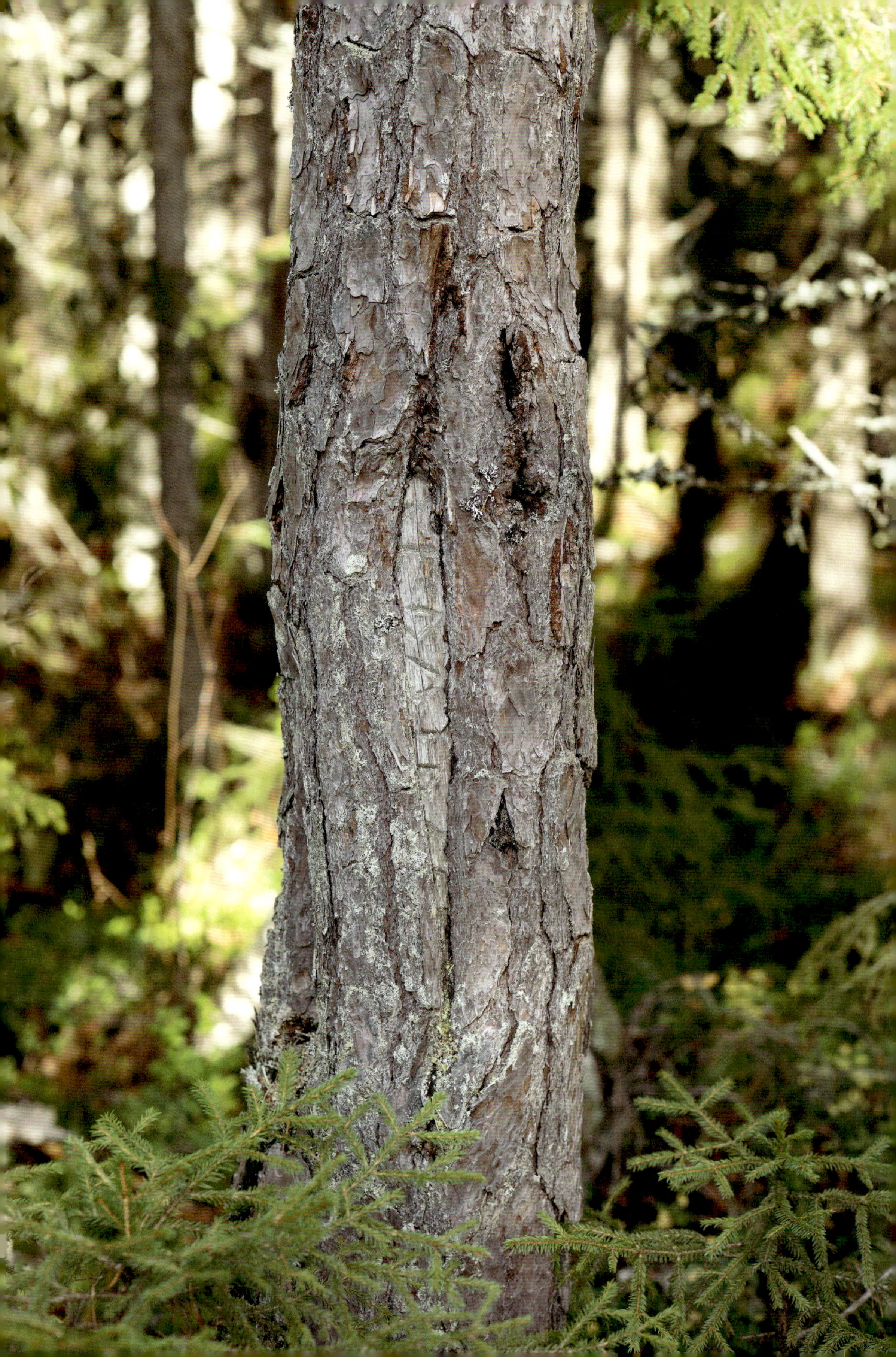

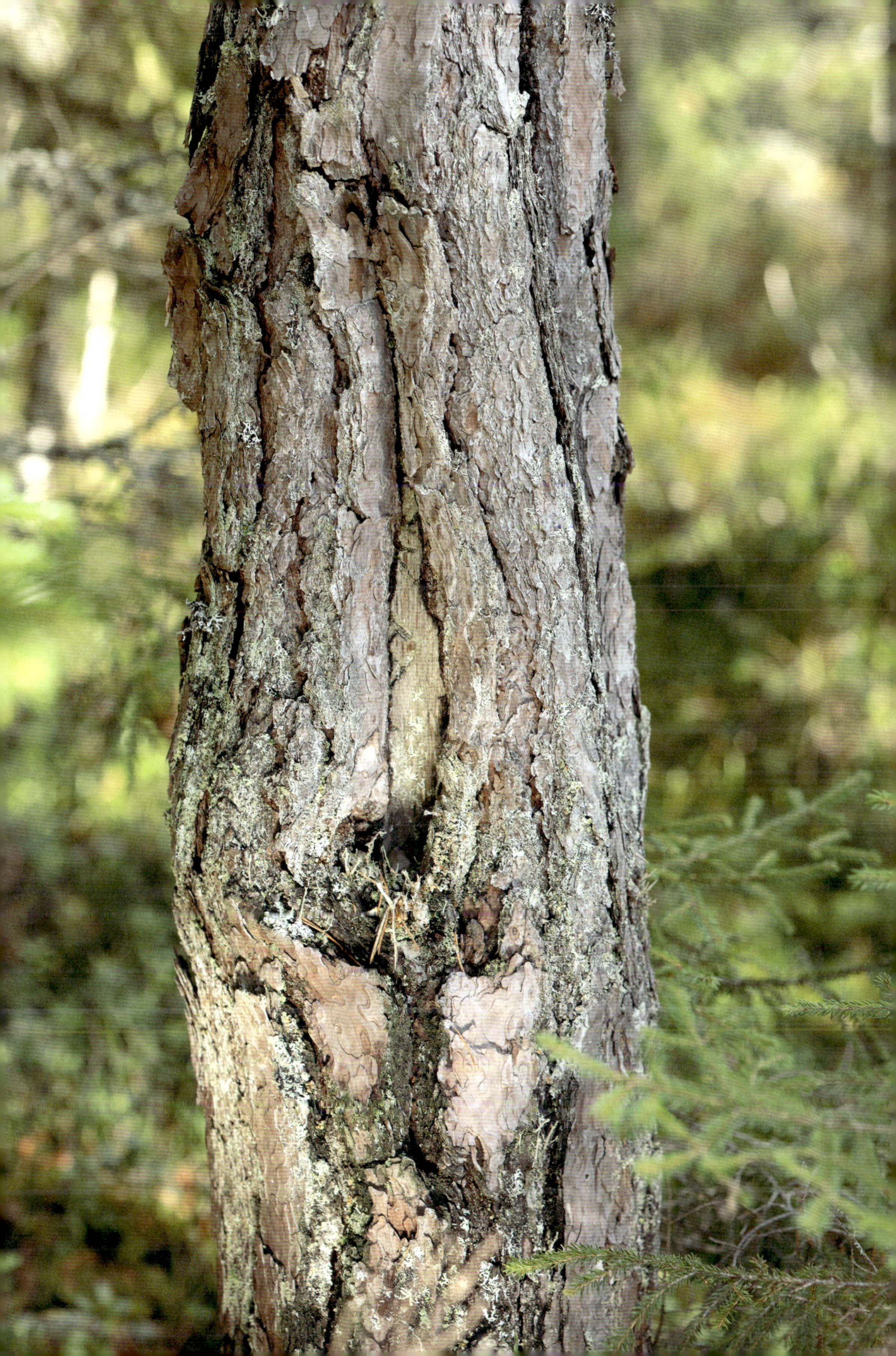

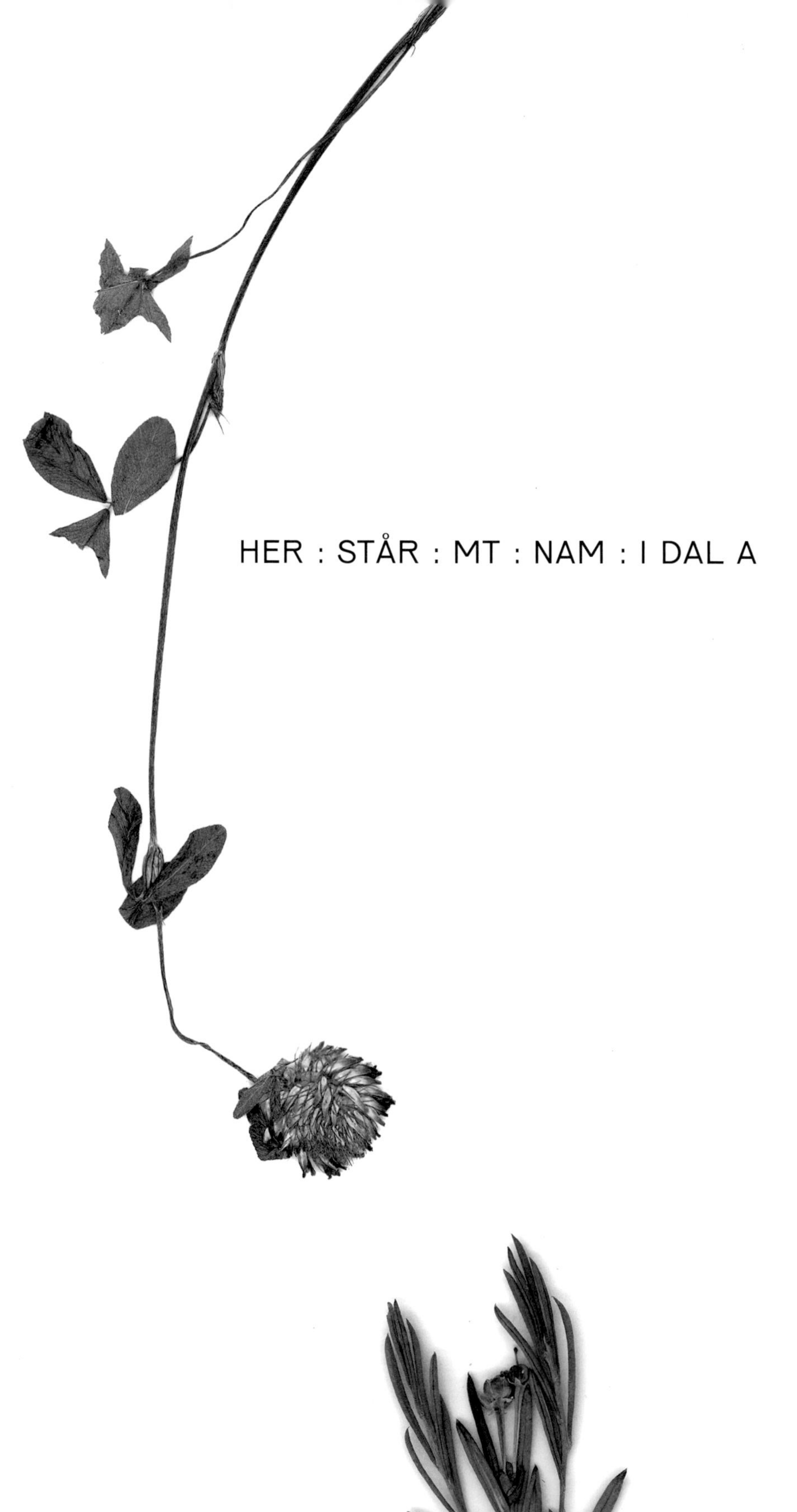
HER : STÅR : MT : NAM : I DAL A

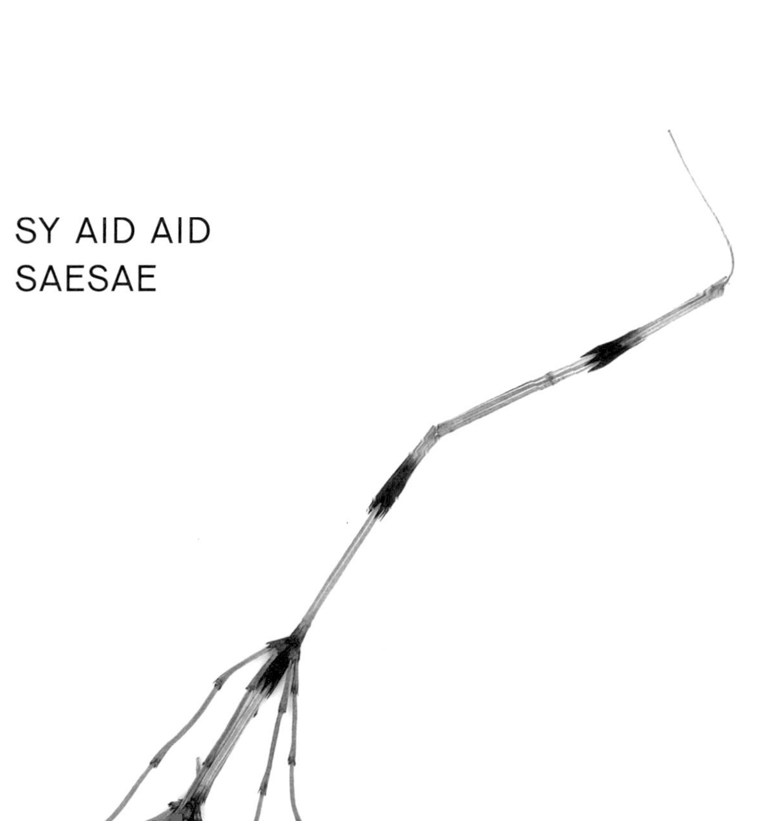

SY AID AID
SAESAE

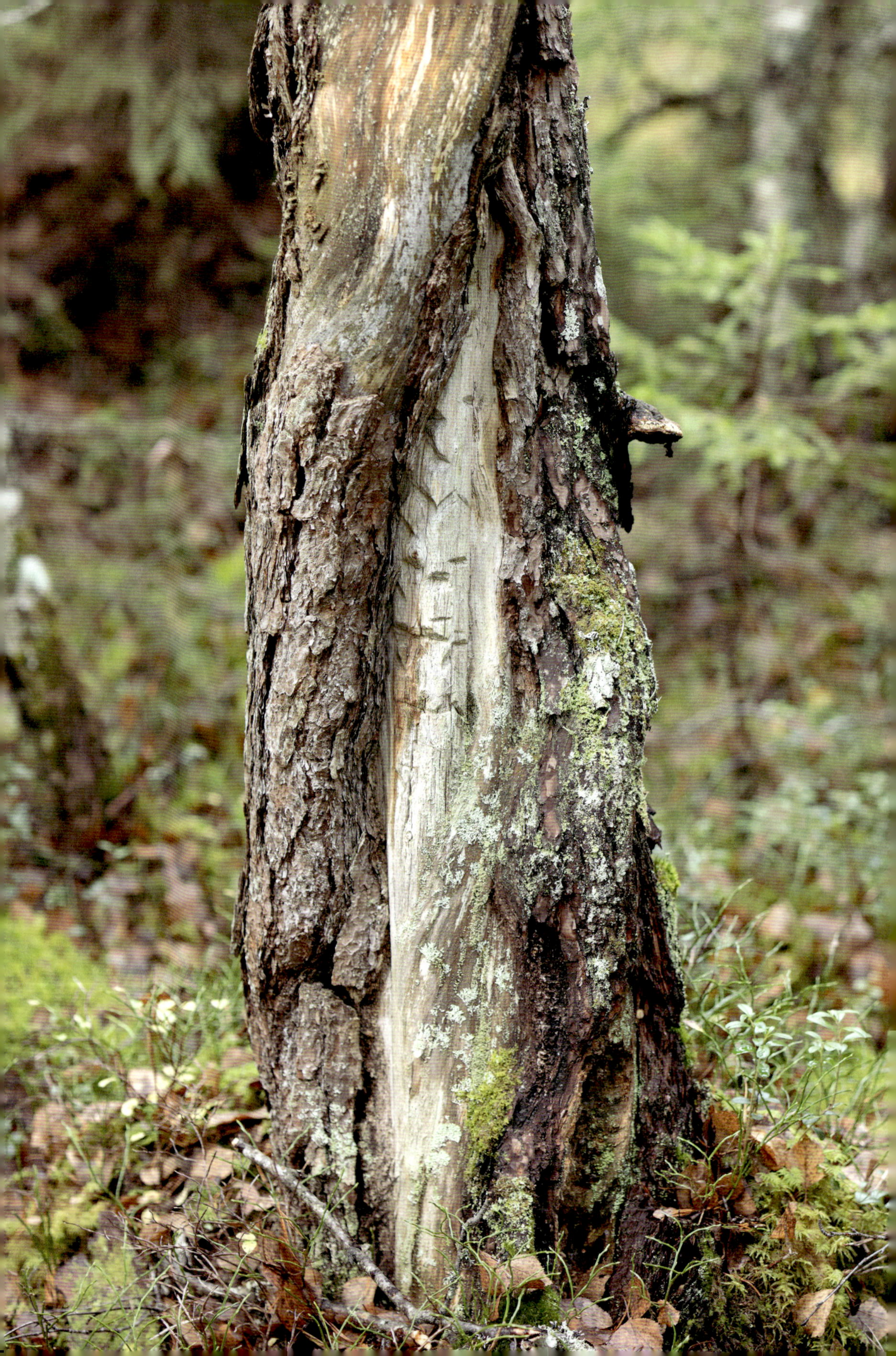

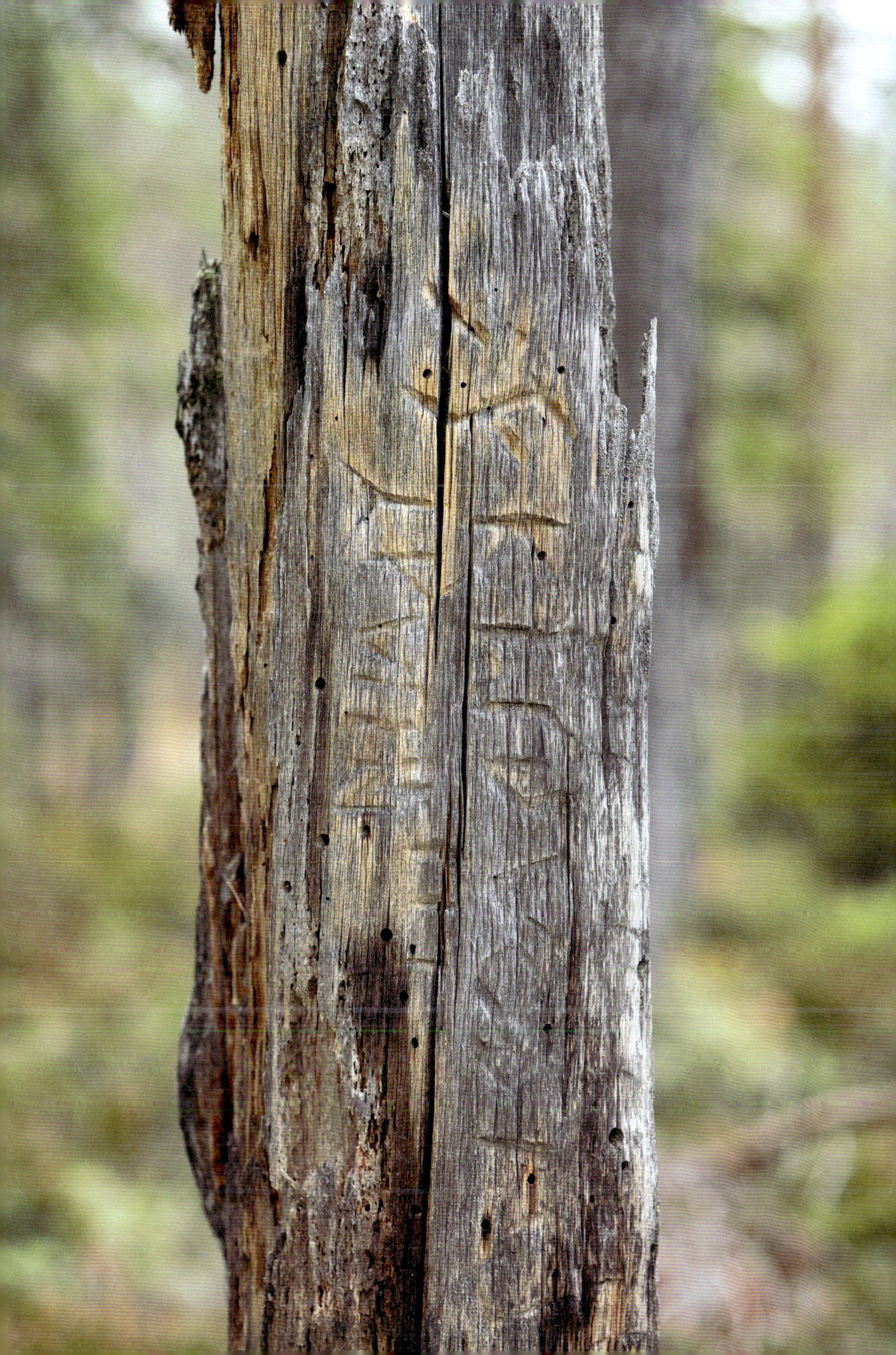

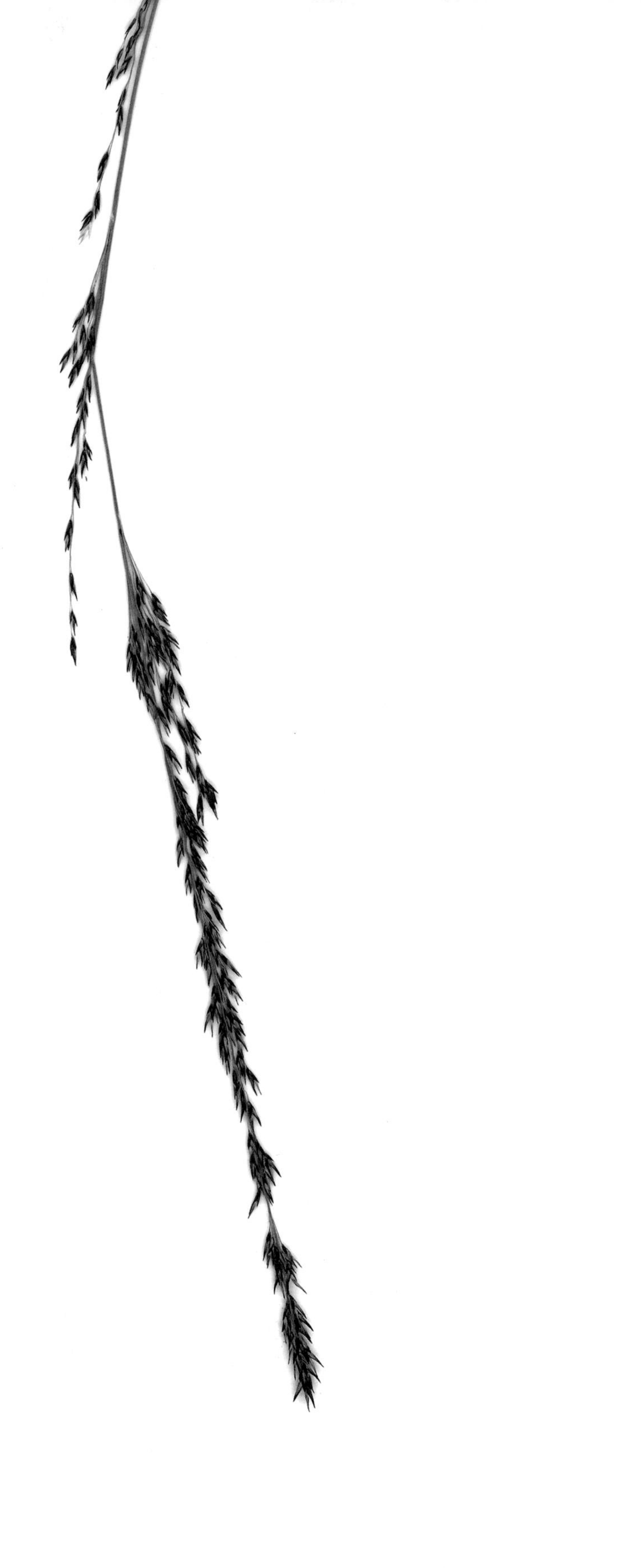

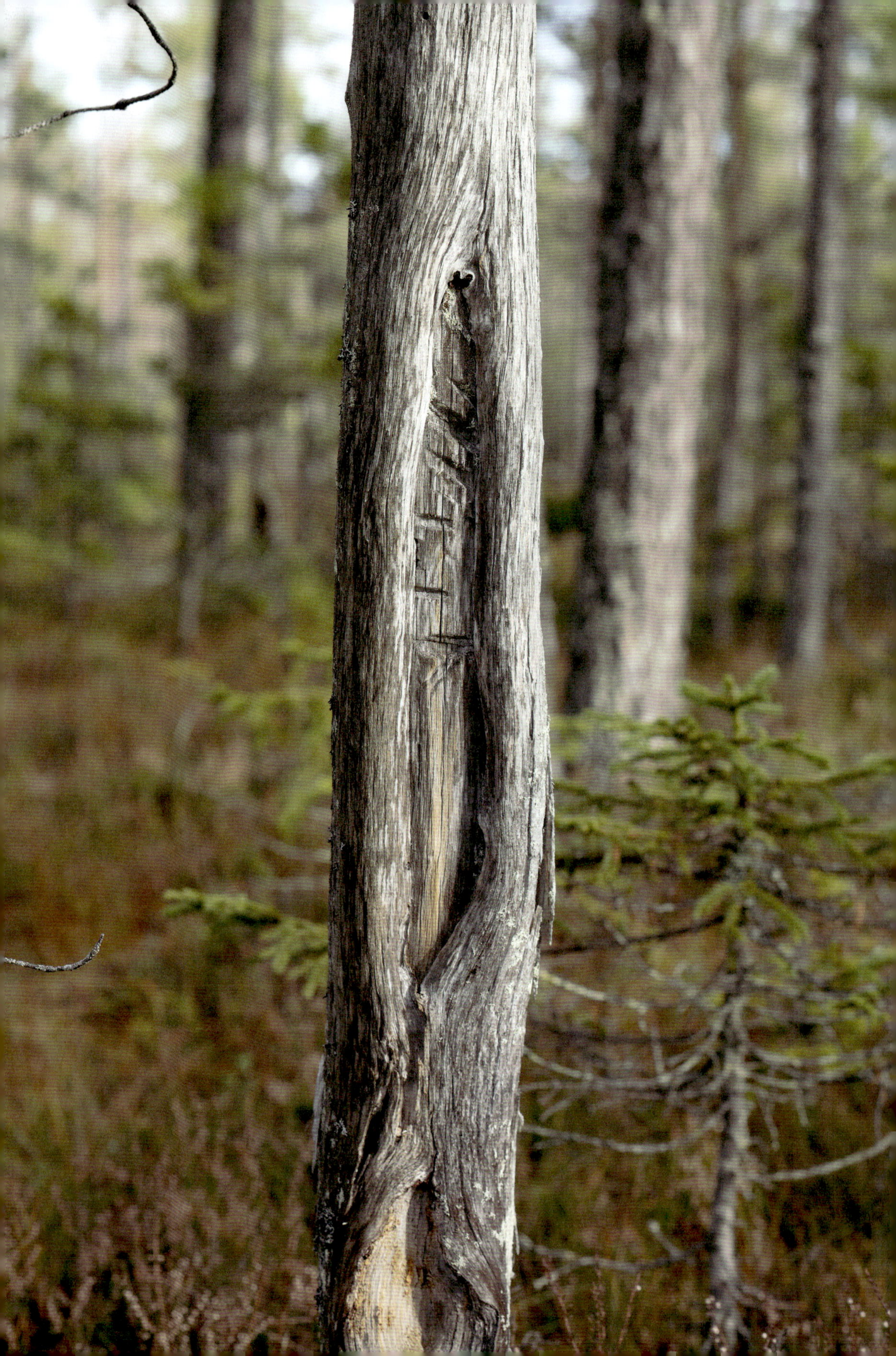

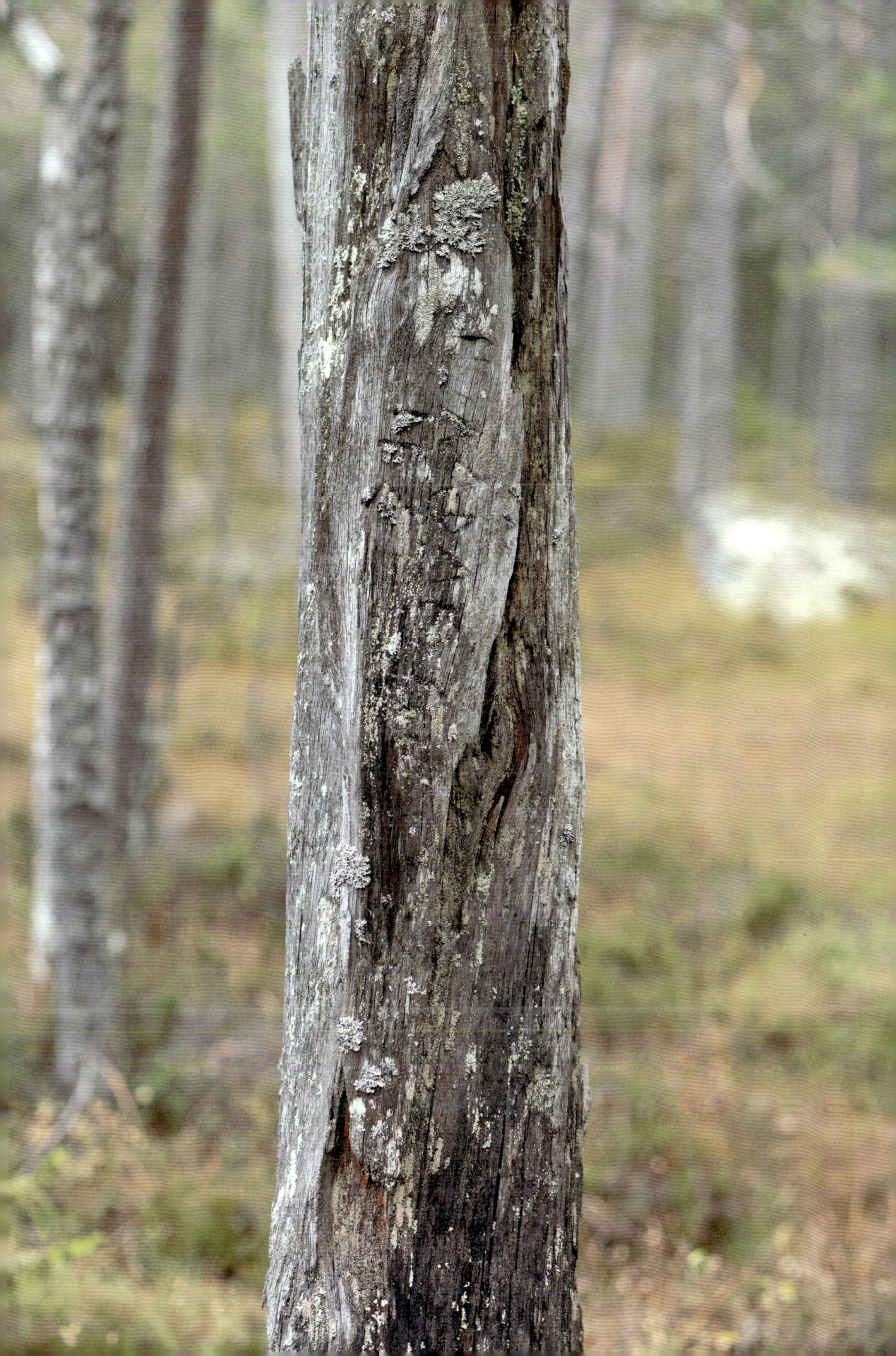

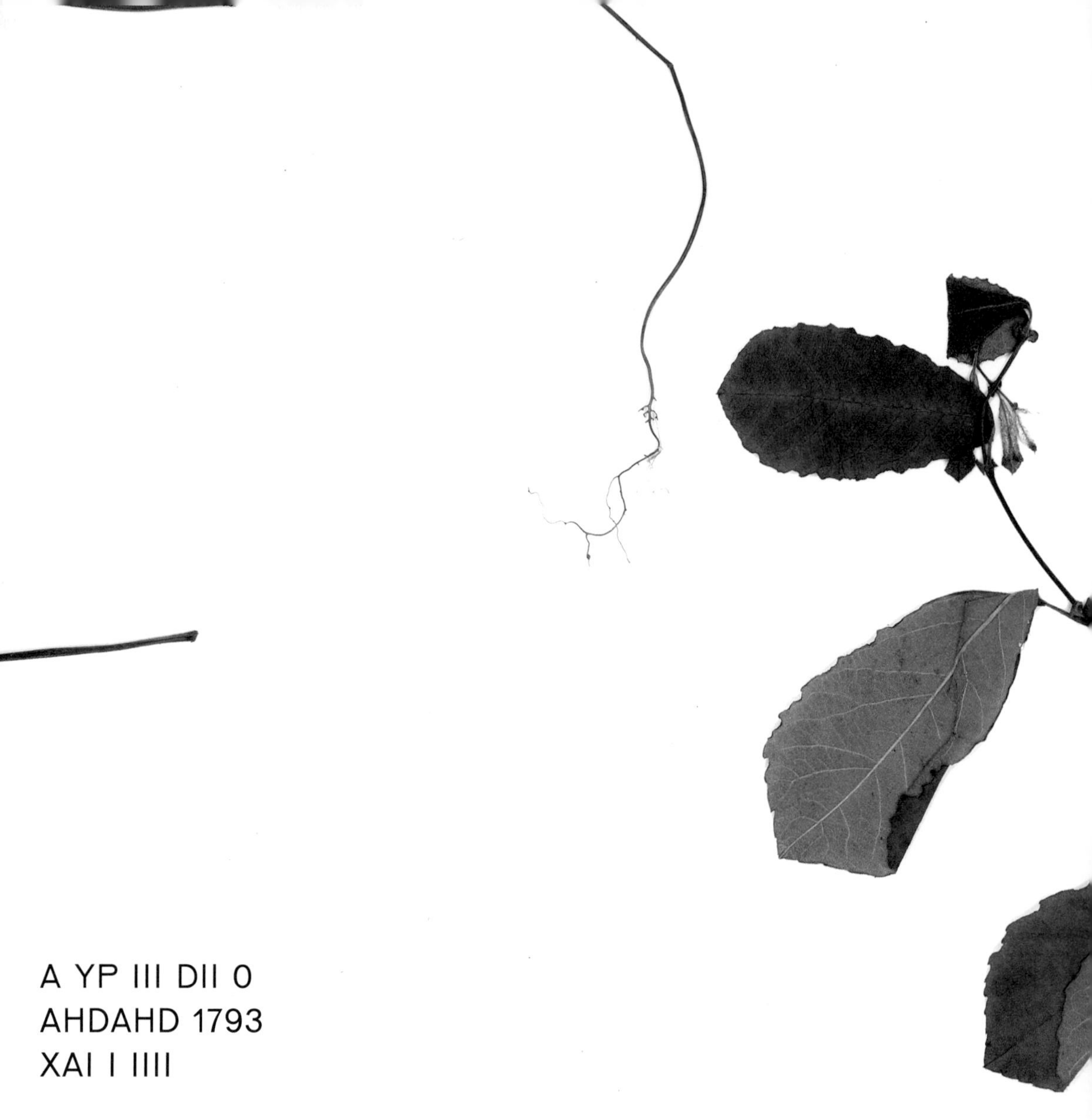

A YP III DII 0
AHDAHD 1793
XAI I IIII

blowing horn
pin cushion
a needle and a thread

stay in the glade   write your name
with a friend

K (x3)
M (x2)
O (x2)
D (x3)
A (x3)

i repeat AOD

B

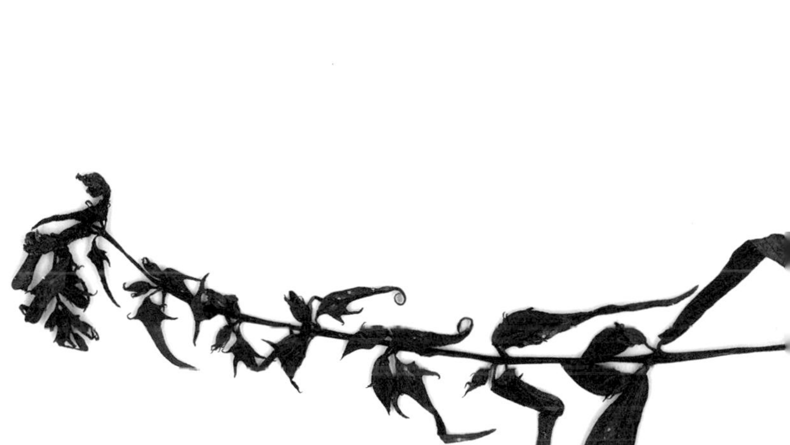

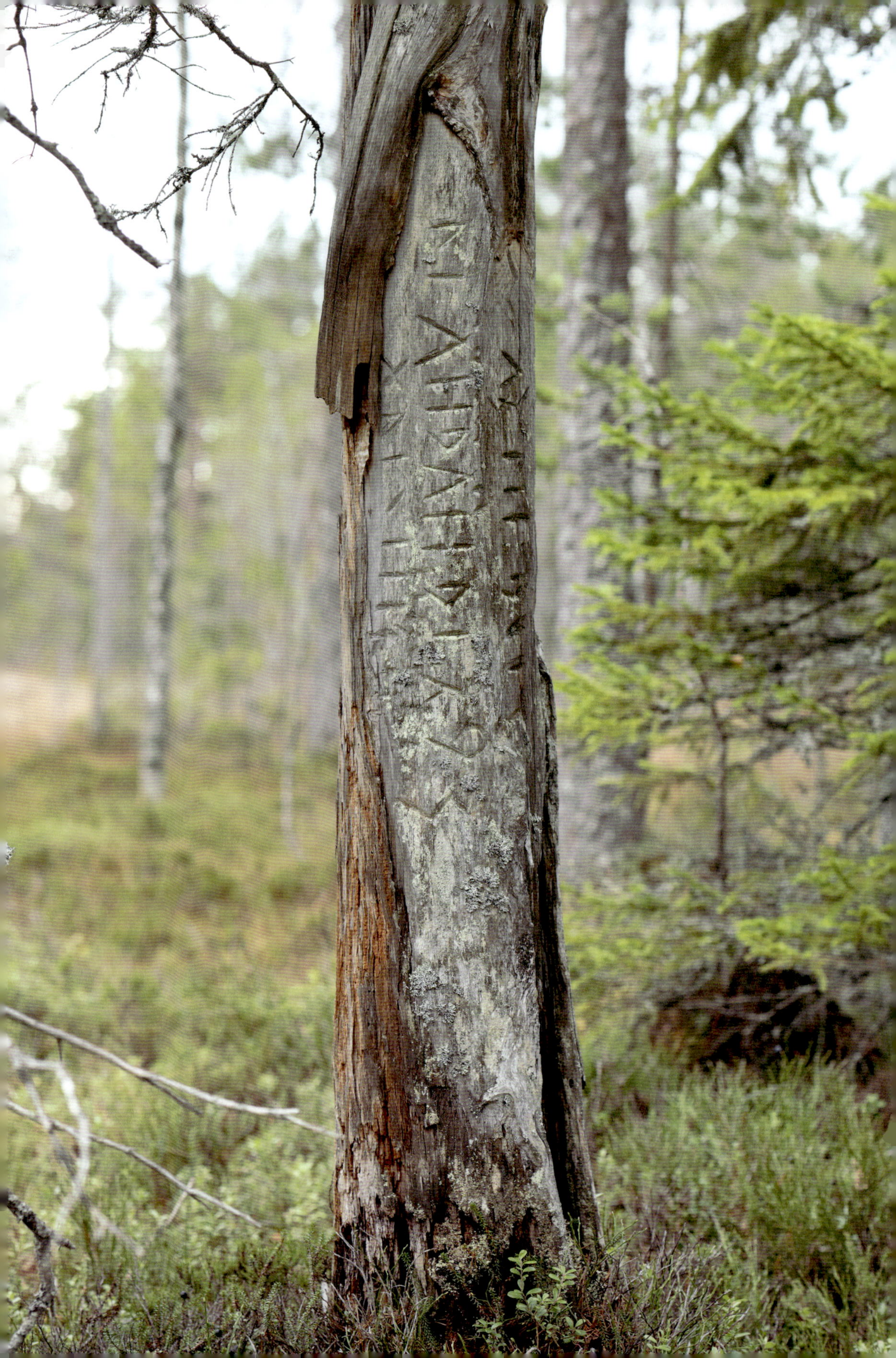

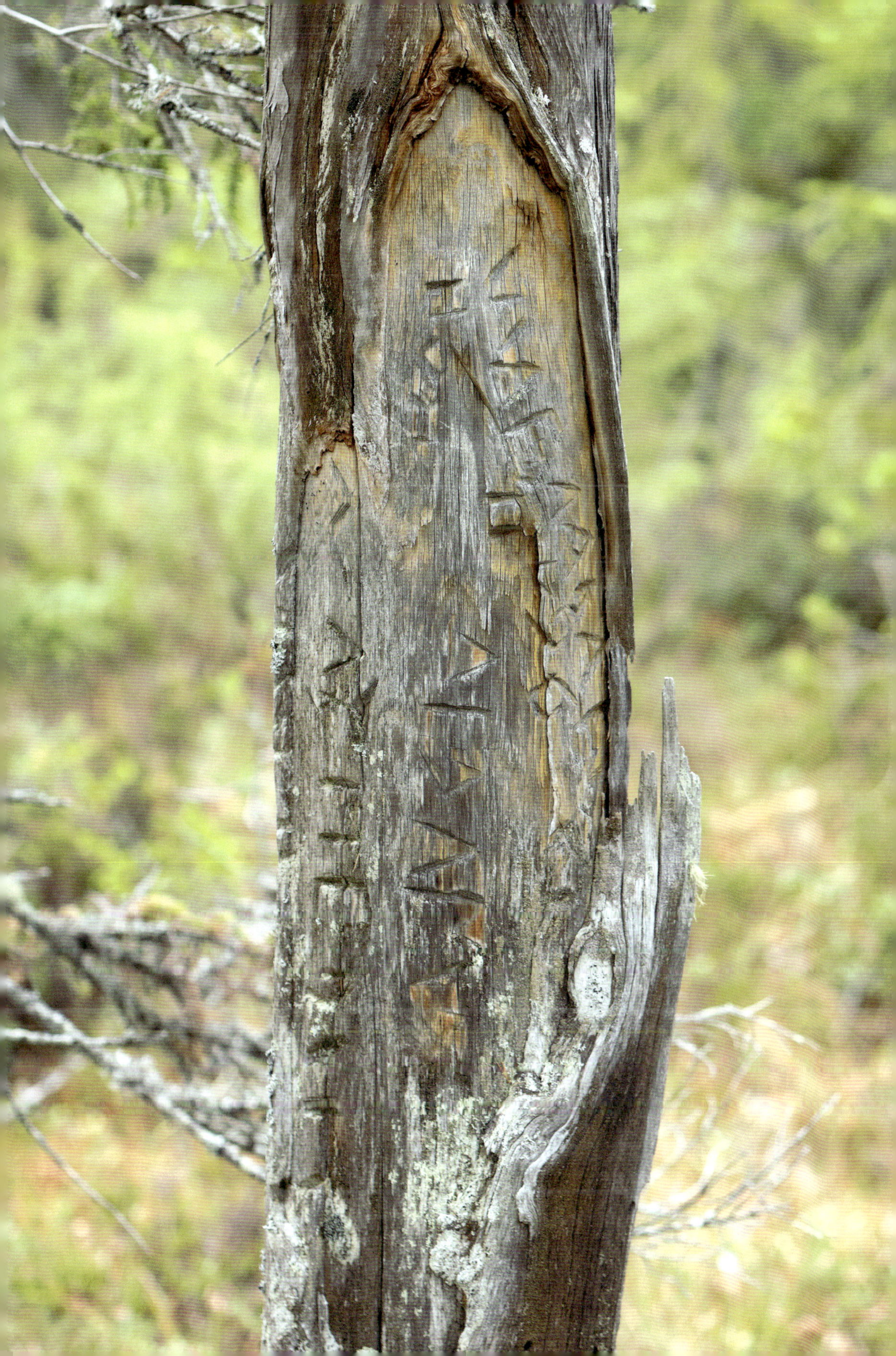

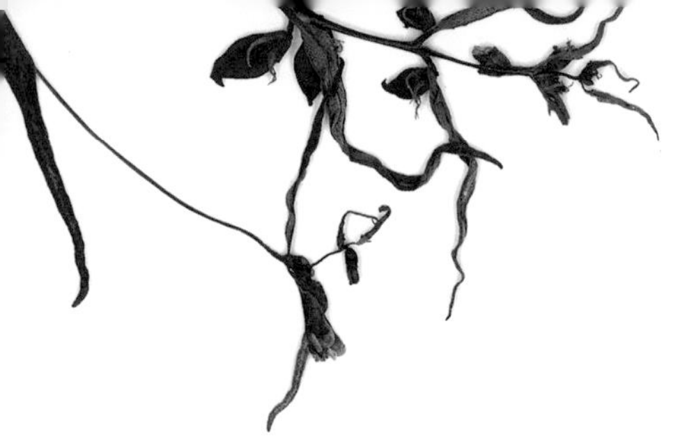

you carved autumn

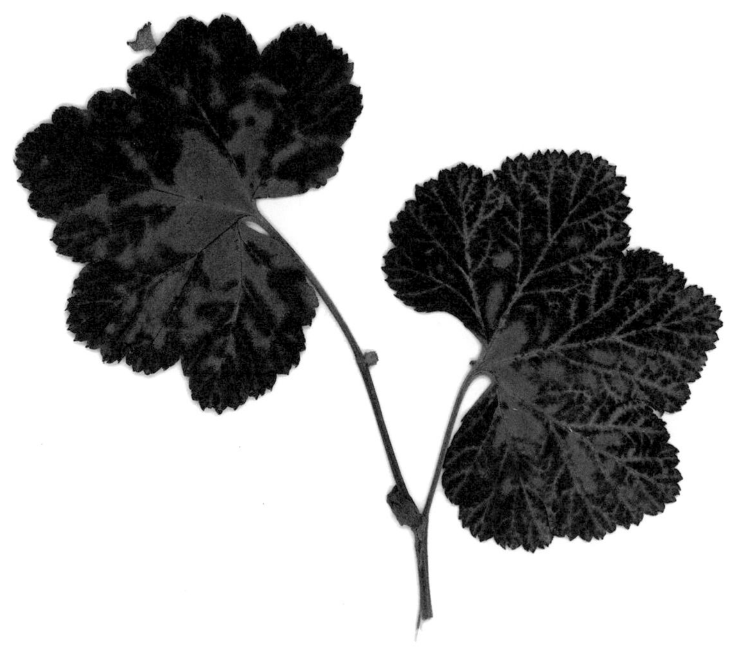

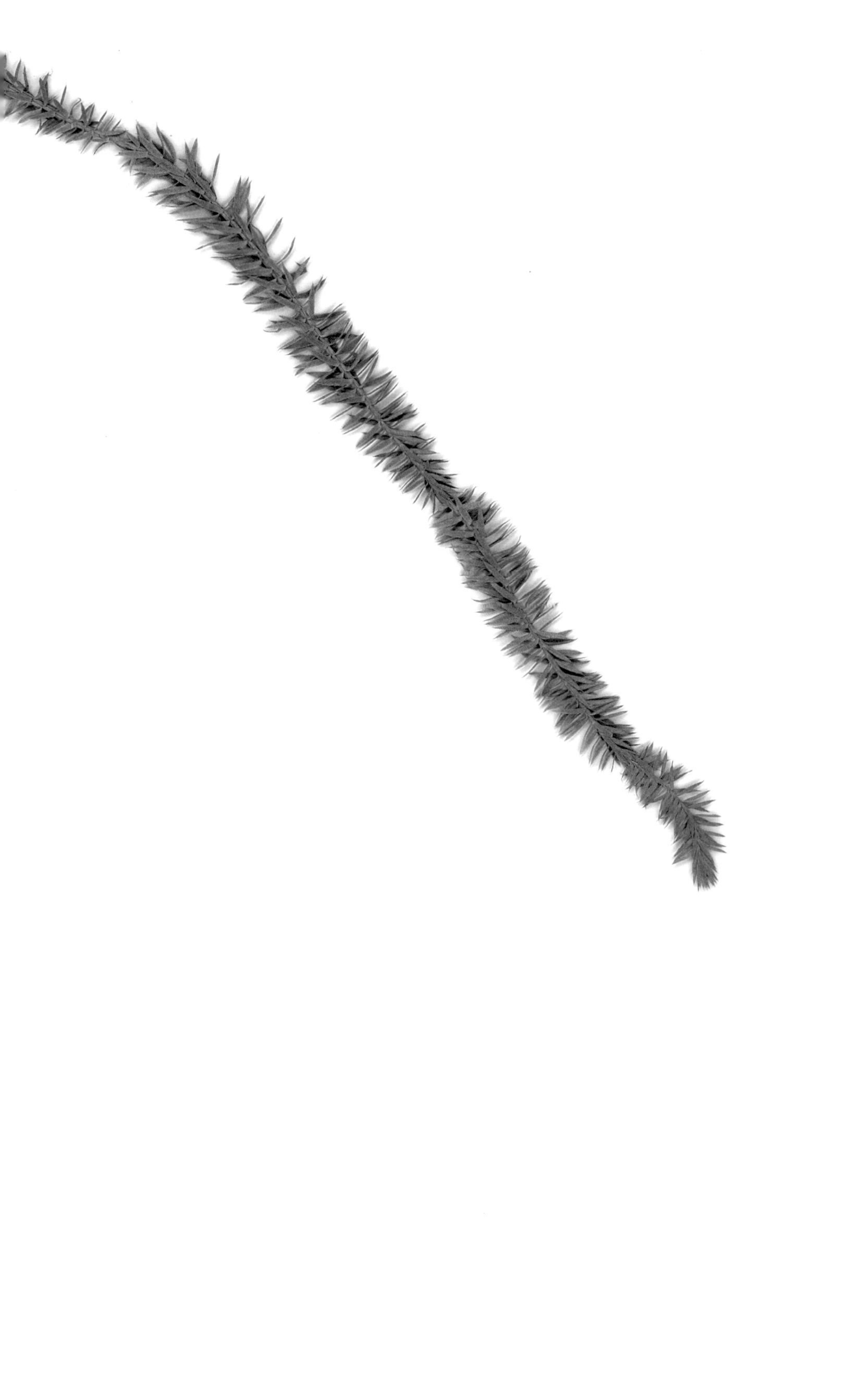

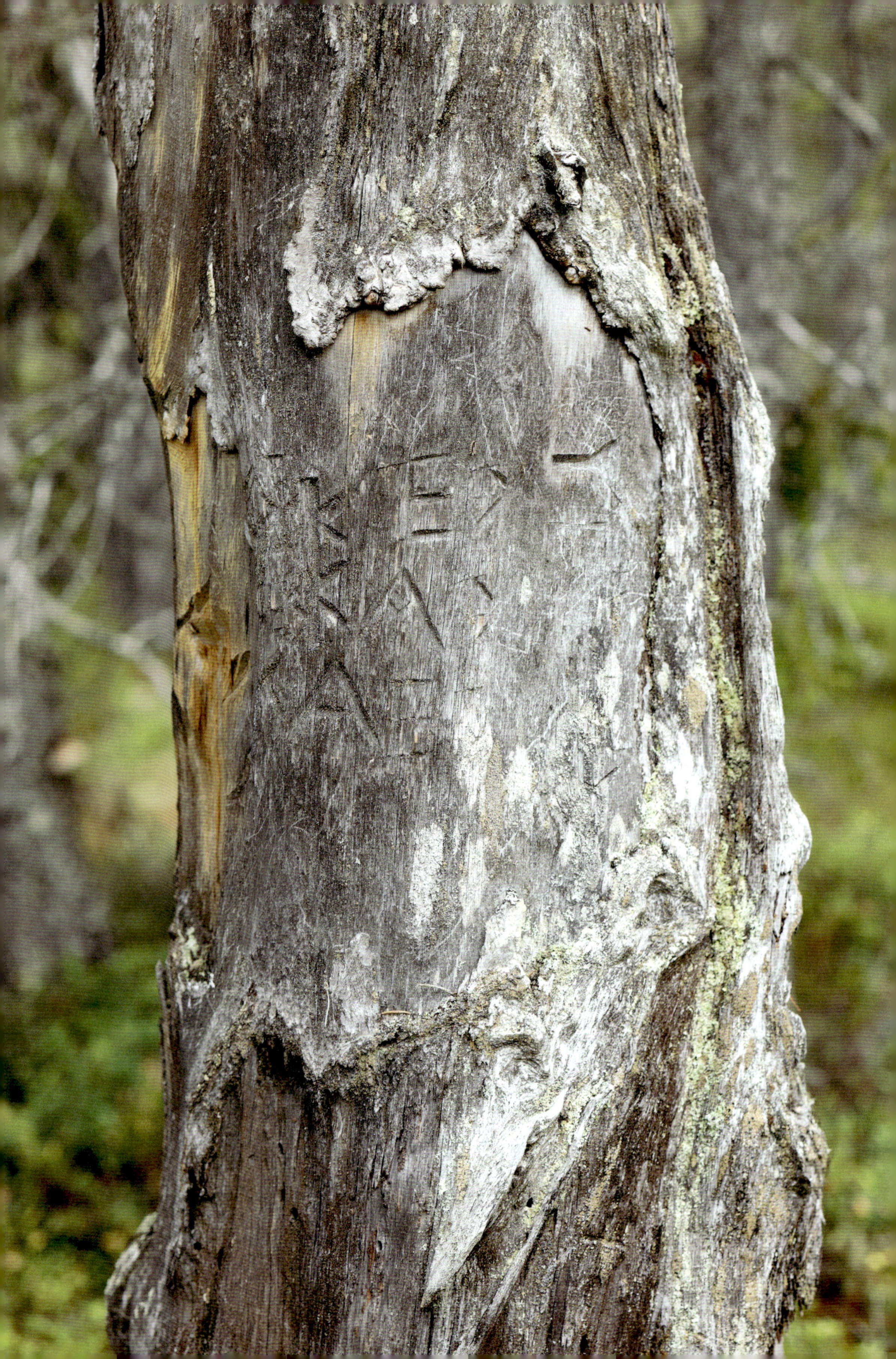

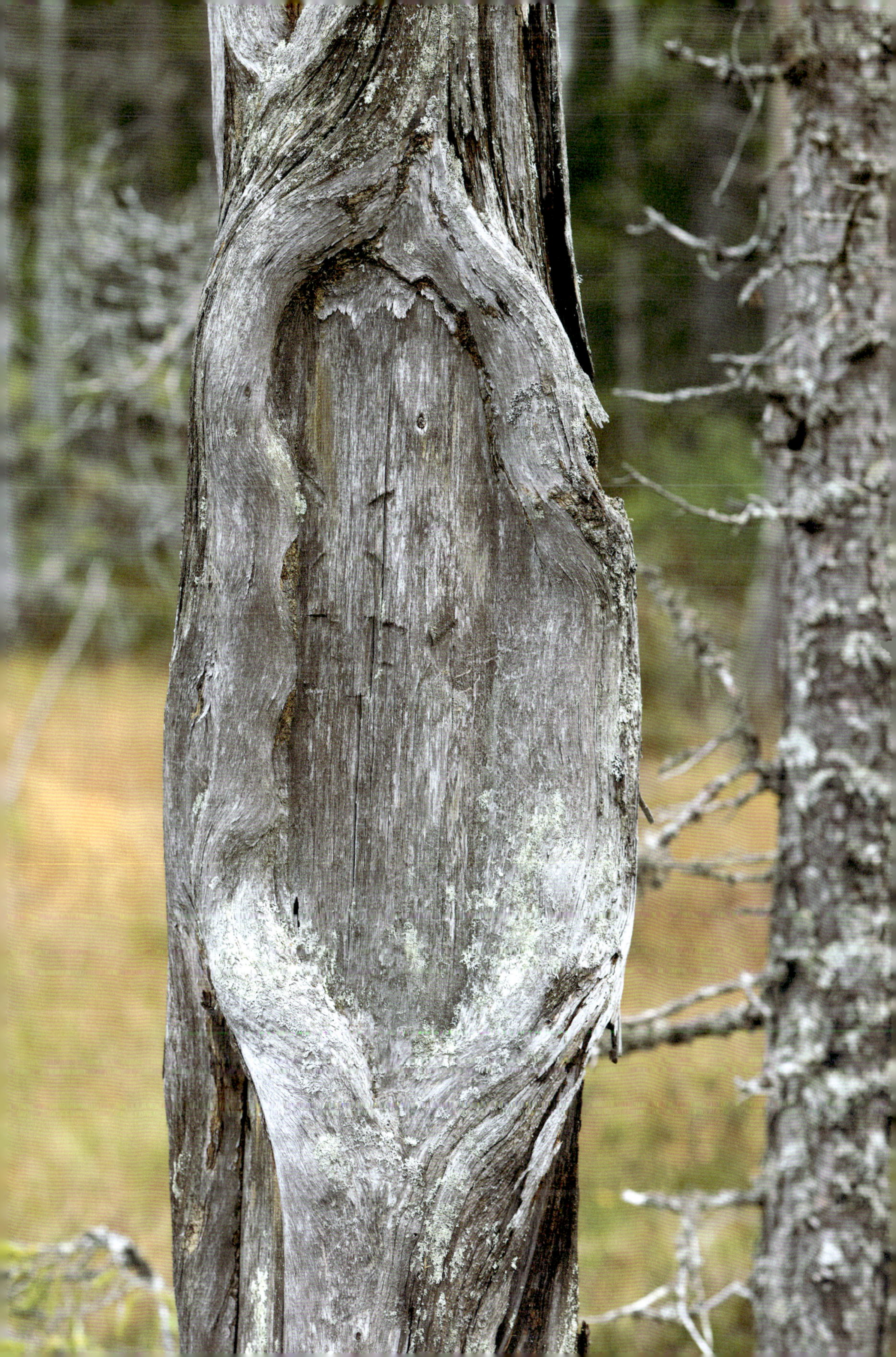

march 2021

the trees are sticking out of the white blankets of snow
it's still cold, but as the sun comes up, the snow begins to melt
   we are driving on a road covered with ice   i'm afraid of slipping

as we come closer to the mountain we enter a gravel road

soon i notice how the road started to thaw in places and become
a muddy mess   the mud is worse than the ice
i make deep tracks with the wheels and feel stressed about how
i am ruining the road   we stop and park the car and start walking

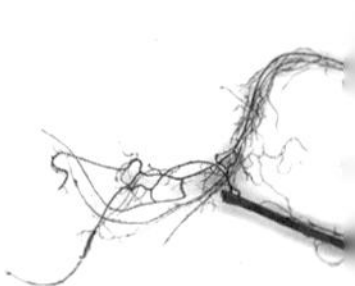

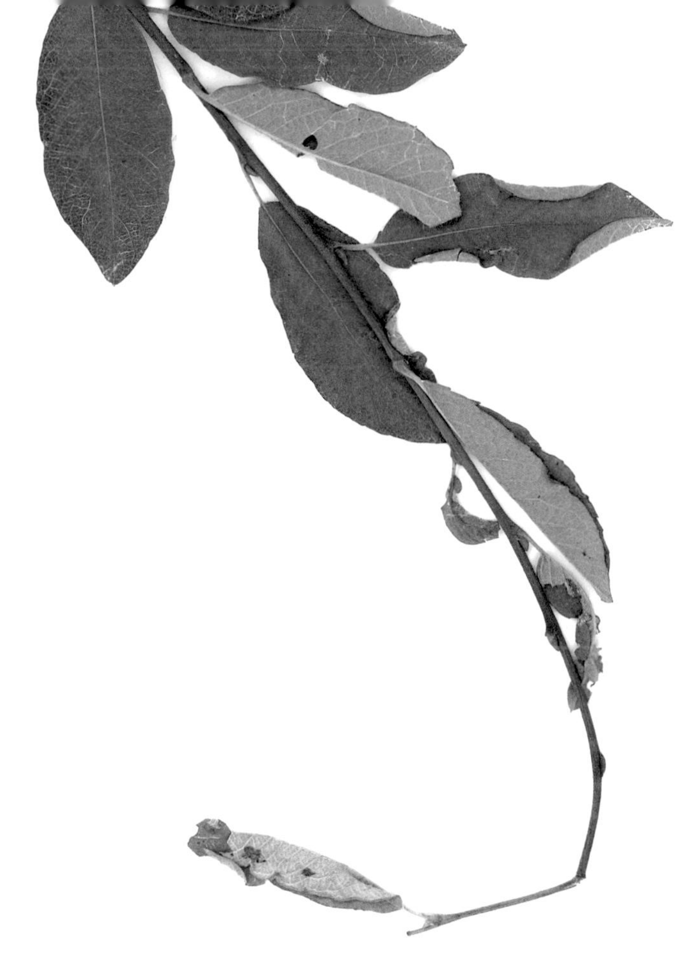

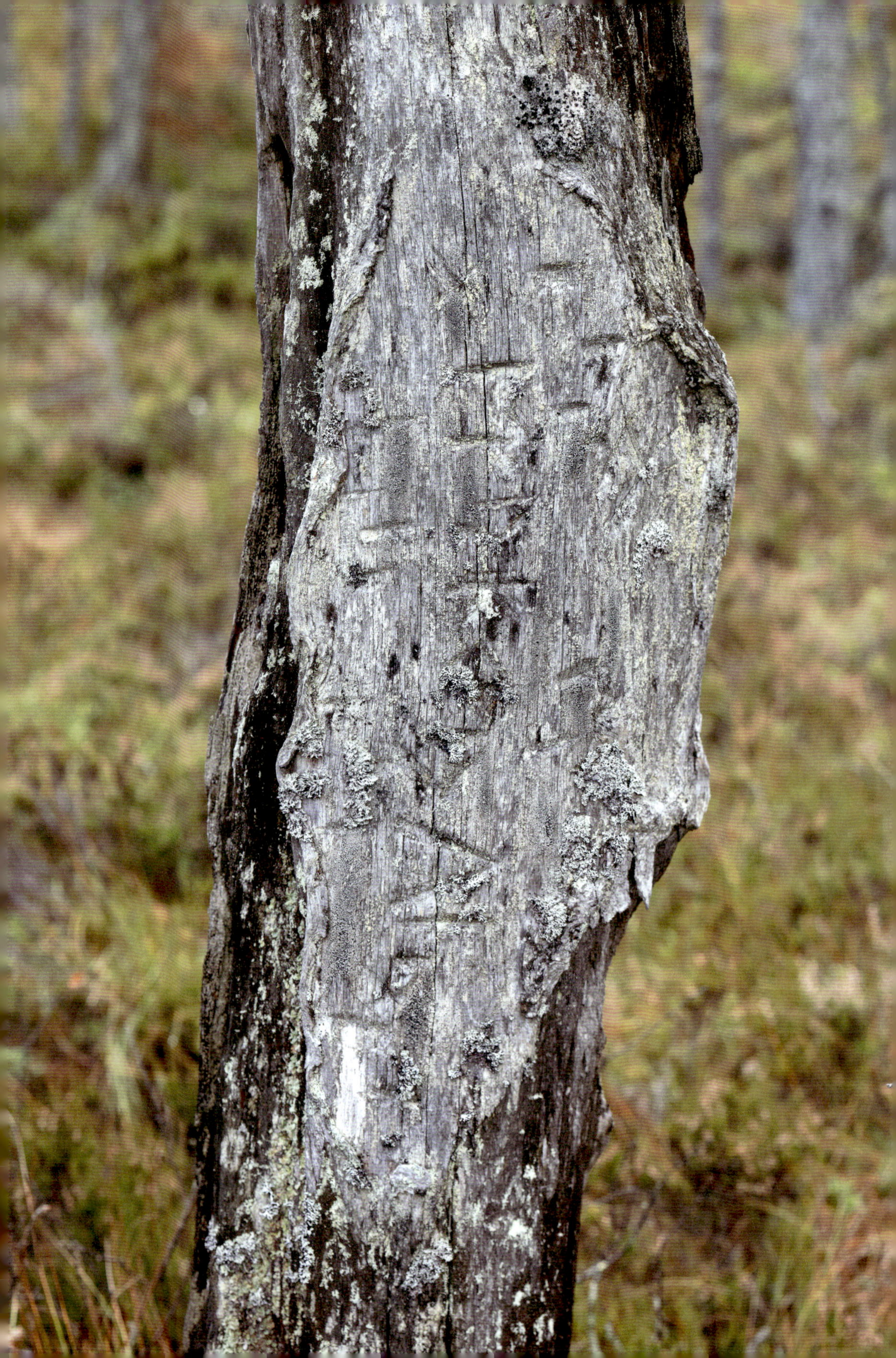

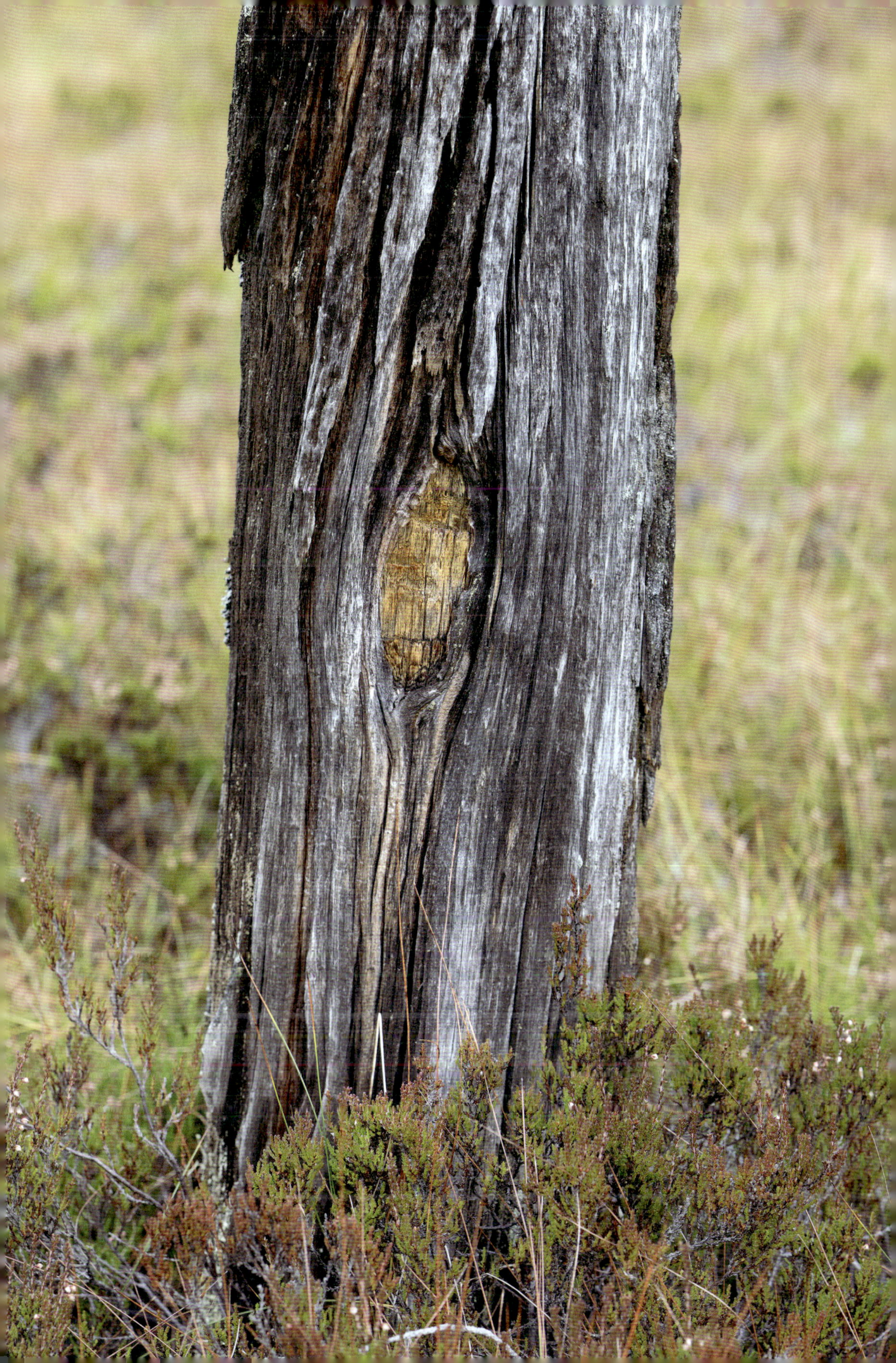

08:00
i sit in front of my computer screen and browse through the pictures
   i look at one tree trunk at a time   trying to decipher
the carved letters that run vertically with the trunk

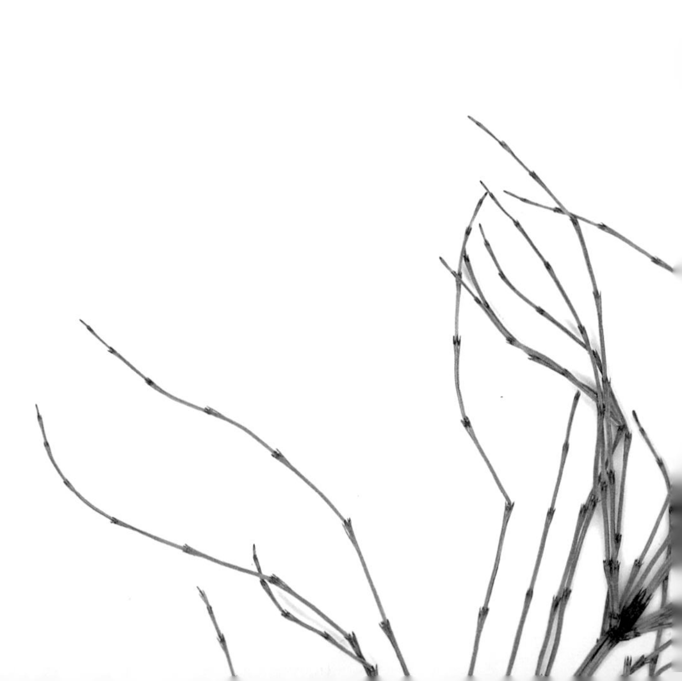

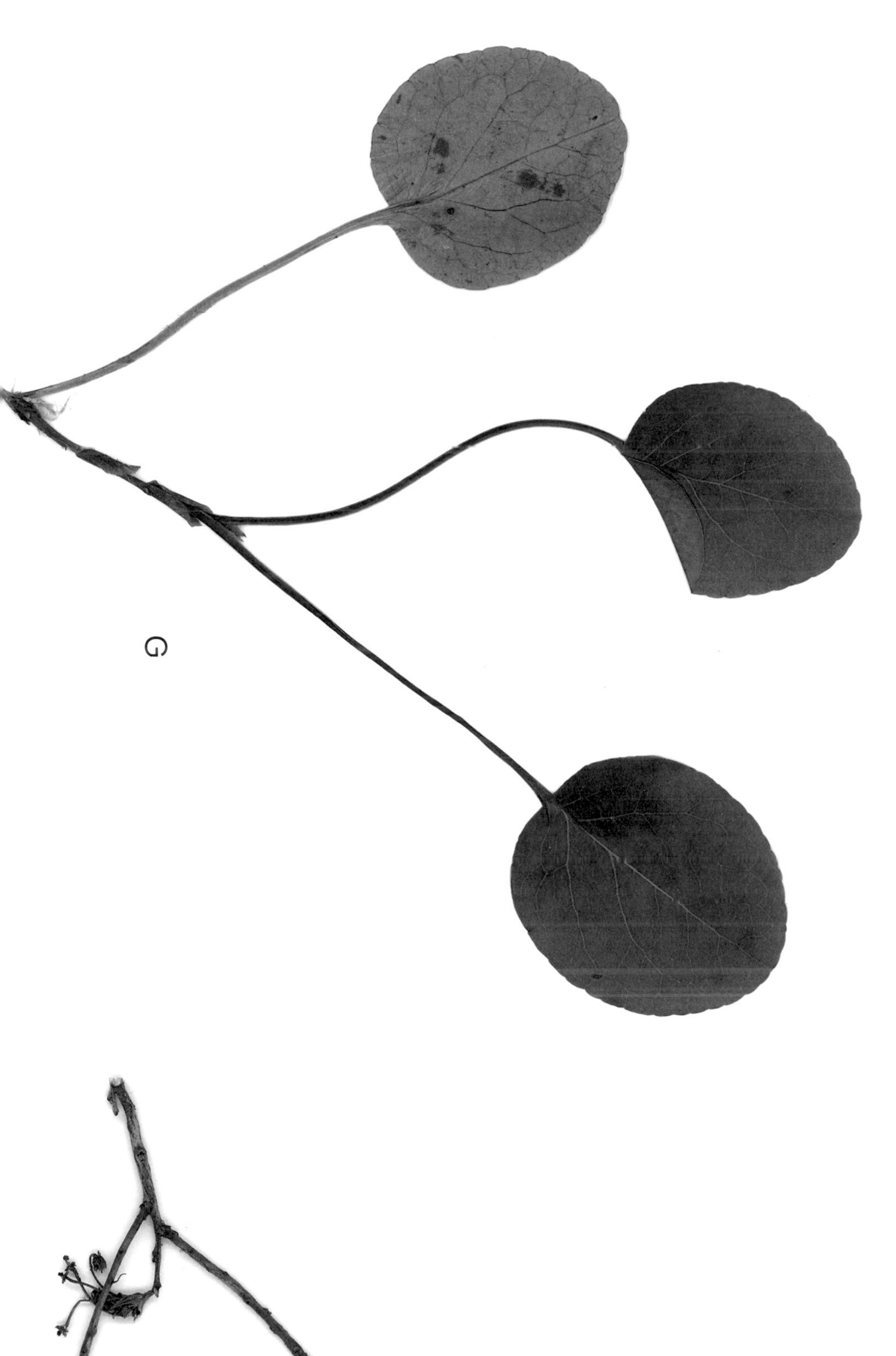
G

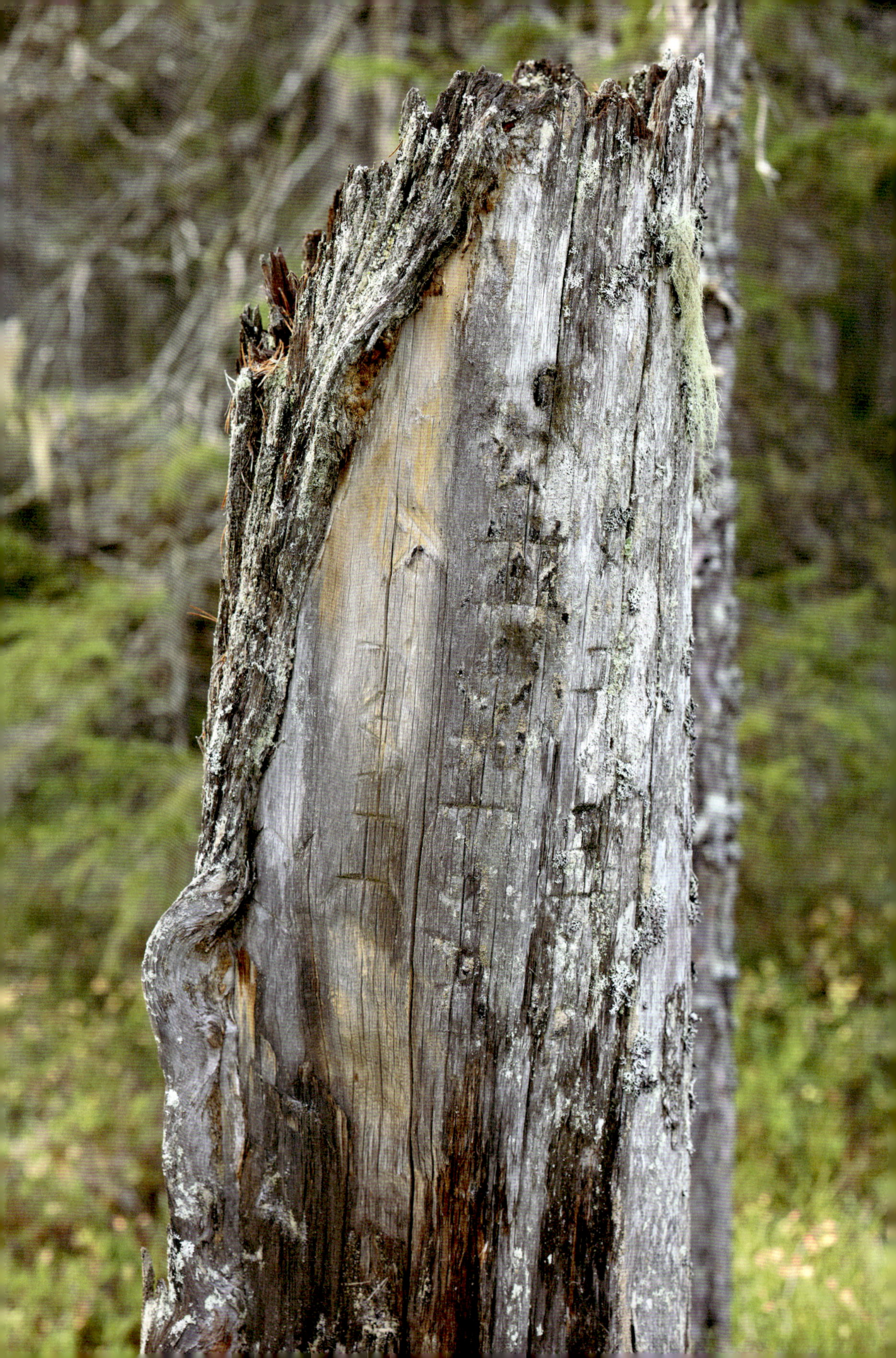

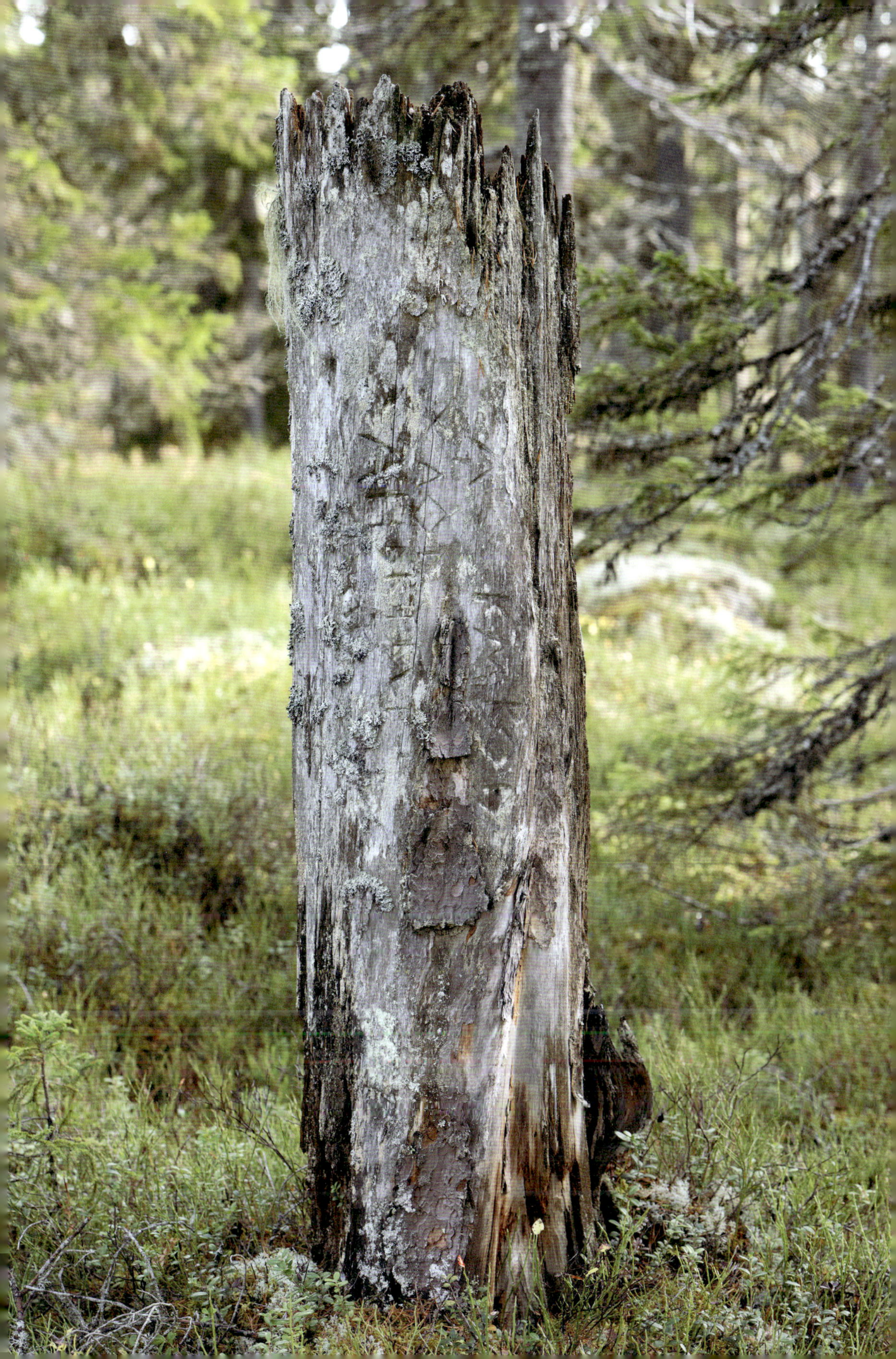

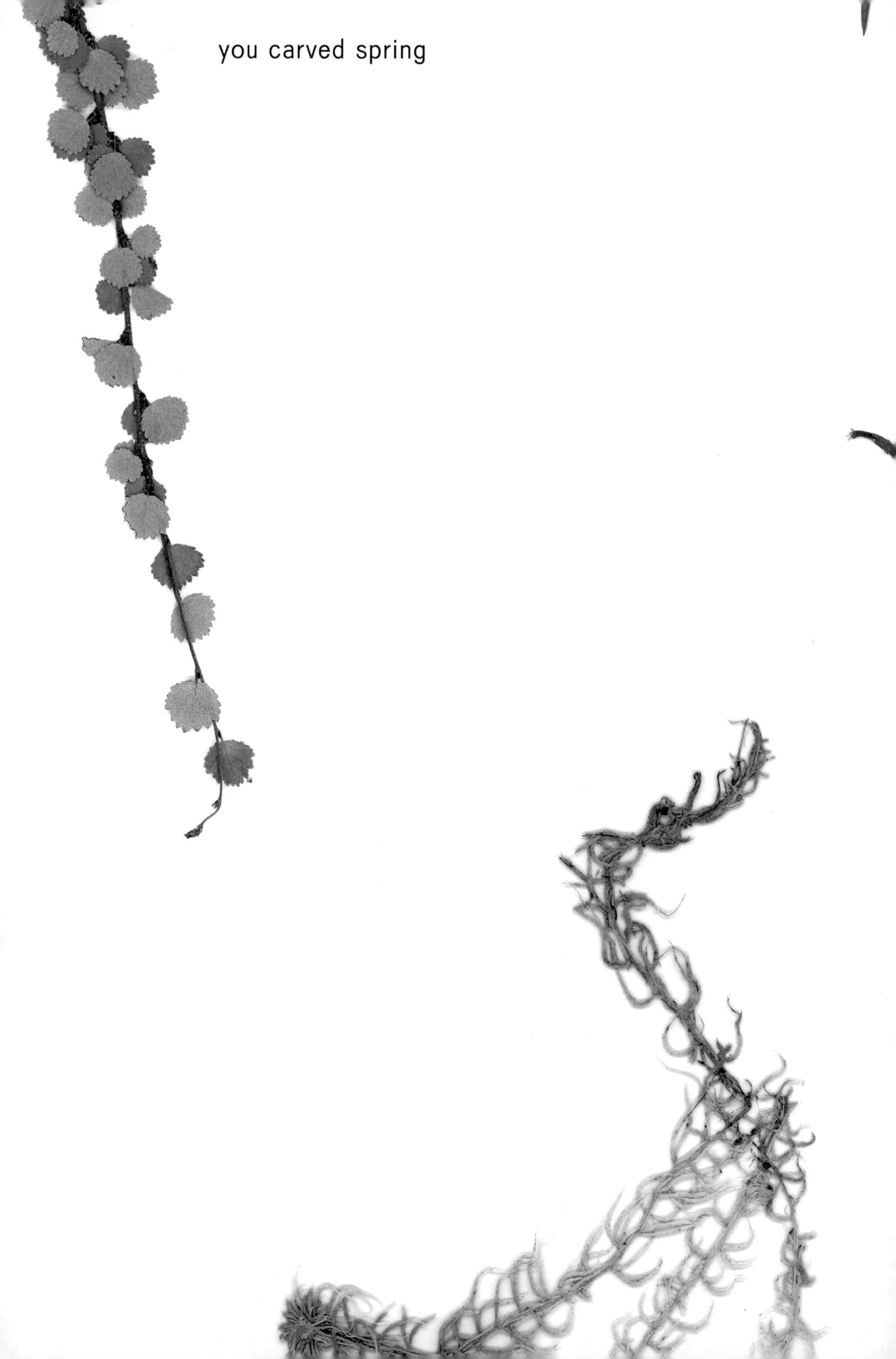
you carved spring

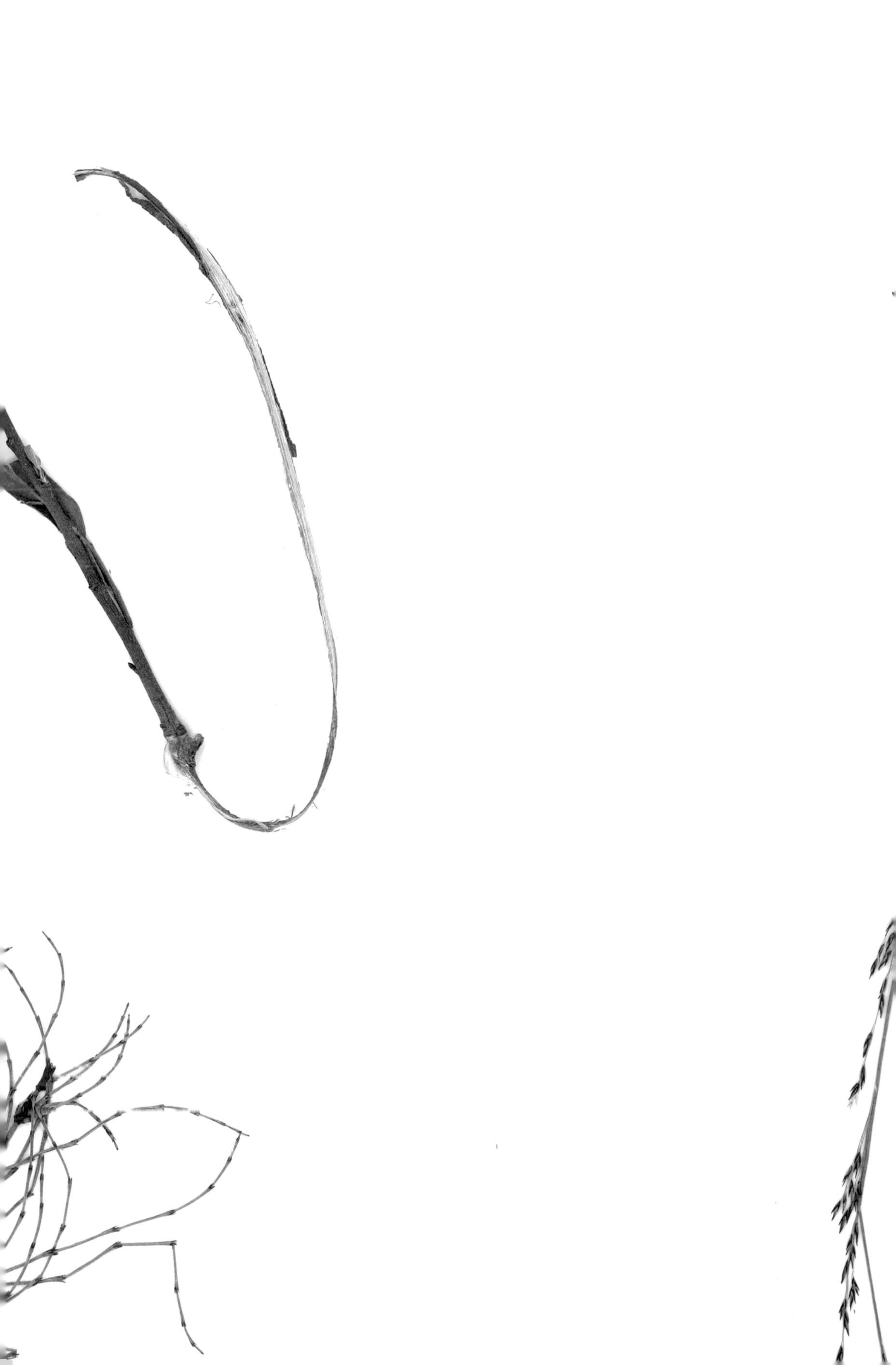

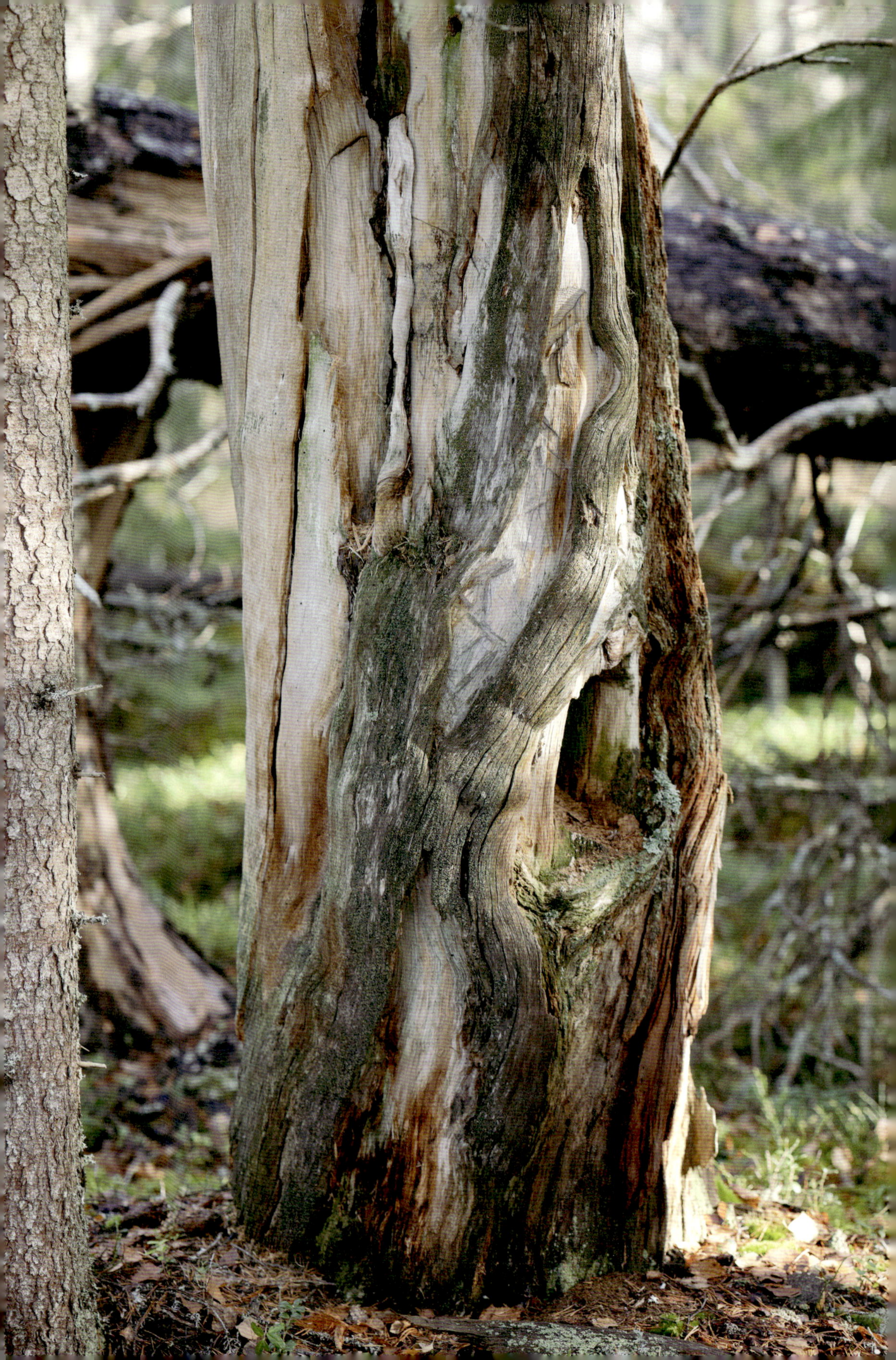

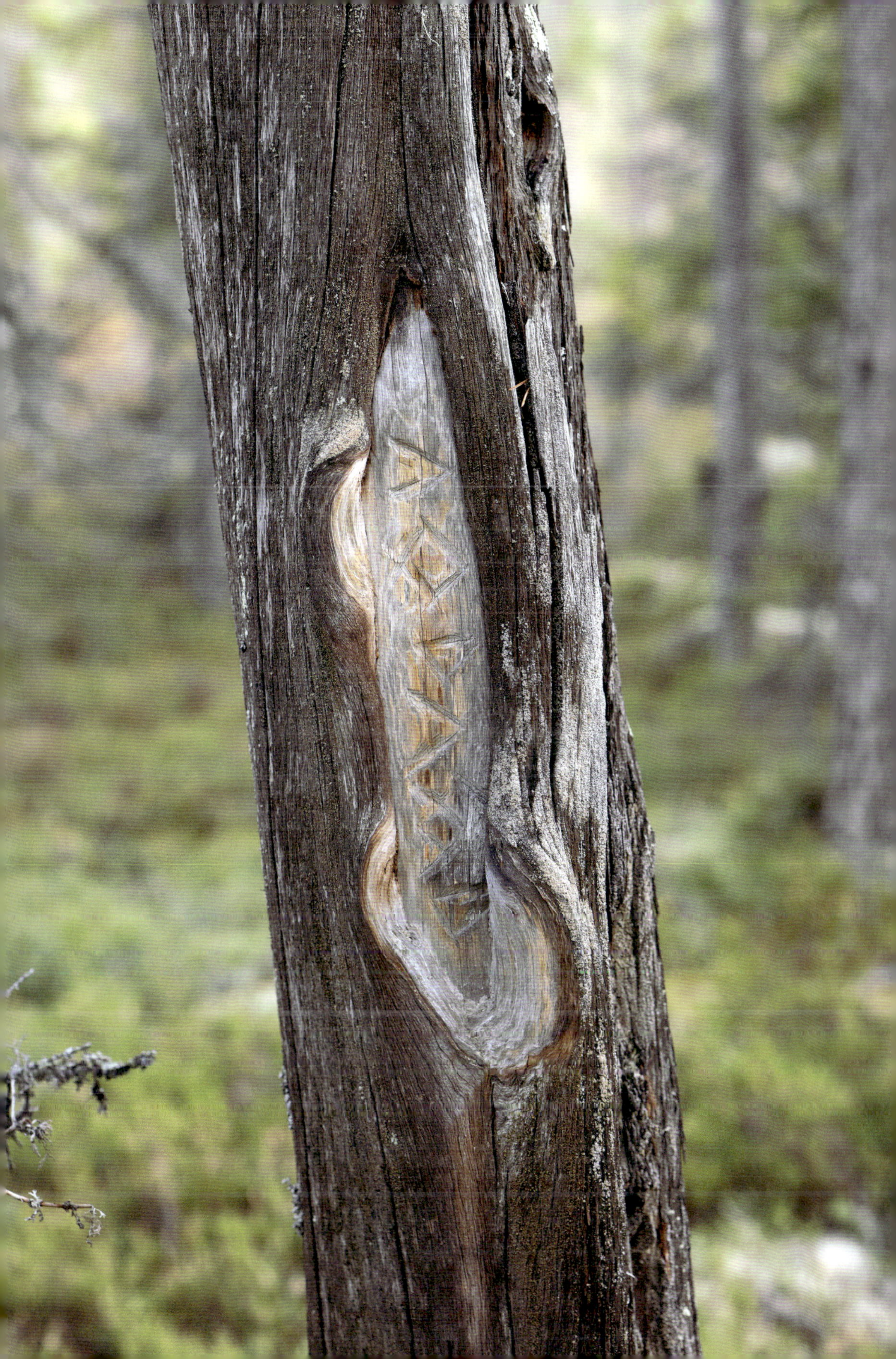

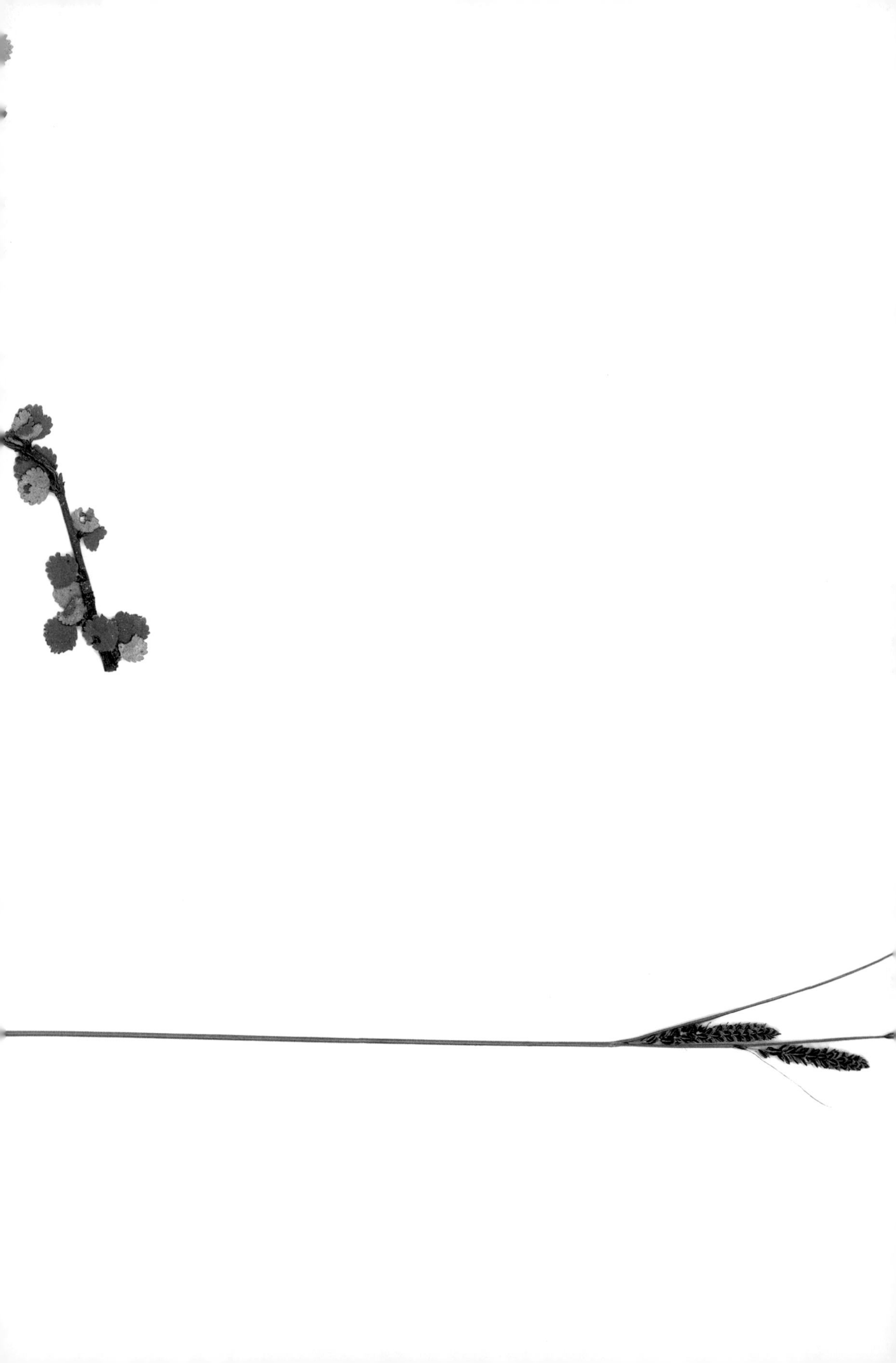

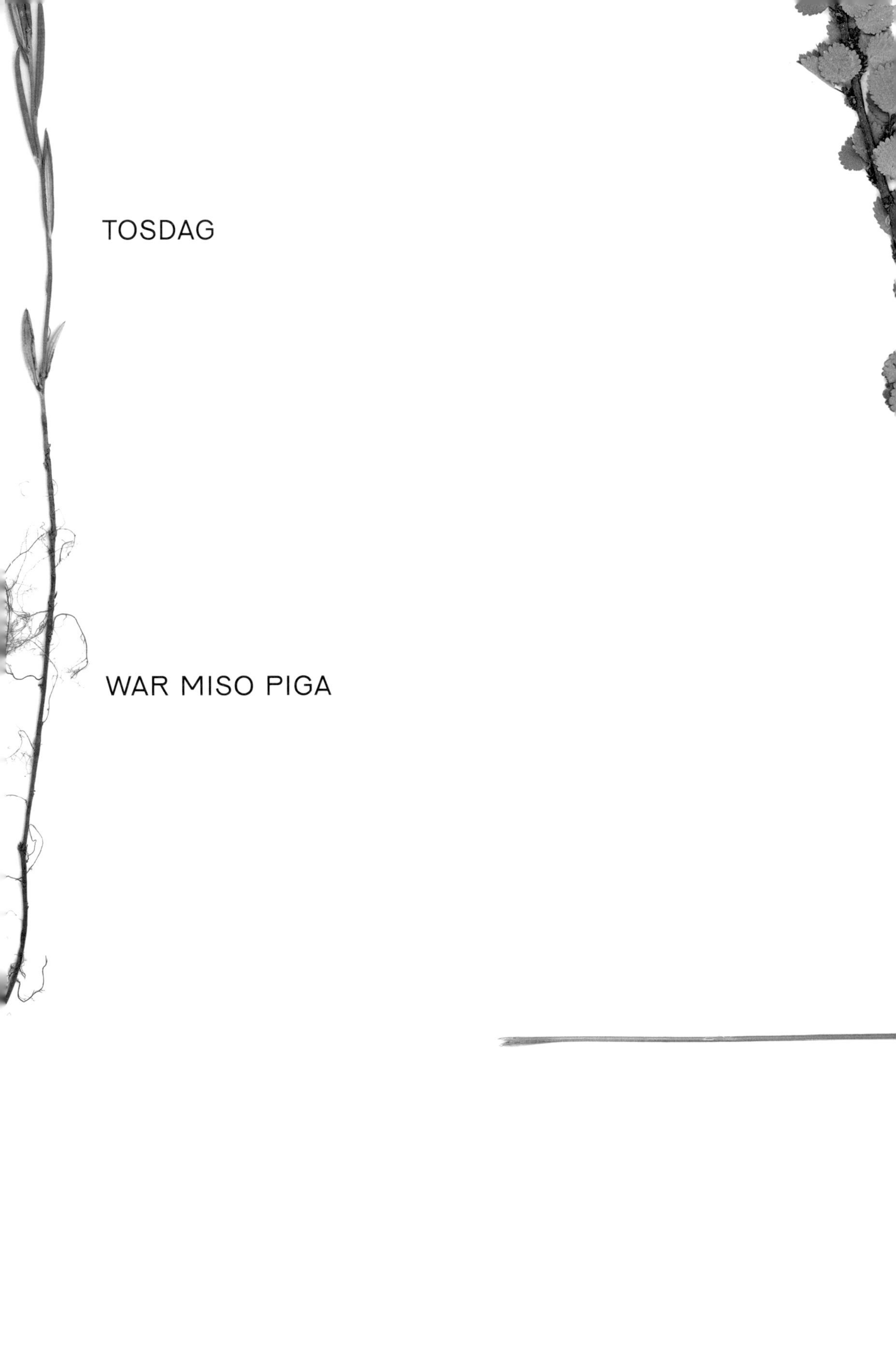
TOSDAG
WAR MISO PIGA

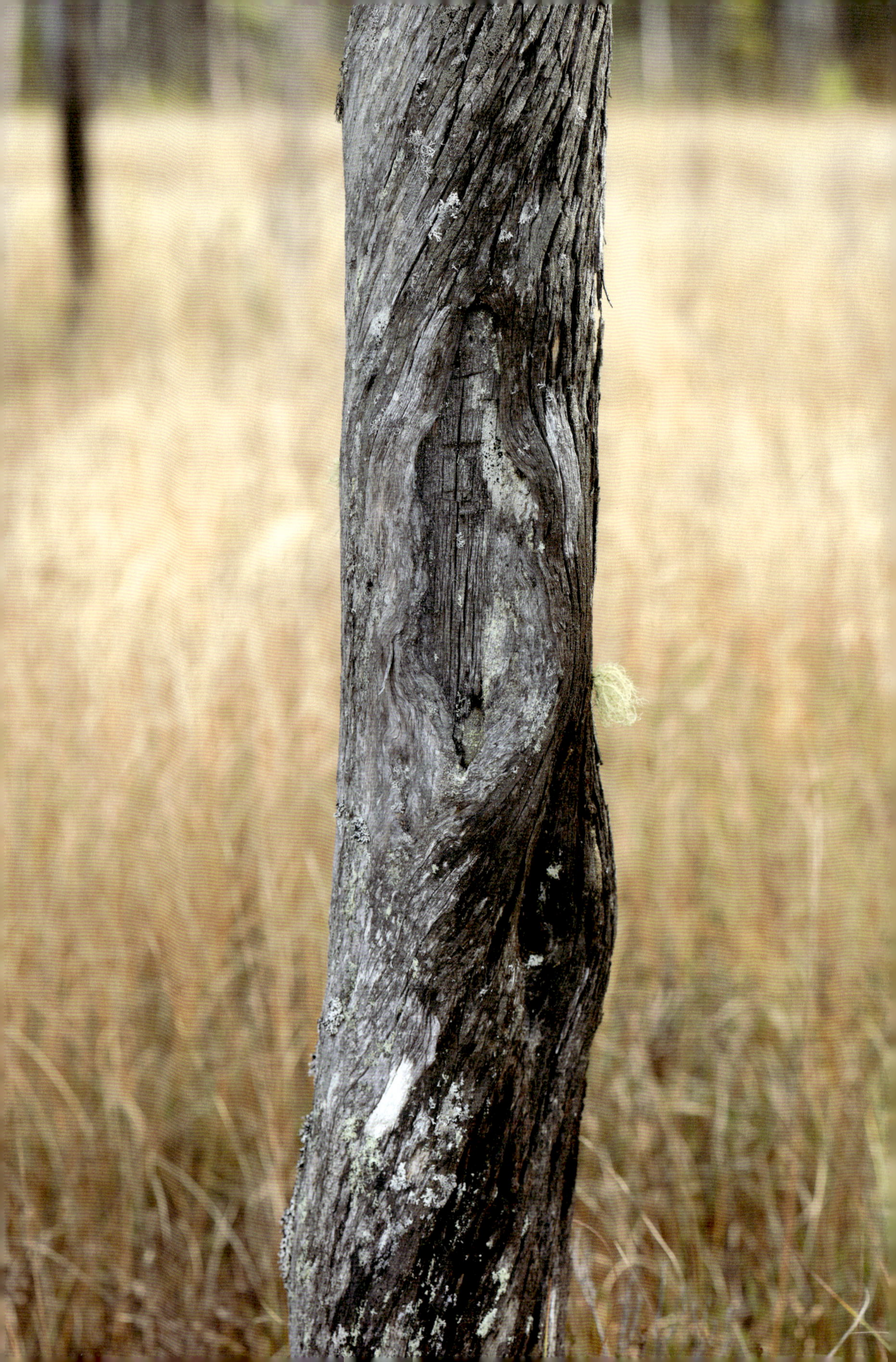

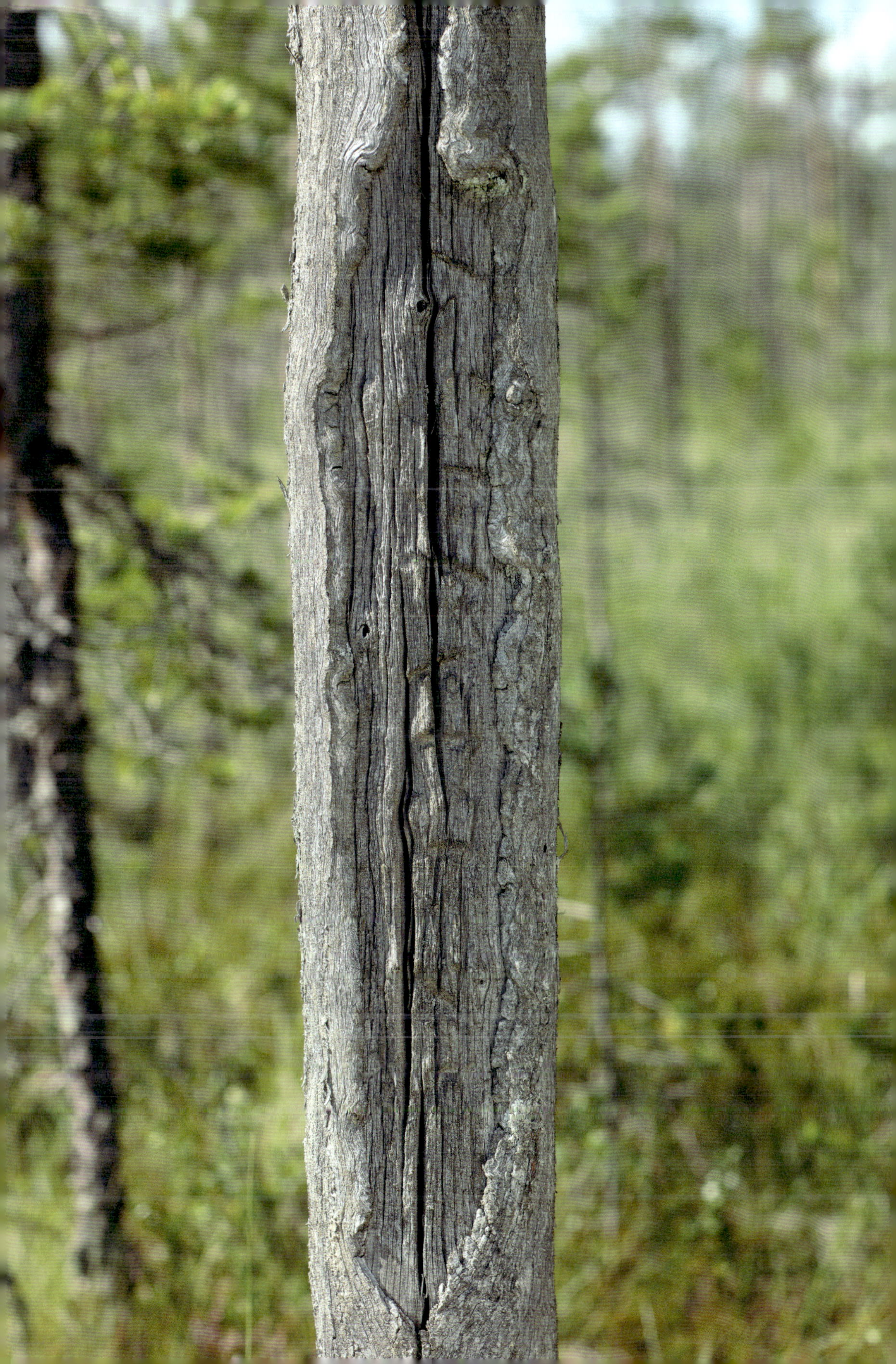

II   I   III X

I '   I   ' '   X

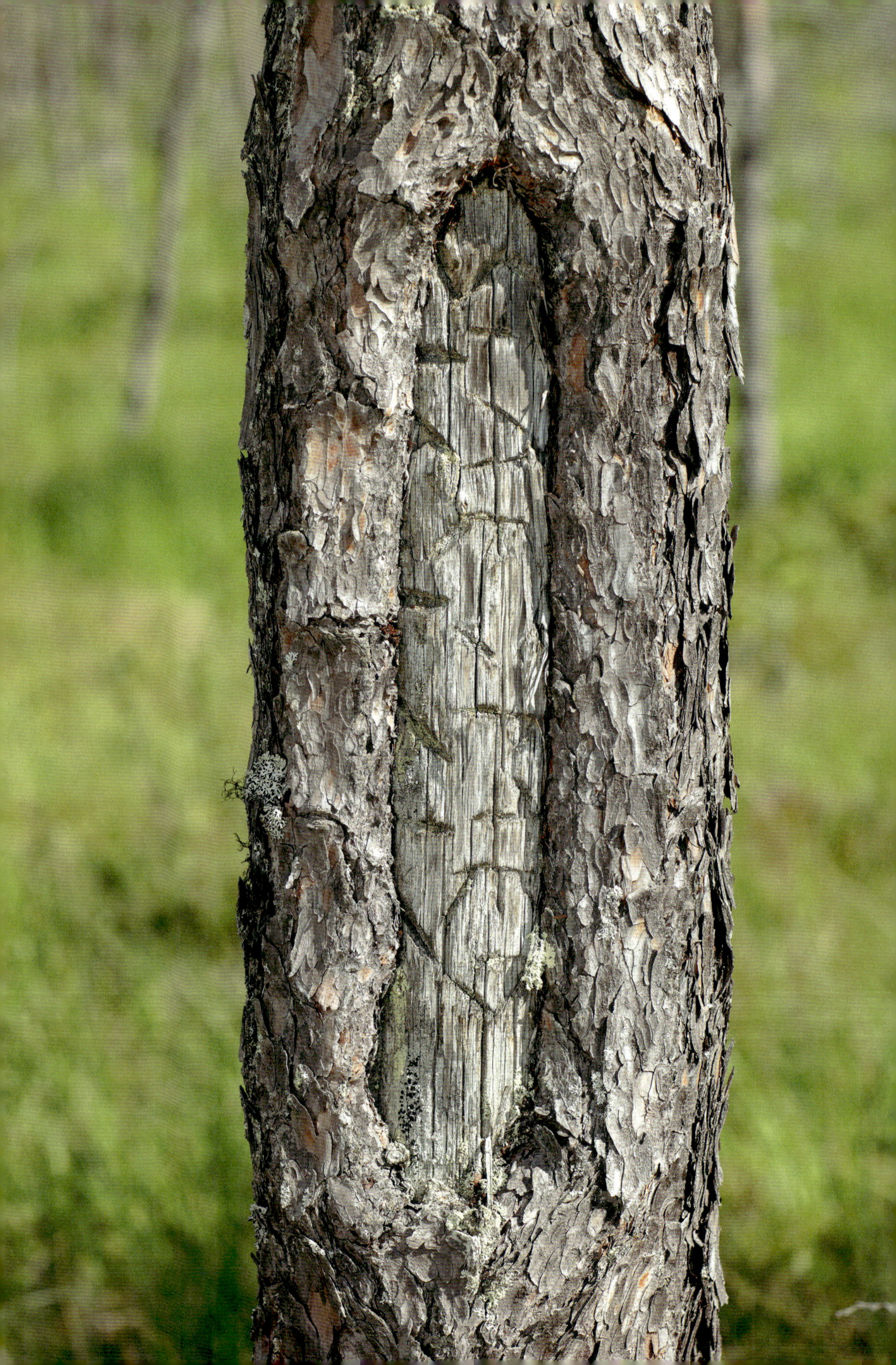

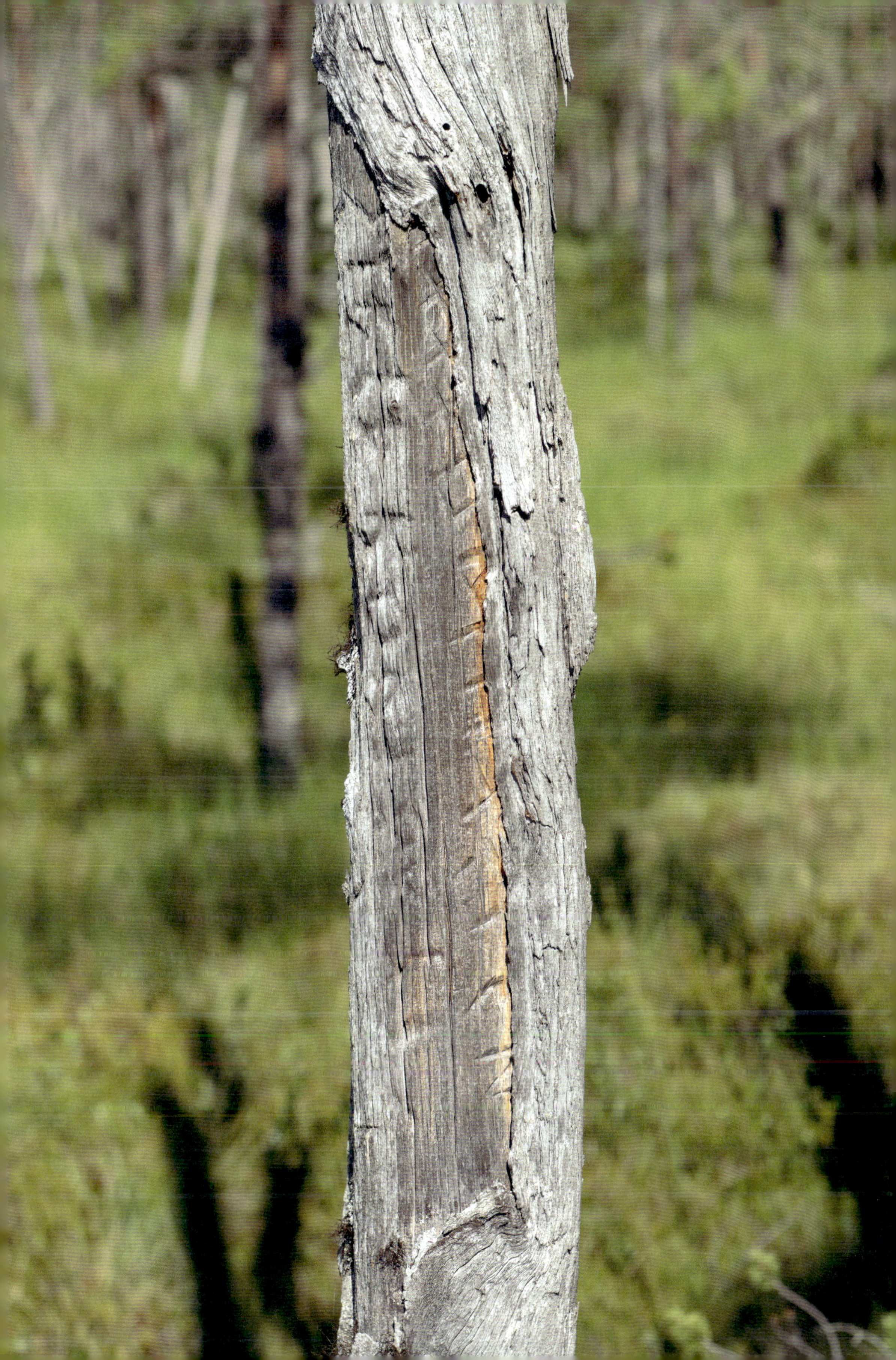

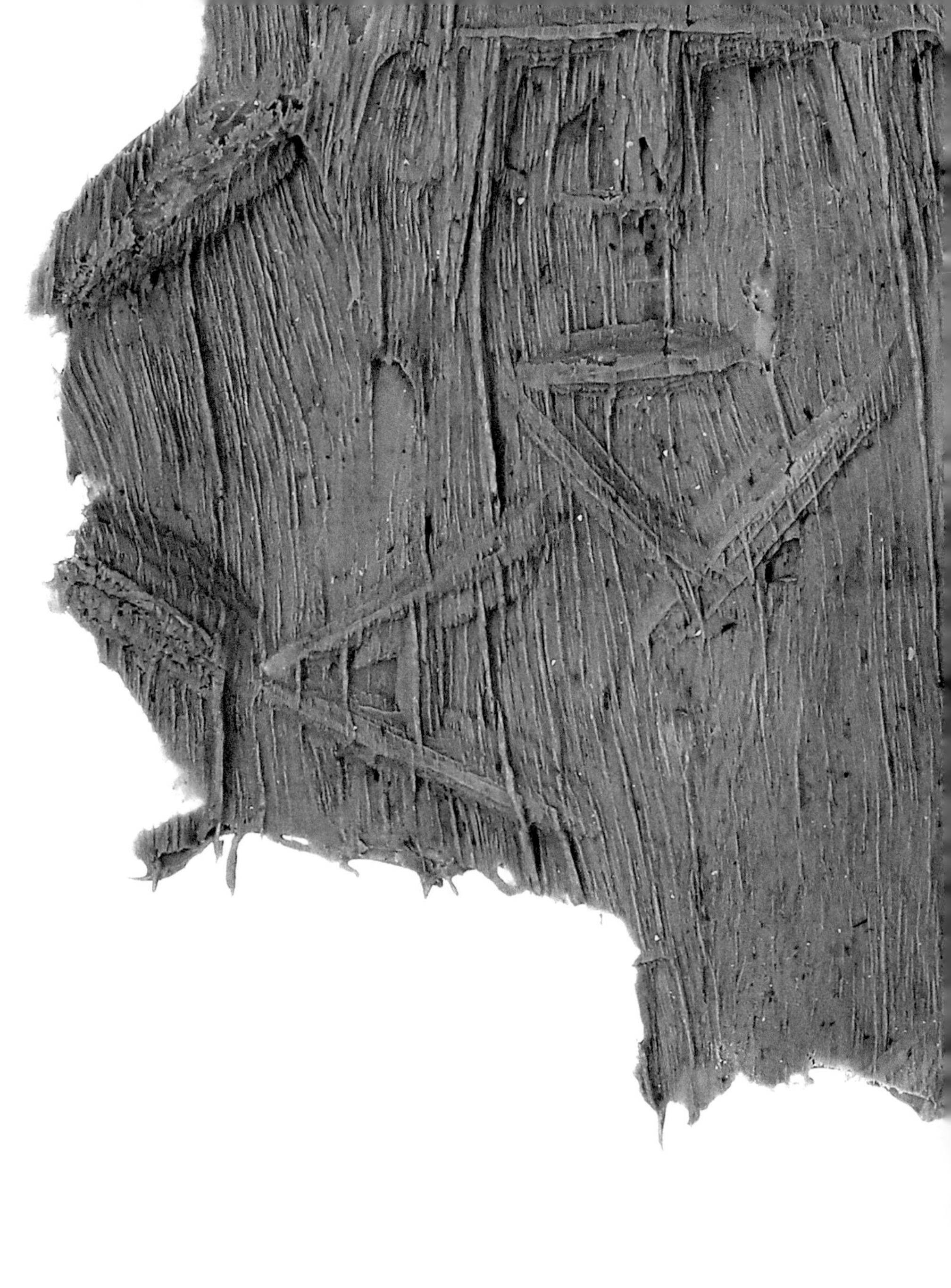

S

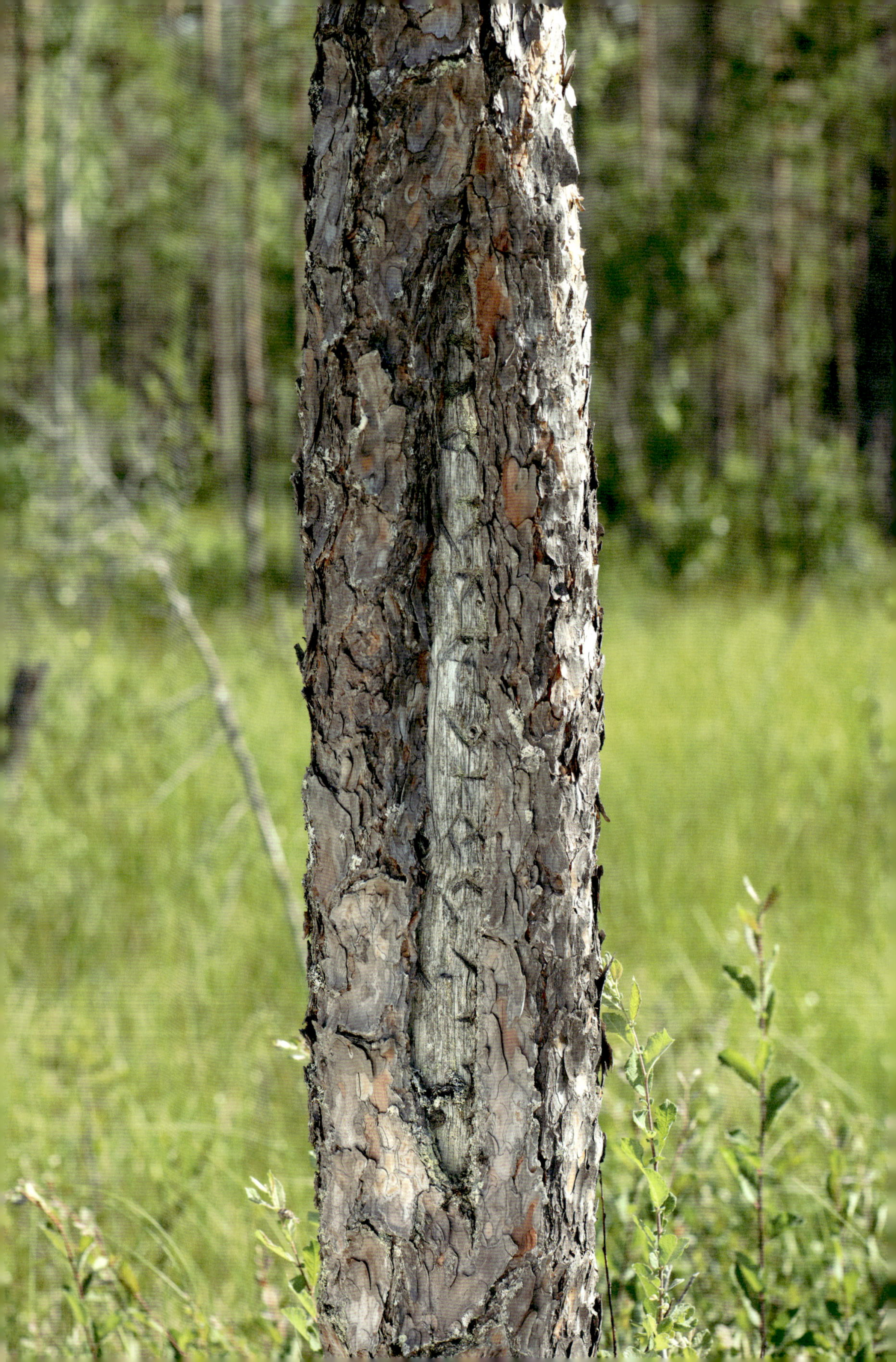

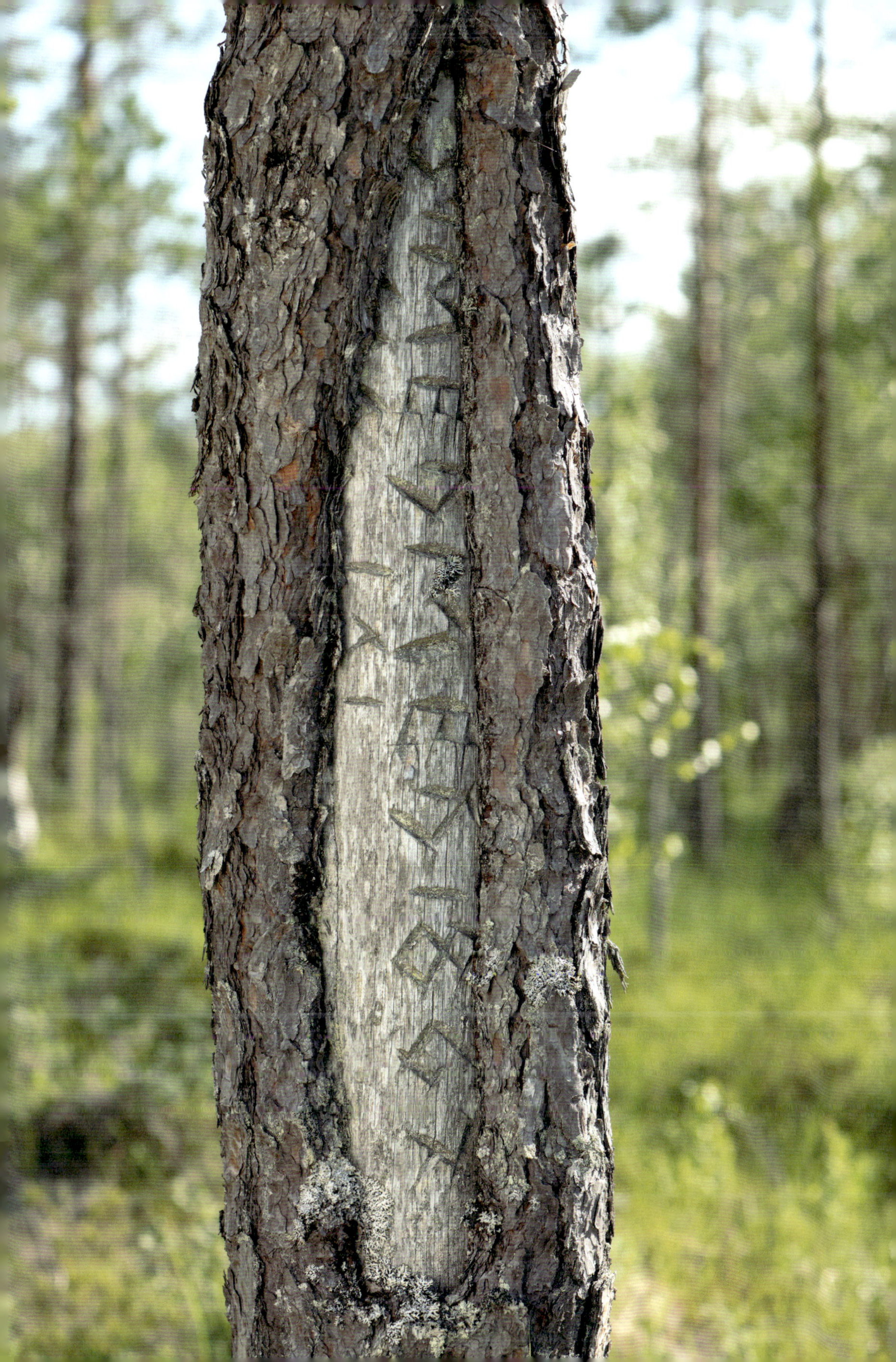

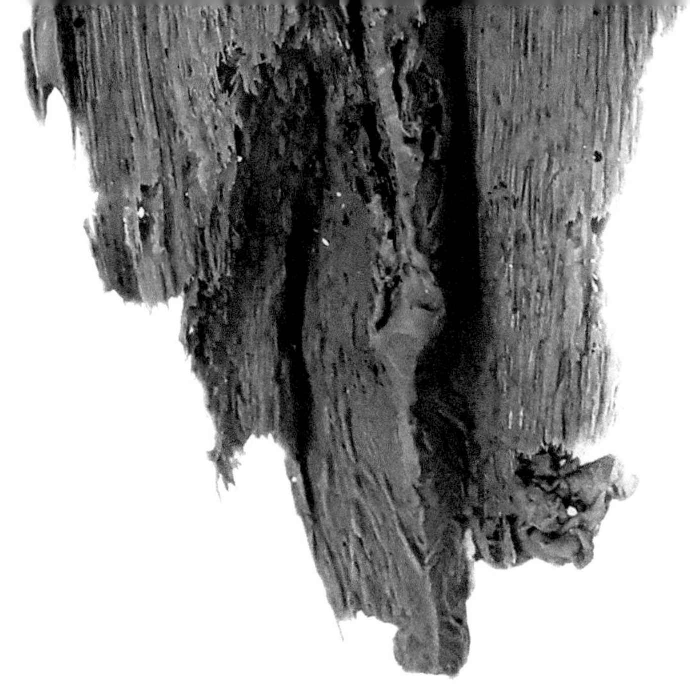

AMD X60

人

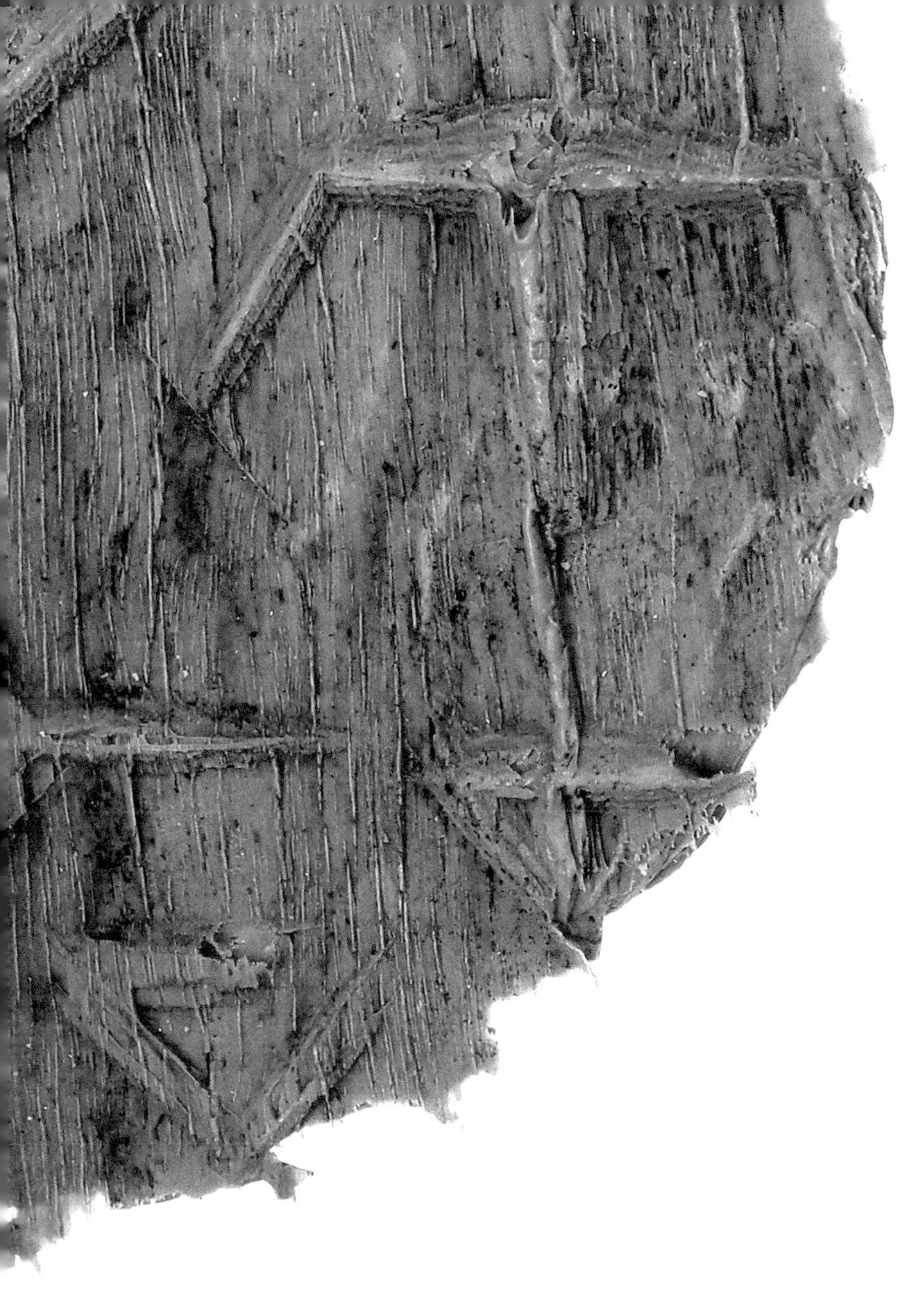

A RO HOS EN

HAR DU   108518

AMSI 8   1850

PAR KARIN LP M

A E LINE B ANNMA

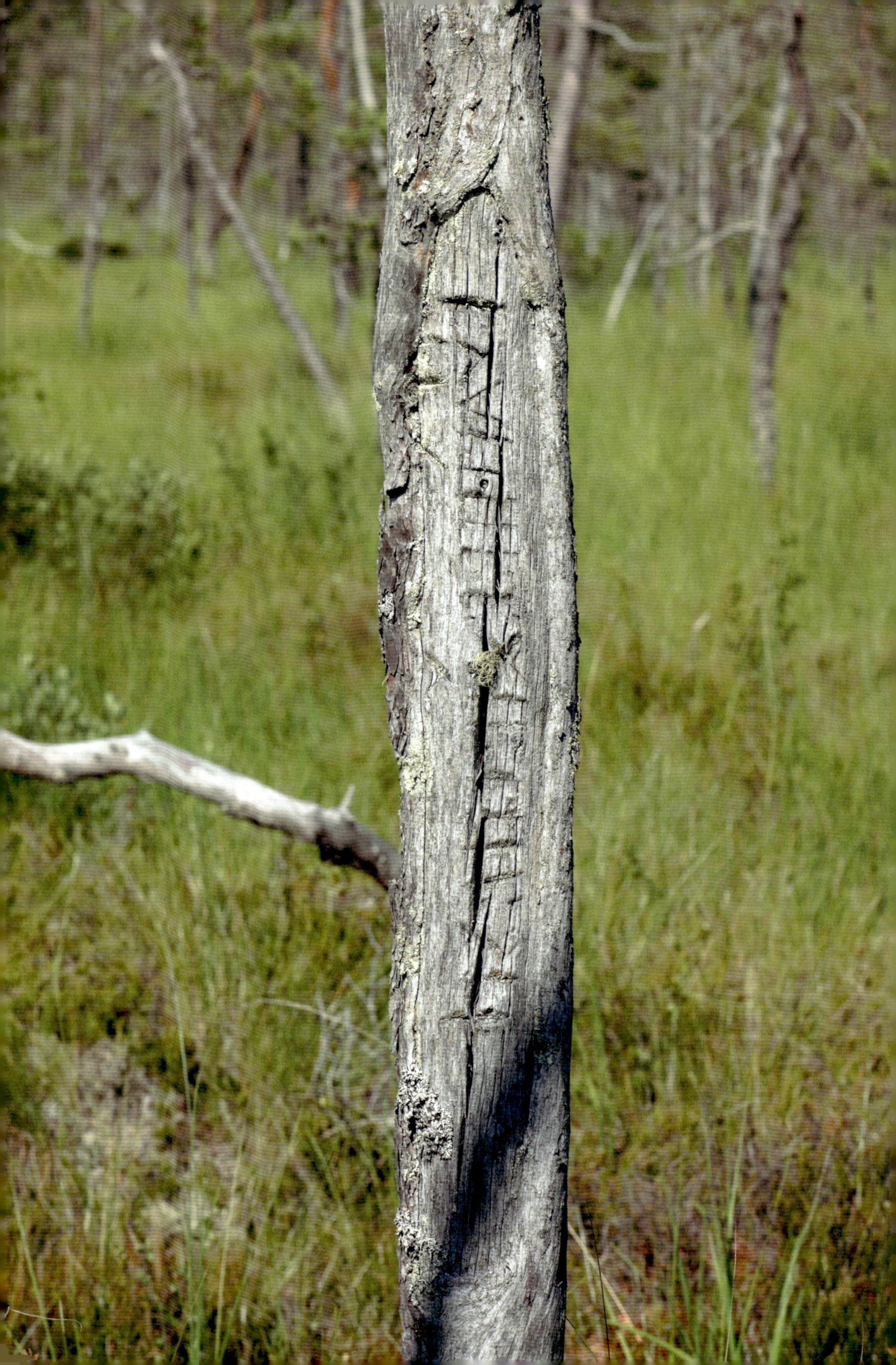

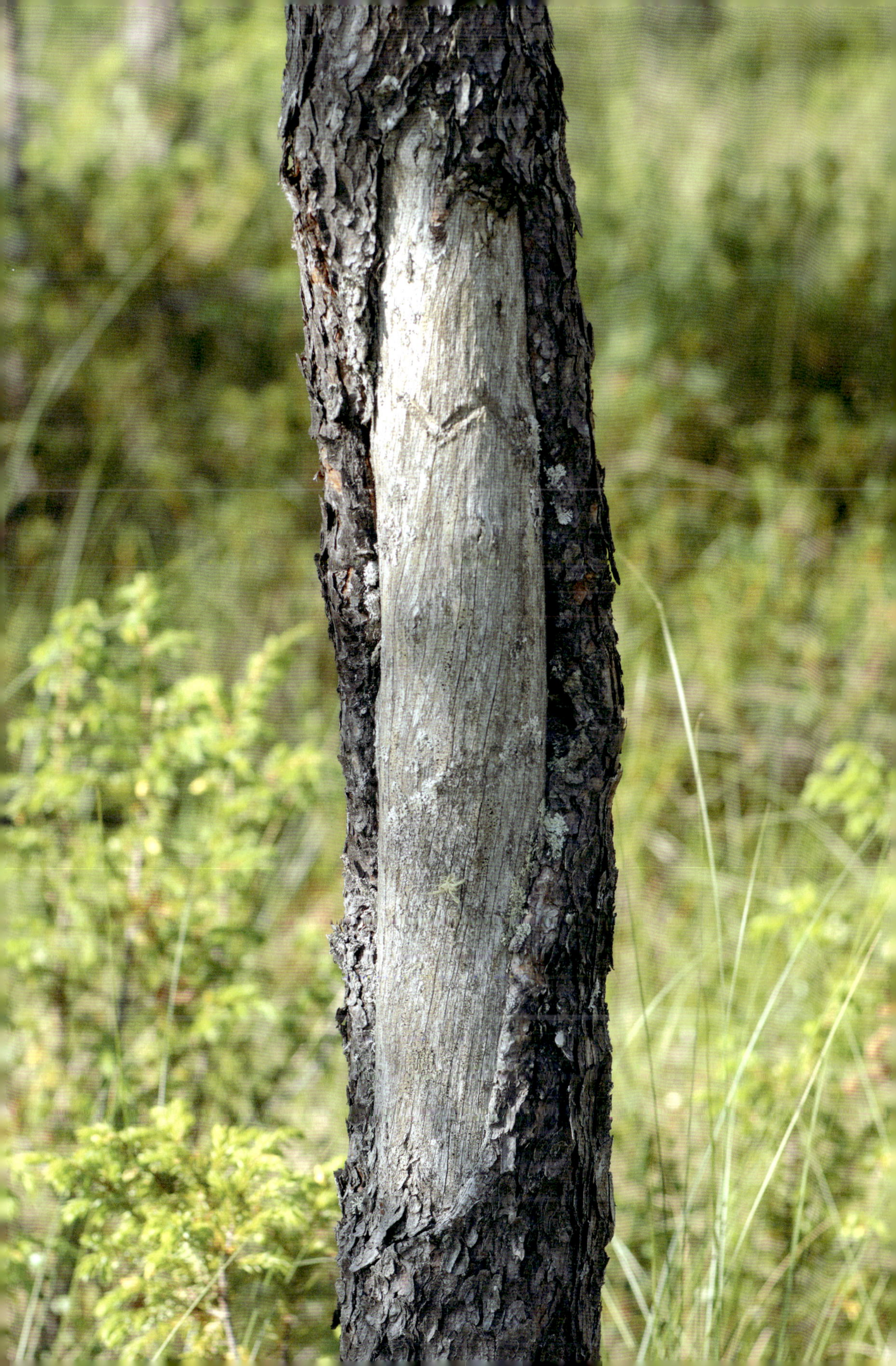

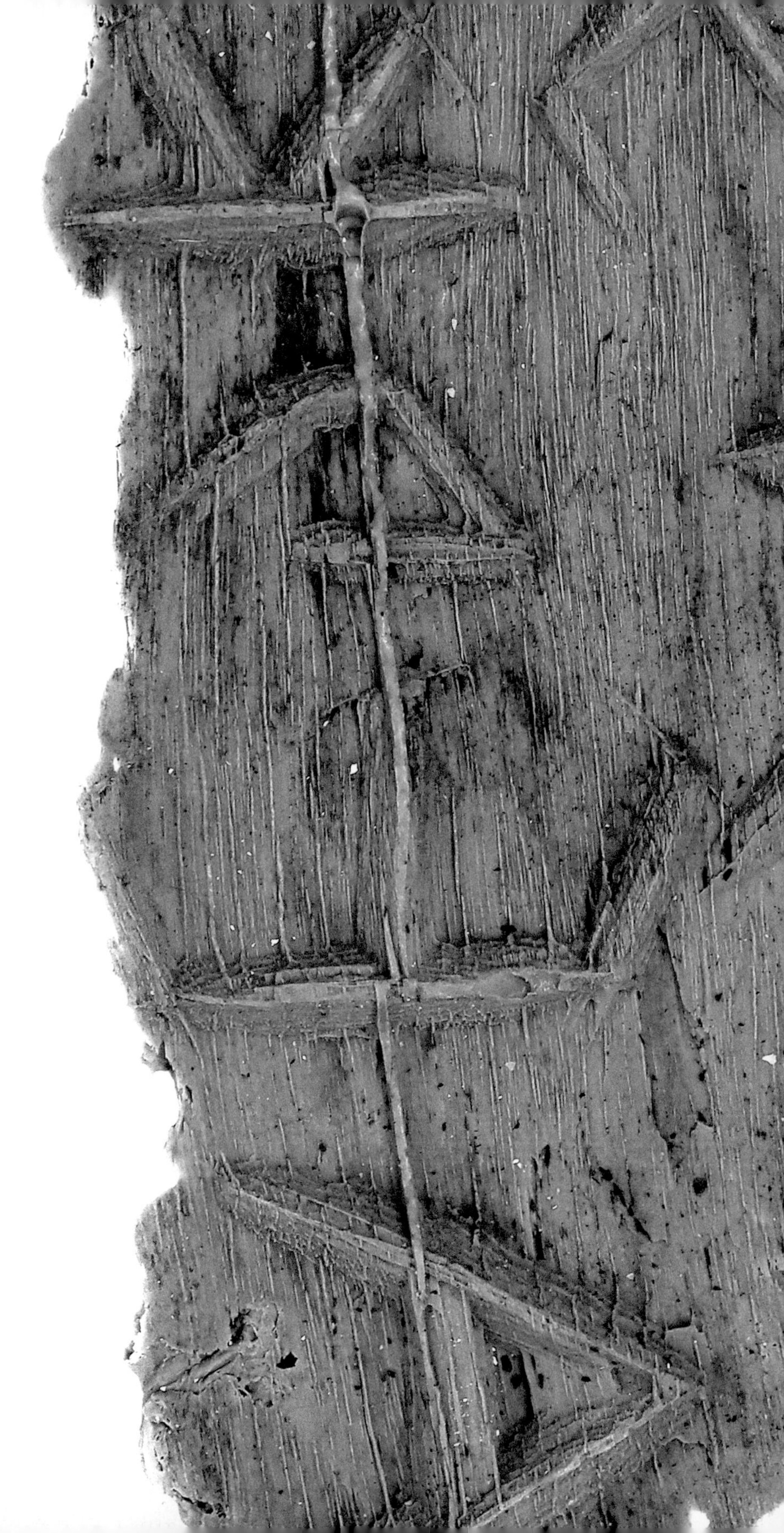

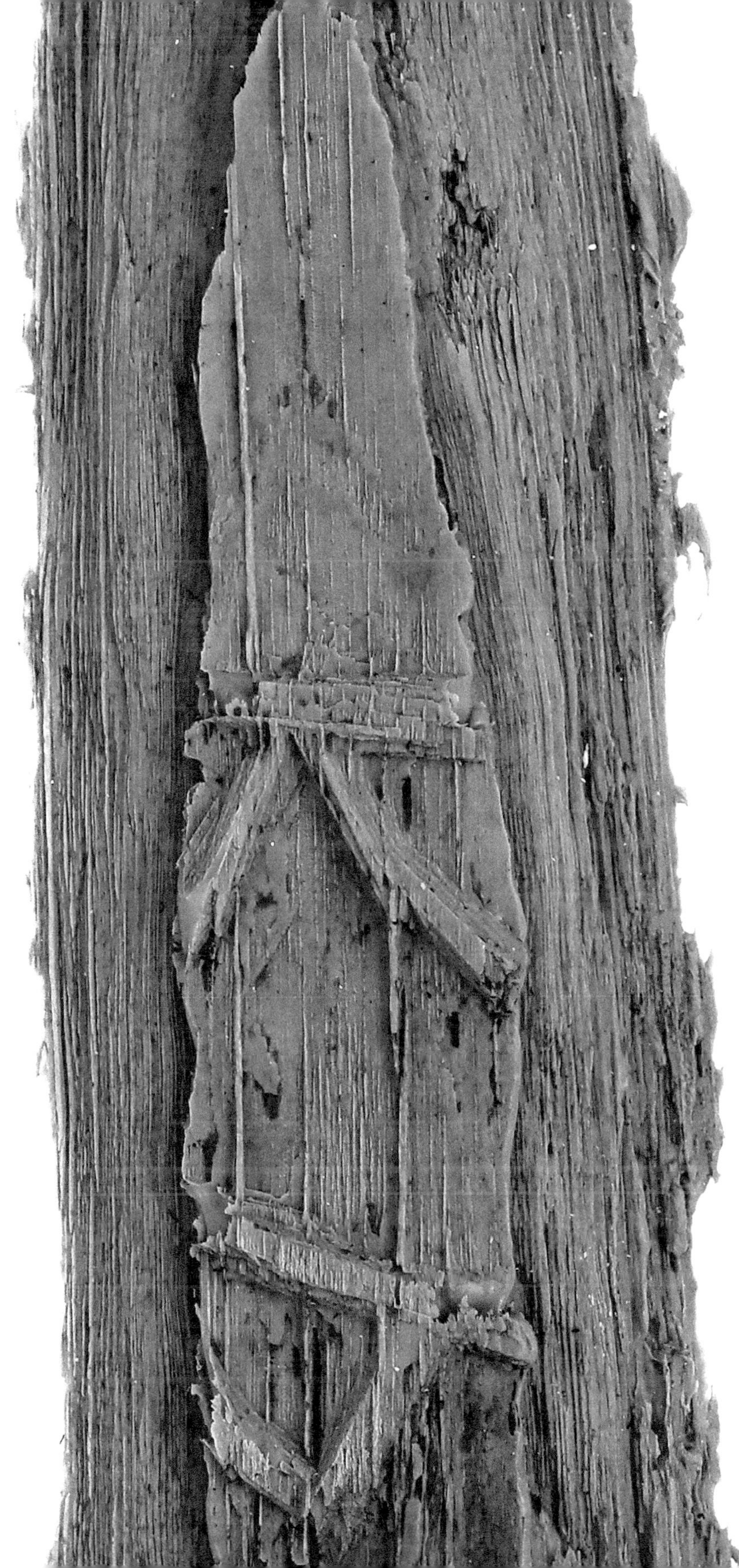

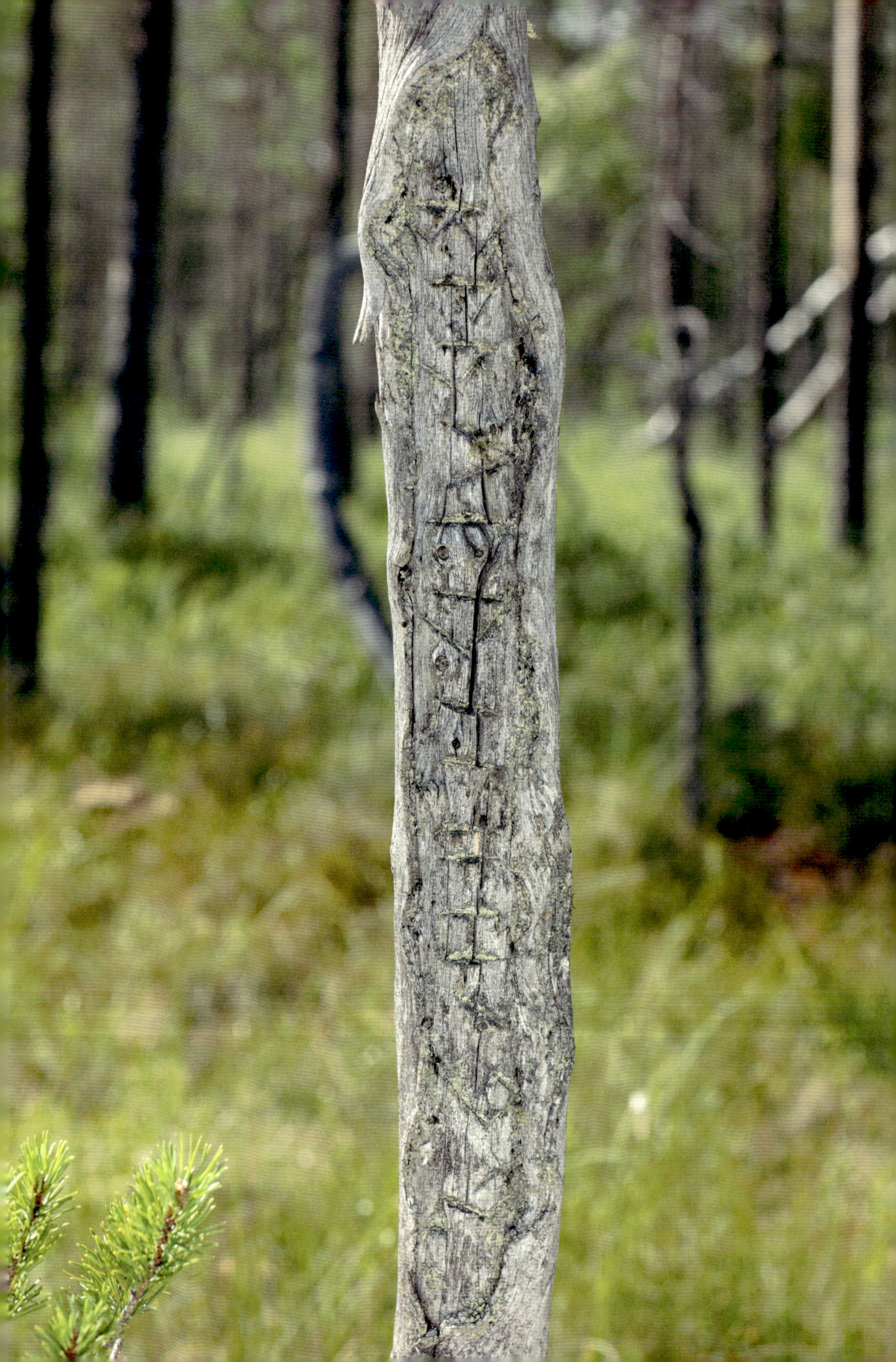

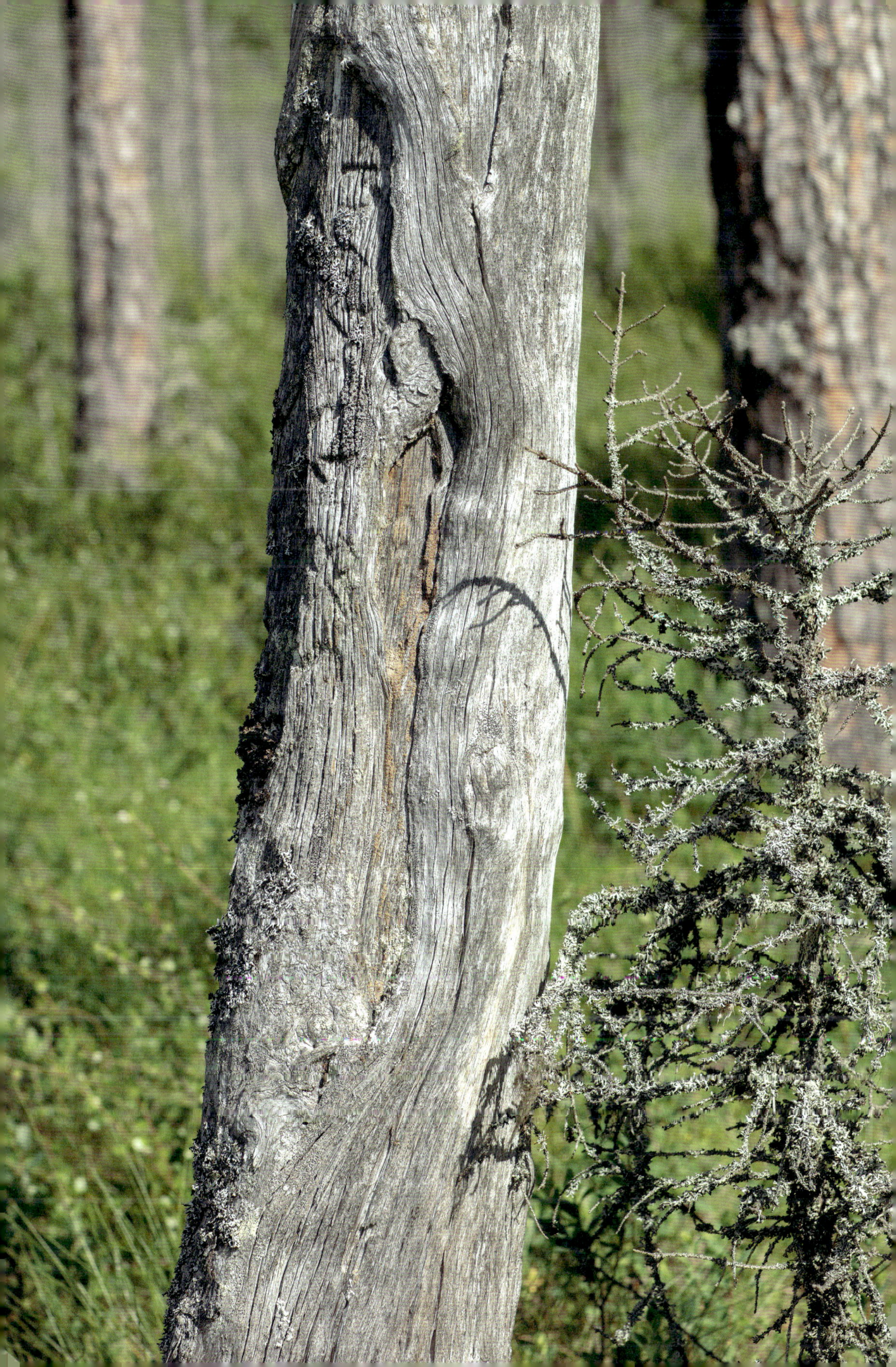

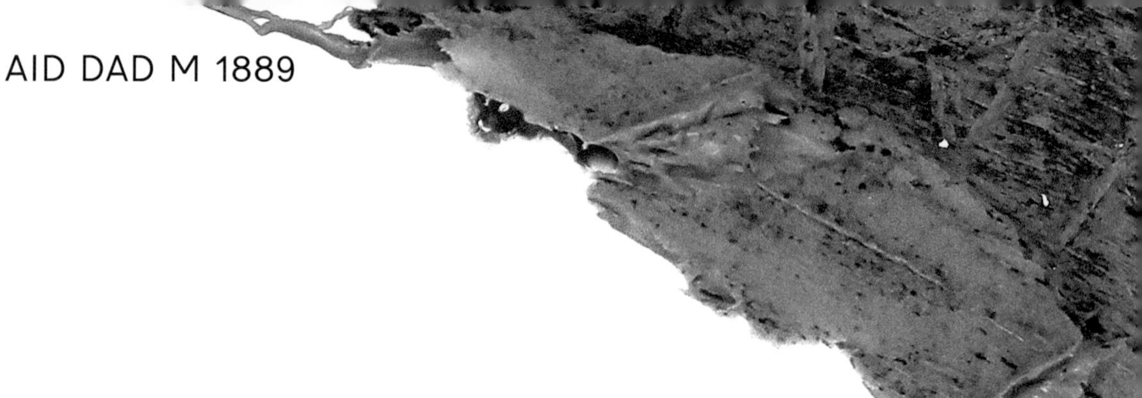

IX4III
D   PILA GODA
WENR   SITA SÖMAREN
DALFÖS   NU HAR
IT IAG NU MER
TI SÄGA
   LIT ÖGNLSNIGT
MINA WENR 1822
X

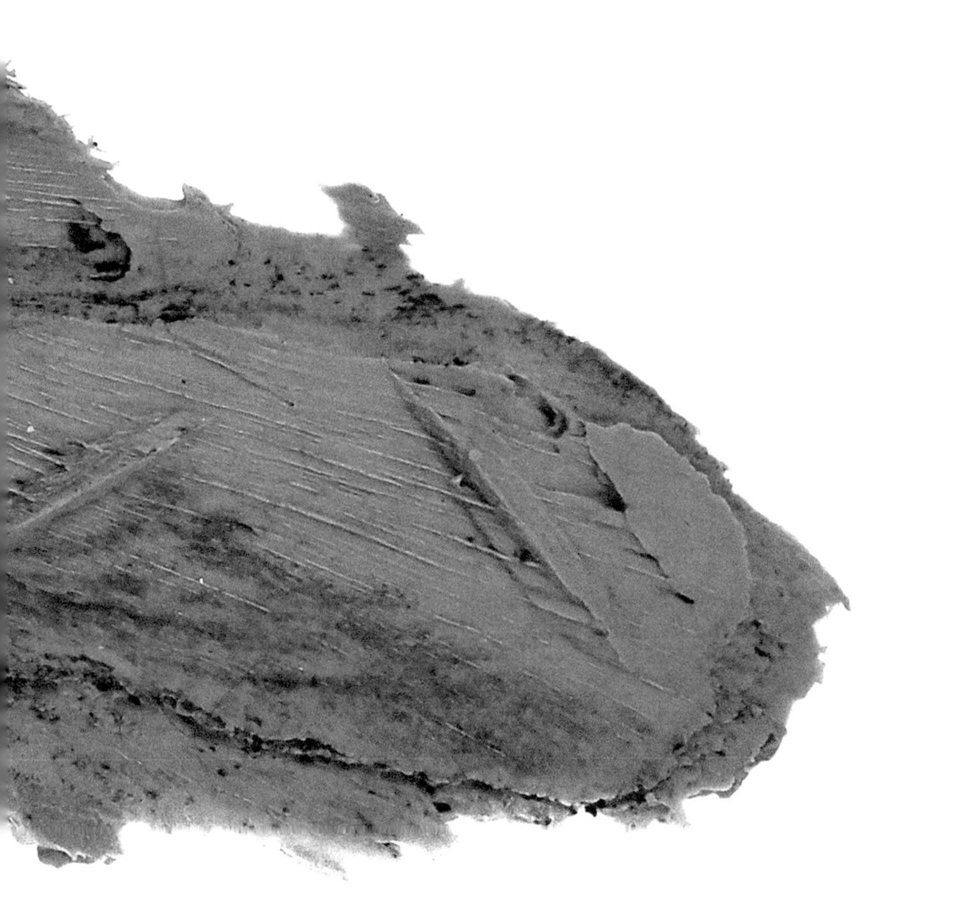

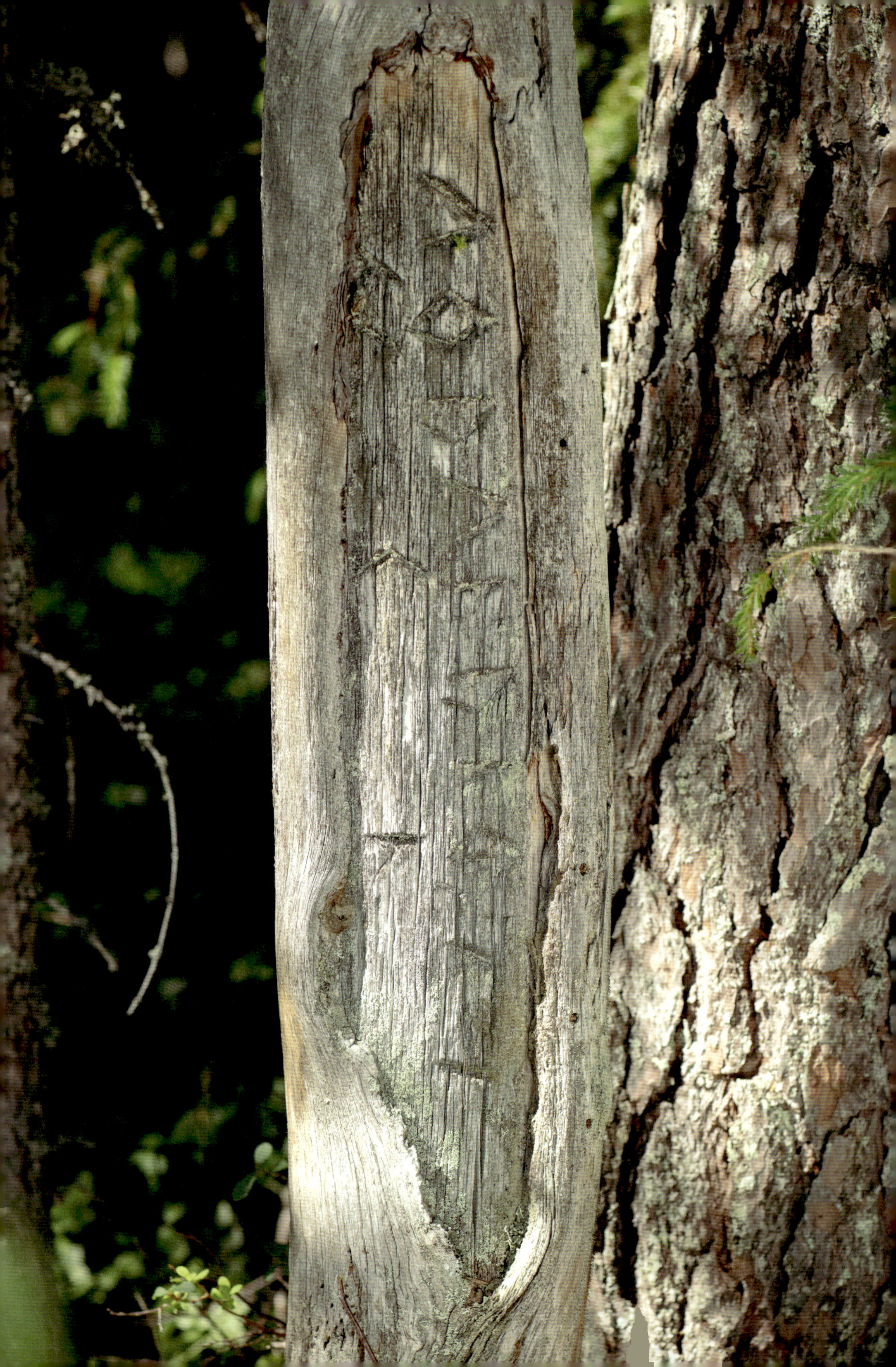

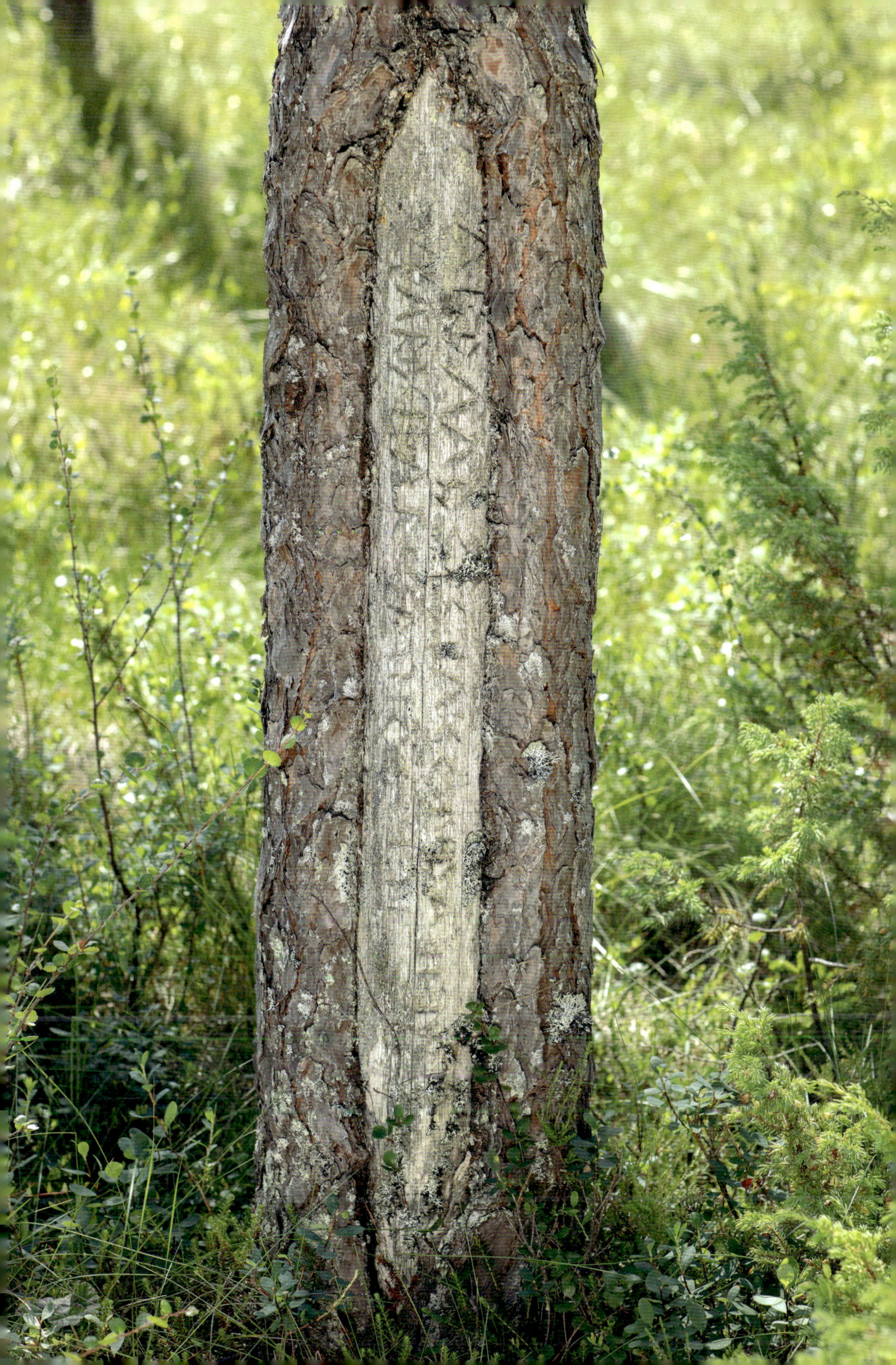

there is a large stone in the middle of the bog
next to the stone grows a tree   it is carved
i sit on the stone   it is flat and dry   i can see far over the bog

thirty-five cows

1821

A for anna
E for eriks
D for daughter

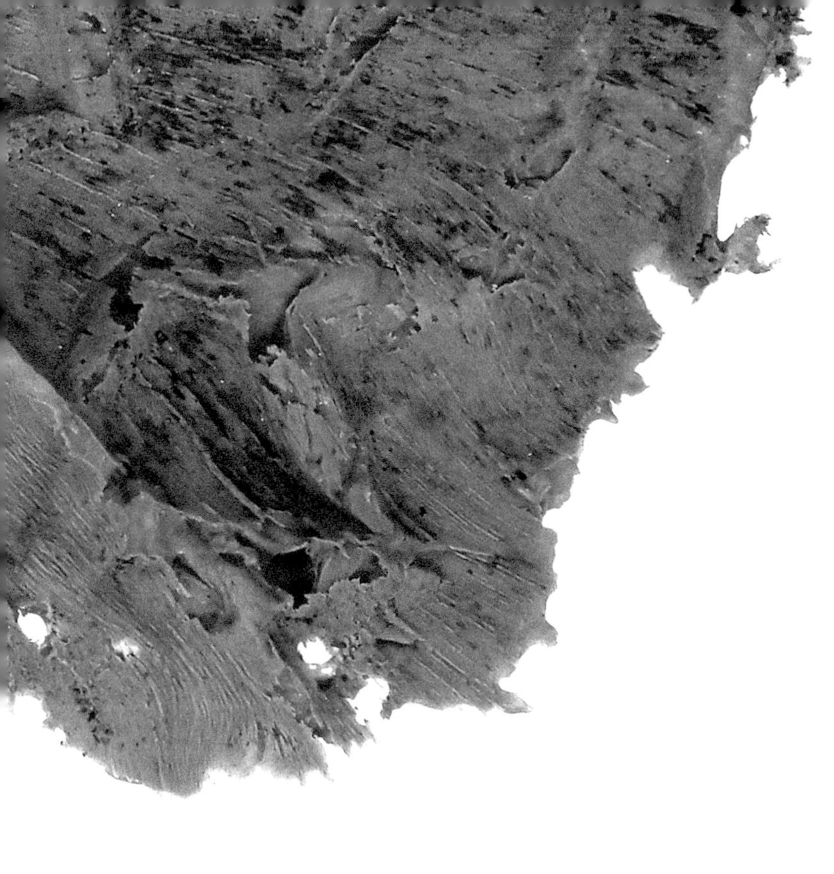

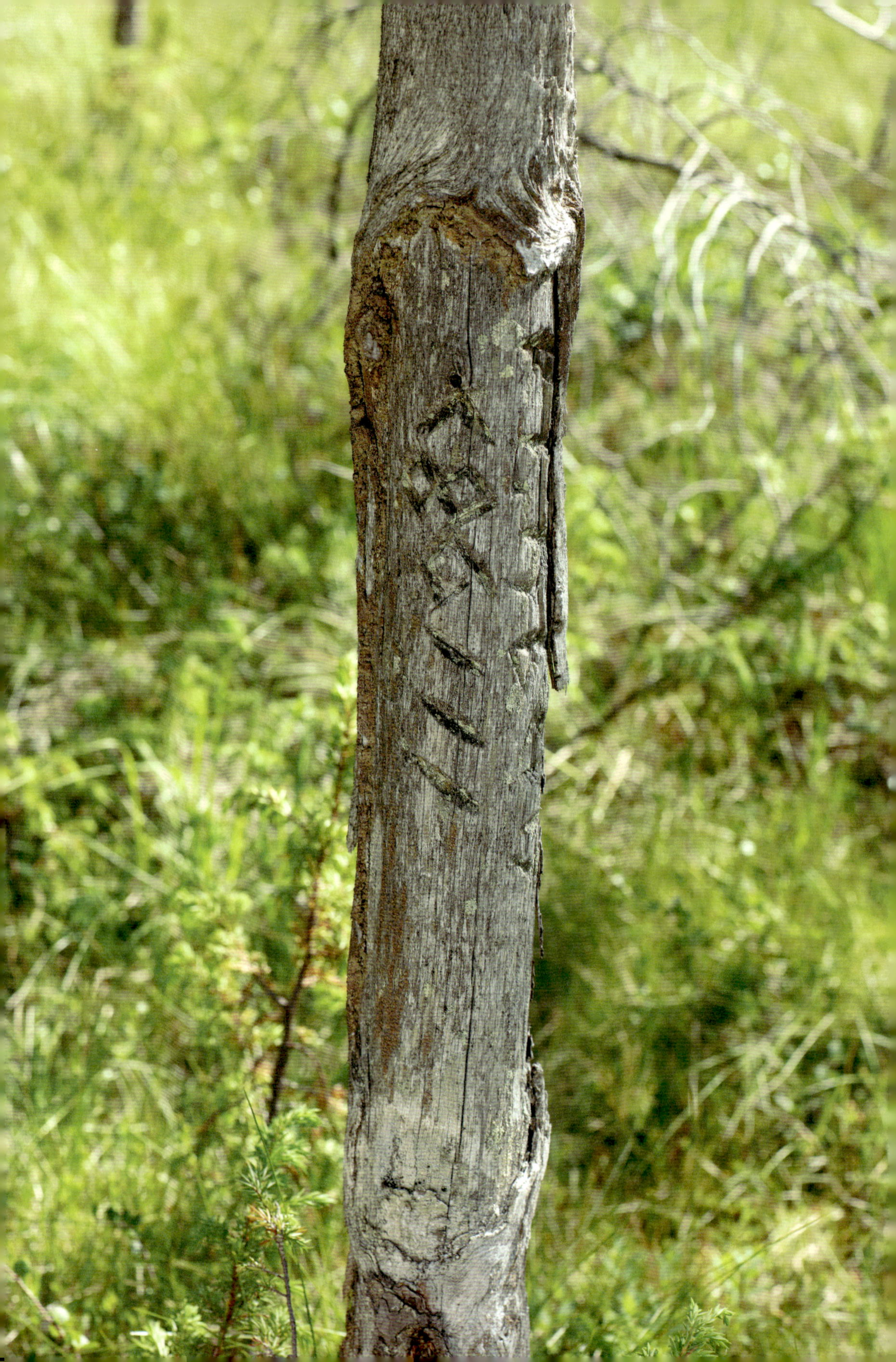

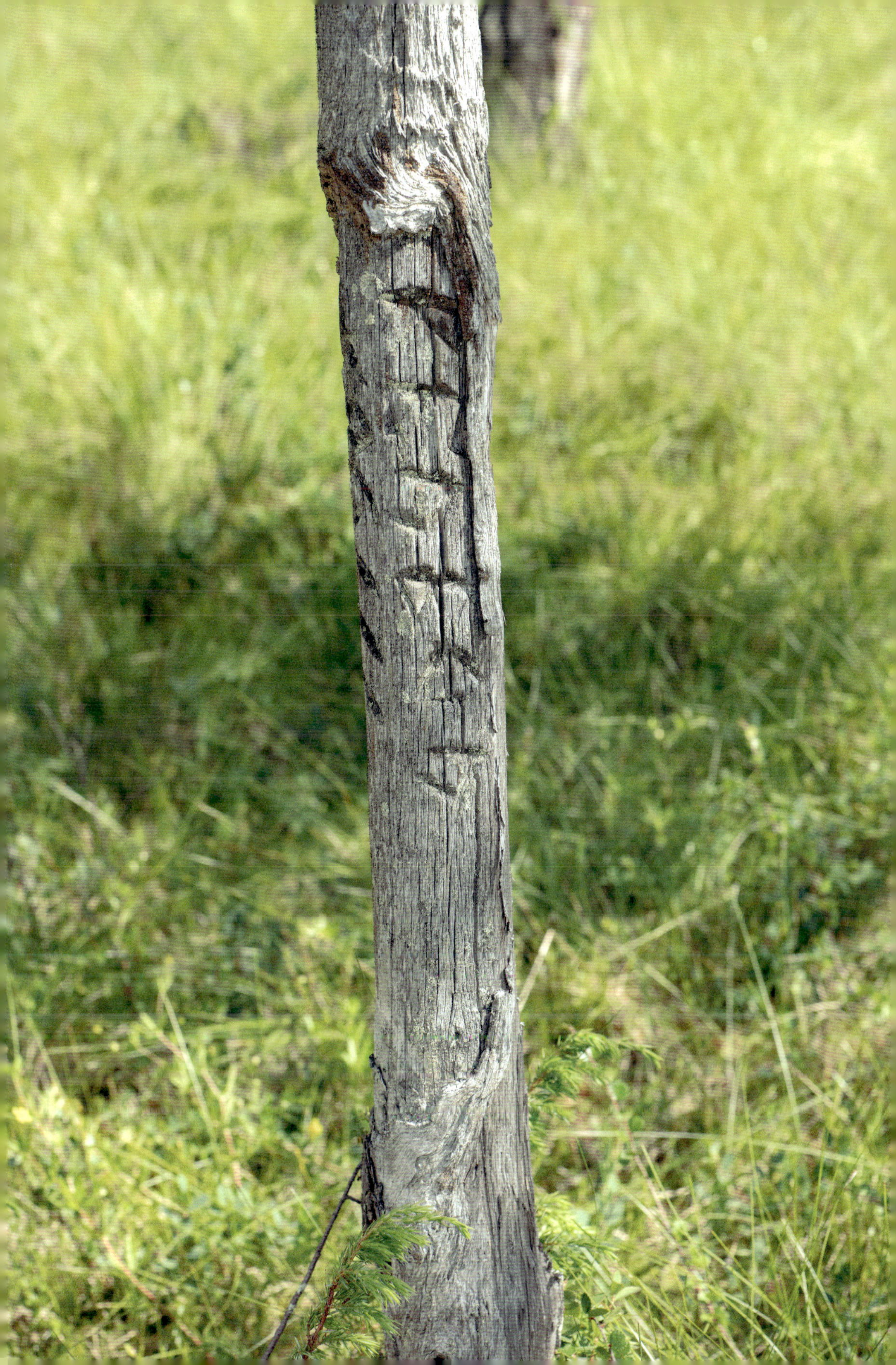

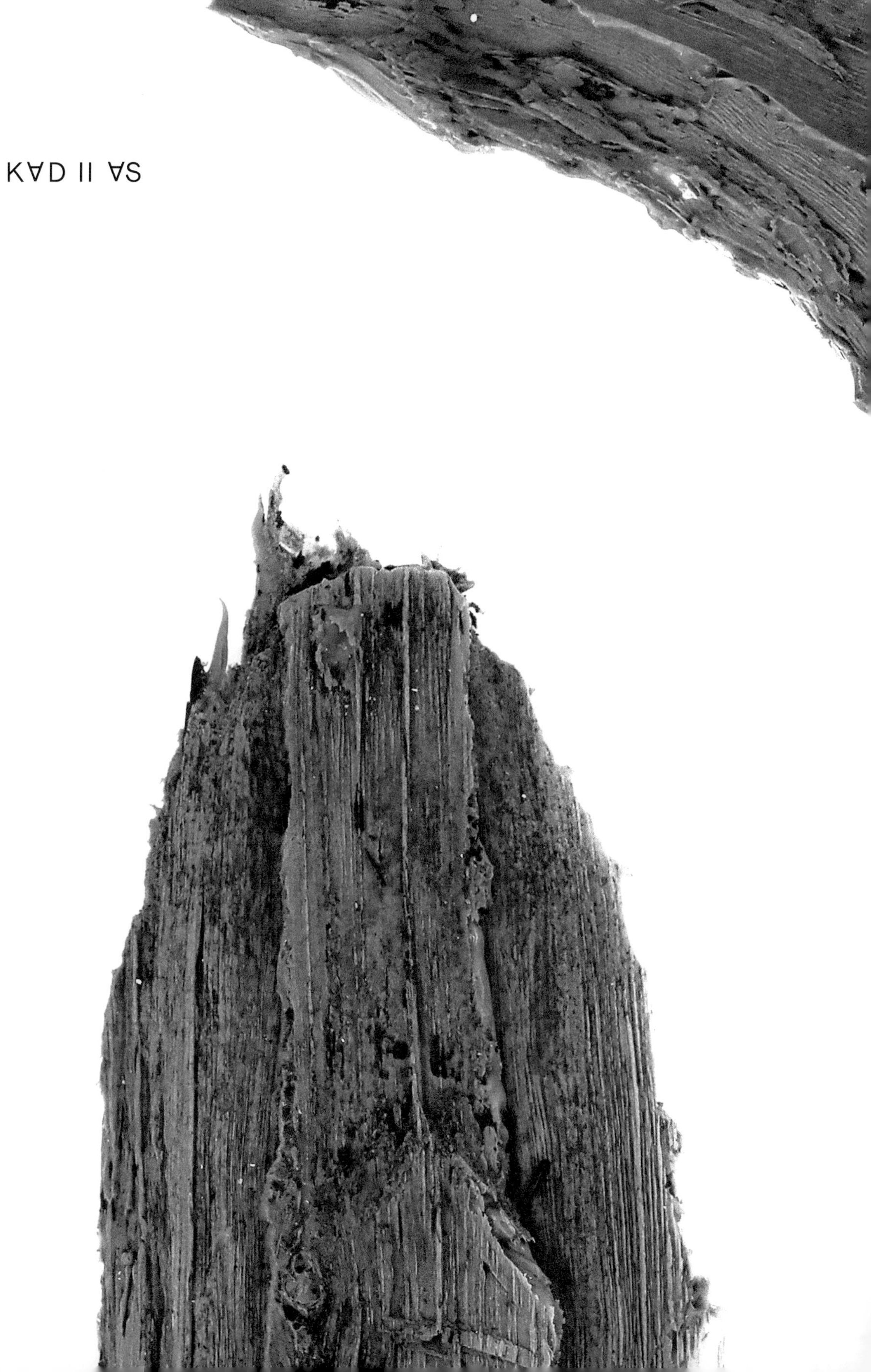

H

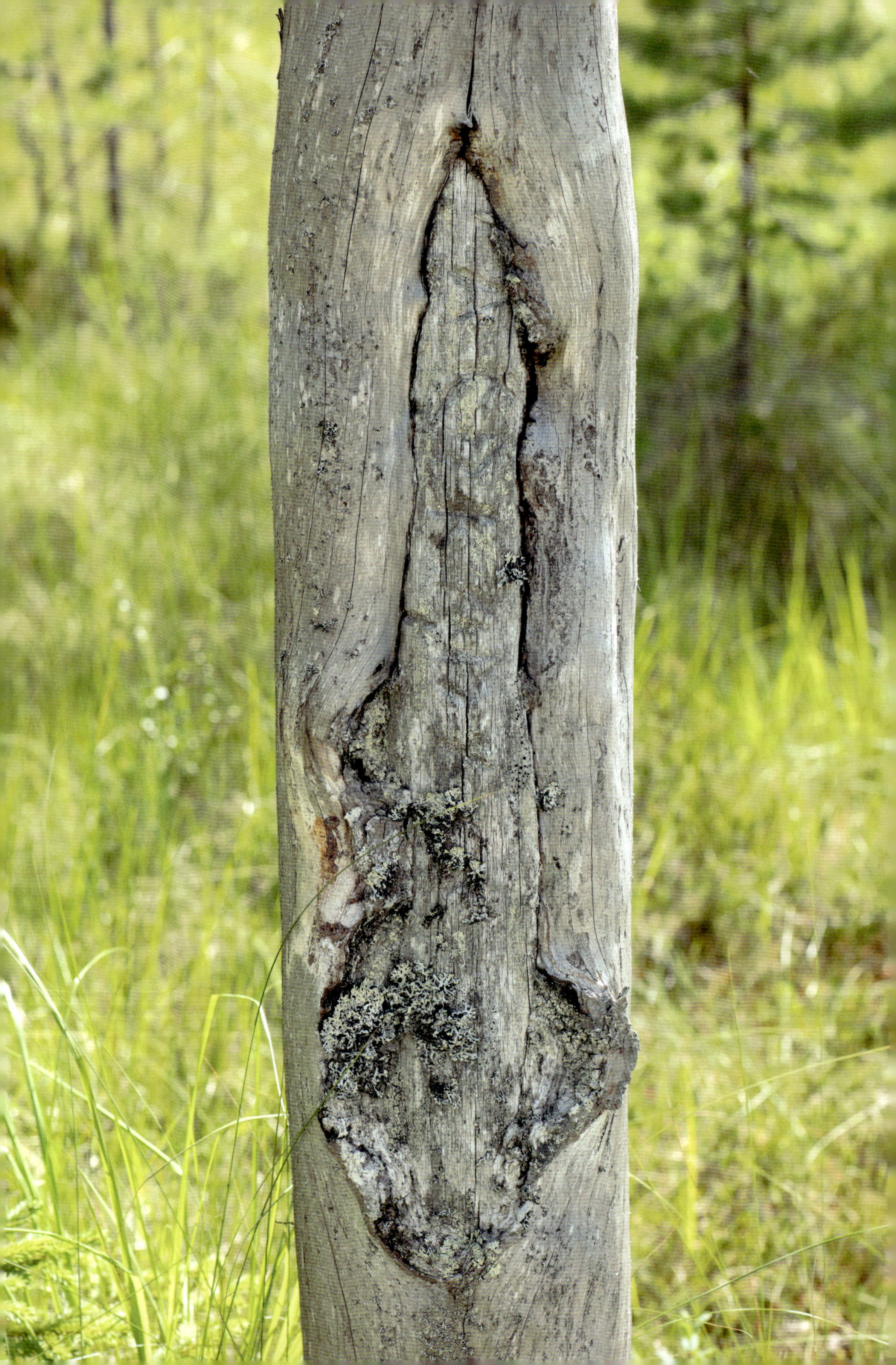

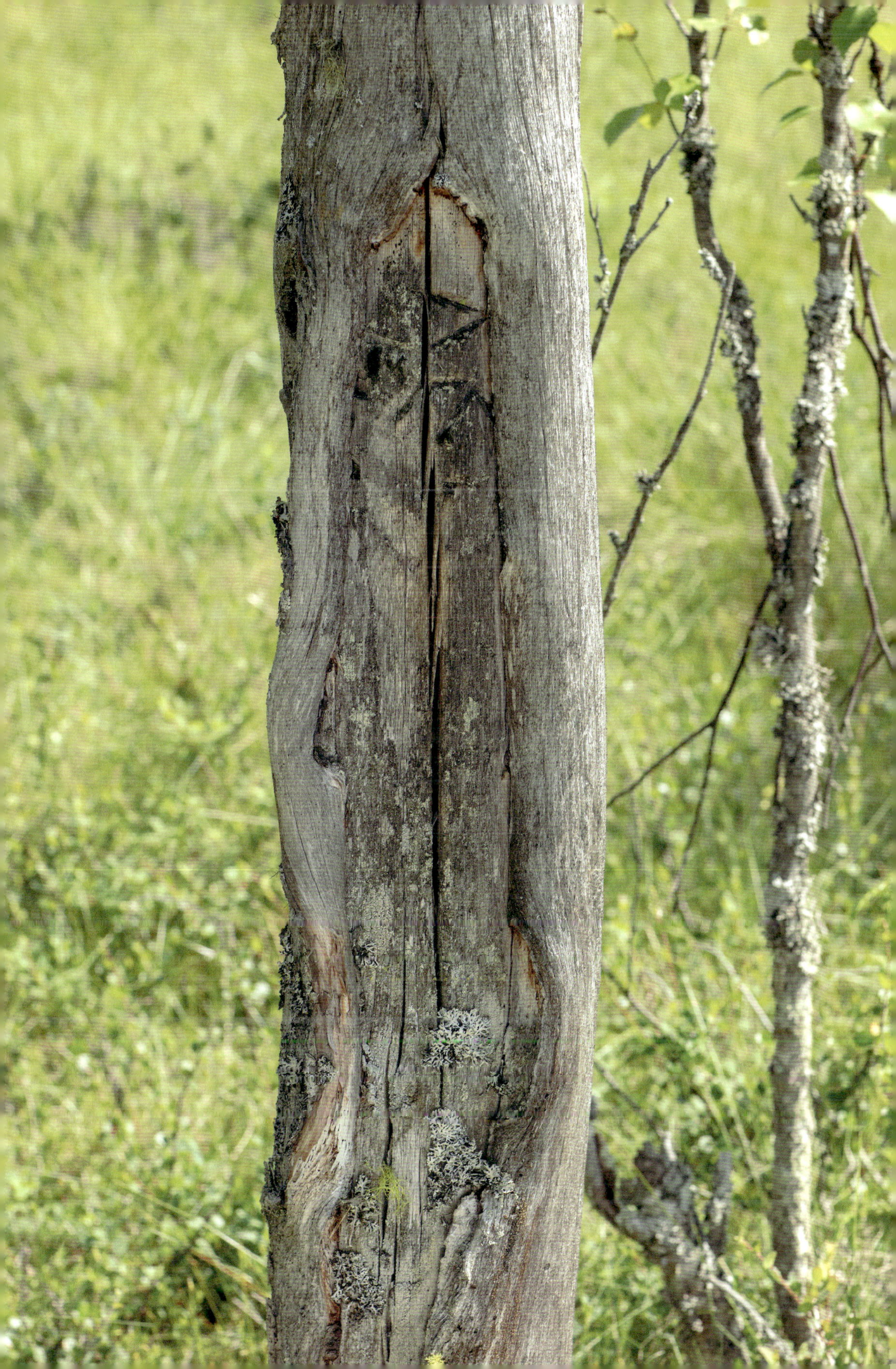

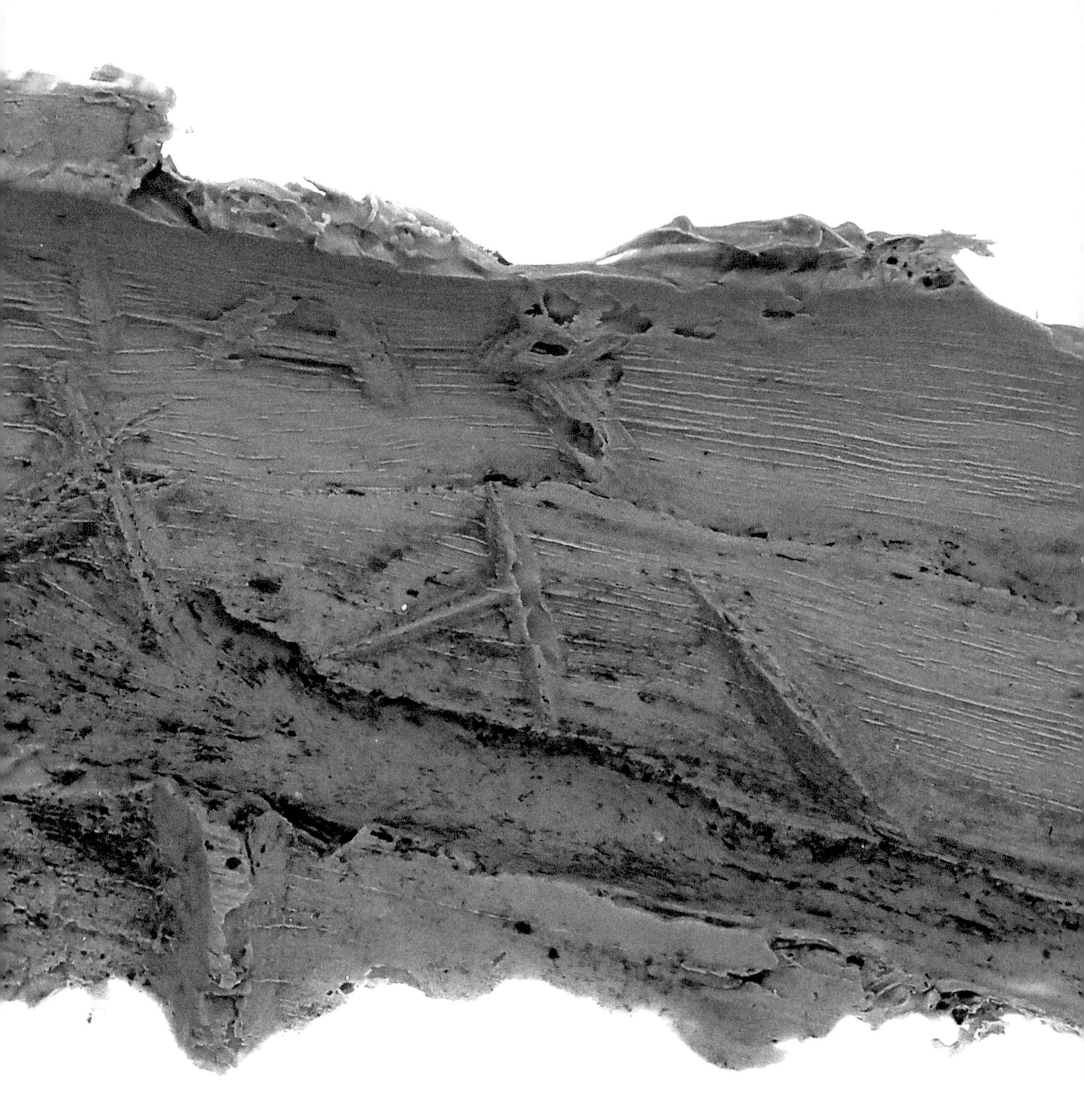

early june until larsmässan

när hon var liten tog dom korna över sjön på en flotte

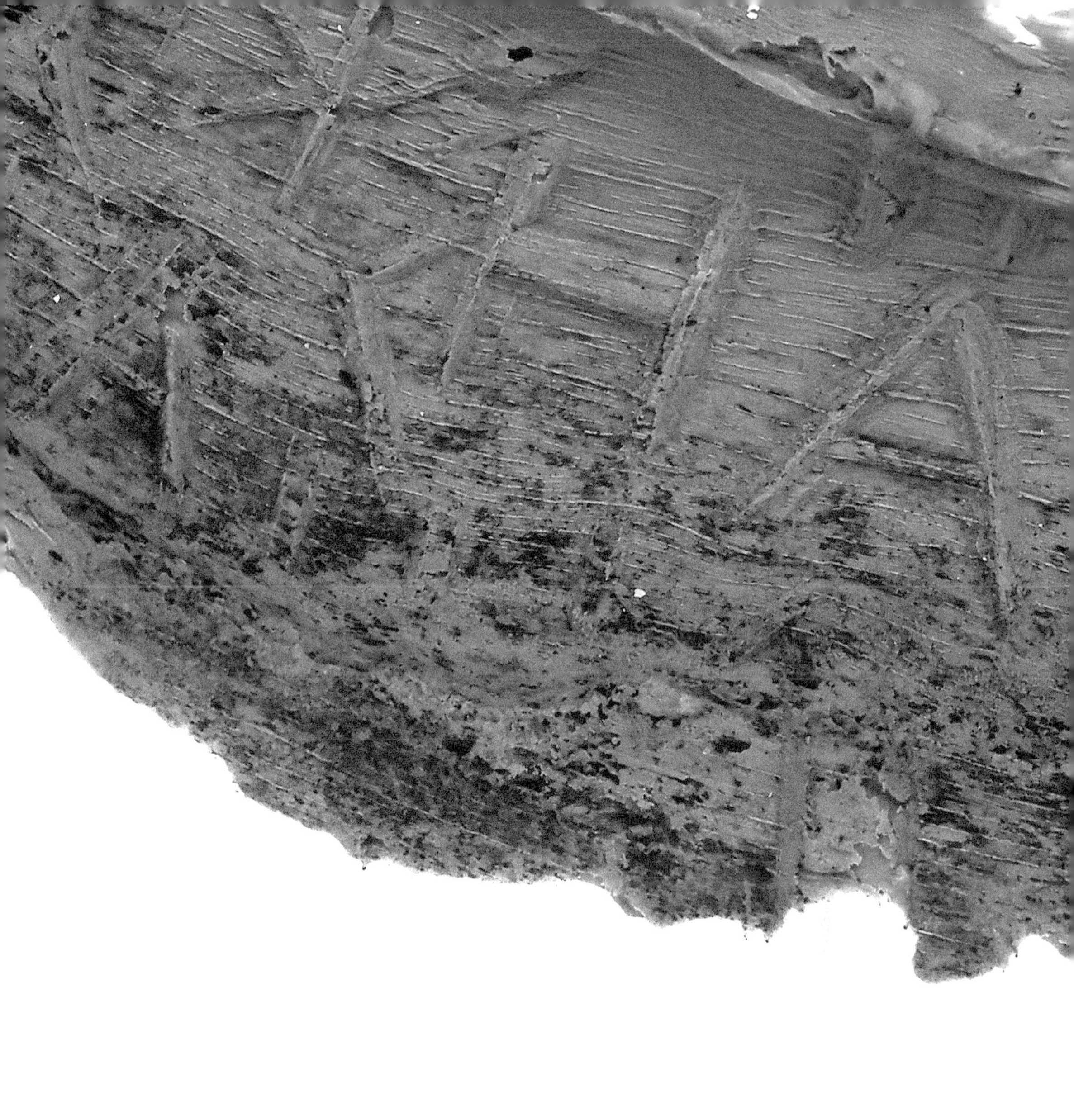

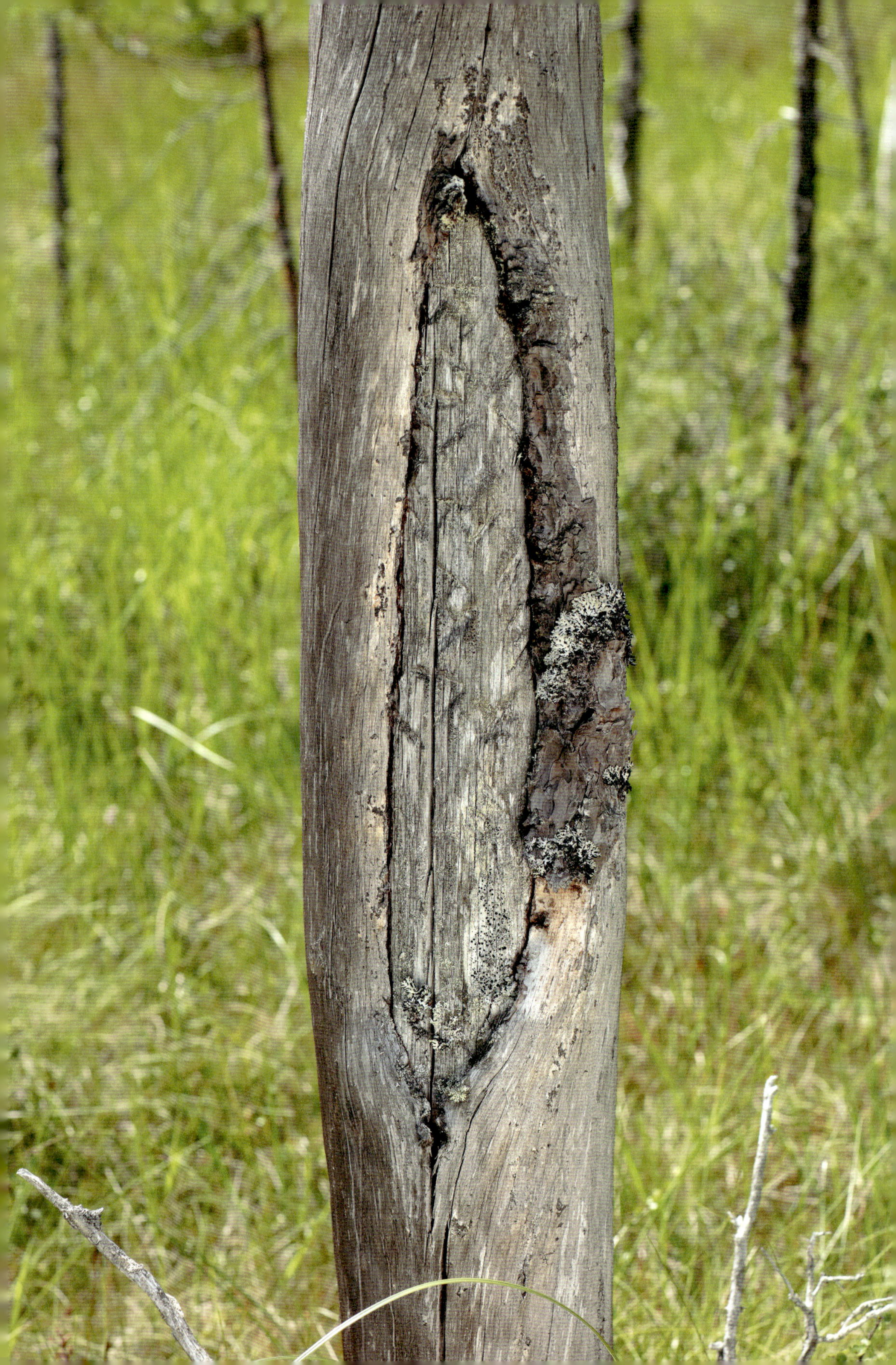

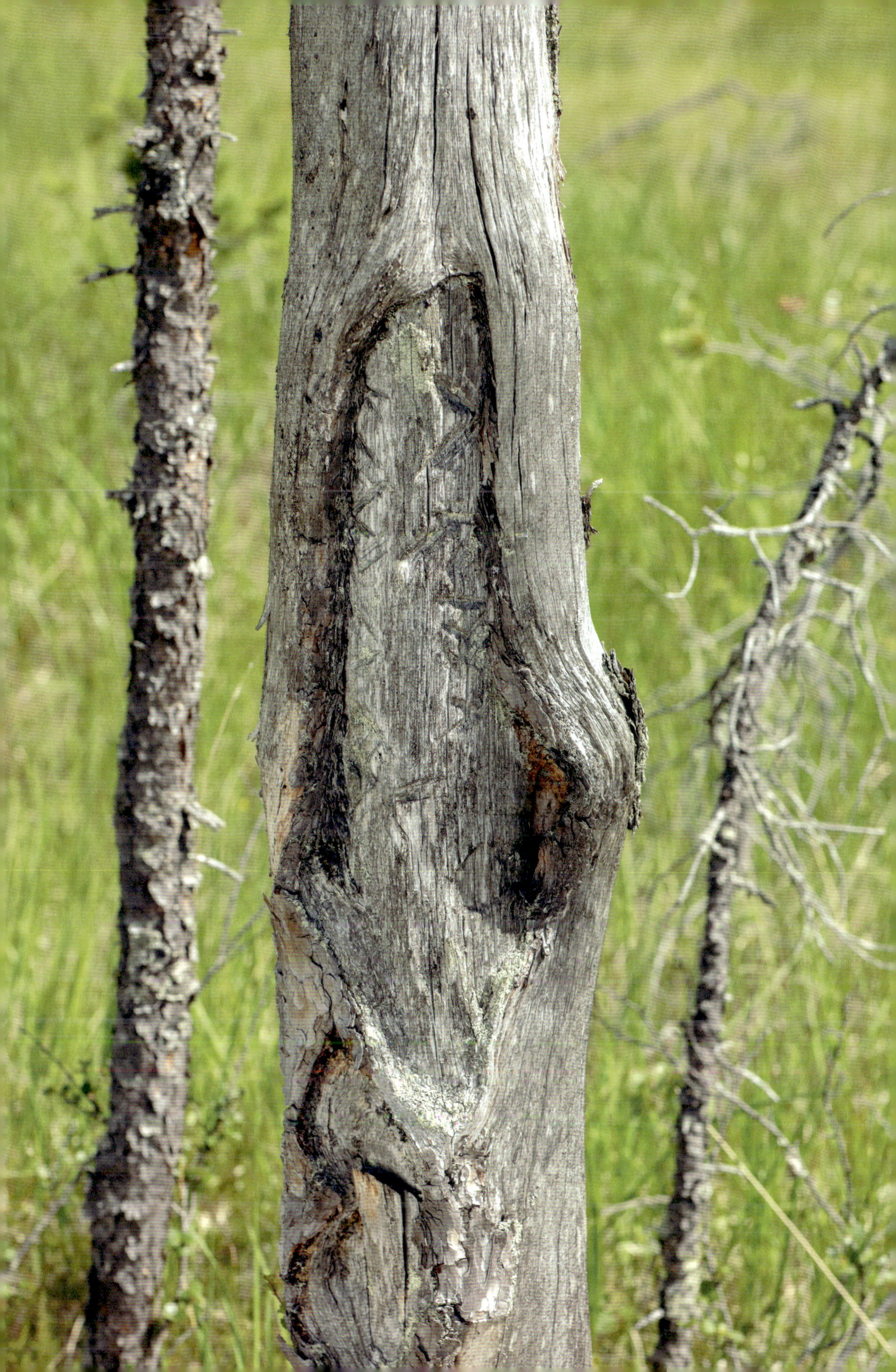

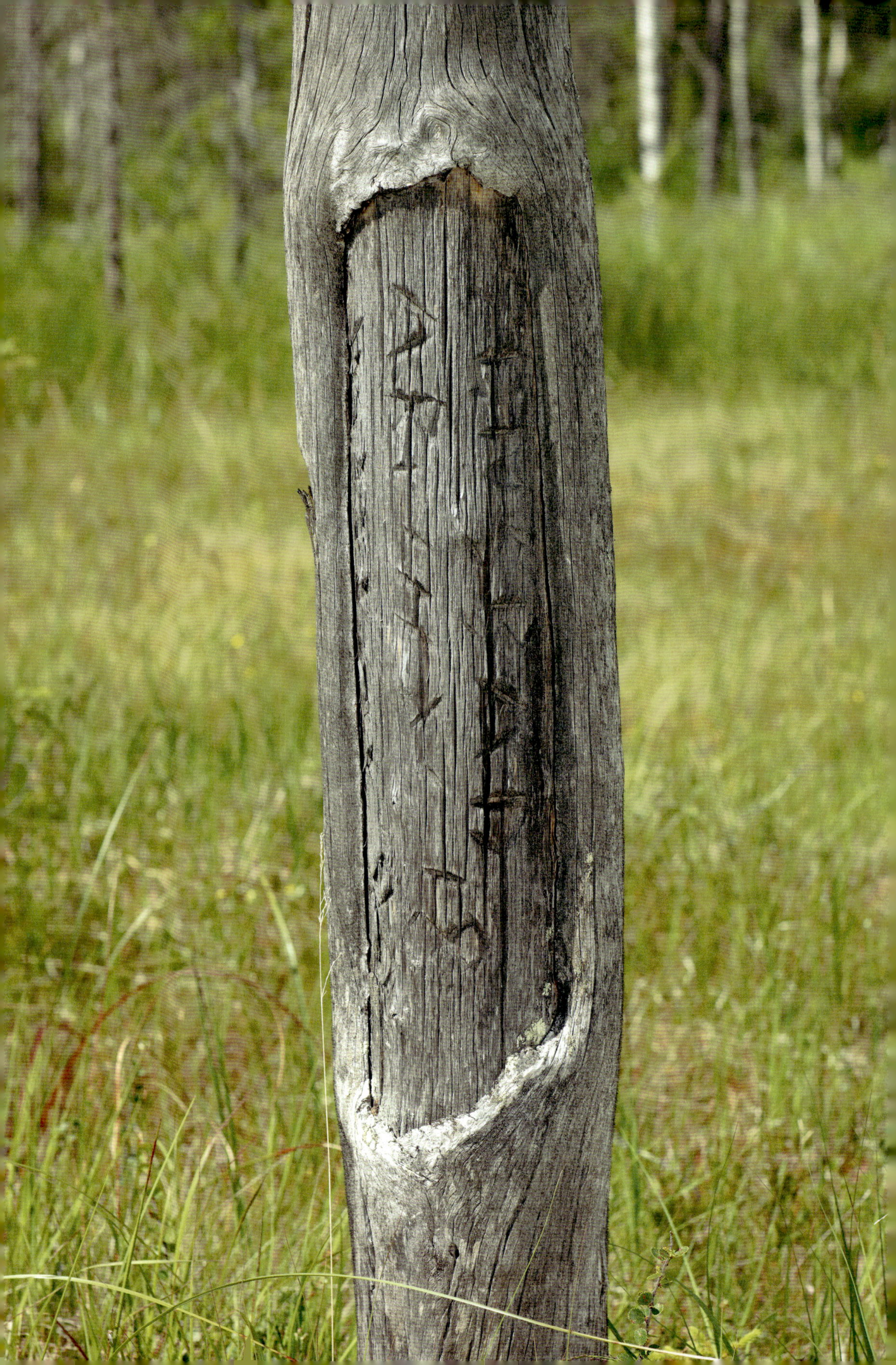

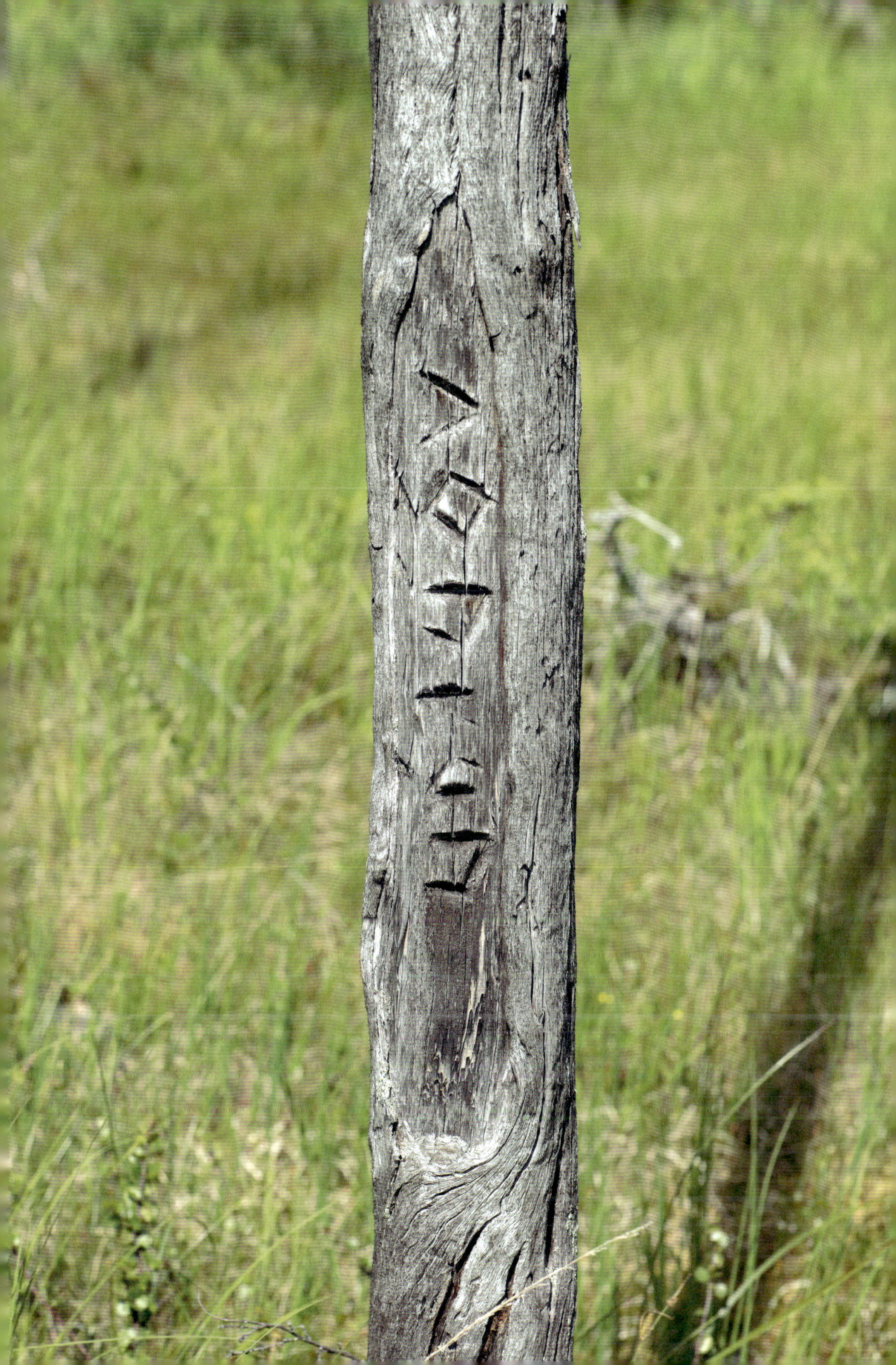

the animals are asleep and you have made a fire
the smoke scares away the mosquitoes

ꓷOM   AA
X

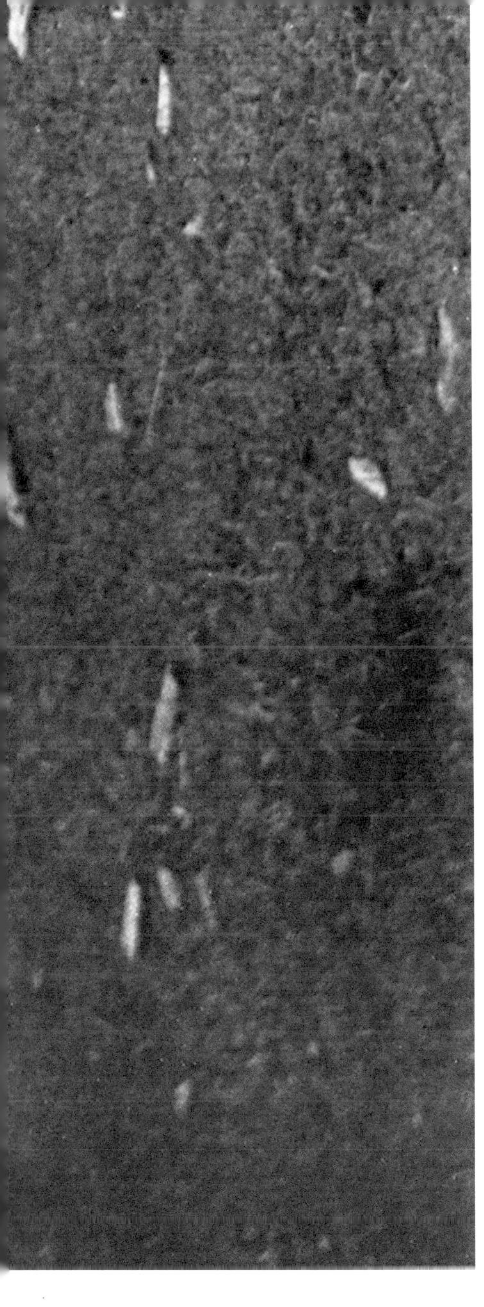

ANDRA SOMMAREN IAG GÅR WAL PÅ 1885
MEN. ACK. WAD. DET. ÄR. LÅNGSAMT

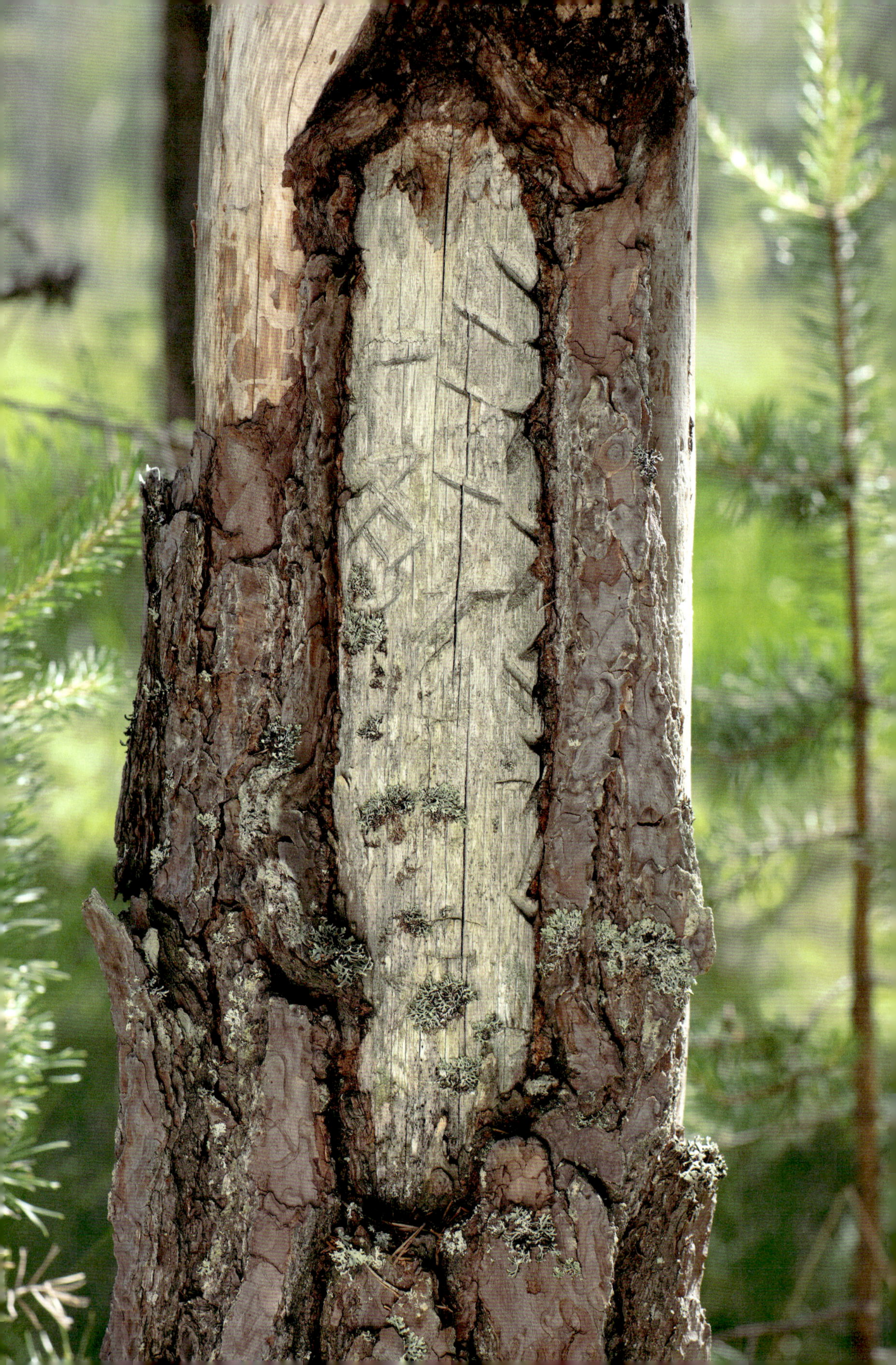

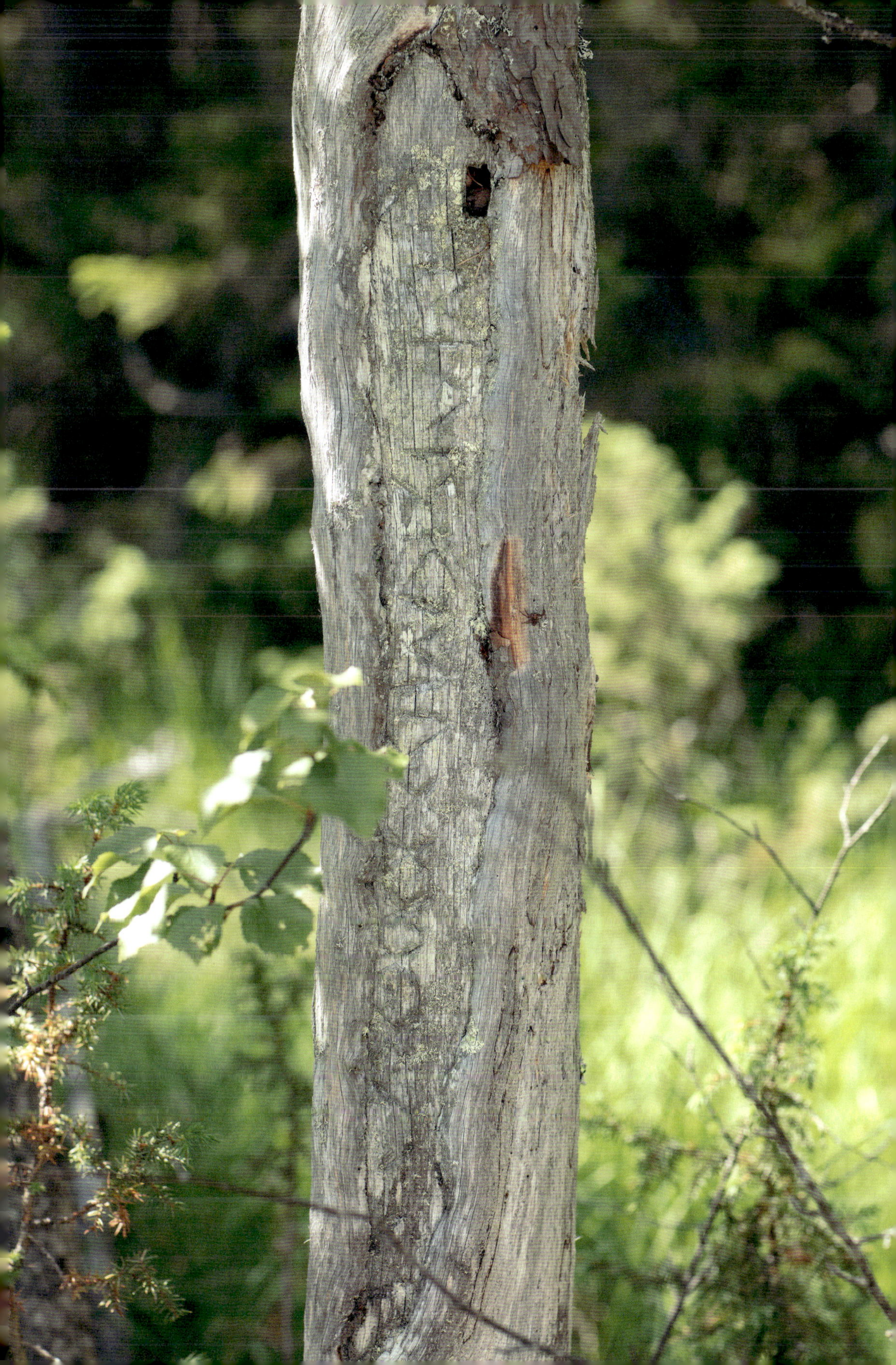

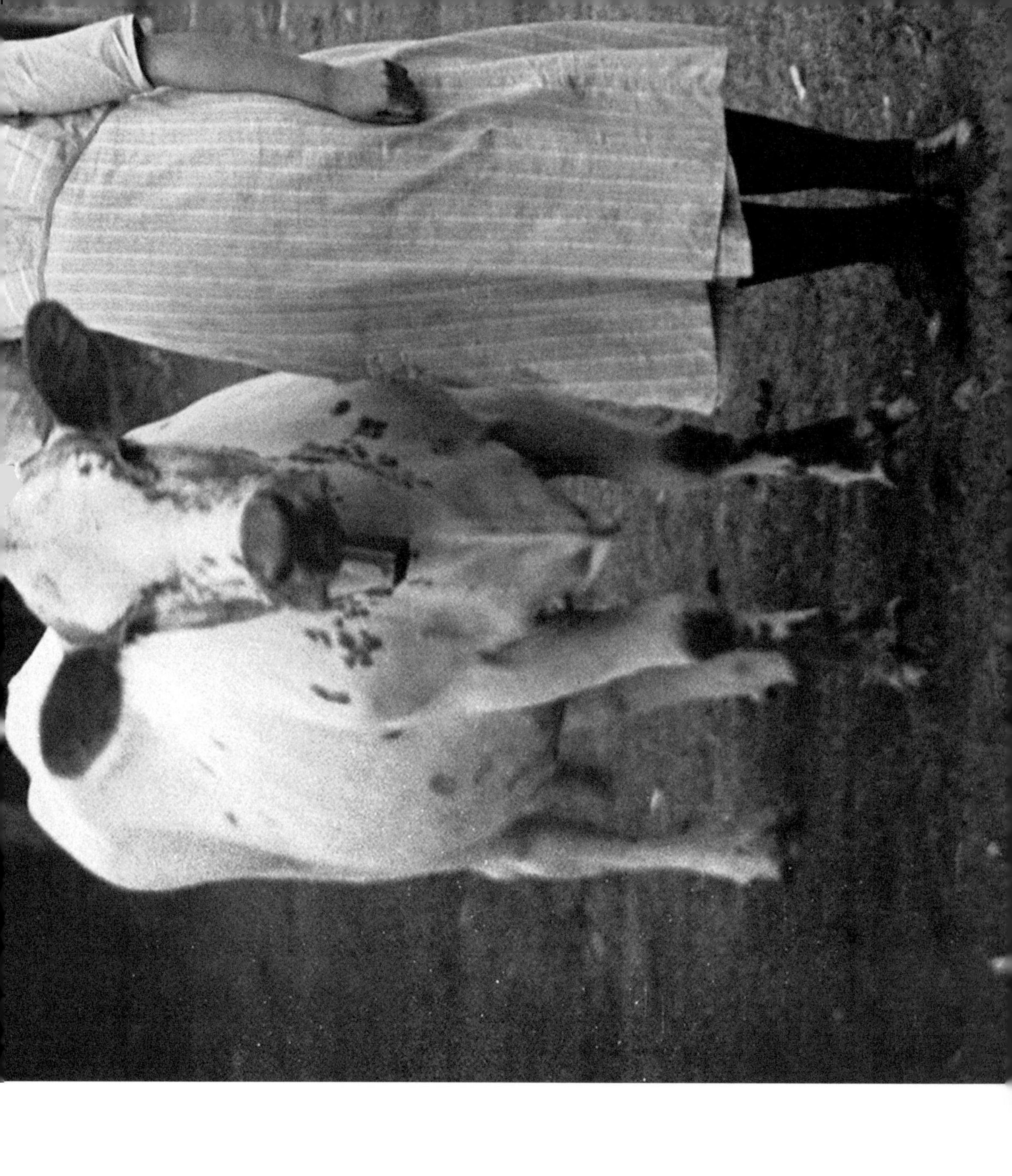

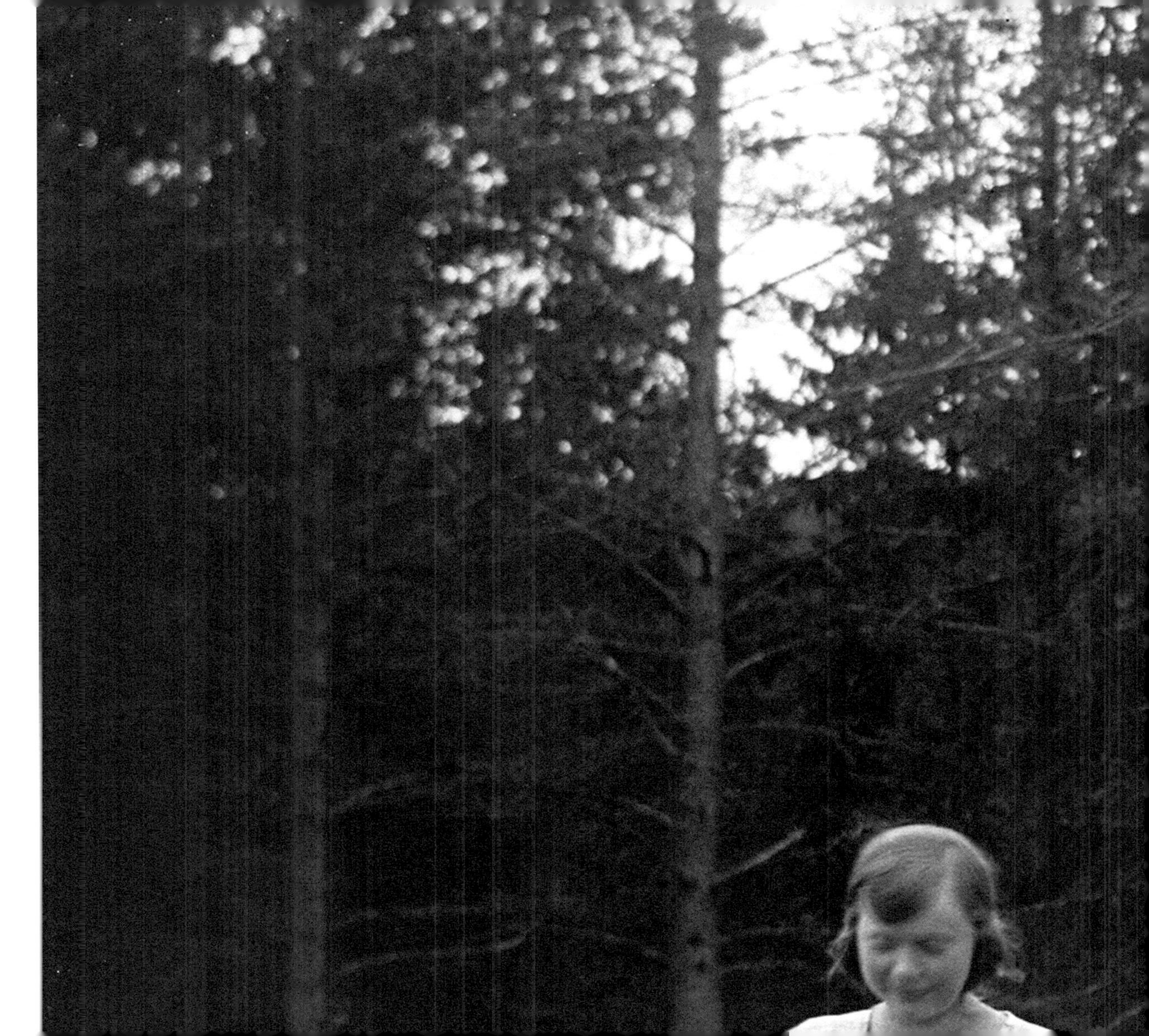

X AA AED XX

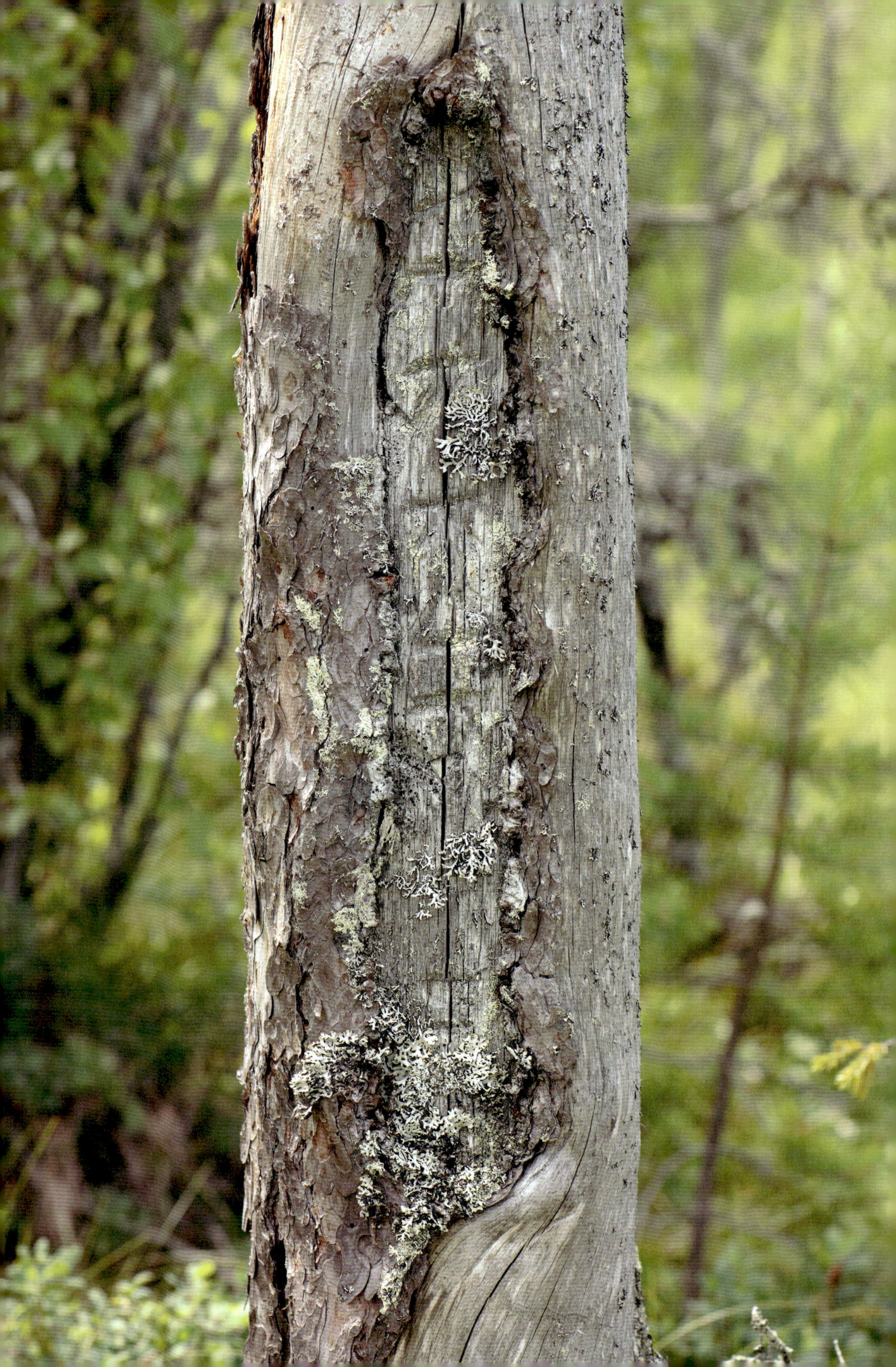

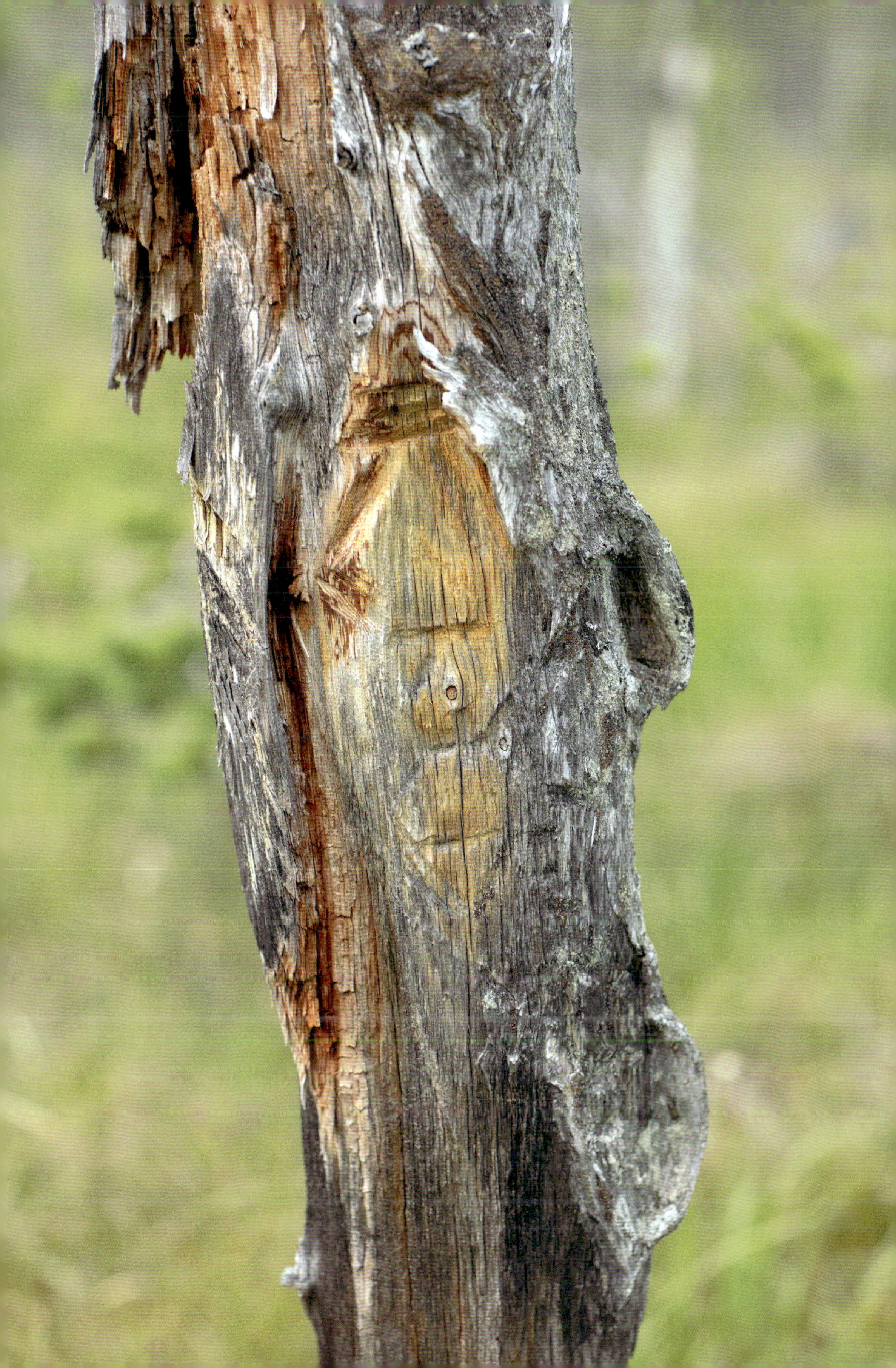

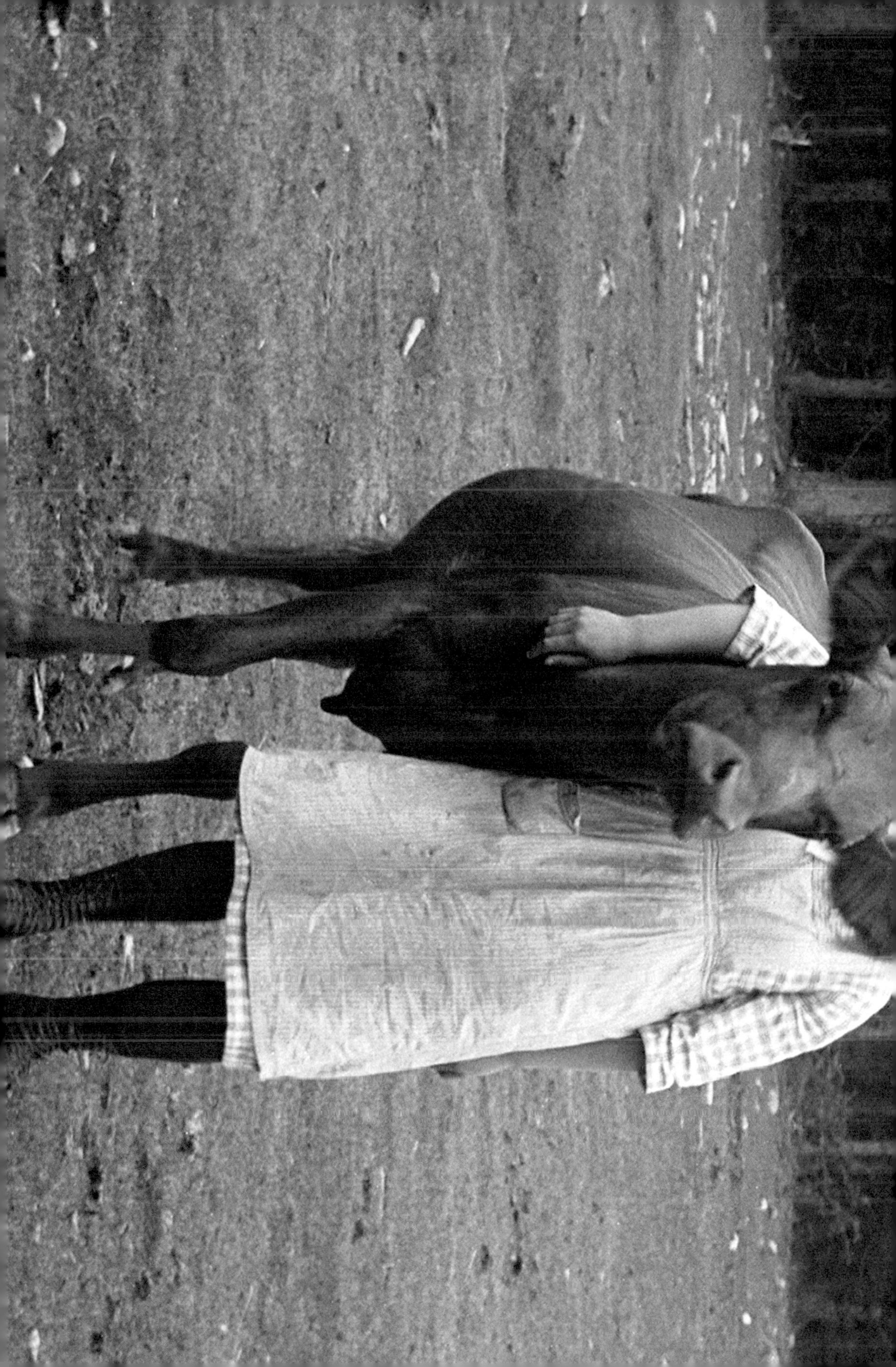

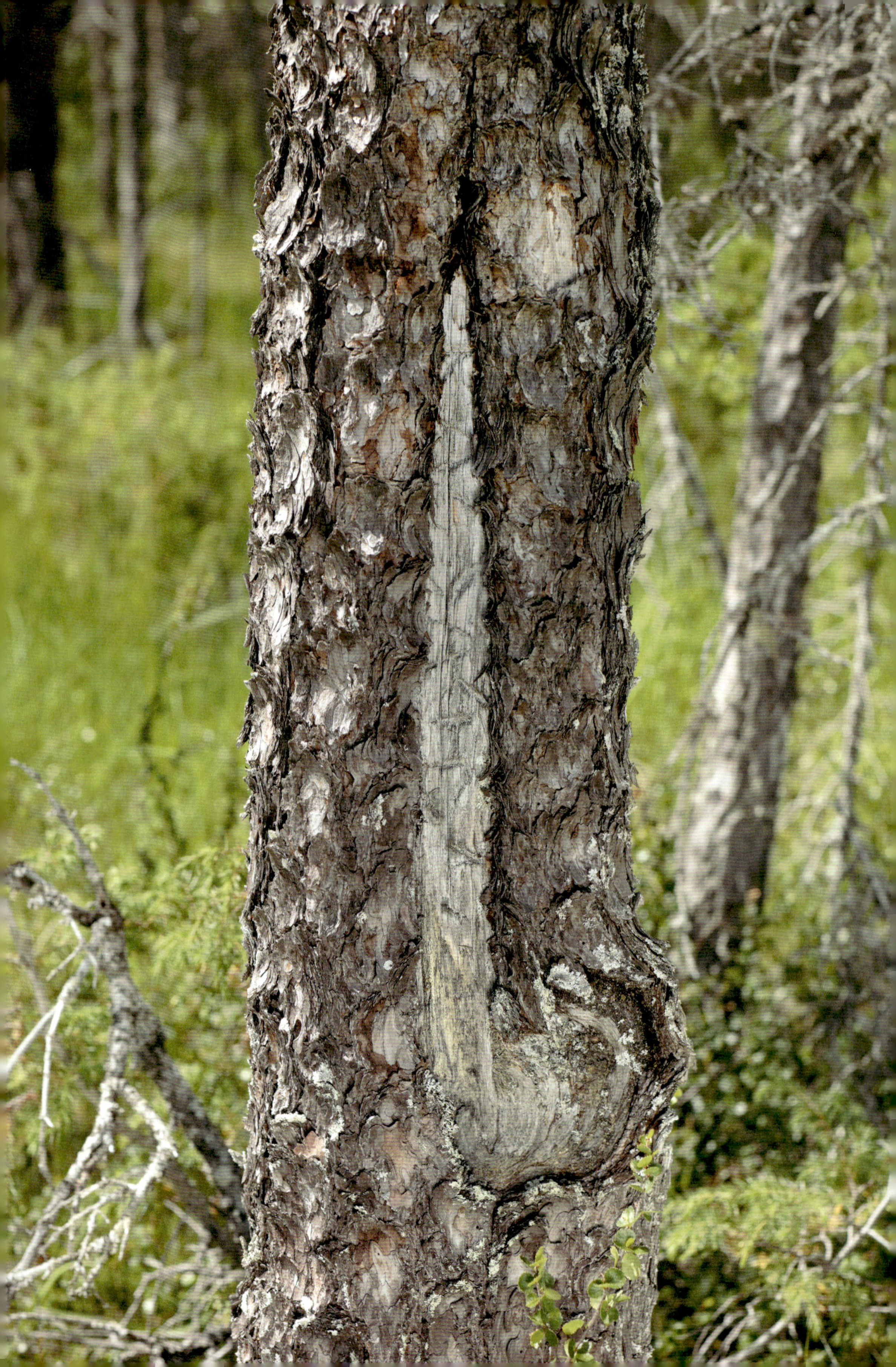

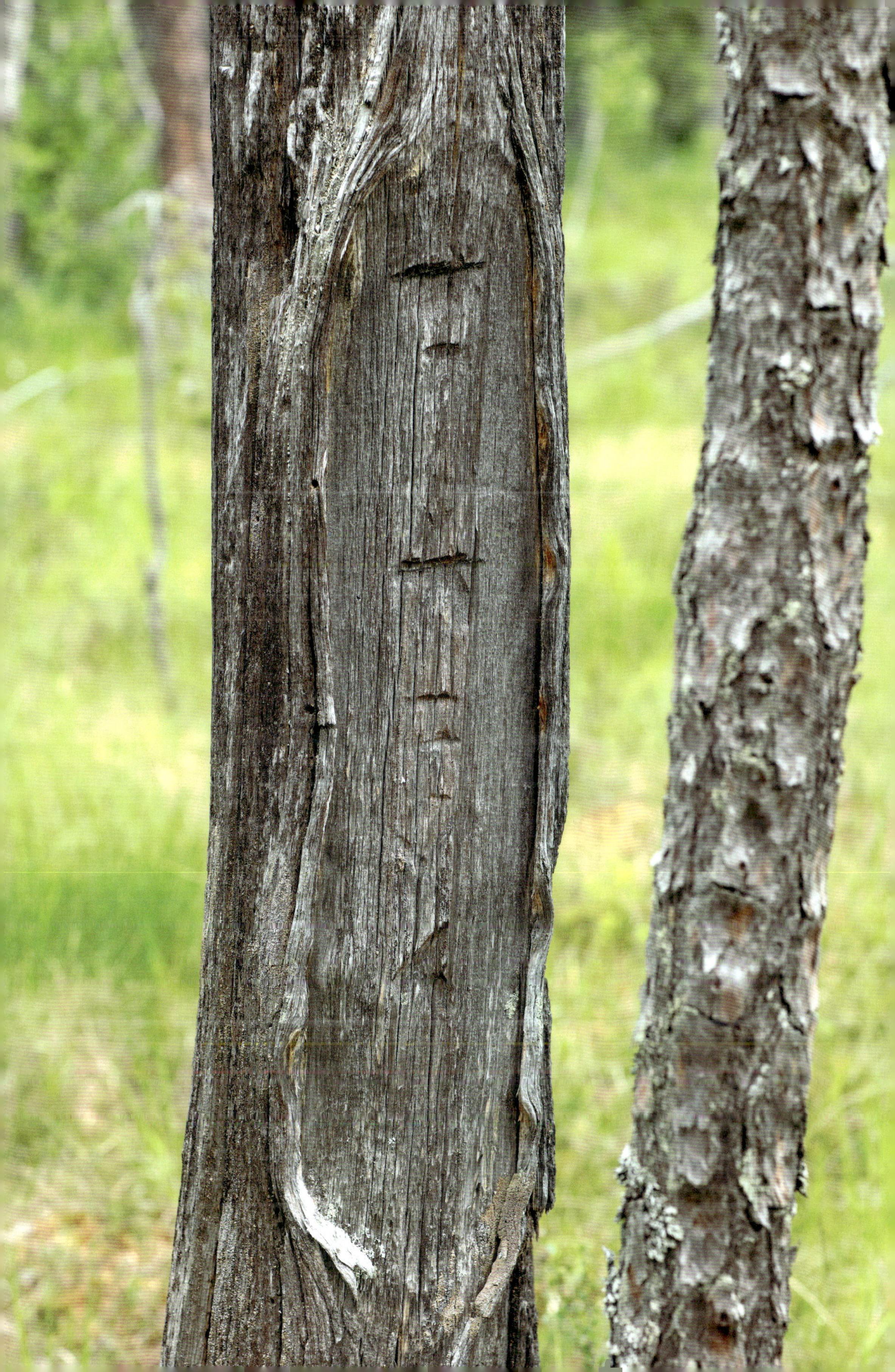

sus a risa

june

to find them, we take the road from rättvik to bingsjö
after passing some small lakes on the left, we turn right on
a smaller forest road that goes north
at first the road is very straight

after gäddtjärnen, the road begins to wind   now we are close

the road has several detours to both right and left
many are not accessible by car
halgonberget is on the left

AOD KOD

the tree is narrow, cannot be more than 1.5 decimeter in diameter
the carved characters are rough, covering almost half the trunk

BOD XXXX

a little further away, another tree
72
SI PÅ MED XXXXX

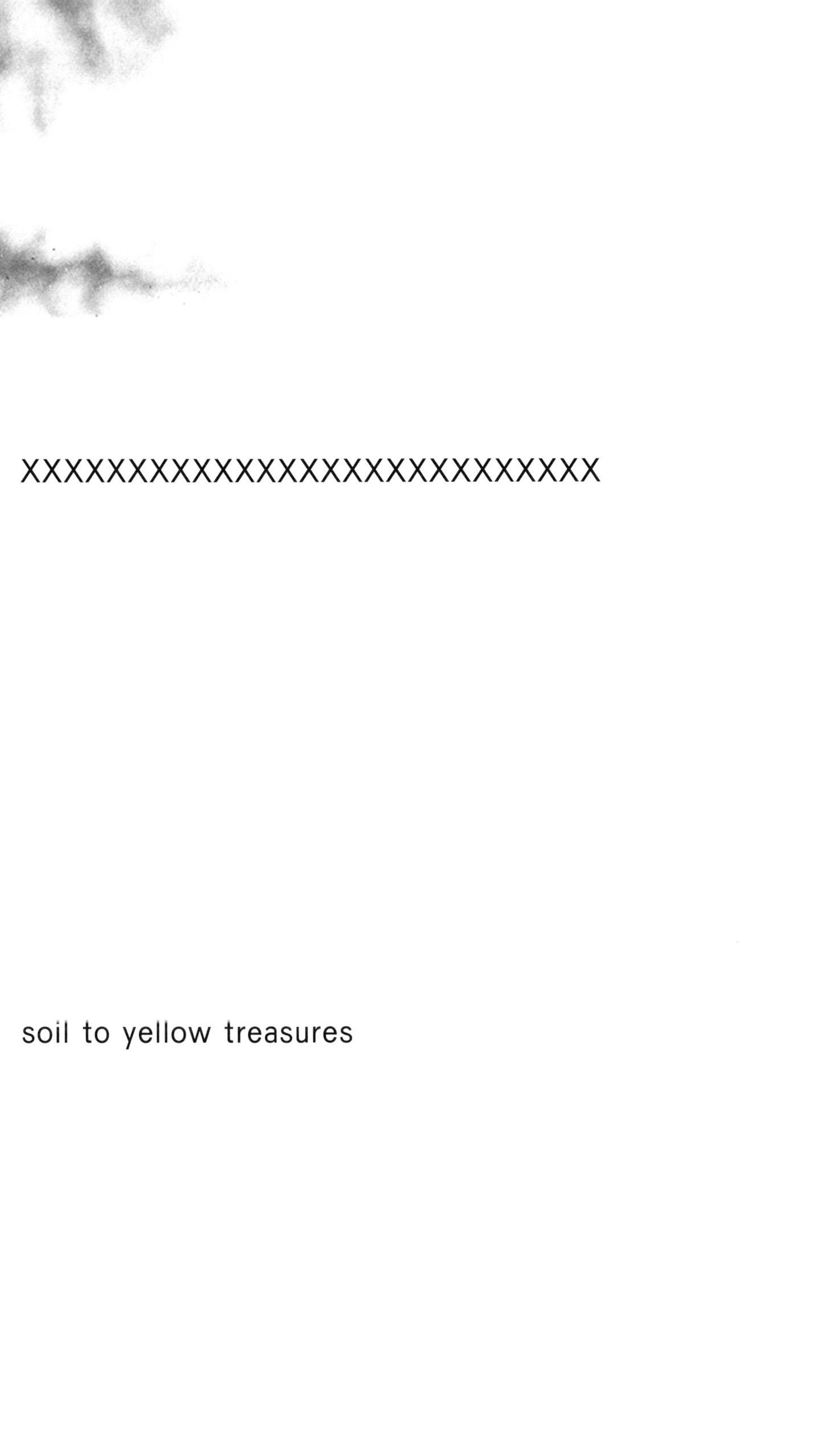

XXXXXXXXXXXXXXXXXXXXXXXXXXXXX

soil to yellow treasures

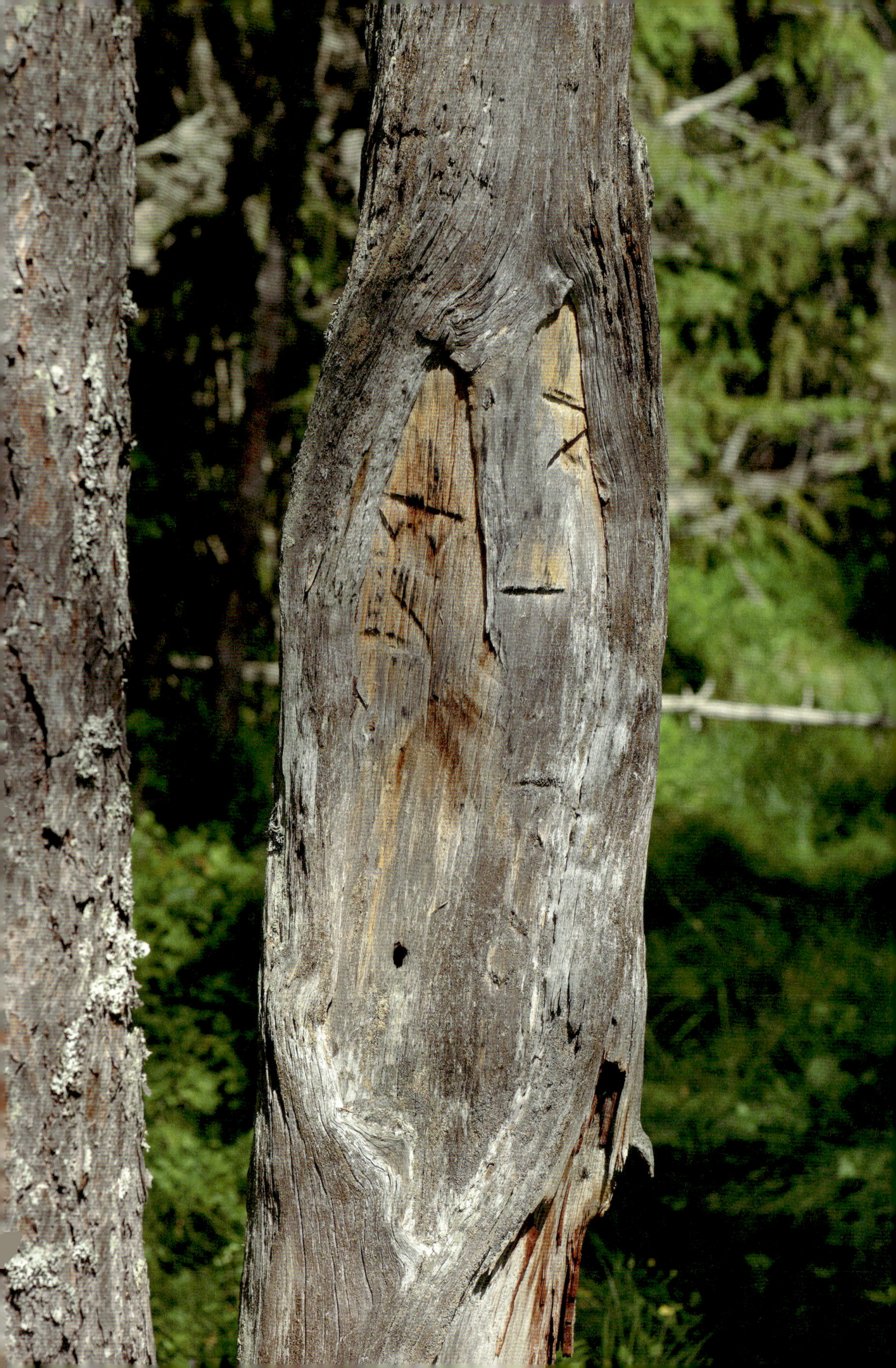

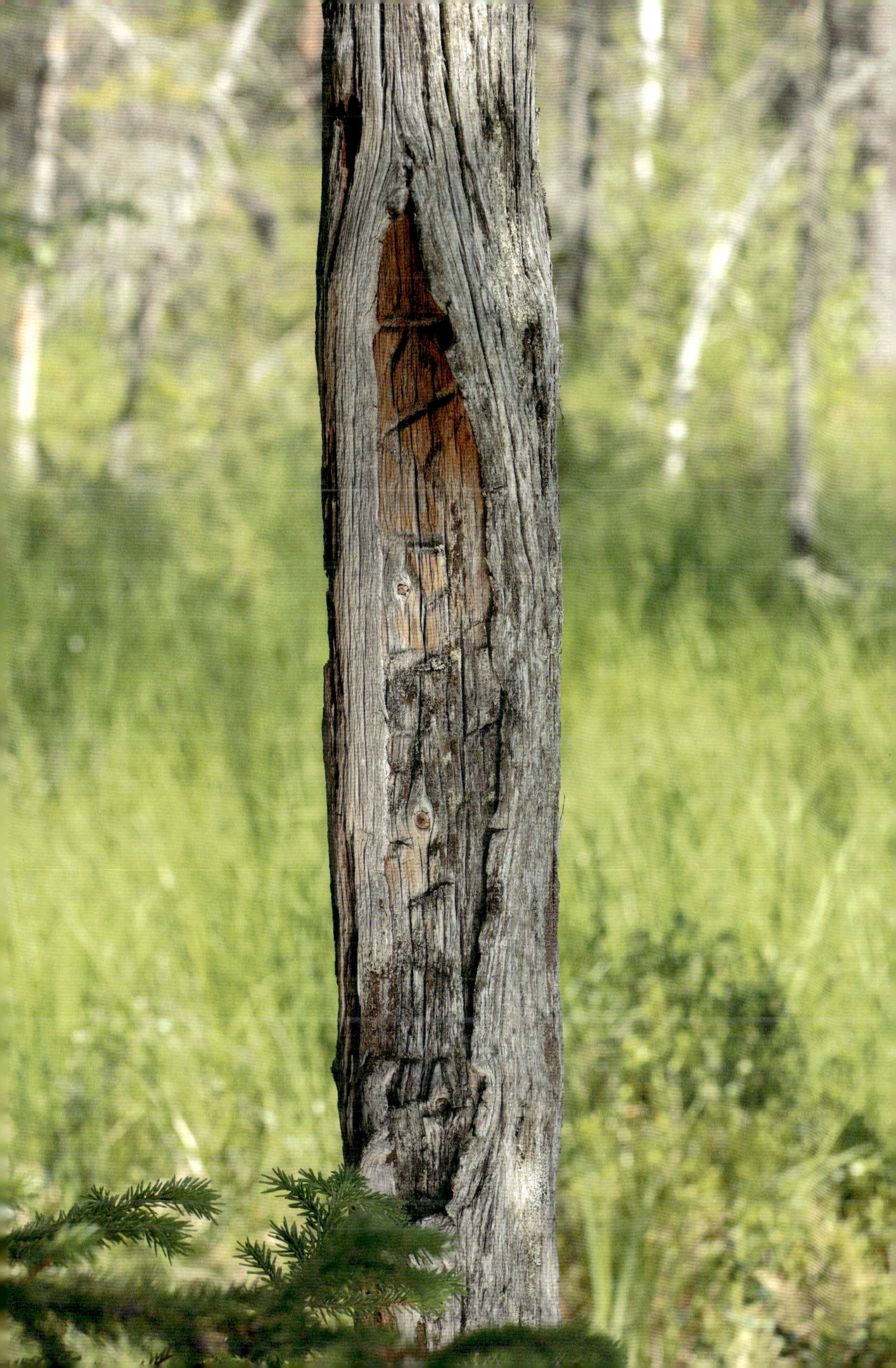

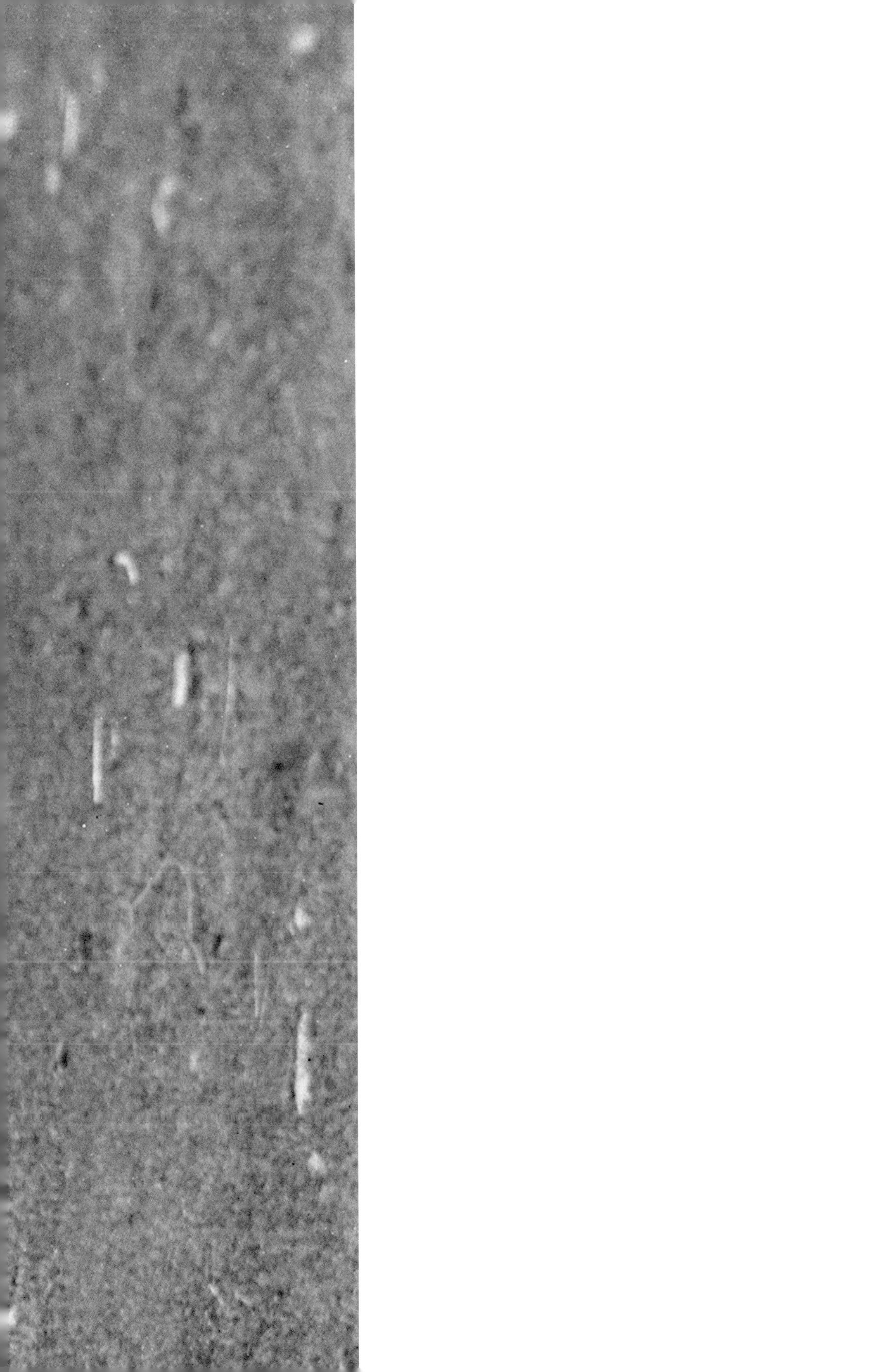

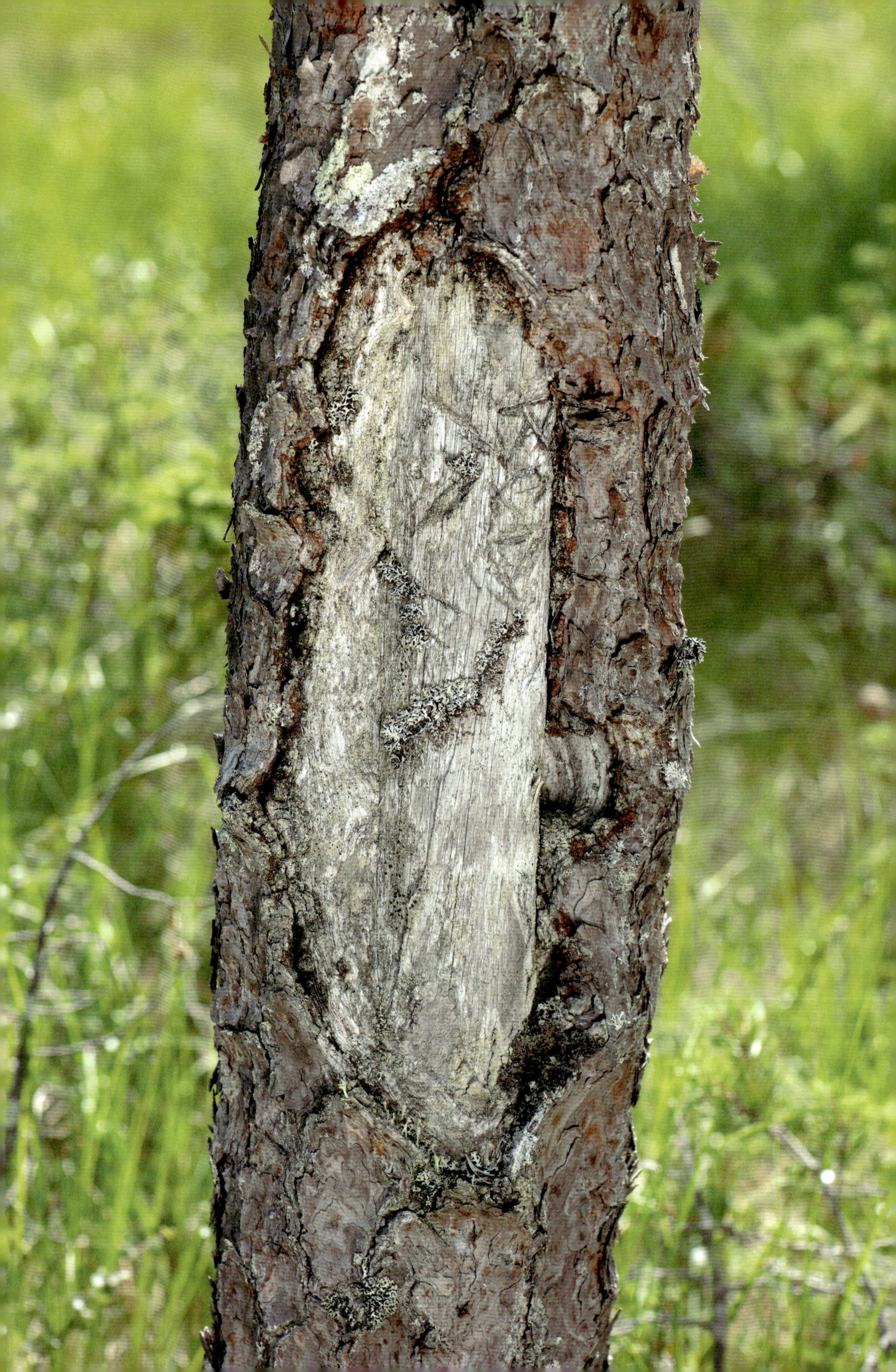

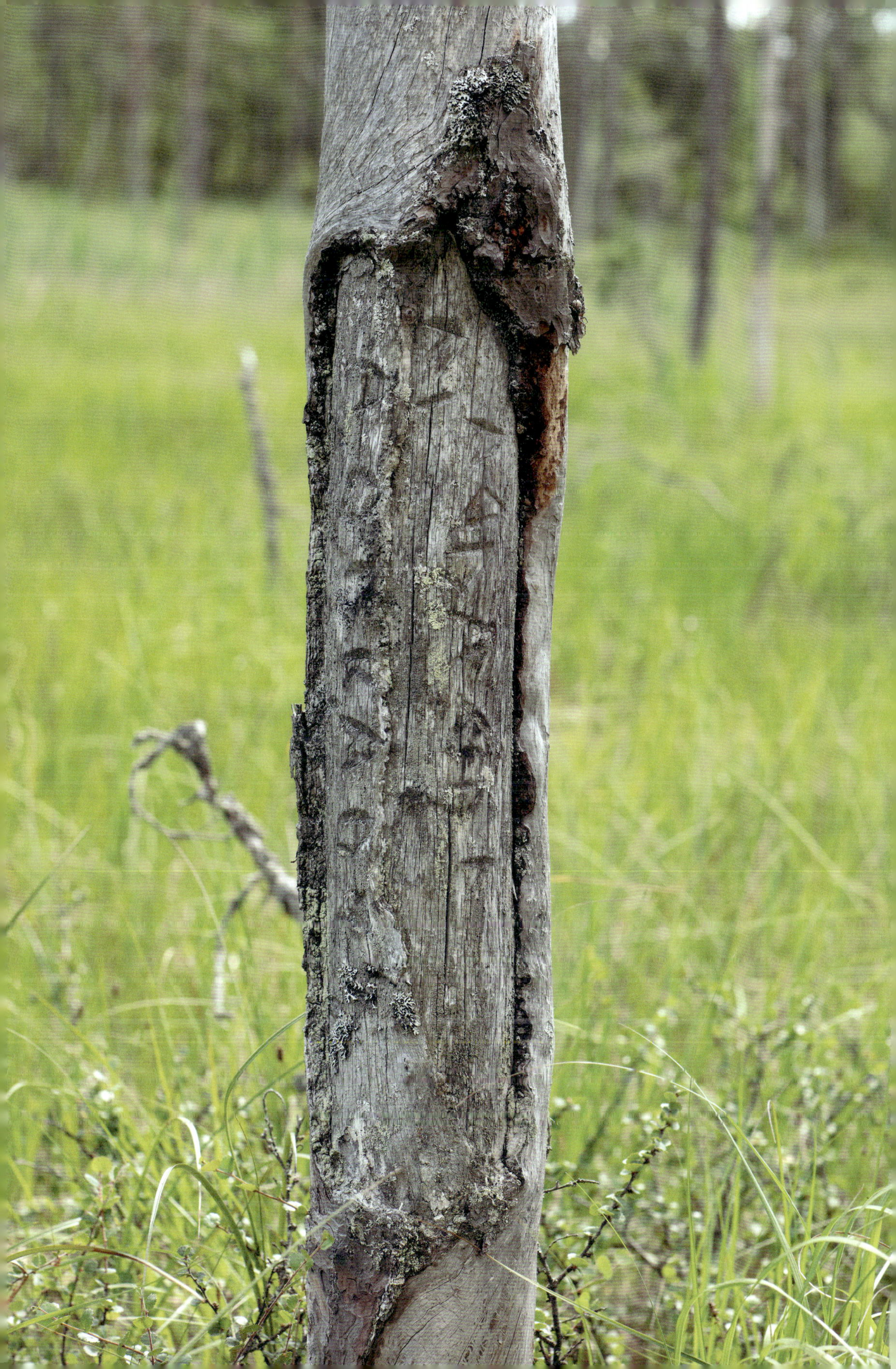

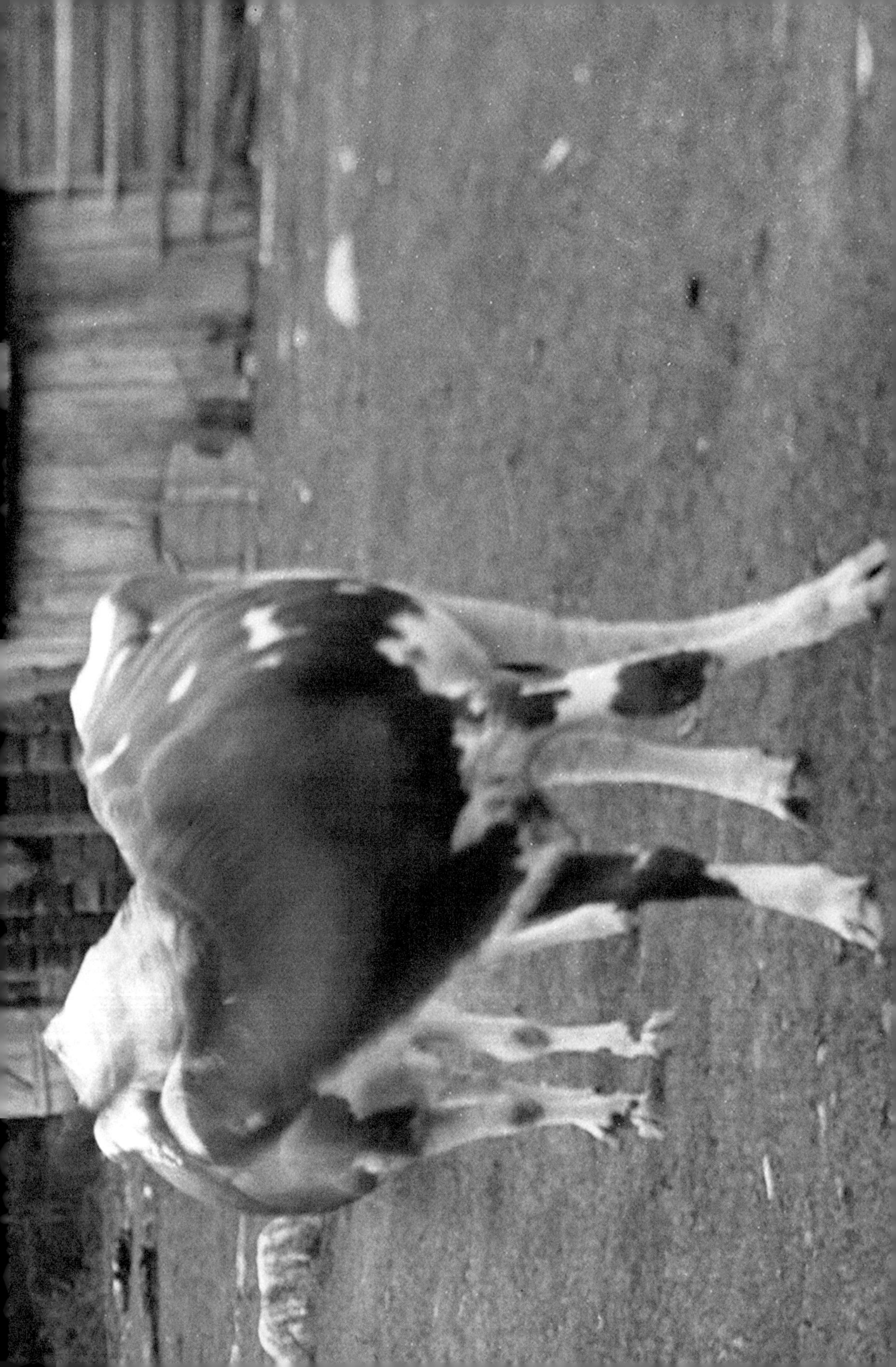

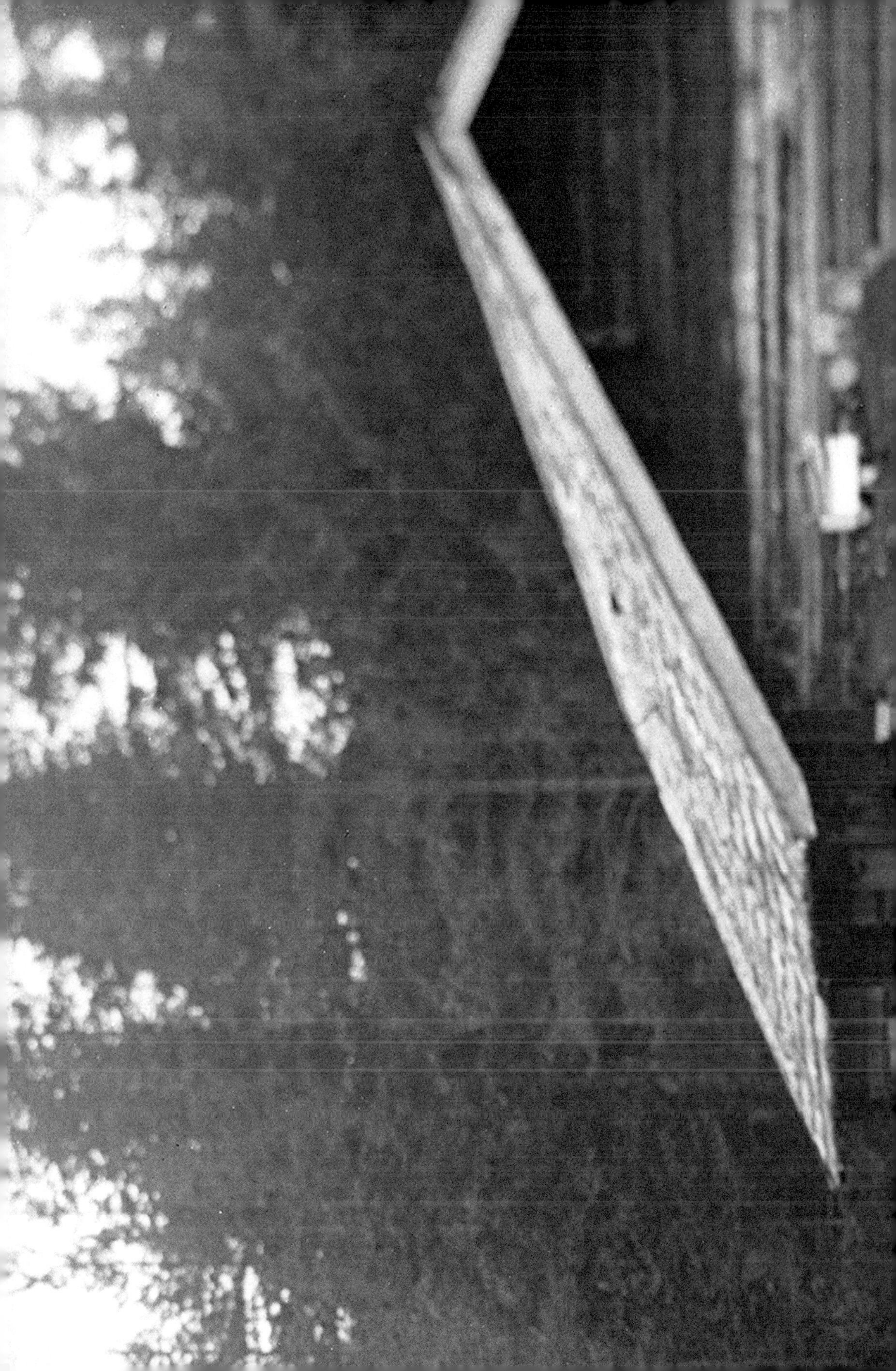

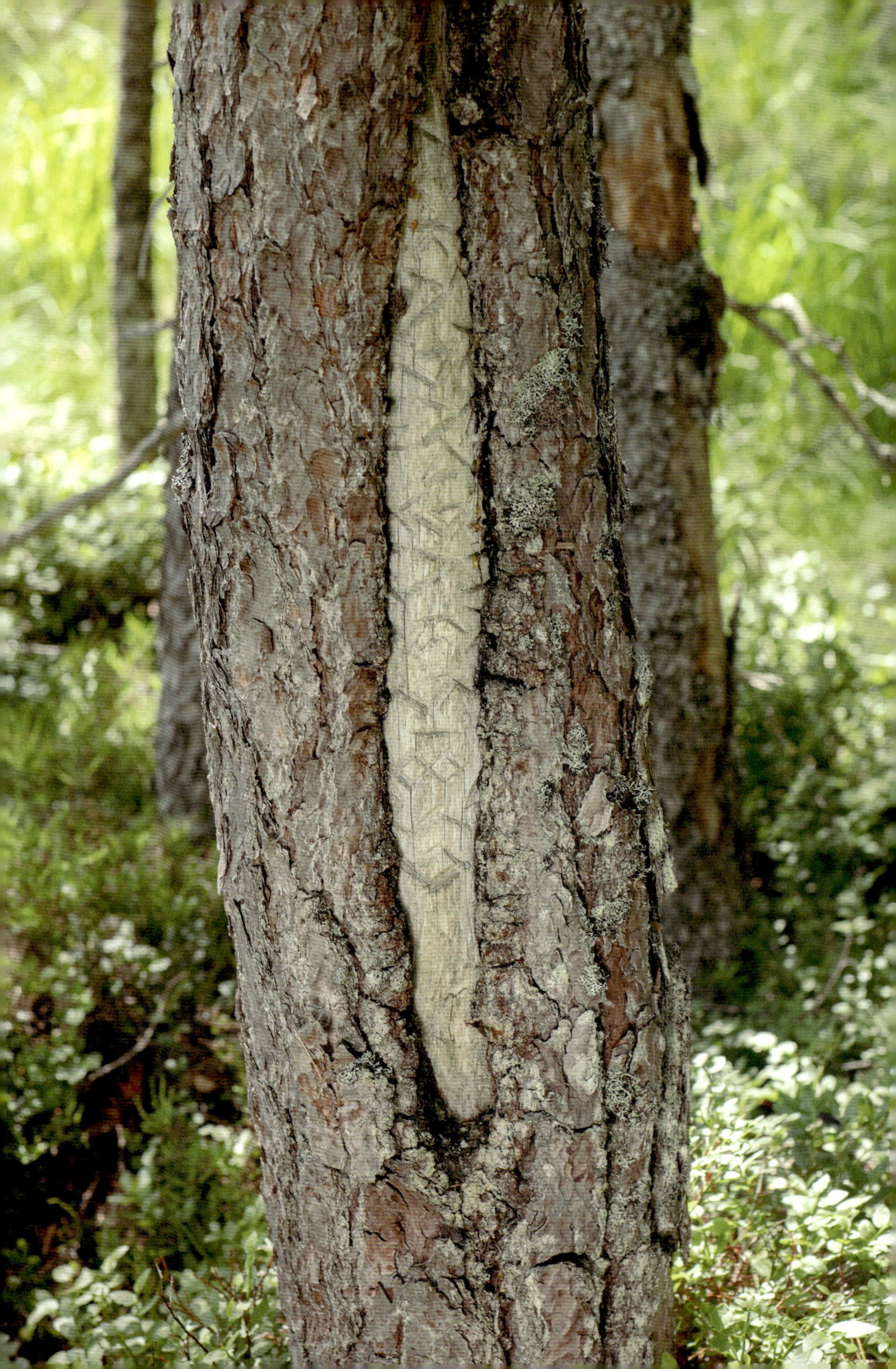

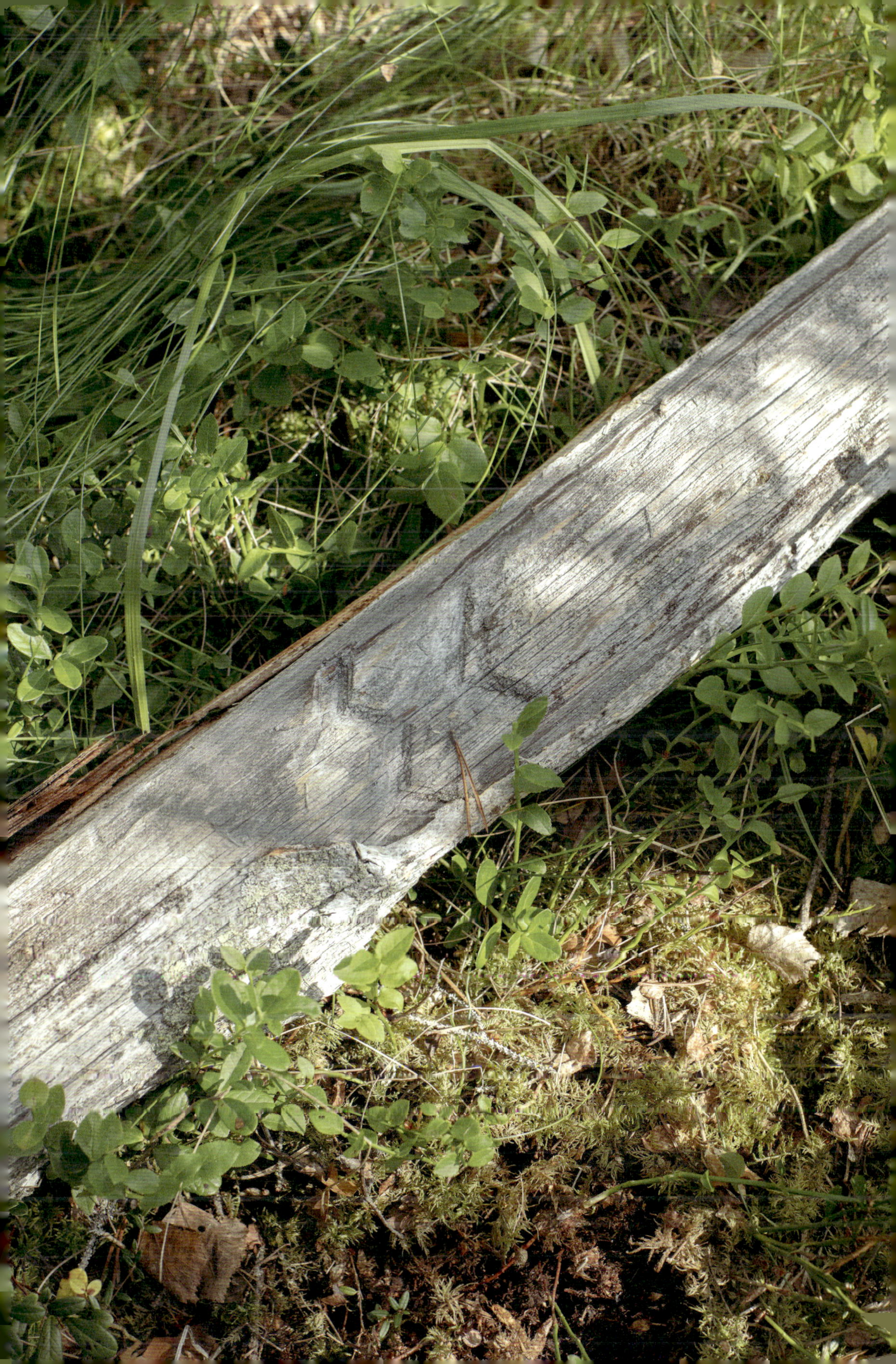

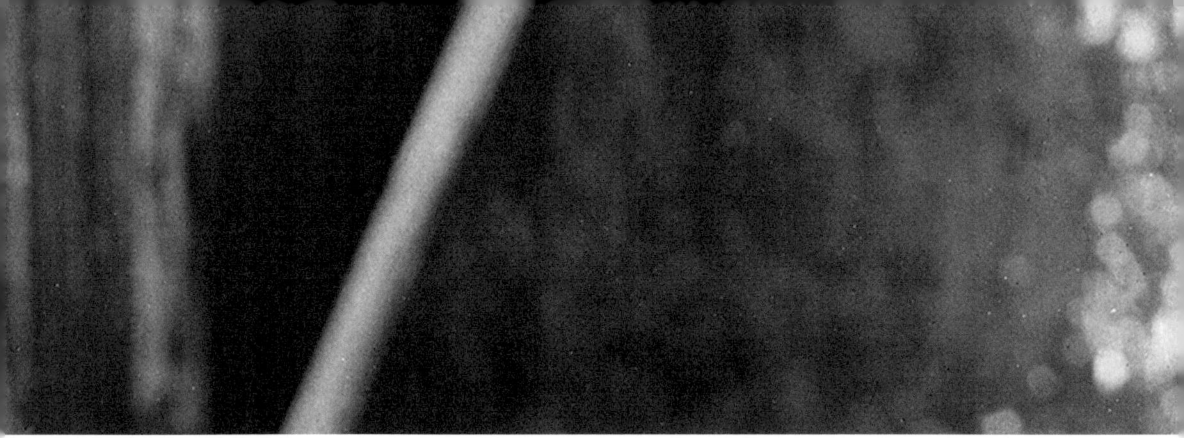

a braided code
A LAZY BITCH

1828

88888888281 zero one 0101 XXXX
76
70 466 49

misspelled

and some skin from a young cow head   for patching

sant   true

0248-15034

HELLO

HI

a öj e va je

two long braids

she turns her head to read

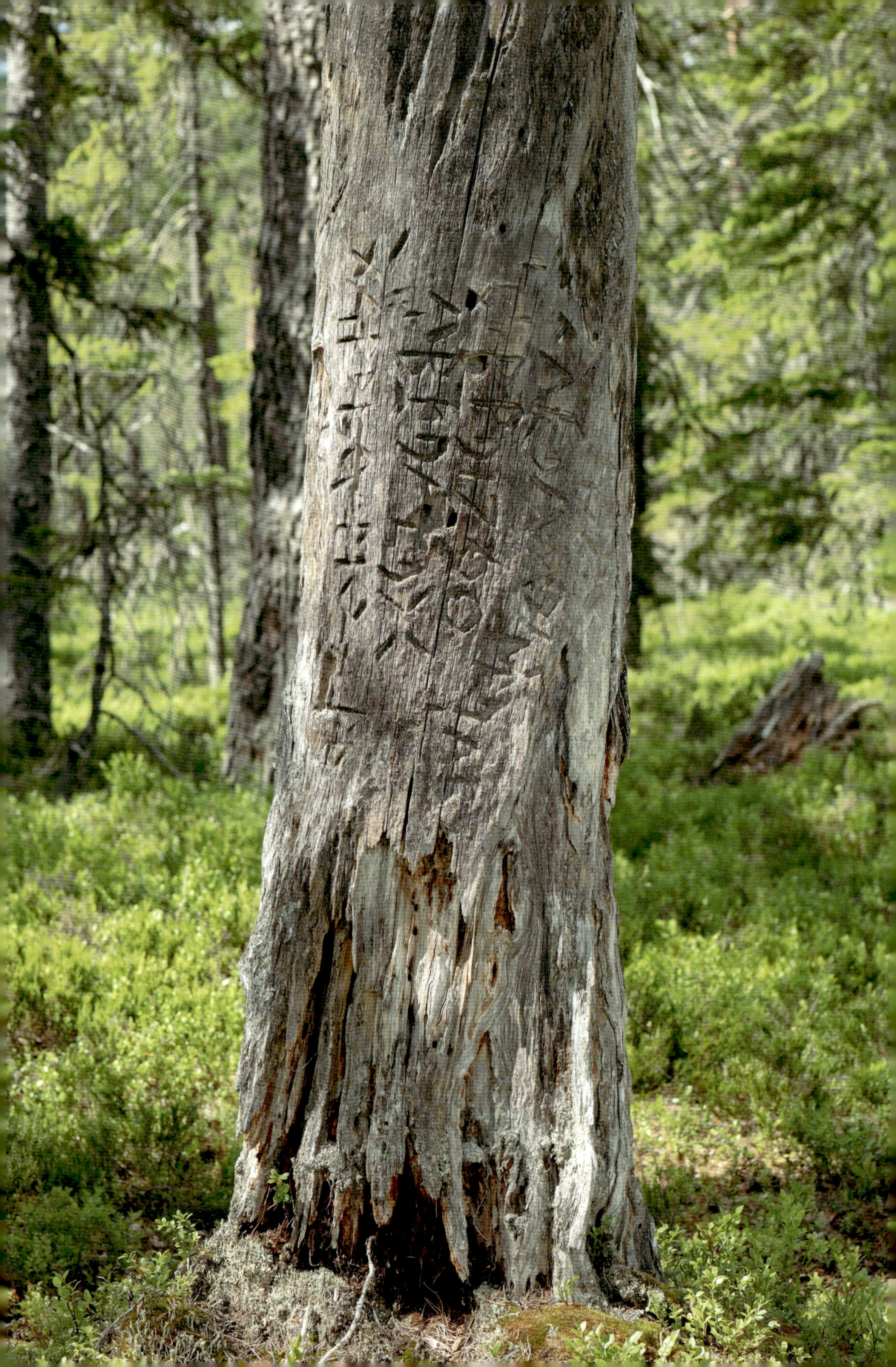

INTRODUCTION
Elina Birkehag

Five letters in a row. E L I N A. The code that makes
my name. As a kid, the E had a few more horizontal lines
than the one I was later taught in school; the N was usually
reversed; the A upside down. It didn't matter, it was legible—
I understood it, and others did too. Once I knew how to write
my name, I couldn't stop. I wrote it everywhere. On my toys
and on my bed frame; on the walls, the doors, the ledges.
On and inside all of my books—even along their uneven edges,
letting my pen glide across the thick stack of pages pressed
between two covers. Leaving marks and traces of myself on
different materials and surfaces was visceral. Pencil on raw
wood, pen on paint. Ink on coated paper and waxy crayon
on plastic. An encounter and exchange between my hand,
the tool, and the surface. Impossible to reverse. The surface
became forever marked, forever destroyed, forever scarred.

BED
AED
KID
BAD
AID
BMD
BED
AED

KAD
KID
KED
KOD
KAD
MOD
AOD
AAD
KLD
MAD
ABD
BOD
ABD
KLD
SOD
BED
BED
BPD

This list contains the initials of the women who also left their
names, by carving into pine trees. While working as shepherds
during the summers in Dalarna, Sweden, these women
marked the surrounding trees with messages that, centuries
later, the forest still carries. The first of the three initials
signifies the woman's first name. The second, their father's
surname. The last, which is always D, means daughter.
Brita Eriksdotter, Anna Eriksdotter, Karin Andersdotter.

When I first saw one of these tree carvings it was summer,
and I was about to turn thirty. I was older than most of the
women who left them three hundred years back, who were
typically unmarried and rather young. I spent my summers
in the area, and as a child, my grandmother had herself been
at the *fäbod,* (the name for the pastures and small cottages
where the shepherds and the animals went for the summer).
But the messages left behind on the trees were unknown
to me. As I followed Brita Eriksdotter's initials with my fingers,
I felt a sudden and distinct connection with the past.
After searching for a few more hours, I found nine additional
trees—seven of them standing close to each other, making
a wide circle. Slowly, I started reading the forest. Tree by tree.

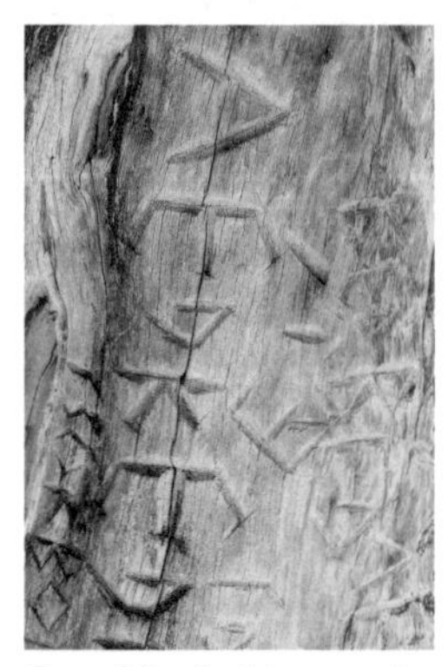

One of the first tree carvings
I found at Halgonberget,
Dalarna, 2021.

AED BED BED AOD 1778 I DALEN IIA AED
KED 1776 I SÖKBODA IES R A A AHD
I S A X AED A AED AAD MDD AI BDD 1760

The underlying idea of *fäbod* culture is to let the animals
graze in remote areas, saving the land nearest to the village
for agricultural purposes. Each spring, the shepherds would
leave their families in the village, lead the livestock to greener
pastures, and live together in the summer cottages, where
they would manage the production of cheese and butter.
This annual routine was a survival strategy and is a significant
part of the cultural heritage of Sweden. Yet while herding
exists all over the world, it is only in Nordic *fäbod* culture that
the shepherds were almost exclusively women. In the Middle
Ages, men and children tended the cattle while the women
did the milking, but when milk production moved to the *fäbods*,
the tasks could no longer be divided, and women took on
both. Two other factors contributed to this tradition as well:
a 1686 law that prohibited teenage boys from spending time
on their own with livestock, due to concerns about bestiality,
and the many wars during the seventeenth century, which
created a surplus of women at that time.

After finding the initials carved into the forest near the old
fäbod farms, I went to the local archives to find out more about
these women. I found a few photographs of women tending
cattle, which were taken at the beginning of the twentieth
century, near the end of the *fäbod* culture, on occasions
when the women were visited by a farmer, a priest, or their
families. The pictures showed women at work. Their hands
held vessels and utensils. Women with long braids stood next
to each other with knitting needles, smiling at the cameras.

Though the carved initials had been unfamiliar to me,
these photographs were not. Growing up, I'd seen plenty
of depictions of the young shepherds. At the beginning of
the twentieth century, the region of Dalarna was known
as one of the most idyllic places in Sweden, with its deep
and dark forests, beautiful lakes, and blue mountains.
The history of hard-working, unmarried, and independent
women herders soon became another draw for tourists.

Elina Birkehag

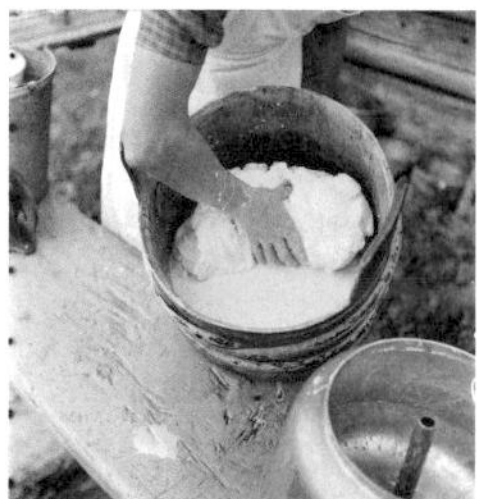

Archive image of a woman
cleaning butter at the *fäbod*.
Nordiska Museet.

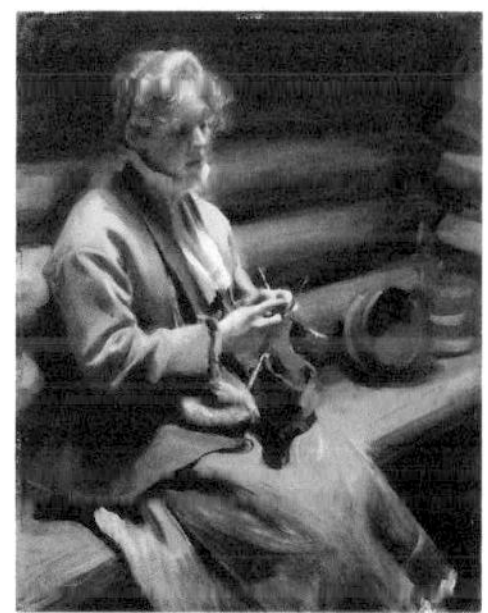

During the twentieth
century, *Dalecarlian Girl
Knitting* by Anders Zorn,
(1901) was one of
Sweden's most famous
and most frequently
reproduced paintings.

Some of the country's most famous painters such as Anders Zorn, Olof Arborelius, and Johan Fredrik Höckert depicted these women as healthy, pure, and surrounded by nature. The flushed cheeks, traditional folk dress, and sensual gazes in these paintings cemented into an image that stayed in the public imagination for years to come. In 1978, the archetype reached a certain climax with the porn movie *Fäbodjäntan* and its main character, Monika. Young and blonde, surrounded by blue mountains and accompanied by folk music, Monika was the culmination of decades of art, writing, and cultural lore that helped shape an erotic image of Sweden's famed female shepherds.

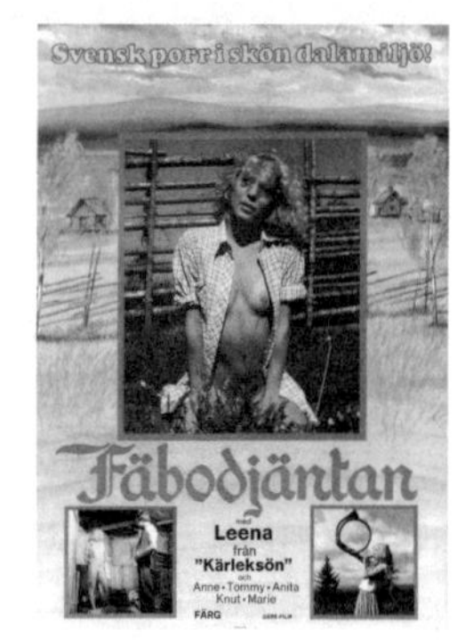

Come and Blow the Horn (Fäbodjäntan), a pornographic movie directed by Joseph W. Sarno, 1978.

Yet in all of those depictions of *fäbod* culture—both real and imagined—I had never seen an image or heard a story that involved the carvings I had come across in the forest. I was struck by this absence; abstract as they are, these carvings are part of the women's stories, and they came directly from them. To me, the carvings witnessed something that isn't captured in Zorn's paintings, or in the archives: they tell of desire, fear, love, missing, loneliness, and boredom. But also of pleasure and friendship. Sometimes these carvings would fill an entire tree trunk; sometimes the women wrote ugly and forbidden words. The carvings memorialize women who had found autonomy, maybe for the first time in their lives. These were women who wanted to be seen, and who had decided to leave assertions of their existence—a definitive mark, a living monument.

<table>
<tr><td>

HÄR, RITAR, JAG, MITT NAMN
T, ILL, HEDER, Å, SKAM LED

</td><td>

HERE I DRAW MY NAME IN
HONOR AND SHAME LED

</td></tr>
<tr><td>

A SED BPD ET : PAR : GODA
KAM : RAT : TER : SOM : Y
: ÖR : Y LAG : DÅ : WI ÄR I
ÄRTTERÅSSEN
MÄN DÅ WI KOMMER HEM
38 DÅ KAN ENT WI LÖPA I LAG
BRA DÅ   LIOT SKRIWA 1849

</td><td>

A SED BPD A COUPLE OF GOOD
FRIENDS WORK IN A TEAM
WHEN WE ARE IN ÄRTERÅSSEN
BUT WHEN WE GET HOME
38 THEN WE CANNOT WORK
TOGETHER WELL THEN
BAD WRITTEN 1849

</td></tr>
<tr><td>

BOD FAN : SÅ LET

</td><td>

BOD DAMN THAT'S BAD

</td></tr>
</table>

SI BBD EN SLV SLABA
EBANKO 1828

X SY : PÅ FEM : WAL : PI : GVR :
AHD MAD AMD KED KMD AL :
LE : HOP : FRA : KE : WI : MI
SOM : ÄR : SÅ : LI : TEN 1849

SNART DEN TIDEN

Transcript of walls in various *fäbod* cottages and tree carvings.
Fäbodristningar i Ore socken by Lasse Bägerfeldt

LOOK HERE A LAZY BITCH
IN EXCESS 1828

X LOOK HERE FIVE SHEPHERDS
AHD MAD AMD KED KMD
EVERYONE IS KIND TO ME WHO
IS SO SMALL 1849

SOON THAT TIME

Translation by author

To carve your name into a tree requires preparation. Pine trees
are stubborn and slow interfaces. In order to make a mark
that lasts, you must first peel off the bark. This can be done
with a small axe. Behind the bark, you will find a smooth
and even surface. Now carve your letters. Hew them diagonally
into the tree's fibers so that the letters bite into the wood.
Your name. An impression on the landscape.

Although Sweden's landscapes are known for their deep,
lush green forests, most of the country's woods today consist
of plantations. Since the 1950s, over 60% of Sweden's
forested area has been clear-cut. Most of the trees where
I found carvings are on the outer edges of a mire or a bog,
places that were ideal for the animals to graze and for herders
to get a good rest. The location has also contributed to
the trees' survival: in the wetlands, pines grow too slowly
for the forestry industry. But the bogs were likely not the only
places where the women carved, and an unknown number
of carvings made in more lush and dense pine forests have
by now been cut down. Like many types of women's work
throughout history, the carvings have been poorly archived
and little written about—when the remaining trees are felled,
die, or decompose, only our documentation of them will
continue to carry the messages of the shepherds.

Today, five years since I saw my first carving, I now know what
it feels like to walk in the wetland, get water in my boots,
and fight the mosquitoes. I know the names of the different
plants, what the Lavskrika (*Siberian jay*) sounds like, and
the taste of the cloudberries as they finally ripen in late July.

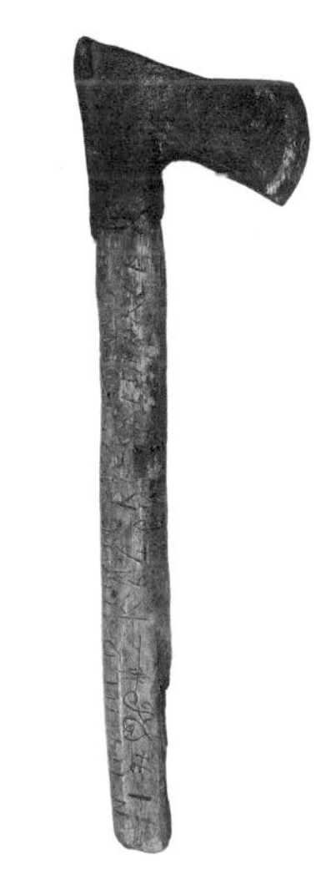

Archive image of an axe
used for carving.
Maria Lannerbro Norell,
Dalarnas Museum.

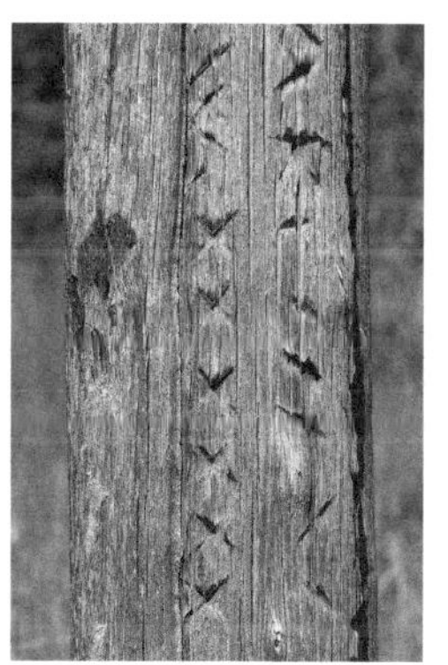

Recurring X on a tree trunk
at Halgonberget, 2021.

Elina Birkehag

I know all of this, and still I can only guess at the meanings
behind some of the symbols, acronyms, and shortcuts carved
into the trees. Some researchers believe that the recurring
rows of X's and I's imply a counting system, where one 'X'
equals either one week or ten days, and an 'I' equals one day.
The counting may have been a way of keeping track of what
fields had been already grazed and now needed time to grow
back. According to one story, the act of carving was itself very
quick, made more precise when the women tapped on the
back of the axe with a stone. The rapid knocking sound this
action produced could be heard all throughout the forests.
Another story tells of a shepherd who was asked why she
carved the trees, to which she simply replied: "It was fun."

Reading and writing were not common skills among the
farmers, and until 1842,* the only place to learn was in church.
The women at the *fäbod* most likely created their writing
system by copying one another. Reading the carved names
today, it appears the women carved both in groups, and also
by themselves. When they returned to the cottages after their
herding, they continued to carve, now on the interior of
the wooden cottages, where they used a knife instead of an axe,
and wrote long, detailed sentences and more elaborate stories,
sometimes encrypting their writing with techniques like
mirroring or braided letters. To see images of the cottages
today brings to mind teenage diaries and notes passed during
class—frenetic scrawlings cover the walls, the benches,
the door handles, the ceilings, and even the cheese boxes.

Much like these carving–covered cottages, neither the history
of these women nor the meaning of their carvings are neat,
legible, or ordered. When I started compiling my research into
an artist book, my intention was never to write their story in
my own words; rather, I wanted to create a space for dialogue,
wonder, and imagination, reflecting theirs. I see this book as
a collective space, one that connects this local phenomenon
with contemporary culture, both inside and outside of Sweden.
I thought that if we tried to look at these carvings from
further distances and varied perspectives, we could understand
them in new ways. I invited Amelia Groom, M. Ty, Quinn Latimer,
Meg Miller, Matilda Kenttä, Linnea Rutz, Jungmyung Lee,

* In 1842, a law was
passed in Sweden, called
Folkskolestadgan, which
gave all children the right
to go to school and receive
basic knowledge in various
subjects.

and Jennie Tiderman–Österberg, all writers and artists I admire,
to contribute texts relating my research to their own practices.
Today, I am very happy to publish these six textual contributions,
which expand upon contemporary subjects such as ecology,
typography, labor, and art—all in close connection to a local
writing tradition that existed, once upon a time, in Dalarna.

During the four years that I have been working on this project,
I always kept a notebook with me, writing down what I read
on the trees, as well as gossip I heard, notes from conversations
I had, and beliefs about life on the *fäbod*. The notebook
oscillates between English, Swedish, and a local dialect from
Rättvik. This text is presented on the backside of the pages
of the tree photographs, together with other materials collected
or made during those four years. This text is my response
to the text I read in the forest. It is a text written to my
grand–mother, her mother, and their mothers.

ELINA 2022

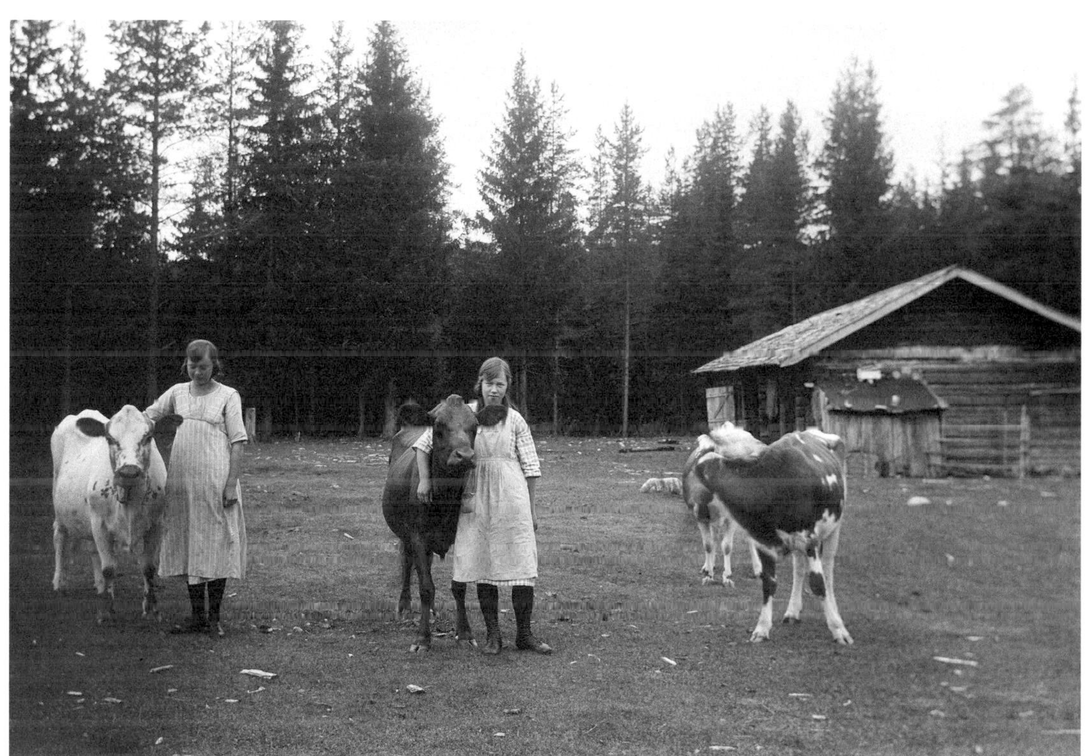

Archive image of girls standing with cattle, Dalarnas Museum.

Elina Birkehag

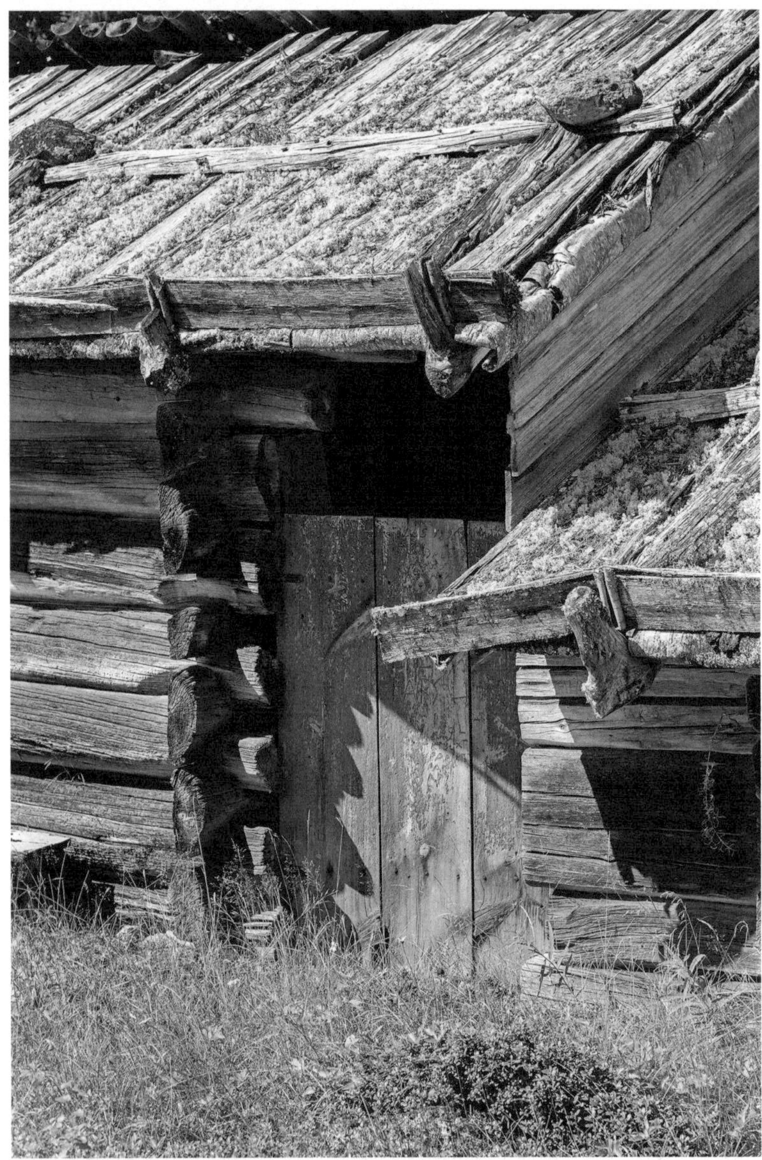

Fäbod cottage at Dansbodarna, Dalarna. July, 2021.

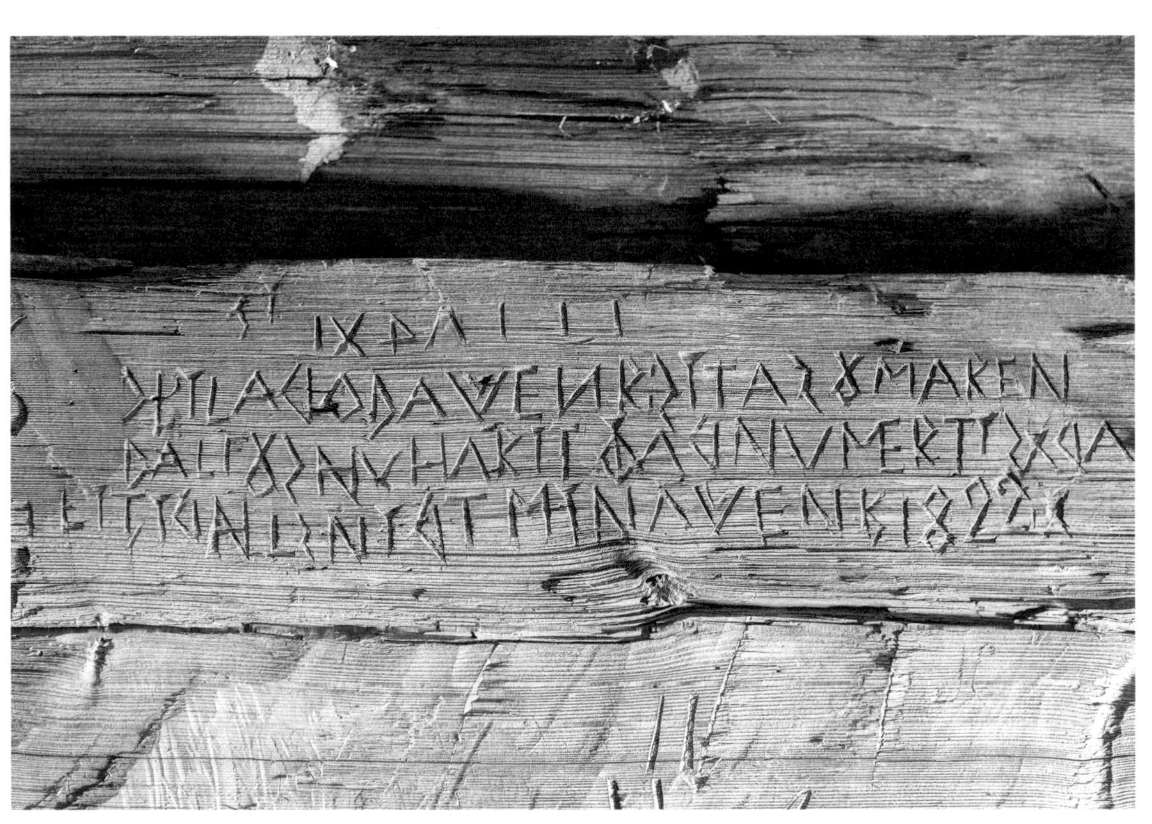

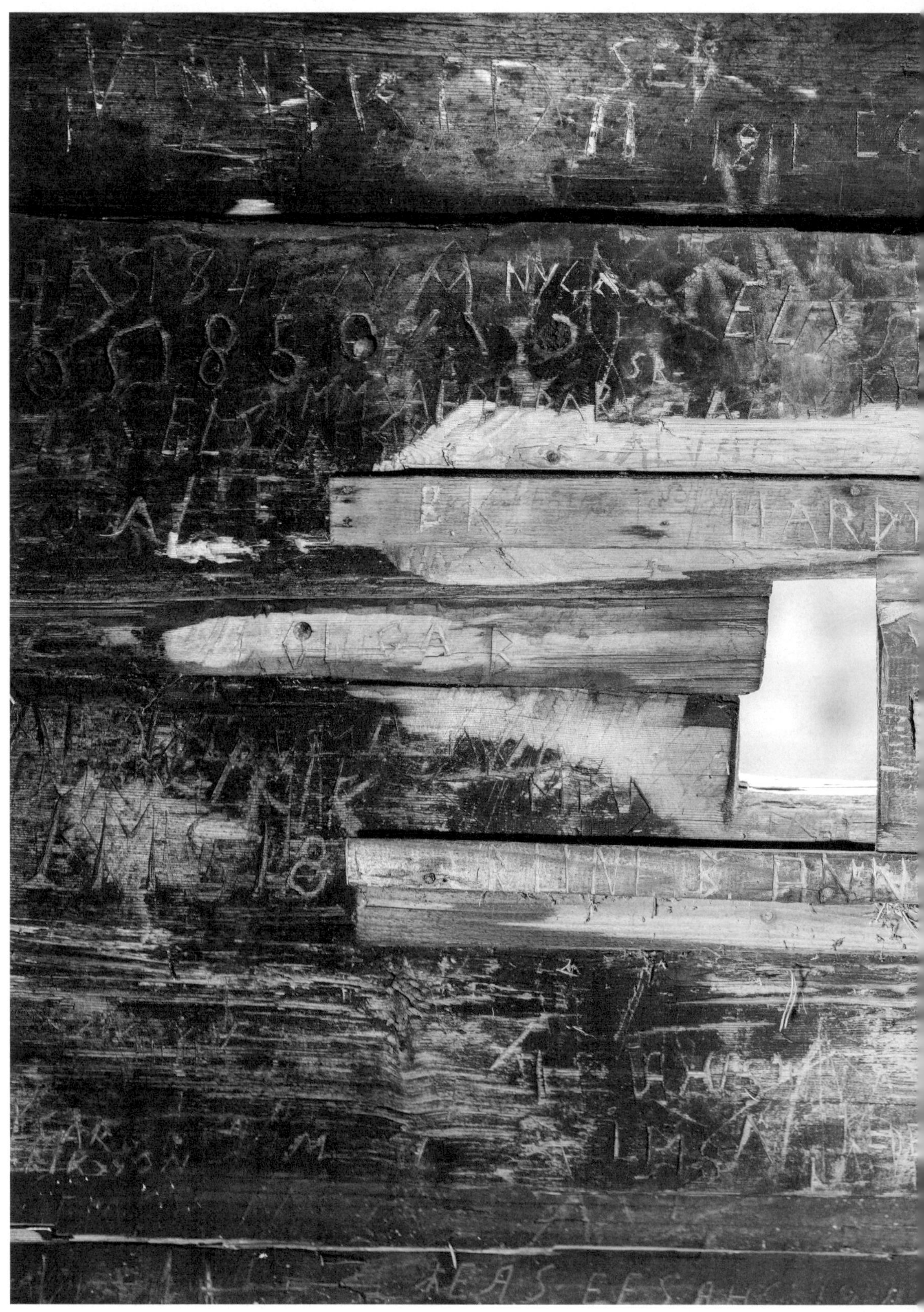

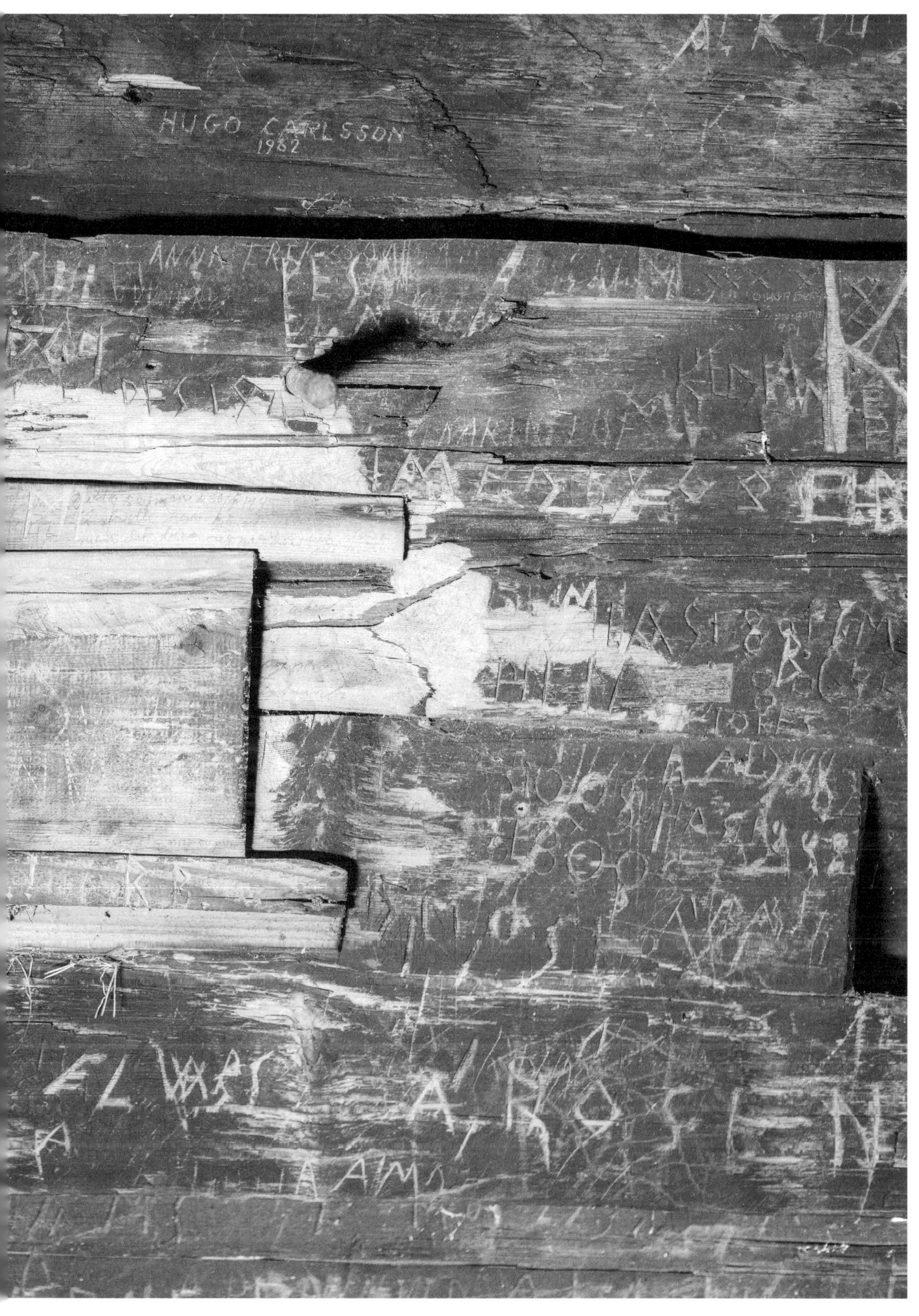

Elina Birkehag

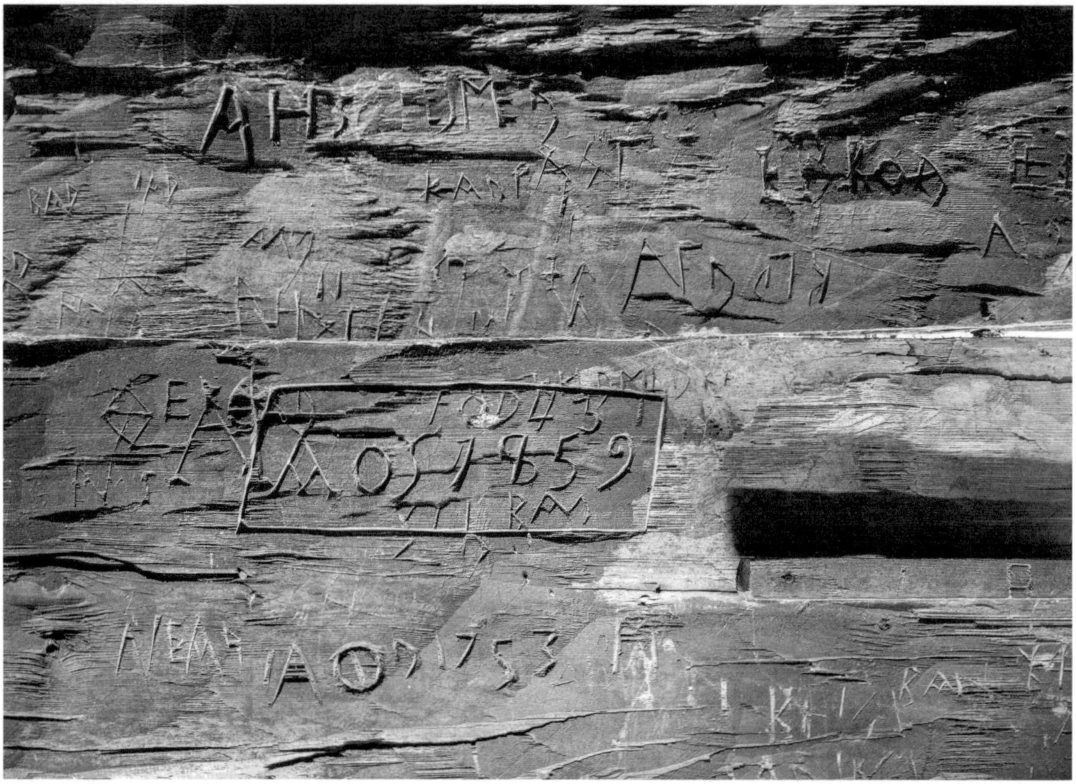

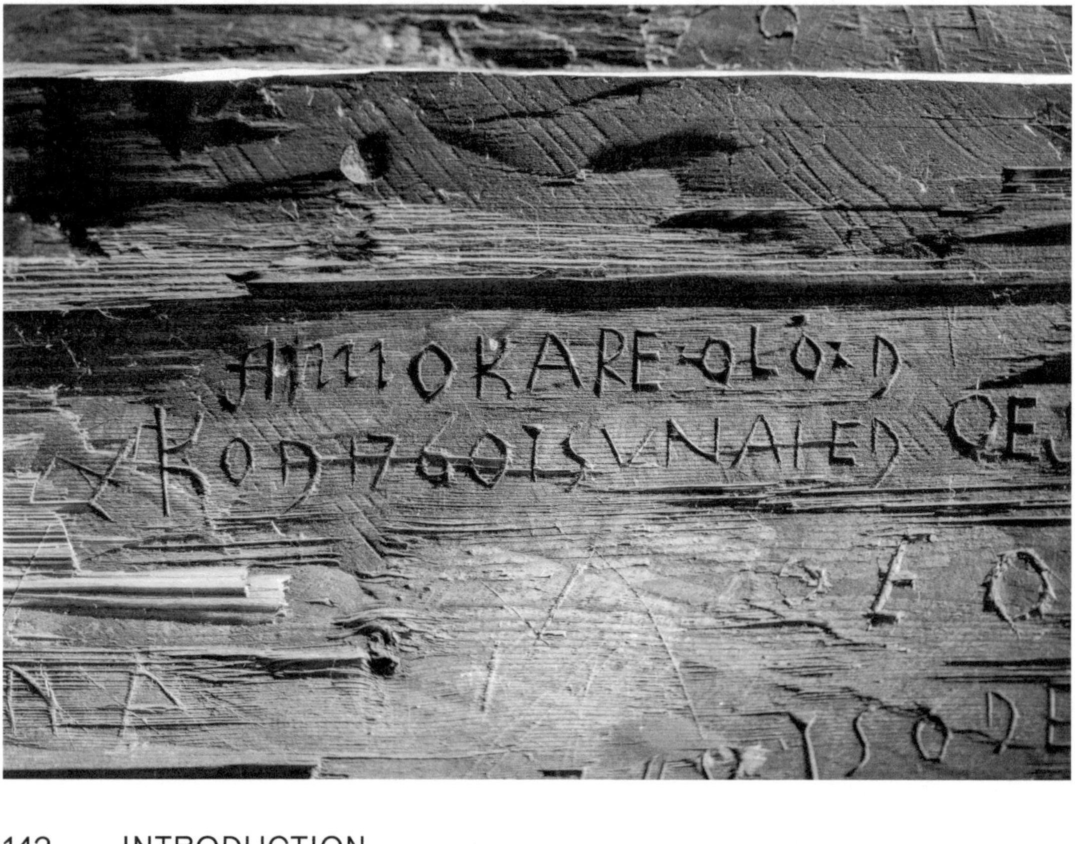

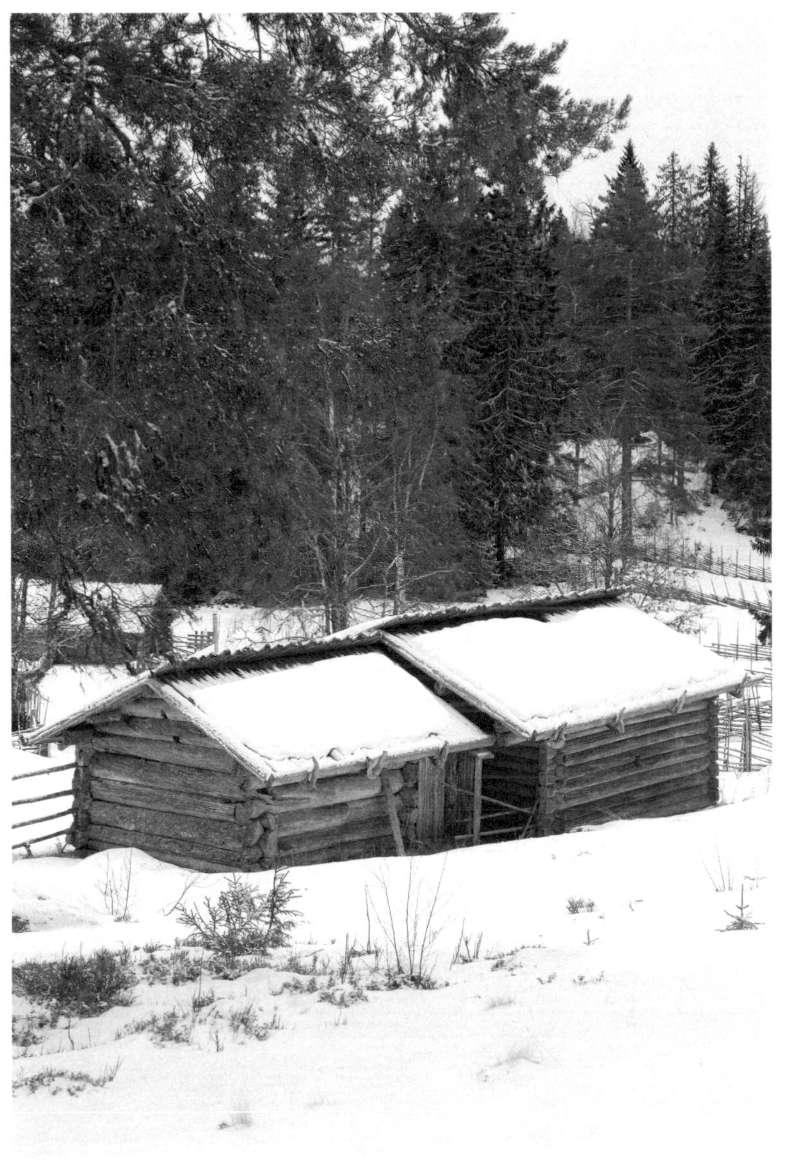

Fäbod cottage in Ärteråsen, Dalarna. March 2021.

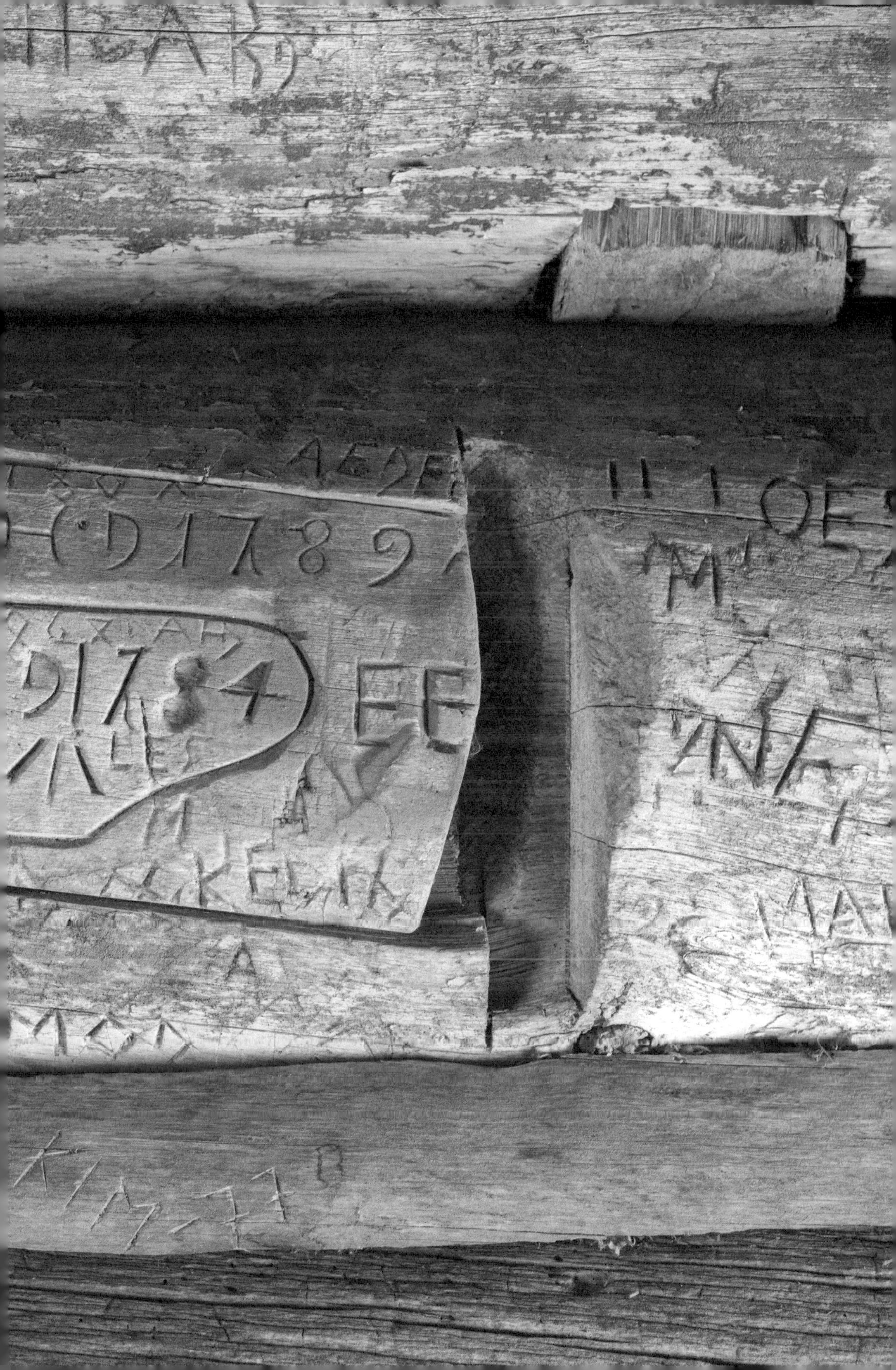

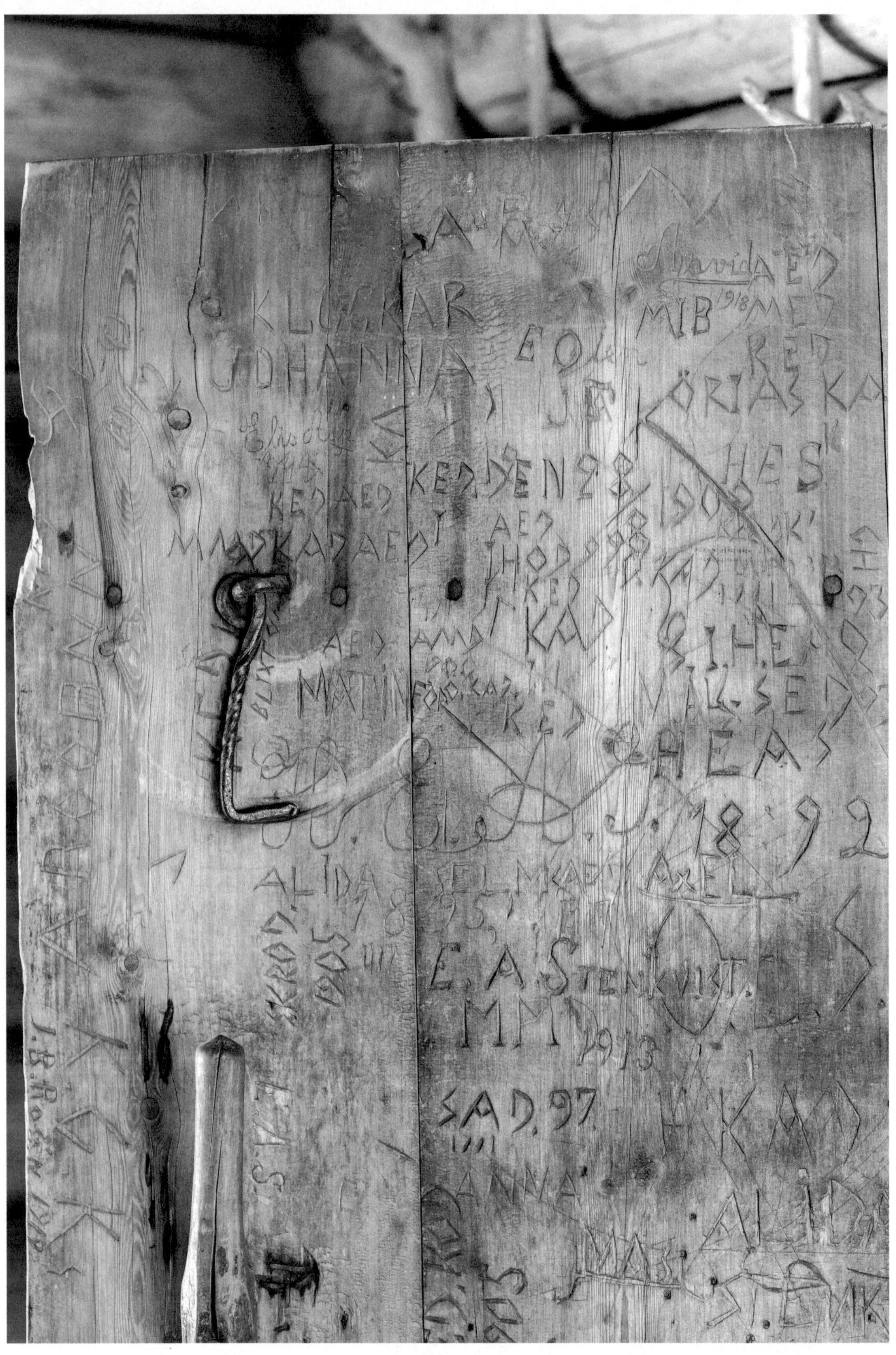

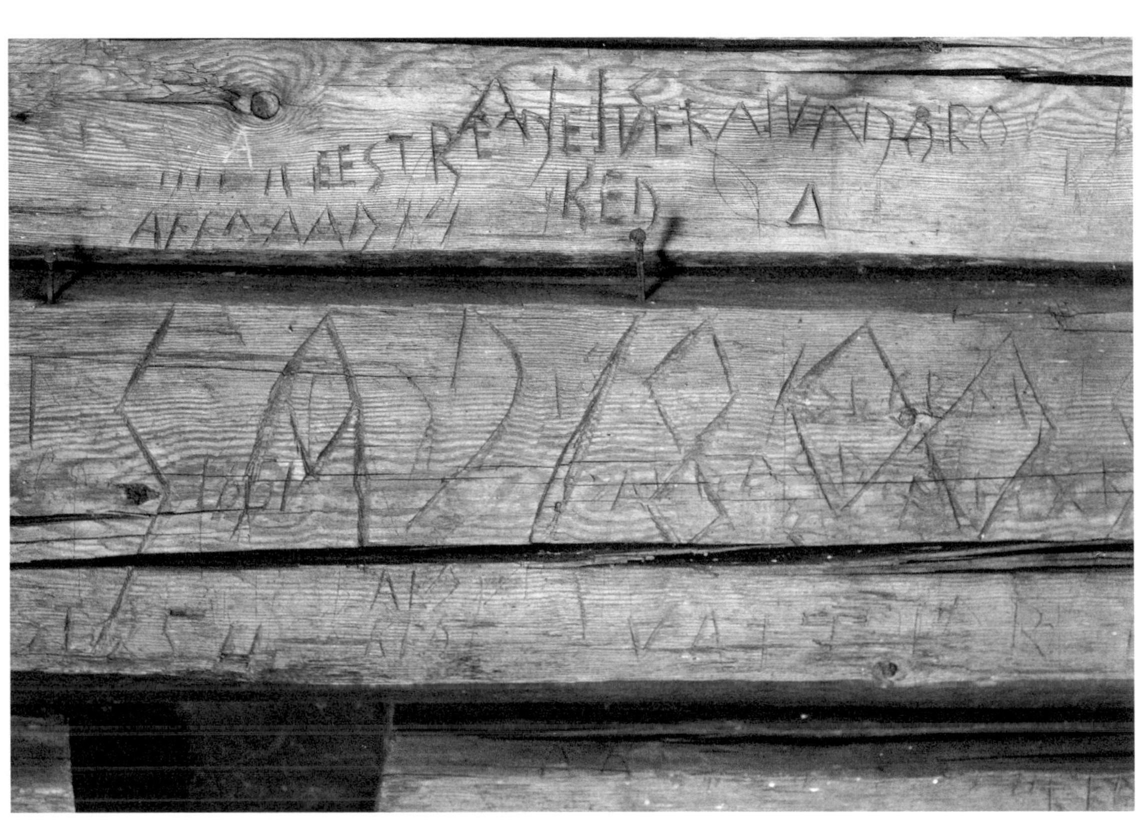

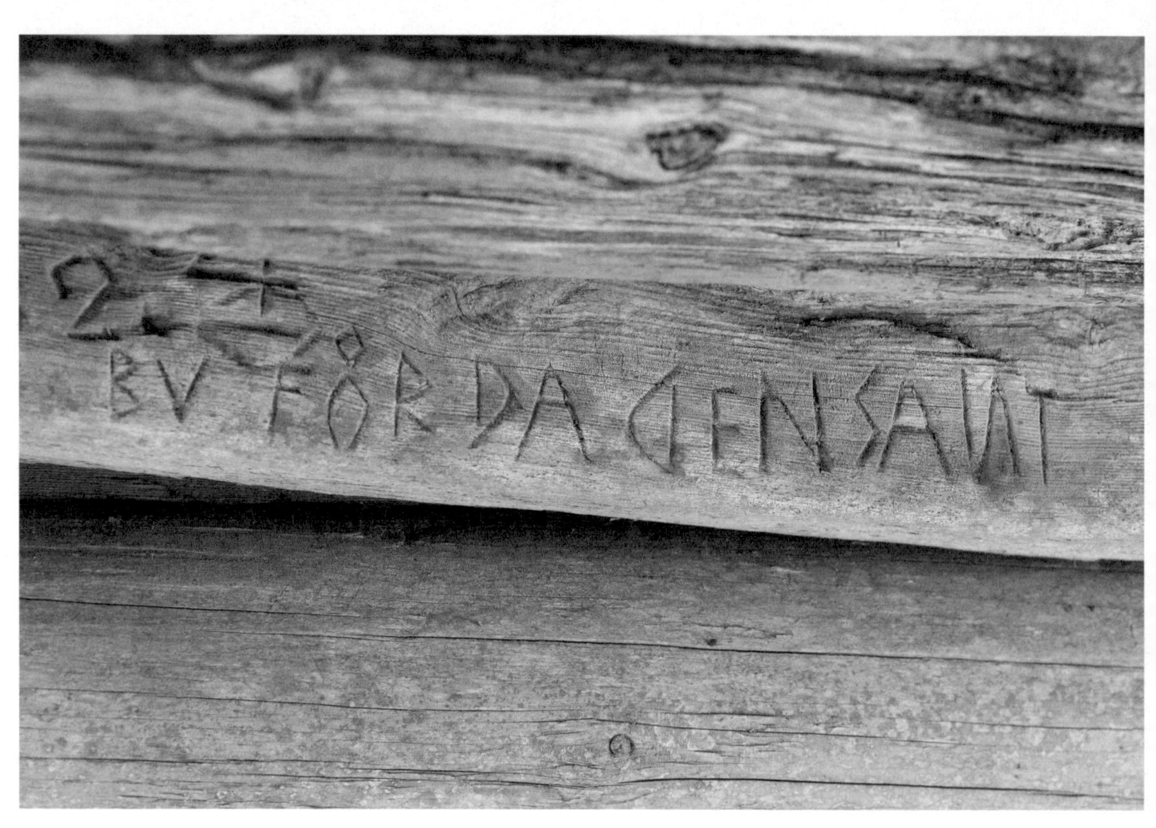

SANT KNIFE
Quinn Latimer

April. There are some women in the forest, some cattle.
There are trees. 700 carvings on trees and 21,000 on the walls
Of the *fäbod*. 700 carvings on trees and 21,000 on the walls
Of the mind, which we incise into pale bark, then bind
Up in a PDF we download and open on the glowfield of a laptop.
Glowfields, monitors, glens of trees, attachments, black resin, and then some opening
In the forest of the girl: language. Its marks like teeth chewing the bark.
Light like mouths dappling the forest floor. Light scratched in, like language.

Cowbells. They are constellating the woods in the forms of
Animals. Wet mouth, dry mouth; its excised marks a rough whisper in the round.
Skin and song: human and non. Nonhuman skin writ with song: both fiction
And history, some autofictive spirit flitting among animal, vegetal, and poverty,
   girl and record
And cow and boy and tree and woman and labor—her writing spirit, getting it down.
Cylinders of trees, smooth or roughhewn then sticky in the hands, in the set
   and seismic mouth
Which tells on another, which tells on oneself. The forest flashing in the mouth as fire
Then flood. Bells of one's animals shattering the woods. Loneliness.
Then friendship like the knife found there, and worn on the belt, at the hip,
Whose bone also writes the skin, sharply. An inscription, a true record.

Sant Language
Sant Cattle
Sant Forest
Sant Whisper
Sant Writing
Sant Women
Sant Circles
Sant Scratch
Sant Friendship
Sant Belief
Sant Boredom
Sant Loneliness
Sant Loss
Sant Labor
Sant Exhaustion
Sant Exclusion
Sant Economy
Sant Animal
Sant Axe
Sant Index
Sant Body
Sant Bark
Sant Milk
Sant Spirit
Sant Surface
Sant Inscription
Sant Excision
Sant Resin
Sant Responsibility
Sant Gossip
Sant History
Sant Theory
Sant Fiction
Sant Writer
Sant Discourse
Sant PDF
Sant Girl
Sant Script
Sant Sap
Sant Shit
Sant North

Sant Text
Sant Tree
Sant Rune
Sant Ruin
Sant Human
Sant Nonhuman
Sant Herd
Sant Breath
Sant Knife
Sant Song
Sant Record
Sant Valla

All true, true, true.

Saint Language
Saint Cattle
Saint Forest
Saint Whisper
Saint Writing
Saint Women
Saint Circles
Saint Scratch
Saint Friendship
Saint Belief
Saint Boredom
Saint Loneliness
Saint Loss
Saint Labor
Saint Exhaustion
Saint Exclusion
Saint Economy
Saint Animal
Saint Axe
Saint Index
Saint Body
Saint Bark
Saint Milk
Saint Spirit
Saint Surface
Saint Inscription
Saint Excision
Saint Resin

Saint Responsibility
Saint Gossip
Saint History
Saint Theory
Saint Fiction
Saint Writer
Saint Discourse
Saint PDF
Saint Girl
Saint Script
Saint Sap
Saint Shit
Saint North
Saint Text
Saint Tree
Saint Rune
Saint Ruin
Saint Human
Saint Nonhuman
Saint Herd
Saint Breath
Saint Knife
Saint Song
Saint Record
Saint Valla

August. Money trees: *green*, they gossip and lyric, in the epic
Futures, in another constructed country and system. Take an index of the future
And its currencies—they all relate to the labor women once did in the forest
With the animals, so take an index of the cattle, of girls tending
Them, an index of the writing done by them, there, among cattle, shit, milk, belief,
   and trees. Shall we
Chop it down, write it down, push it out. Cut a litany or sing a refrain of
   one's attachments,
Languages, labors, theories, betrayals, shatterings, animals, freedoms, incisions,
Poverties, riches, metals, milk products, forests, friendships, hunger, poetics.

Poetics. Of times spent laboring alone and together, pastures and pastoral
Memories and poverty conditions and the attendant texts. Find a theory for this.
Scratch that. Scratch it all into a tree, leave a record of your most ludic attachments,
Lucid conditions, your most exhausted PDF, send it across the woods, open it

Like a mouth or text in the glen of trees, the clearing shimmering in late summer
Heat, swim each page of the document, its thin or deep currents, dark pool of ones
And zeros, it's all water, thirsty cattle, their heaving sides constellated with flies
Like stars, heavy bodies marking the shores of northern meadow
With a haptic heat and lean
Breathing. Herd them. Call them. Read them. They are not texts,
Mineral and violent and ardent, they are stardust. Grassy breath.

If you hide
In your writing, you also appear
There, inscribing trees with an ardor and rigor and the women you find there,
In it, casting language like a knife or a voice across the summer forest, cold bells ringing
Out, touching the trees with rough hands, hot hands, cool mouth,
New language, old letters, feverish memories told together, wolves
And bears pacing the purple perimeter, hungry for inscription, rent and reed of
Carvings, writing. Memory like a knife slipping
Into the tree, some strong grip yanking it down, opening its skin.

Language like a knife slipping in. Grass in the mouth. Animals
In the round, chewing. What north of the mind is this. What essaying
Animal body, what solar refrain of northern summer. Why do we send the girls to labor
With cattle, why do we like working girls, writing girls, cast-off girls, grieving girls,
    but not
Sovereign women, why do we send them to a forest constellated with animals,
    why must they care
For them as for language, letters which for 300 years do not burn
But sink deeper into nonhuman skin, clarion, then obscure. Their voices caught, later.
The distance between the knife and the voice is the distance
Across the forest, which they cross, herding their cattle, each sharp hoof
Punctuating each page of pasture with its dark commas, wetly writing it.

Clean the tree with your mouth. Take a picture of it with your mouth.
The violent, impatient god turned the girl into a cow—we all know this.
The white cows of his father were all girls—we know all this. The girls in
    the forest won't
Stop writing—we know all this. A blade of grass grows in the throat, exits
The mouth, scratches the strobe of sun with its lick of green—we know all this.
The script stabbed into the tree is Latin or Dalacarlian rune—we know this.
The song is a mark, a series of marks, epigrams or autofictions or lyric screams
Knifed into skinned surface both human and nonhuman, something in between,
    I mean.

Quinn Latimer   153

Poetics of the girls in the forest left to labor and live
With their animals, their most elegant axe. Not theirs. Nothing theirs except records
Scripts mouths lyrics epics labors incisions skins support surfaces songs voices letters.
And this should mean something. Skin and song. Skin and song.
They cut the air, the women—all cognition—and then they cut the trees.
When you decided those years with your knife were your real life
What did you mean?

There are some women in the forest, some cattle.
There are trees. 700 carvings on trees and 21,000 on the walls
Of the *fäbod*. 700 carvings on trees and 21,000 on the walls
Of the mind, pale bark, dark monitor, lean script that sinks into nonhuman
Skin, deeper. Trace it with your dry animal finger.
Put it in your mouth. Then push it out.

Sant, sant, sant.
            True, true, true.
Sant, sant, sant.
            True, true, true.
Now press the blade in,
Let the axe sink in,
            now write it down.

THE WOOD FOR THE TREES
And other things we cannot see

Meg Miller

I

The trees of a forest communicate, though to us it sounds
like silence. We can hear the rustling of leaves and the
creaking of trunks, the wind howling through a tree hollow.
But that's not how trees talk to each other. Trees converse
via underground networks so vast and interconnected that
some have taken to calling them the "wood wide web."[1]

The main material of the wood wide web is mycelium,
the network of fungal threads from which mushrooms sprout.
We see mushrooms everywhere in forests, emerging in
billowing white heaps or scalloped folds; popping from the
earth after a day of rain. But mushrooms are just the part of
a fungus that's visible above ground—below the surface, miles
of mycelium form fibrous webs that extend throughout
the forest floor. The individual threads are delicate and fine;
they branch infinitely and cluster together, appearing like
plates of bright white fur. The networks they form are massive,
complex, and alive.

Because the fungi live in darkness, they form symbiotic
relationships with trees to survive. They trade nitrogen and
phosphorus from the soil below for water and photosynthate
from the sunlit world above, an exchange made through
the trees' root systems. Trees that have the same type of
fungi are connected by these subterranean networks, which
connect to other networks, meaning that even different
species are bound together by the wood wide web:
cedar murmurs to maple; birch to hemlock to Douglas fir;
Douglas fir to ponderosa pine.

1
The term was coined by
Suzanne Simard in her paper
"Net transfer of carbon
between ectomycorrhizal
tree species in the field,"
published in *Nature* in 1997.

The networks also allow for another type of trade, one in which
nutrients and carbon travel from tree to tree, when needed.
It allows for trees to send other trees chemical signals of
distress or warning, if one is being cut down, for example,
or attacked by parasitic insects. An older tree that's dying can
bequeath its stored up carbon to the younger trees around it
through this network, a transfer of knowledge that preserves
the legacy of the old forest for and in a newer one. Suzanne
Simard, the scientist who pioneered research on how trees
converse, colloquially calls these older trees "mother trees,"
because they look out for the younger ones, and because—
although they speak across species—they also recognize
and nurture their own kin.

Simard first published her research on the networked
communication of trees in 1997, but it is only recently that
it has been widely accepted by the scientific community.
At first, Simard was dismissed by many of her peers, who
saw her research as counter to the idea that species must
compete with each other in order to survive, per Darwinism.
Simard's research tells a different evolutionary story than
the one that solidified over the last century: her discovery
confirms that while trees compete, they also collaborate.
The well-being and survival of one tree is linked to the well-
being and survival of others, just like all social creatures.
The forest is an ecosystem woven together by subterranean
fungal networks, through which trees communicate and
coordinate the forest's survival, using what has been referred
to as the "secret language of trees."

II

What makes a language secret? At its most basic, a secret
language is one that can be understood by one group and
not by another. But all languages are gibberish to those who
have never learned them. Perhaps it is more about intention:
secret languages are intentionally encoded to be meaningful
to an in-group and illegible to outsiders. Or maybe, like the
underground language of trees, a secret language must just be,
in some way, hidden.

For six years, the artist Amy Suo Wu has built her practice
around researching steganography, which she succinctly
defines as "the art and science of hiding in plain sight."
Steganography can be coded language like jargon, slang,
or in-speak, or it can take the form of words hidden inside
pictures, or encoded into textiles. But unlike cryptography,
steganography is not encrypted—it is only hidden to those
who overlook it. "At the heart of steganography is the
instrumentalization of the seemingly innocuous," Wu writes.
"The skin of a steganographic object blends in with its
environment, deflecting the unknowing gaze of the onlooker."[2]

My favorite example of steganography in Wu's *A Cookbook
of Invisible Writing* is a syllabic script called Nüshu (literally,
"women's language" in Chinese). Nüshu was developed
in the ninth century by women in the rural Jiangyong county
of China's Hunan province; today, it's still the world's only
script used exclusively by women. Made up of dots and three
different types of strokes—horizontals, verticals, and arcs—
the script is derived from square Chinese characters, but the
results are simpler and vertically stretched, elegantly elongated.
The strokes are curved diagonals that branch and cluster,
and which can be so thin as to be described as threadlike.

Nüshu was passed down from mothers to daughters and
spoken among sisters and friends. The women who created it
didn't have access to formal education in their feudal society;
Nüshu was the only language they could read or write. Women
wrote letters to each other in Nüshu, recorded their lives in
clothbound booklets, created songs and ballads, all in their own
private script. They embroidered the wispy calligraphy on silk
clothes, handkerchiefs, and belts, inscribed song lyrics on fans,
asked their friends to bury their papers with them after their
deaths. "Women's work" like sewing and embroidery provide the
archive of most of the Nüshu artifacts that remain today.

Men in Jiangyong county couldn't read Nüshu. But as Wu
writes, it wasn't because Nüshu was explicitly intended to
exclude them. Rather, the men just never bothered to learn it.
The women created, in the absence of one, a writing system
that they could use to correspond with each other and record

2
"Dark Cousins: #1
An Introduction to
Steganography"
by Amy Suo Wu,
Source Type, 2021.

their own histories; to form a sense of belonging, autonomy,
and social cohesion. In that way, Nüshu was coded, but
it was never intentionally hidden. What made this language
secret was that it was unvalued and overlooked.

In her book, Wu notes that while cryptography requires some
sort of key or mathematical formula to decode, steganography
(sometimes called cryptography's "dark cousin") relies on
cultural apathy or misunderstanding to remain coded. It stands
to reason then that teenagers, perpetually and notoriously
misunderstood, are masters of open code. In a 2010 paper
on teens and online privacy, media scholar danah boyd uses
the term "social steganography" to describe social media
posts written by teenagers so that they're understood by their
friends but misinterpreted by their parents. Unable to control
their own digital or physical privacy, the teens boyd talked
to attempted instead to limit access to the meaning of their
messages. They did this by, for example, encoding the meaning
in song lyrics, inside jokes, or circumstantial references that
only some followers would understand. Taking advantage of
the fact that they were so often misunderstood or not taken
seriously, viewed as frivolous or immature, the teens subverted
their own surveillance, allowing for them to communicate
privately in "networked publics."[3]

III

In Dalarna, Sweden, another teenage steganography runs
parallel to the network of tree chatter happening underground,
mimicking the collaboration of the birch and Douglas fir,
but visible to us only if we care to look. Grand old Scotch pines
can be found in the forests there, thick, gnarled, and covered
in carvings. Shepherds from the seventeenth to the early
twentieth centuries—almost all of whom were unmarried women,
the majority of whom were teenage girls—left messages
for each other on the tree trunks and in stone. The shepherds
carved their initials, the dates, notes to each other,
and assertions of existence. *Here we draw our names.*

Tasked with taking the family's livestock to graze in greener
pastures, these girls were given a responsibility they didn't hold

3
"Social Steganography:
Privacy in Networked
Publics" by danah boyd,
2010.

in normal village life, and a lot more freedom. They worked
collectively on the *fäbod*, or summer farm, to herd and milk the
cattle, churn the butter, make the cheese. They slept together
in wooden chalets, summer–camp style. There they also
made their mark, with teenage freneticism; blanketing every
inch of the wooden interiors, from the walls to the ceilings
to the furniture, with their coded language. They wrote with
melodrama (*we've lost three cows*) and hubris (*I draw my
name with honor and no shame*); they swore (*we feel damn
good*); they got homesick (*I long for home*). They wrote
to themselves, to each other, and to future shepherds,
with a language and a sentiment that would be understood
by others like them.

Beginning in the late eighteenth century, the shepherds would
let the cattle roam freely while they worked at the chalet,
calling them home at the end of the day with the hypnotic,
reverberating melodies of *kulning*. But in earlier days,
the girls would take the cattle to pasture themselves, leaving
the activity of the base camp to herd them alone for the entire
stretch of daylight. It was probably painfully boring, out in
the forest glade, watching the cows chew grass from under
the shade of a pine. There's nothing so slow and sap–like as
the passage of time for a teenager on duty, siloed from the
drama, gossip, and far more interesting happenings of literally
anywhere else. So they talked to each other through the trees.
With an iron ax, they'd remove the bark and carve their
initials onto the smooth wood, along with a short message for
the next herder. They marked time—for themselves, as a way
of quickening their solitude, and for us, by carving the seasons
and years that they were there.

Some were written in the Dalecarlian runes, a local variety
of the runic alphabet, used to write various Germanic languages
before the Latin alphabet was adopted. As the last surviving
runes, Dalecarlian runes looked similar to Latin letterforms,
though more angular and with no horizontal strokes—better for
carving into wood. Sometimes, the shepherds' messages were
encrypted by "braided writing," a simple form of cryptography
that will be familiar to anyone who has passed notes in class
(HKLHSD 1786 = HLS KHD 1786). Sometimes they were

mirrored, or written in reverse. But mostly, the tree writings were an open code, a form of in-speak visible to all, but whose meaning is held only for those who see the social significance. The carvings were left behind for a specific audience: their authors knew that another girl would come after them, minding the cattle under the hot sun, desperate for something to read. She would look out for, see, and understand the social code.

Many more would overlook it. The fact that these carvings have not been better documented or written about more widely is evidence of that. Much of the old forest has by now been cut down for logging, but the carved trees that remain preserve their legacy and pass on their messages. Some of the trees are charred from forest fires; others have grown new bark, moss, or tree knobs around them. Still, the Dalecarlian shepherds chose the right vessels for their missives: pine trees can live up to 700 years with no human intervention, and stand another 300 years after their death.

Societies consciously recognize and actively preserve only what they value, but the unofficial toil of memory work is often "women's work." Embroidered into clothing, carved into trees, written into decades-old scientific papers, this work might linger on the edges, or be shrouded in innocuousness. It might hide in plain sight until someone is ready to look, which is the only key needed to break the code. Attention is a crucial precursor of understanding, and to give something your attention you must first see it. The shepherds must have known that too; they often began their messages with *SI*, meaning "look here."

SOME TIME WITH UNLUCKY WOMEN
Matilda Kenttä & Linnea Rutz

If we cannot make babies,
maybe we can make some time (U and me)
Some time, some time, some time
Prince, *Erotic City* (1993)

BEGINNING OF 17TH CENTURY, 300 YEARS AGO

Local women are entering meadows of hay in May. They are bringing the cattle
from town to summer grazing. Leading the animals to the energy of this
season's fertility.

THE MEADOW
some sort of lichen
wood sedge
bog rosemary
maybe cranberry
septfoil
cloudberry
cottongrass
roses

Three hundred years ago, luck was limited to the goods. Women transported the cattle
from meadow to meadow. While the animals grazed, the women transformed
their milk into butter. The basis of their production were the good conditions for luck.
Luck was processed in material and bound to chores and house work. Milk-luck,
harvest-luck, crop-luck, bread-luck, spinning-luck, butter-luck. Local women could
act on their capacity to manipulate or change relationships in nature, creating
better conditions for luck. This was where the real magic happened.

RECIPE 1: BEHAVIOR OF BUTTER

Make during the cool dawns; never during thunder; always under the influence
of the dewy fumes; whisk gently white until yellow; if you're unlucky add saffron;
your whisking arm will separate the fat from the milk, the whey from the butter;
pearls of butter will rise to the surface; gather the pearls; always use moist tools;
press away the water from the pearls; add salt and press and roll; shape it,
let it rest in darkness; carve xxx into the surface; don't pay his taxes; sell it for gold;
eat it. This is how you do it.

An unlucky woman could have a hard time. Chores and house work limited by luck
made some unlucky local women spend more time on the distribution of luck
in the area. An unlucky woman could use her competence for pulling luck from
someone she found too lucky with a spell.

RECIPE 2: BJÄRA SPELL

Take nine different threads of leftover yarn, hair from your neighbor's cow, a blue
nail from your neighbor's toe; sit in a sauna three Thursday evenings and spin it
together; on the third Thursday cut yourself in your left pinky finger and drop three
drops of blood on the clew, say: *You will run for me on earth, I will burn for you
in hell;* throw it over your left shoulder, the clew now comes to life with a small
red glowing tongue, hissing to you: *What should I bring? What should I bring?*
And will then run to pull your luck.

During hikes to fresh meadows, local women made hearths in circles of rocks.
Resting with bread and butter. If they were lucky, they could waste some time
carving signs and signatures into bark. Burning fat, saving fat, leaving traces.
The trees mark areas for lingering. They rest for some time.

THE MEADOW
some time, some time, some time
glades of wet grass
chalet architecture
a rose larvae
hot sun telling the time
sweat running down thighs
unmarried women
hiking

Lingering generates friendship. It is time to take a break. Inside the woods they were free to divide their time between labor and leisure. Maybe the summer also provided them the time and space to be lazy. On the farm, just taking a break occupied time from the exploitation of their bodies carrying out domesticated work. Women's laziness is always a refusal, a "No" that provides openings for relaxation, sharing time while hanging out around the fire, receiving information, and giving something back. This is where the real magic happens.

RECIPE 3: ABORTION HYMN

Young local woman: It has been some time.........
Old local woman: Mh–hm
Young local woman: I met with the boy from the north farm on midsummer eve...
　He made me a wreath of roses from the farm garden. I took him to the field.........
Old local woman: I understand
Young local woman: I don't want his child.........
Old local woman: Get blueberries, get lemon balm, get lilies and Aquilegia,
　get roses and sage, get spearmint. Fat takes fat and rose takes rose.

This was the bouquet of medical herbs she needed for mixing a potion for abortion. The local woman knew her surroundings. She knew that when the cow eats the rose she can work it into butter and when she picks the rose she can mix it into medicine. This was where the real magic happened. Fertility and lust lead to endless labors: that is a knowledge that women have known and shared as long as there have been reproductive conditions. Defender of lust. Her healthcare practice. When lust or violence lead to consequences of the procreative body.

Friendship–magic, luck–magic, rose–magic, text–magic, work–magic, time–magic, healthcare–magic, milk–magic, tax–magic, sex–magic, carving–magic, bouquet–magic. Silvia Federici–magic:

> Eradicating these practices was a necessary condition for the capitalist rationalization of work, since magic appeared as an illicit form of power and an instrument to obtain what one wanted without work, that is, a refusal of work in action. 'Magic kills industry'.
>
> Federici, Silvia, *Caliban and the Witch: Women, the Body and Primitive Accumulation,* Autonomedia, New York, 2014, p. 142.

Before the eradication of magic—as industry kills magic—the local women entered the modern factories, and their time was sealed in line with the standardized working conditions of men. Their magic was thus secured in local women's capacity to manipulate or change relationships in nature and social life.

Rose is a rose is a rose is a rose.
Stein, Gertrude, *Geography and Plays*, The Four Seas Company Publishers, Boston, 1922.

While arranging roses in her Paris apartment in 1913, Gertrude Stein wrote *Sacred Emily.* A rose manipulated and repeated many times. Inside Stein's construction, the rose becomes a sign and a signature. Still, her rose doesn't enter the new century's modernist building. It stays as a messy, sticky hint. The rose was not referring to the redness, ruddiness, or fleetness of the romantic eras. The rose was repeated. The rose was sometimes standing still, sometimes moving, and sometimes lingering. Stein as a local woman also had a capacity to manipulate or change relationships in nature and social life. This was where the real magic happened.

Stein's texts are like bouquets. Her bouquets offers repetition of objects and words without a standardized and disciplined timeline. A bouquet is both a signature and a part of nature. Bouquet, from old French, meaning chunk of trees. A bouquet often connotes an event. A resting area, a date, a graduation, a small operation, an unnecessary treat, money, decoration, and care. A care worker at a mental institution having to de-thorn the roses.

Can repetition produce magic? Keeping a routine and keeping to return to local areas, to repetition. Calling upon the remembering of a hymn. Soaking in the remaining letters on a chunk of trees.

EPILOGUE

Sitting in front of a vase with tulips in Amsterdam. It is the 27th of September 2021. The exact composition of a bouquet for abortion might not be as relevant today as it was in the seventeenth century. Though in the time of our writing, overseas, legislators still eradicate contraceptive practices as illicit forms of power. Abortion still and again has to become a compound of aid in areas other than public institutions.

Texas Abortion

six test
ten toxins, no taxi exit
rot on! rats!
is it no xenia
sex

ex's
ex
text
sat
rotation
tax
taxes
axes
eats
seat
tea
sea
eat
axe
robot
tons
nest
rest
rost
rent
sent
set
abs
east
box
base
extortion
anorexia
obstinate
taxations
toxins
attain
extra
inbox
bans
barns
be
are
so
at
nor

Natural Enemy

greedy loneliness
brilliant butter
natural enemy
mobilized
tamed

It is Wednesday
Maybe an occasional sunset
a path, a rose, a test, a pill, a paper

Spontaneous
dairy
dare

NORDIC FÄBOD CULTURE
Jennie Tiderman-Österberg

Five thousand years ago, a large part of the Northern
Scandinavian peoples were nomadic hunters. This was a time
when the boundaries between wild and tame animals were
not as clear as we tend to think they are today. Humans
followed the seasonal movements of the wild herds, and from
these movements, the economy emerged. It was not until
later, about three thousand five hundred years ago, that human
beings in these areas started to cultivate the land, and thus
became increasingly residential. This also included the
domestication of cattle. The key to understanding animal
husbandry therefore lies in the activity within the relationships
between humans, nonhuman animals, and the environment
they both share. These relationships eventually gave rise to
the Nordic *fäbod* culture.

FOREST PASTURES

The static image of a homogeneous landscape, which forms
for many when thinking of the Scandinavian countries,
does not capture the variation into which the image dissolves
with the changing of the seasons. The barren, icy waste-
lands of the mountains in winter become lush and green with
the movement into summer, and in the Nordic south,

the soil is fertile and fit for agricultural economies. In the hilly
terrain of the middle areas, the soil is lean and rough.
It is in the latter areas that the *fäbod* culture was situated.
Due to the hilly landscape and the lean soil, it was not
possible for the economy to be based on agriculture alone.
The land simply could not offer the necessary resources.
The solution emerged in the form of an economy based on
animal husbandry which provided milk, meat, and coats for
clothing. But when you keep animals, you need to feed them.
Since the land could not offer enough resources to feed both
humans and animals, the farmers needed to come up with
a solution for feeding the animals without making an impact
on the small arable lands near the villages. Since the forests
were commons, the solution was clear: use the forests
as pastures. In this solution, we can still see active and crafty
farmers. The solution shows us how they benefited from older
knowledge of how to survive by attending and relating to their
environment. It shows that they had the skills for living *with*
nature, not just *in* it. And it shows that they knew their lives
were dependent on, and entangled with, their surroundings.
In order to survive, they acknowledged this dependence. To live,
they recognized other living things.

HERDERS

Herding exists all over the world, and it is an old practice.
The Abrahamic religious texts are full of herders and herding
metaphors: the Lord is a shepherd, and we are the herd.
Herding is also one of the key elements in *fäbod* farming in
Scandinavia. The earliest sources of *fäbod* cultural embryos—
the seasonal transfer and herding of animals in the forest
commons of the *fäbod* region—date from the eleventh century
in German medieval chronicler Adam von Bremen's writings:

Såsom hos araberna låter man sin
boskap beta långt ute i ödemarkerna.
Och nordmännen lever av sina husdjur
på så sätt, att de använder deras
mjölk till föda och deras ull till kläder.
Adam von Bremen, as citied by Ivarsdotter, 1986.

As the Arabs, they graze their cattle
in the farthest wilderness. And the
Northern peoples live by their cattle
in a way where the milk becomes food
and the furs become clothing.
Translation by author

However, we cannot say that what von Bremen refers to here
is *fäbod* farming as a developed transhumanist phenomenon
where the *fäbod* is part of an agricultural economy; Even so,
we can at least see an embryonic form of the practice of
outlying lands being utilized as pastures. Later, approximately
during the sixteenth century, we find more and more
sources that tell of a systematic herding culture, where the *fäbod*
functions as a satellite farm during the summer season.
The forest pastures were carefully distributed to those who held
animals. This division of pastures indicates that the *fäbod*
culture rested on notions of equality. Each village had a *fäbod*
area and each area was shared by several households.
The share stood in direct relation to the ownership of land
in the village: if you had large arable lands and owned more
animals than your neighbor, you generally had a larger share
of the forest commons at your disposal. The establishment of
a *fäbod* farm in the forest commons was thus both a collective
and a household enterprise. The idea of equal distribution
is also evident in other regulations. First, it became
compulsory in many areas to transfer your cattle to the *fäbod.*
The village council decided when to transfer the cattle
and when to come back to the village. Every household in
the village migrated to the *fäbod* on the same day, at the same
time during the day. This created a current of hundreds of
cows, goats, and sheep leading up to the forested mountains.
Second, the division of land was read out loud in church.
If someone broke the boundaries, this could lead to legal
conflicts. As a matter of fact, the earliest sources on *fäbod*
culture in Sweden are sixteenth century trial minutes
from court cases where farmers disagree on the pasture
boundaries. The herders thus had great responsibilities
resulting from these notions of equality, and one of the tasks
was to make sure that the animals grazed on the correct
share of the commons. This also places the community,
rather than the individual, at the center of importance.
The community set out the rules, the individual was obligated
to follow them. And even though herding may seem
like a lonely endeavor, the herders collaborated to tackle
their responsibilities.

A STORY OF WOMEN

In other parts of the world, male shepherds are common.
The iron fists of patriarchy have placed women in the domestic
sphere—caring for children and the intimate dimensions
of the household. They could not stroll freely on the wrong side
of the thresholds to their homes. Women have been thought
of as too weak to face the dangers of herding. Fighting off
predators and resisting the harsh forces of dramatic weather
were not permitted for women. Yet, in the *fäbod* culture,
the herders were women. Why was this so? In medieval
sources on herding practices in these parts of Scandinavia,
we also find male shepherds. Young boys herded goats and
sheep through the muddy streets of the rural villages to get to
the pastures beyond. In early sources on extensive grazing,
for example in the writings of Adam von Bremen and Olaus
Magnus, we cannot find anything about the gender of the
herders. But if they were women, we can guess that it would
have been so unusual that this would have been mentioned.
However, a shift must have occurred in the seventeenth
century. From this time on, the records tell stories about
female herders. In Jacob Svedelius' thesis from 1683, we find
a poem about *fäbod* culture and, in a draft, we can read:

Vara om morgnarna i skinnkjolen min,
i hudskorna ute mjölka, lösa ur fähus
mitt små och storboskap. Oxen med
korna, bocken med getterna, killingar,
kalven, skall jag med slekorna raskt,
med påsen om halsen, ryggsäcken
baktill, yxan framtill och bössan på
axeln, spela i lur och ropa i hals det
värsta jag orkar, boskapen så locka
att i bergen skräller och höres i skogen.
Jacob Svedelius' thesis from 1683, Pastor in Parnasso.

I'll be there early in the mornings,
dressed in my leather skirt and shoes
of pelt, milking. Releasing the cattle,
both large and small. The ox, the cows,
the buck, and goats. Baby goats
and the calves. I shall in haste, with my
pouch around my neck, my backpack,
my axe, and my rifle, blow my horns
and call out loudly as much as I can.
Luring the cattle so that the mountains
rattle, resounding in the forest.
Translated by author

Here, we read about herders in *skirt*, shouting to lure the
animals. We can draw the conclusion that what is referred to
here is a female shepherd, since, in this context, a skirt was
a garment with female connotations. But why did this gender
transfer of herding practices occur?

There are several possible explanations. First, Sweden was
at war for most of this century, which led to the deaths of
many boys and men, who were the soldiers. This meant that
women needed to take on the burdens of farming, with all
that it entailed. Second, if herding was one key element in
fäbod farming, milk husbandry was another. For centuries,
taking care of milk had already been considered and
distributed as a woman's job. Since milk husbandry was such
an important part of this way of farming, the person most
fit for that job—a woman—was sent to the *fäbod* with the
animals. Third, it became illegal for men to work at the *fäbod*
by the end of the seventeenth century. The King sent out
a decree that stated that the risk for bestiality was too high if
a man worked with female cattle. Still, when this decree was
signed, women had carried the *fäbod* labor for quite some
time already, which means that the decree is not a plausible
explanation for the gendered division of labor. Rather,
the division reflects the skills connected to the various kinds
of labor in a farmer's household at this time. The knowledge
and skills of women were most fit for taking care of the
milk and the cattle on the *fäbod*, whereas the men were
responsible for the forestry and the cultivation of the arable
lands in the village.

SISTERHOOD, SENSUALISATION, AND SEXUALIZATION

We have seen that the *fäbod* culture rests on values of equality
and community. This is also found in the organization of
the labor on the *fäbod* farm. The female herders supported
each other in their everyday work, both in herding and in
the preparation of milk products such as butter and cheese.
In this location-specific matriarchy, sisterhood was foundational.
However, throughout the centuries, this was heavily challenged
in many ways—challenges reflective of larger societal issues.
An unmarried woman from the peasantry generally had
low individual socioeconomic and religious status until the early
twentieth century, when she finally was emancipated from
the control and influence of her male relatives. Marriage was
thus necessary for a woman to be able to have a tolerable
future. As stated earlier, Sweden was at war for long periods

throughout the seventeenth century. Men lost their lives as soldiers, and there was a significant gendered imbalance within the population. This was a hotbed for competition and conflicts between women. As if this were not enough, in the late seventeenth century, the most extensive period of witch trials affected women from the peasant class severely. Women pointed at other women and accused each other of the terrible crime of witchcraft. It was a dangerous time to be a woman, especially for farming families in the *fäbod* regions, where most of the witch trials took place. Anxiety and desperation spread through the society, and thereby also through the *fäbod* women.

Despite the turmoil and tribulations faced by the *fäbod* women, they became highly sensualized and sexualized by male ethno-graphers, painters, and poets from the mid–nineteenth century onward. Throughout the National Romantic movement, with its most intense period in the late nineteenth and early twentieth centuries, Sweden needed a cultural costume to unify its realm. There was a tendency to turn to rural areas in order to find ancient cultural expressions that could fit the idea of the nation. And there she was: the *fäbod* woman with her cattle and her horns, practicing traditions that were thought of as both ancient and uniquely Swedish. She was perfect for the job. She was portrayed in poems as innocent, yet sensual. In traditional clothing usually used for ceremonial occasions, she stood with her wooden trumpet before a backdrop of bluish mountains and a vivid rural landscape. Around her, the weather was always beautiful. She stimulated the male fantasy of a lonely girl in desperate need of male attention. Even Richard Dybeck, the nineteenth century antiquarian, wrote about the female *fäbod* herders in a sensual way, and explicitly described how the voices of the *fäbod* women made him feel lured and excited. This erotic male fantasy famously peaked in the 1970s when a pornographic movie was produced with a *fäbod* woman at its center. The image of the mystic female herder, full of carnal lust that could flow freely in the wilderness, now reached its zenith.

With the above as a background, we can see that the *fäbod* woman (*vallkullan, butausen, säterjäntan, gattaren*) has been highly mystified, mythologized, sensualized, and sexualized

through the male gaze throughout the centuries. But this
picture might change if we let the *fäbod* women speak
for themselves.

NINETEENTH CENTURY:
A DAY AT THE FÄBOD IN HER OWN WORDS

Livia Sjöblom tells us that:

Dagen började klockan fyra, ty man skulle först göra ost innan man gick ut och mjölkade, för att vasslen skulle hinna koka ihop så pass innan man gick till skogen, så man kunde koka mesosten färdig på kvällen då man kom hem. Så mjölkade man vid sextiden klockan halv åtta skulle man vara färdig att gå till skogen, så kom man inte hem förrän klockan 6 på kvällen.
Vi hade olika "lötar" (betesplatser) för varje dag. Så betades till klockan tolv, då vilrummet uppsöktes. En eld gjordes upp på vilrummet, våt mossa lades på så det bara rökte, detta för myggens skull, som var så besvärlig. Runt omkring elden lade sig nu djuren och vallkullan sov med huvudet på skällkon. Som genom en tyst överenskommelse lågo alla stilla omkring två timmar så var det att söka ny mat för djuren så de skulle reda sig till nästa dag.

Berta Olsson's diary

The day started at 4 a.m., because you needed to curdle the cheese before milking the cows. And the whey needed to be reduced before going out in the forest. You then did the whey cheese when you arrived home in late afternoon. Then you milked the cows by 6 a.m. and at 7:30, you needed to be ready to go to the forest.
We had different parts of the pastures for each day of the week. The cattle grazed until lunch time when we sought out the resting place. There we lit a fire and we put some wet moss on it. Smoke flew about, keeping the mosquitoes away. They were so bothersome. The cows settled around the fire and "vallkullan" slept with her head placed on the leader cow (skällkon). Through a silent agreement, we rested like that for two hours. After that, it was time to find fresh grass for the cows so that they could be satisfied until the next day.

Translation by author

Livia continues her story by telling us that she had a small
pouch on her shoulder with flour and salt to give to the cows
to get them to follow her. This was a part of her equipment.
She also had a backpack with a bottle of milk and a sandwich.
She also carried an axe and a knife because there were
bears in her area. She had a weave made from hair–yarn

Jennie Tiderman–Österberg

to protect her from the rain. She could not walk empty-handed.
She always had her knitting. That was a part of her job.
She knitted socks that would keep their feet warm during winter.
They knitted for the whole household, and maybe also
for their extended family or for their neighbors. The rule was:
always think ahead. Waste neither time nor resources.
Plan your day carefully and in detail. Prepare the whey products
before going to the forest so that it will be almost done
when you arrive home. Nothing was left to chance. Not even
things belonging to an abstract and spiritual realm. Folkloric
traditions incorporated rituals of protection against dark
and malicious entities that were believed to pose a possible
threat to both animals and herders. These rituals could be
performed each day, or sometimes just after arriving to the
fäbod at the start of the season. Carvings were made on cow
bells and on timber walls. Knives of steel were placed under
thresholds. Dried pieces of magical herbs were carried in
pouches and spells were read out loud in the forest. This too
was something incorporated into a *vallkulla's* responsibilities.
Fäbod woman Anna Blomquist tells us that many hostile
entities, such as trolls and ladies of the woods, had their own
animals. And they too used to lure them using herding calls.
One woman who worked at the same *fäbod* as Anna learned
one of these calls. That tune proved to be the most efficient
way of calling the cattle home.

In the forest, the herders used either signals from horns or their
voices to call the cattle and to keep them together. These
signals were also used to get the cattle to follow the herder
and to send messages to other shepherds. Karin Saros tells
us about this in letters that she wrote to her sister while
working at the *fäbod*:

Stigen slingrar sig uppför backen
och det är en vacker syn att se oss
försvinna ut i skogen. Där uppe på
krönet stannar Flintull Anna och för
hornet till munnen och vallåten ljuder
lång genom rymden.
Karin Saros, Dalarnas museum archive

The path is winding up a hill. It is
a beautiful sight to see us disappear
into the forest. At the top of the hill,
Anna stops and picks up the cow
horn. The sound of the herding tune,
reaching out very far into space.
Translation by author

When the herders arrived home to the *fäbod* farm in late
afternoon, all animals needed to be counted. No one could
be missing. If there was a missing animal, a herding signal
was used that meant "my cow is lost, help me look for her."
All who heard the tune participated in the search. If and when
the cow was found, another signal was used: "She is found."
Everybody could relax. If she did not return, anxiety hit.
If a cow was lost, resources disappeared. That could mean
starvation.

When everyone had arrived home, the cattle were tied up inside
and prepared to be milked again. After taking care of yet
another large portion of dishes, the *fäbod* women prepared for
the upcoming day. Everything needed to be exactly in place
in order to avoid any delays. No time could be wasted on
searching for a missing milk vessel. When all work was done,
a herding tune rang, meaning "time to go to bed." The *fäbod*
women then entered the simple timber cottages and lit a fire
to keep warm during the night.

Here, it needs to be said that walking with the animals in
the forest was not always the only long-distance stroll that
the *fäbod* women did each day. If there were several herders
working at a *fäbod*, they shared responsibilities, as mentioned
before. During the time when the farmers harvested the tall
grass in the villages to keep for winter fodder, it was required
in some regions for one or two of these women to assist
in the harvest. They walked ten or twenty kilometers each
morning to get to the village, and they returned on the same
path at nighttime.

The labor at a *fäbod* farm might be covered in a romantic
shimmer by the National Romanticist. But the *fäbod* women
can tell us of a different story—one of hardship, but also
of freedom and peace. As Karin Saros tells in her letters:

Vi var född till arbete och ansvar
och det har följt oss hela livet.
Det låg liksom i blodet. Nu börjar
livet på allvar med ansvar och arbete,
men också harmoni och trevnad.

We were born into labor and
responsibility. It has followed us our
whole lives. It runs through our veins.
Now, life starts with great earnest,
but also with harmony and joy.

Jennie Tiderman-Österberg175

Här finns inga dåliga nerver, oroliga
magar eller sömnlösa nätter. Första
veckorna är det solsken varje dag,
men längre framåt sommaren, ofta
regn. Vi måste gå i skogen våta hela
dagarna, hur det regnar, ty djuren
måste ju ha mat där. Vi gör då upp
stora eldar och värmer oss ibland.
Också har vi vadmalströja som stänger
regnet ute, men den torkar knappast
på en natt i taget.

Here [at the *fäbod*], no poor nerves,
stomach aches or sleepless nights exist.
The sun is shining for the first weeks,
but as time goes by, the rain comes.
We walk through the forest completely
wet because the animals still need
to graze. We light great fires to keep
us warm. We have wool shirts to
protect us from the rain, but those
do not dry overnight.

Hard work and responsibility are recurring themes in Karin's
story, as they are in the narrative of another Karin, namely
Karin Edvardsson:

Jag hade så hemskt med kreatur,
det var alldeles för mycket. Jag var
uppe halv 4 varenda morgon, och jag
kom i säng tolv och ett på nätterna.
På morgon när jag satt och mjölkade
så somnade jag och vaknade av
att mjölkhinken ramlade ner i golvet.
Jag hade 11 mjölkkor, och en sex,
sju kalvar, åtta getter. Ystade varenda
dag och kärnade smör flera gånger
i veckan. Och korna var elaka när man
skulle springa runt och leta efter dem
klockan tre på dagen. Ja, jag vet inte
hur det gick. Men så var jag färdig
också när det var höst. Och sen var
man ju rädd att det inte skulle vara
riktigt. Att när hemfolket kom så skulle
allt vara precist. Man hade någonting
som heter ansvar.

I had so many animals to care for.
It was too much. I got up at 3:30 a.m.
each morning and I went to bed at
midnight. When I was milking, I fell
asleep and the sound of the bucket
falling to the ground woke me up.
I had 11 cows to milk, six or seven
calves, and eight goats. I curdled every
day, churned butter a few times
a week. And sometimes the cows
were awful when you ran around
looking for them. I don't know how
I did it. But then again, I was completely
worn out when autumn came.
And I was afraid that my work would
be all wrong when those who owned
the cows came to visit. Everything
should be precise and correct. You had
something that is called responsibility.

Despite this weight on Karin's shoulders, she also describes
the freedom felt at the *fäbod*:

När man en fin sommardag får ställa
sig bakom gluggen och mocka dynga,
så svetten lackar– är det det som är
romantik? Nej, romantiken för min del...
det var att jag fick ha en fäbodstuga
för mig själv. Jag fick ha min egen säng
och jag var liksom min egen herre
på täppan.
Karin Edvardsson, Dalarnas museum archive

When you, on a nice summer's day,
shovel manure in the fumes of your
own sweat, is that romantic?
No, the romance for me was to have
a cottage on my own, and my own
bed. It made me feel as if I was
the master of my own house.
Translation by author

Yet being alone could give rise to feelings of loneliness.
Mats Kristina Nilsson tells:

Där fick jag gå ensam. Det växte där
en jättestor asp. Och den blev mitt
sällskap genom många veckor och
månader. Den där aspen berättade så
mycket för mig. Den fladdrade i ett
vindkast. I skogen svarade trastarna.
Då blev jag romantisk och funderade
vad som fanns bortom bergen.
Mats Kristina Nilsson, Dalarnas museum archive

I was all alone there. But a large aspen
tree grew there. It was my company
through many weeks and months.
That aspen tree told me many things.
It fluttered in the wind. And in the
forest, a thrush bird answered. I got
a bit romantic, and I wondered what
was hidden behind the mountains.
Translation by author

The theme of longing is also found in Karin Saros' letters:

De dagar då jag går utmed sjön, söker
jag mig ut på någon udde och kliver
upp på någon sten där vågorna sjunger
omkring mig. Då längtar jag nog ut till
det okända, som ofta griper den unga
själen. Men då vi kommer in i skogen
igen söves sinnet på ett annat sätt och
väckes av att någon ropar "Kari, var är
du", eller ibland, en vallåt, som betyder
att vi ska flytta oss ett stycke. En enda
sommar kan bli ett helt kapitel i en ung
människas liv.
Karin Saros, Dalarnas museum archive

When walking along the lake, I search
for a cape. I step on top of a rock
while the waves are singing all
around me. Then I am longing for the
unknown, that which so often grabs
a young soul. But when I get back to
the forest, my senses start to slumber
again. They are awakened when
someone calls "Kari, where are you,"
or sometimes, a herding tune which
means that we should move along.
One summer could be a whole chapter
in a young girl's life.
Translation by author

Jennie Tiderman-Österberg

We find opposing feelings in these stories. We find freedom,
but also hardship and responsibility. We find romantic lights,
but also gloom and the longing for something different.
We find a desire to go into the unknown, as well as embodied
sensations of strength arising from labor and the opportunity
to organize without male supervision. At the same time,
we find anxiety and the fear of doing a bad job, which could
lead to the bad reputation of being lazy. The *fäbod* women
were longing for home during autumn, but they also could not
wait to go back to the *fäbod* the next spring. Diversity is
displayed both in feeling, and in the modes of organizing labor.
The everyday is blended with moments of reflection and
spirituality. This brings nuances to the *fäbod* story—nuances
capable of creating, in the perception of the *fäbod* life,
deviations between its image in the romantic paintings
and poems on the one hand, and its depiction in the
documents left by those who spent chapters of their lives
there, on the other.

In these traces, we find strong women, whose frailties only
add layers to their strength. These are women who took
responsibility for an important part of the household economy;
women who organized their work in detail in order to be
as efficient as possible; women who fought off predators
and cared for their animals almost as if for family members;
women who walked miles and miles no matter the weather;
women who developed and refined milk husbandry so
that the family would not starve; women who were otherwise
oppressed, but free during summertime. These are women
we can admire, and above all, can learn from.

REFERENCES

Björkroth, M. (2019) "Fäbodlandskapets död". In *Årsboken Dalarna 2019—Fäbodlandskap och vallmusik*, p. 78-92. Falun: Dalarnas Fornminnes- och Hembygdsförbund.

Dalarnas museum sound archive DM BA 0068, DM LRD 0047, DM BA 0357, DM LRD 0047, DM LRD 0055, DM BA 0145, DM DLS 0001, DM DLS 0002, DM DLS 0010.

Dybeck, R. (ed.) (1846). *Svenska vallvisor och hornlåtar, med norska artförändringar*. Stockholm.

Forsslund, K. (1918-1939). Med Dalälven från källorna till havet. Stockholm: Åhlén & Åkerlund.

Ivarsdotter, A. (2004) "And the cattle follow her, for they know her voice... On communication between women and cattle in Scandinavian pastures". In *PECUS - Man and Animal in Antiquity*, The Swedish Institute in Rome.

Ivarsdotter, A. & Ramsten, M. (1992). "Folkmusiken som nationell och provinsiell symbol". In *Musiken i Sverige [Jonsson, L. & Tegen, M. ed.]. 3*, p. [237]-250).

Ivarsdotter [Johnson] A. (1986). *Sången i skogen: studier kring den svenska fäbodmusiken*. Diss. Uppsala Universitet, Uppsala.

Ivarsdotter [Johnson] A. (1984). "Voice physiology and ethnomusicology: Physiological and Acoustical Studies of the Swedish Herding Song". In *Yearbook for Traditional Music*, vol. 16, pp. 42-66.

Kvinnors minnen https://vimeo.com/333061504

Kättström Höök, L. (2019). "Folktro på fäbodarna." In Thorell, E. & Tiderman-Österberg, J. (eds). *Fäbodlandskap och vallmusik*, p. 54-63. Falun: Dalarnas fornminnes- och hembygdsförbund.

Lannerbro Norell, M. (2019). "Fäbodristningar i skogen". In Thorell, E. & Tiderman-Österberg, J. (eds). *Fäbodlandskap och vallmusik*, p. 40-53. Falun: Dalarnas fornminnes- och hembygdsförbund.

Larsson, J. (2019). "Lagpigor och döttrar i Orsa vallängder". In Thorell, E. & Tiderman-Österberg, J. (eds). *Fäbodlandskap och vallmusik*, p. 31-39. Falun: Dalarnas fornminnes- och hembygdsförbund.

Larsson, J. (2014). "Boundaries and Property Rights: The Transformation of a Common-Pool Resource" in *The Agricultural History Review, 62*(1):20-40.

Larsson, J. (2009). *Fäbodväsendet 1550-1920: ett centralt element i Nordsveriges jordbrukssystem*. Diss. Uppsala: Sveriges lantbruksuniversitet, Uppsala.

Nordiska museet, E.U. "Folklig telegrafering", "Boskapsskötsel". Excerpter Vallmusik.

Olaus Magnus (2010[1555]). *Historia om de nordiska folken*. Swedish translation 1909-1925, Michaelisgillet. Möklinta: Gidlunds förlag.

Ramsten, M. (2019) "Fäbodarnas ljudlandskap". In *Fäbodlandskap och vallmusik*, p. 122-136. Falun: Dalarnas fornminnes- och hembygdsförbund.

Tiderman-Österberg, J. (2020). "Why Sweden's Ancient Tradition of Calling Home the Herds Is Women's Work", in *Smithsonian Magazine*. https://www.smithsonianmag.com/smithsonian-institution/why-swedens-ancient-tradition-calling-home-herds-womens-work-180975904/

Tiderman-Österberg, J. (2020). "Kulning: The Swedish Herding Calls of the North", in *Smithsonian Folklife*. https://folklife.si.edu/magazine/kulning-swedish-herding-calls

Tiderman Österberg, J. (2019 a) "Dit lockropen tog mig" In Thorell, E. & Tiderman-Österberg, J. (eds) *Fäbodlandskap och vallmusik*, p. 190-205. Falun: Dalarnas fornminnes- och hembygdsförbund.

Tiderman-Österberg, J. (2019 b) "Kom Kullorna! Kom Vallros". In Thorell, E. & Tiderman-Österberg, J. (eds) *Fäbodlandskap och vallmusik*, p. 172-189. Falun: Dalarnas fornminnes- och hembygdsförbund.

Tiderman-Österberg, J. (2019 c) "Reflektioner och processer". In Thorell, E. & Tiderman-Österberg, J.

(eds) *Fäbodlandskap och vallmusik*, p. 150-159. Falun: Dalarnas fornminnes- och hembygdsförbund.

Tiderman-Österberg, J. (2019 d) "Vi befinner oss i det förflutna". In Thorell, E. & Tiderman-Österberg, J. (eds) *Fäbodlandskap och vallmusik*, p. 214-225. Falun: Dalarnas fornminnes- och hembygdsförbund.

Tiderman-Österberg, J. (2019 e) "Vallmusik-några fakta". In Thorell, E. & Tiderman-Österberg, J. (eds) *Fäbodlandskap och vallmusik*, p. 100. Falun: Dalarnas fornminnes- och hembygdsförbund.

Wehlin, J. (2019). "Fäbodarnas förhistoria". In Thorell, E. & Tiderman-Österberg, J. (eds.) *Fäbodlandskap och vallmusik*. Falun: Dalarnas Fornminnes- och Hembygdsförbund & Dalarnas museum, pp. 16-27.

Jennie Tiderman-Österberg

I WAS HERE
Jungmyung Lee

while using the toilet in a public restroom you wait for nature's call turn your
head around to find something fun to pass time the walls become an etch–a–sketch
you scratch and leave your nickname LUV your gf/bf's initials 4ever <3
you arrive at a 1,951–year–old landmark it gives you an itch to add your name
In large capItal letters a heart your best pal's name In large capItal letters 4ever
in the most hidden corner not because your intent is to deface the landmark
but to make your name more permanent <3 during the school term you secretly
plan on carving something cool you don't want to carve into the top of the desk
anymore as your teacher warned you that you were vandalizing school property
you scrape your name your crush's name and a huge heart around the two names
4ever on the bottom of the desk <3 your eyes spot an arrow on a rim of a bookshelf
 at the school library pointing at a book shortly after hesitating whether to bother
opening the book yes! why not! your eyes are exposed to the very line that reads
'i couldn't stop thinking about you while reading this book, I love U' <3 you get
bored with scratching the same line over and over you drop the idea of inscribing
your name and your idol's name after only managing a heart later on it is found
by someone else and they complete it with the name of a celebrity you never stan
</3 you stumble upon an article about a study on how people who carved
their names into park benches (or outdoor art installations, city sites/landmarks,
and other structures intended for the enjoyment of the general population)
remained together an average of three decades longer than couples who did not
engrave their names into property you think it's ridiculous that indelible carvings
contribute to the longevity of one's relationship you laugh at it you wait for your
date who's prone to running late there's nothing else to do but etch the f–word
and the name of the disgraceful leader of your country </3 your eyes scan the lines
that people have carved in a public bathroom of a bar you never liked because
of the music choices they make all of a sudden your eyes tear up when you spot
'don't forget you are worthy' you can hear a feeble sentimental ballad you feel
the warmth as you see a couple of hearts as if they are responding to the phrase
until you see LOL</3

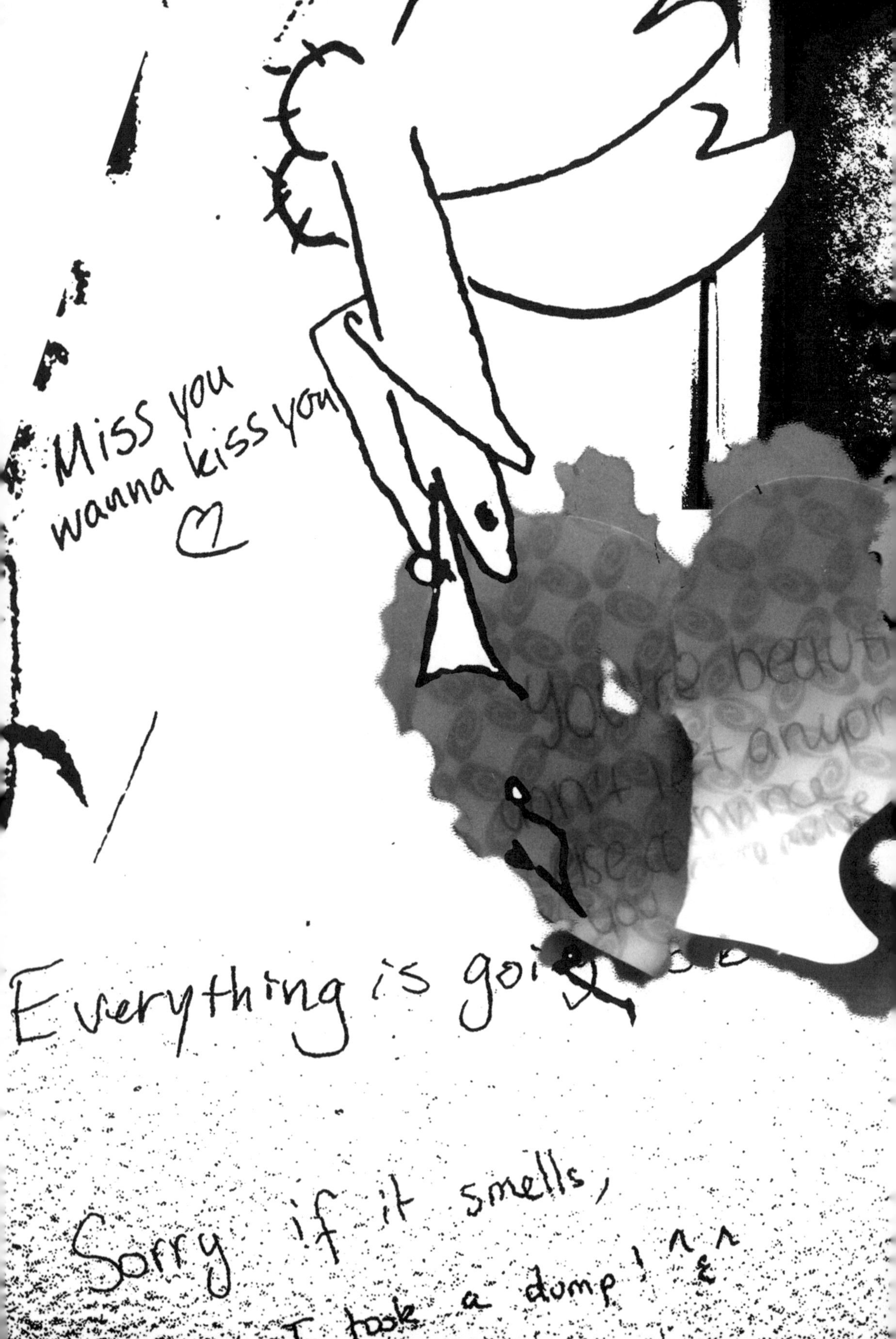
Miss you
wanna kiss you
Everything is goi...
Sorry if it smells,
I took a dump! ^-^

"Would Pee here again"
You know
"I would not Pee here again"
all in Love
OK ♥
LoL
even rather
doesn't

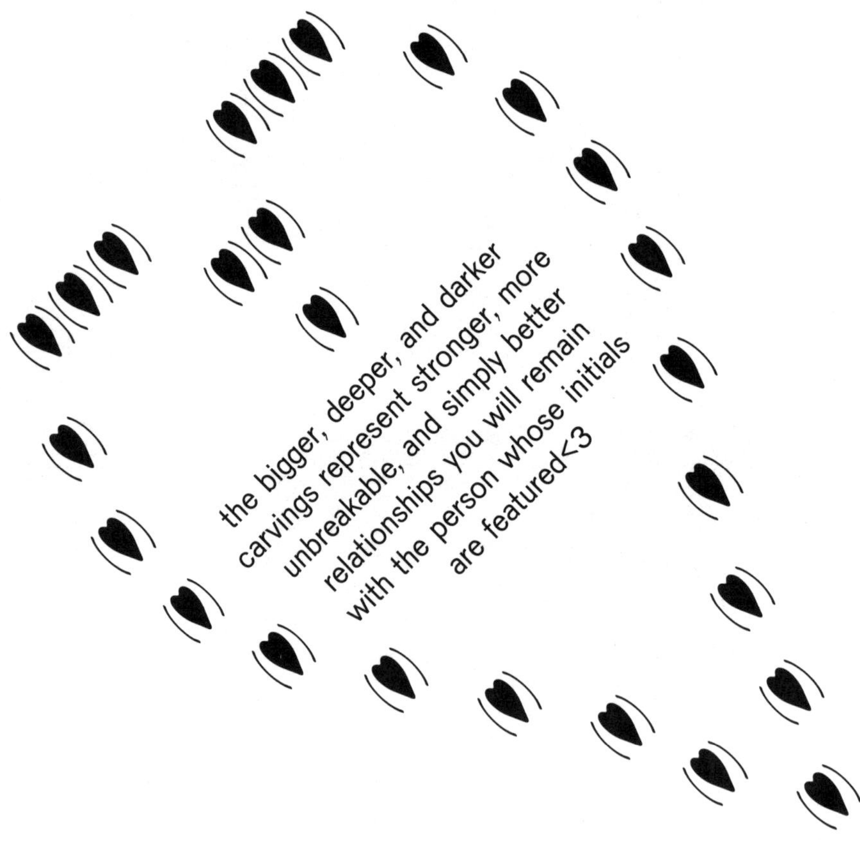

the bigger, deeper, and darker
carvings represent stronger, more
unbreakable, and simply better
relationships you will remain
with the person whose initials
are featured<3

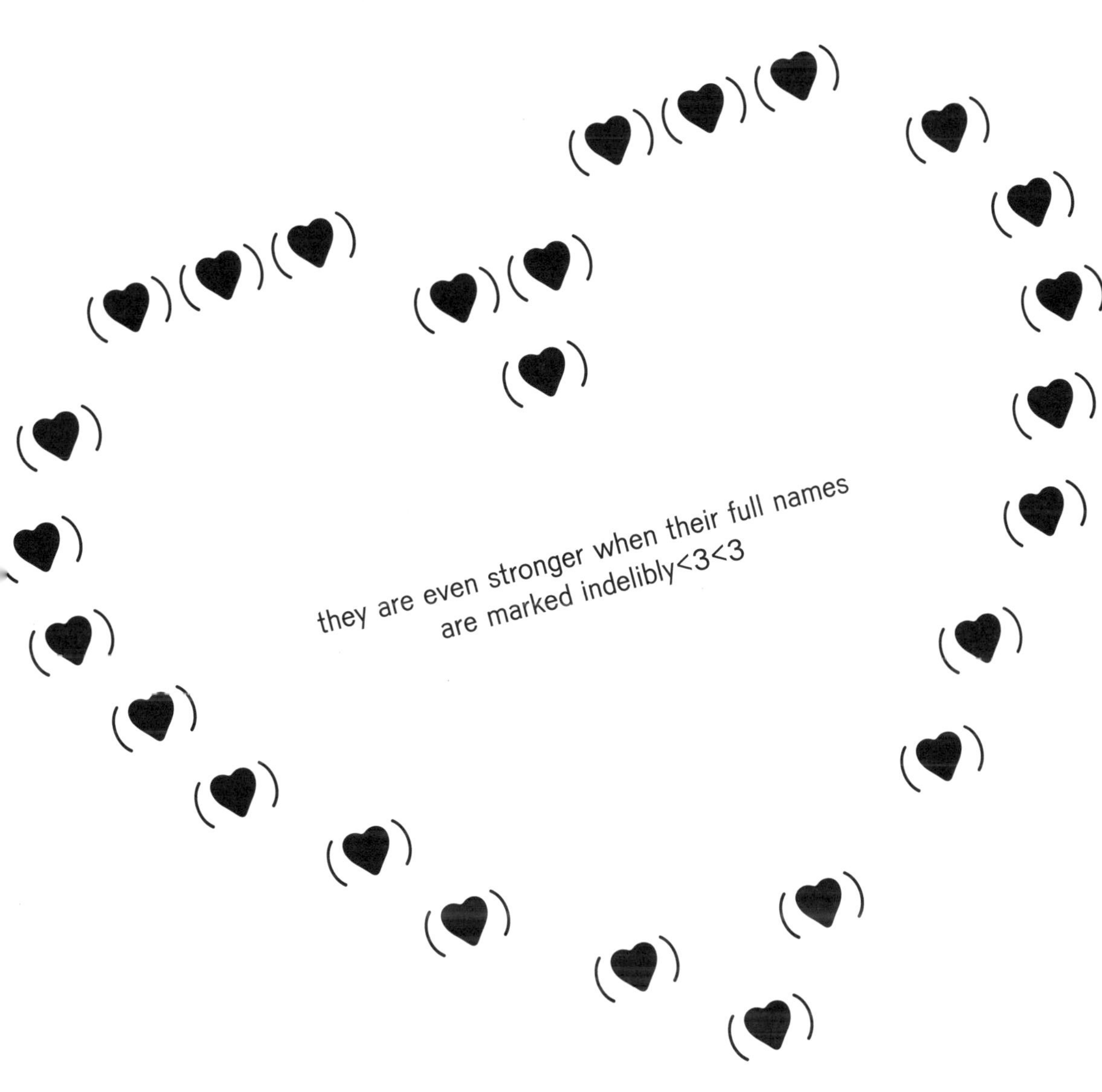

Jungmyung Lee

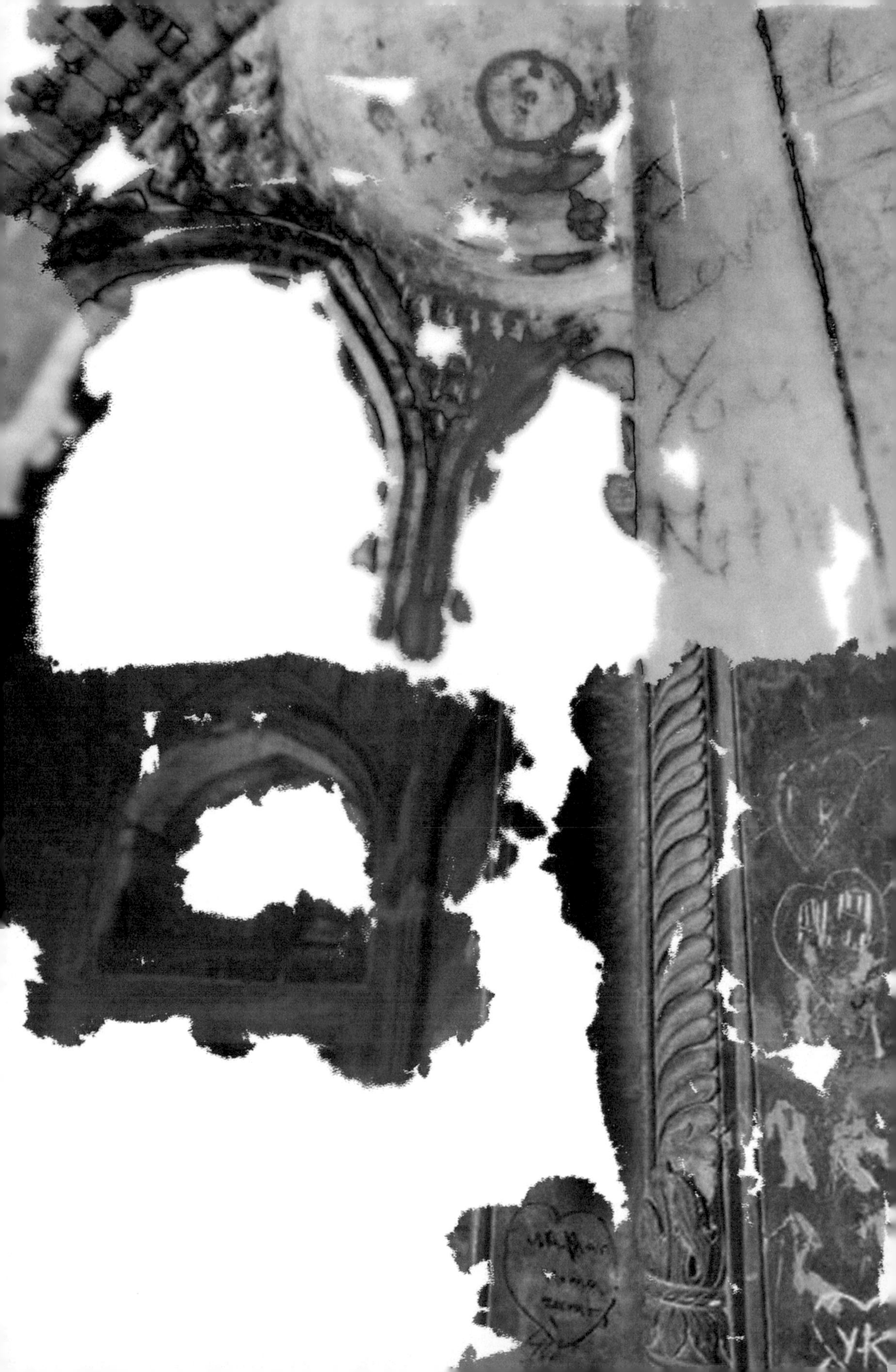

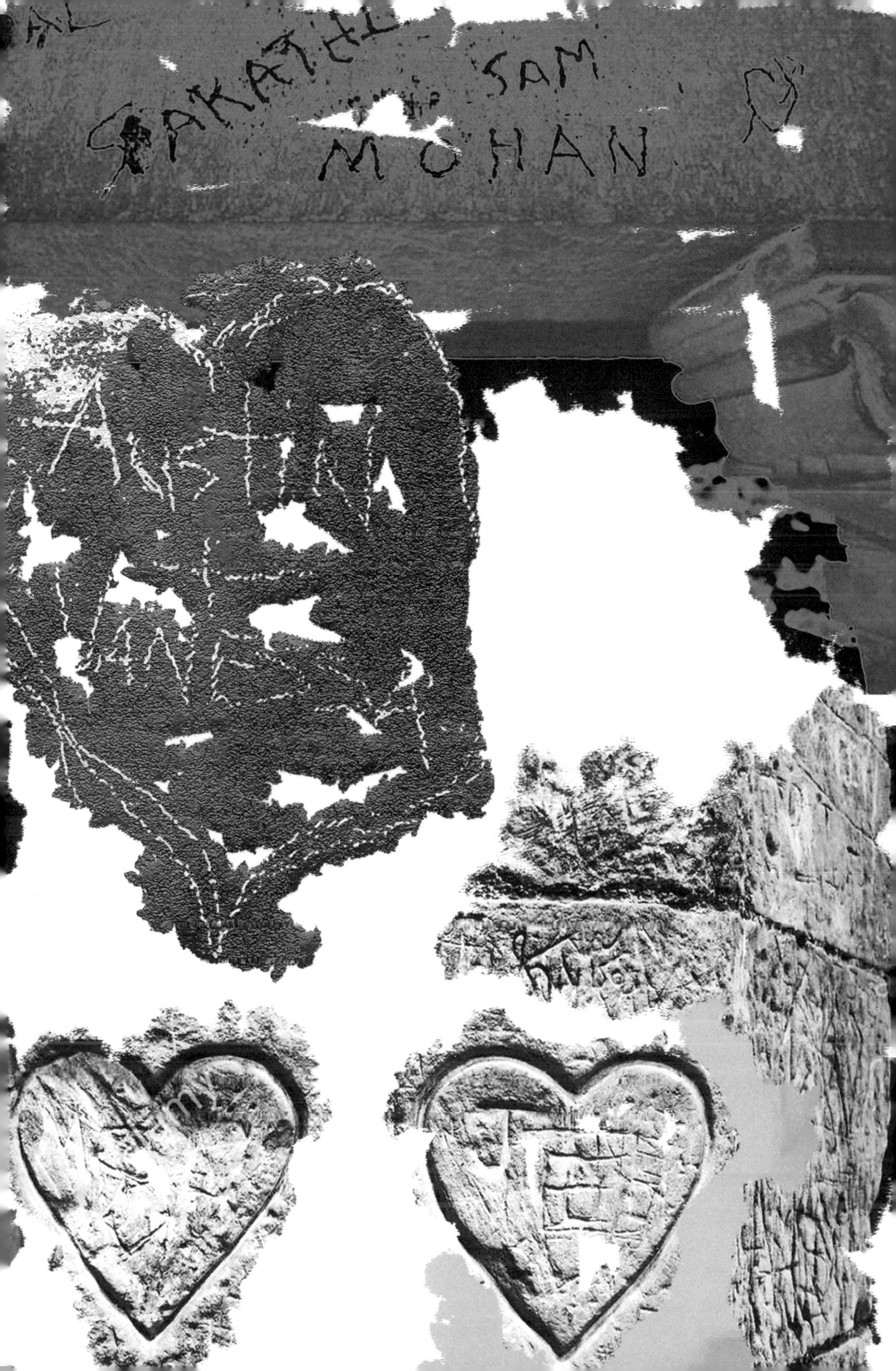
AL
SAKATH
SAM
MOHAN
AUSTIN

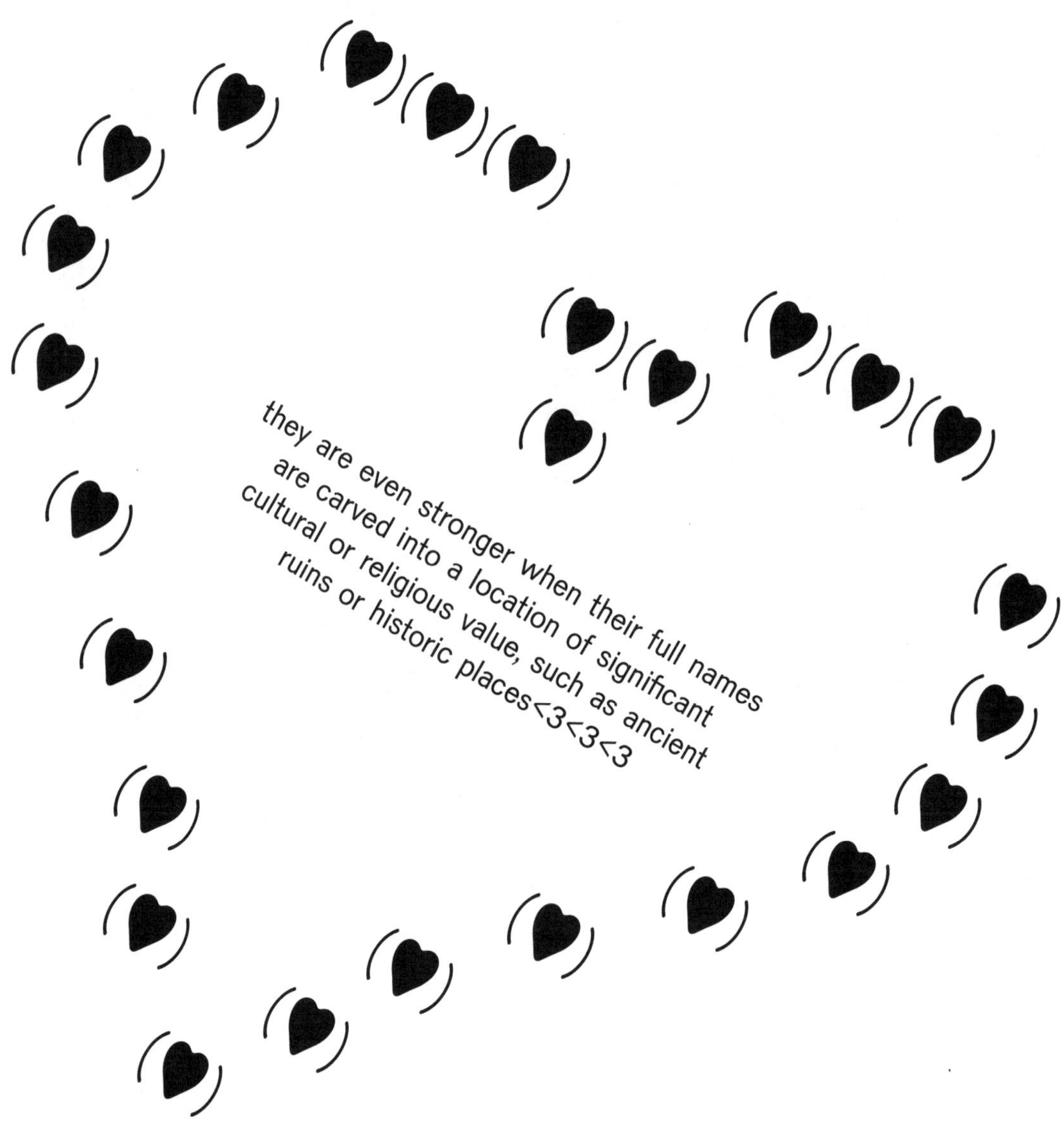

they are even stronger when their full names
are carved into a location of significant
cultural or religious value, such as ancient
ruins or historic places<3<3<3

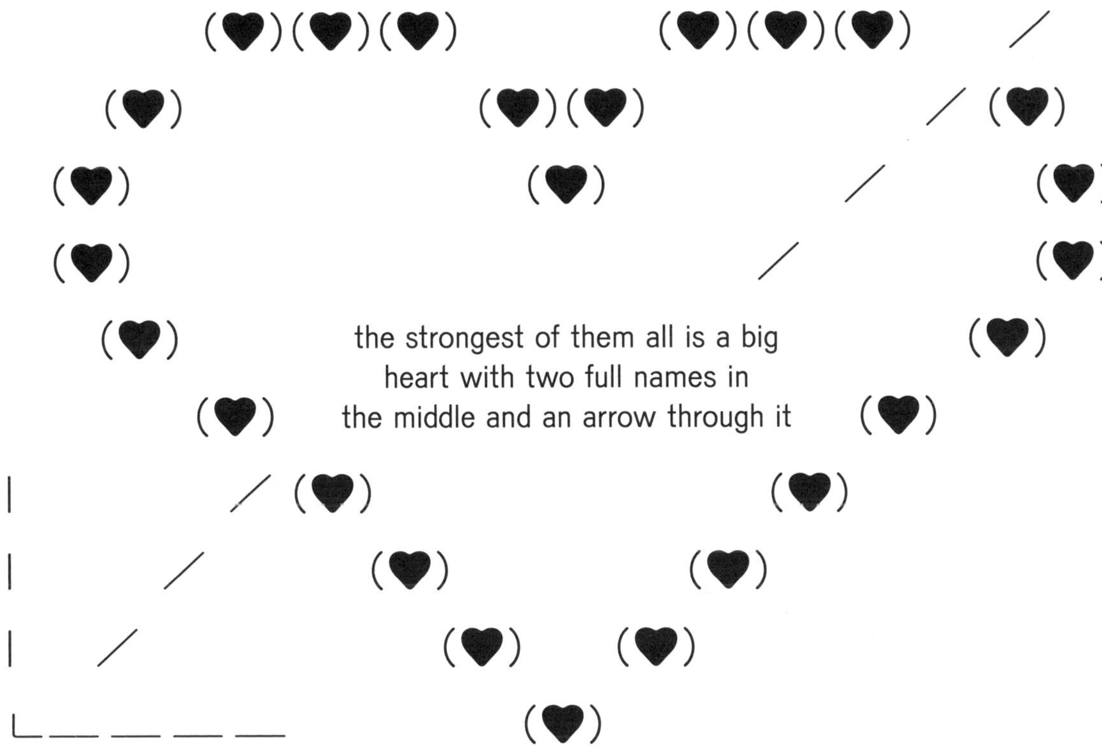

Jungmyung Lee

CLAUD
+
RAY
7-7-1

AMBER
+
TOM
9-20-13
ROBERT
+
SARAH
12-13
I LOVE
YOU!
JEFF

TO SPEAK OF TREES
Amelia Groom & M. Ty

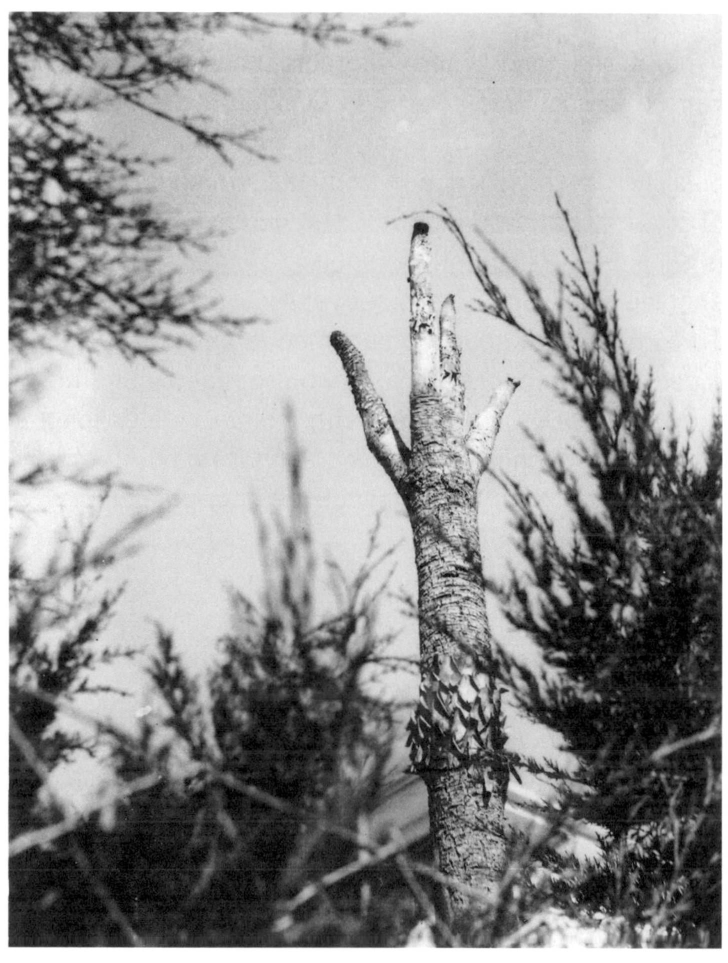

Claude Cahun and Marcel Moore,
Palmier Gelé, 1939.
Courtesy Jersey Heritage.

A tree encountered as an outstretched arm, with its index
finger pointing to the sky. The avant-garde artists Claude Cahun
and Marcel Moore took this photograph on Jersey Island,
a British Crown Dependency in the English Channel. The year
was 1939. The couple had recently relocated to the island,
and they mailed a copy of this pareidolic image to their friend
André Breton, who was back in Paris. 1939 was also the
year in which France and Britain declared war on Germany.
When Nazis invaded the Channel Islands the following summer,
the archipelago became the only British territory to fall

under German occupation. Cahun and Moore decided to stay on Jersey, and from 1940 until their arrest and imprisonment in 1944, they carried out a clandestine antifascist resistance campaign, while hiding Cahun's Jewish heritage and disguising their queer love by passing as a pair of heterosexual bourgeois "sisters."

When Cahun and Moore photographed this tree-hand, Bertolt Brecht was in exile in Denmark. His poem "An die Nachgeborenen" ("To Those Who Follow in Our Wake," published in 1939) opens with the ominous lamentation, "Truly, I live in dark times!"[1] The darkness of the times is such that "A smooth forehead / Points to insensitivity," and "He who laughs / Has not yet received / The terrible news." Throughout the poem, the unnamed forces of fascism impose a zero-sum economy of attention. Laughter and unfurrowed brows can only be equated with indifference or ignorance— and, in the second stanza, *talking about trees* effectively means turning away from the exigencies of the political:

> What kind of times are these, in which
> A conversation about trees is almost a crime
> For in doing so we maintain our silence about so much wrongdoing!

In Euro-American traditions of lyric poetry and landscape art, trees are routinely romanticized as exemplars of an idyllic and ahistorical Nature. When we were invited to contribute to this book on Elina Birkehag's research around the inscriptions that female shepherds left on the trunks of hundreds of old pines in the Dalecarlia province of Sweden, we found ourselves wanting to trace how the equation of trees with political irrelevance has been reiterated and revised. In this essay, we turn to the work of a number of queer artists in the US who have unsettled the colonial segregation of human history from the natural landscape—and, in doing so, offer a capacious sense of what politically engaged work can look like, beyond anthropocentric models of direct intervention. Taking a cue from Cahun's writing about the necessity of *L'action indirecte* ("indirect action") in strategies of resistance, we draw out minor acts—like Cahun and Moore's playful confusion of morphology in *Palmier Gelé*—that do not simply reinforce

1
Bertolt Brecht,
"To Those Who Follow
in Our Wake" (translated
by Scott Horton)
in *Harper's Magazine*
(January 15, 2008),
accessed November 1,
2021, https://harpers.
org/2008/01/
brecht-to-those-who-
follow-in-our-wake/.

or condemn the Western opposition between nature and culture, but recompose it, by messing with figure/ground distinctions and inviting contamination across anthropogenic and arboreal formations.[2]

*

In the late 1990s, the artist Zoe Leonard started photographing trees in New York City that had entered into slow, transformative relations with the metal enclosures that were erected around them. Trunks are shown bulging out of their iron barricades. There's a tree that has partially absorbed a line of barbed wire while breaking it apart. Railings have buckled under the slow pressure of arboreal growth, and thickets of metal have been swallowed into voluptuous wood. One picture in the *Tree+Fence* series shows a close-up of a tree that has pushed itself into a chain-link fence with such dedication that it has become inscribed with the diamond patterning of its wire grid.

[2] Partial translations of Cahun's 1933 pamphlet *Les Paris sont ouverts* appear as "Poetry Keeps its Secret," (translated by Myrna Bell Rochester) and "Surrealism and Working–Class Emancipation," (translated by Franklin Rosemont) in Penelope Rosemont, ed. *Surrealist Women: An International Anthology* (London: The Athlone Press, 1998), 53–57

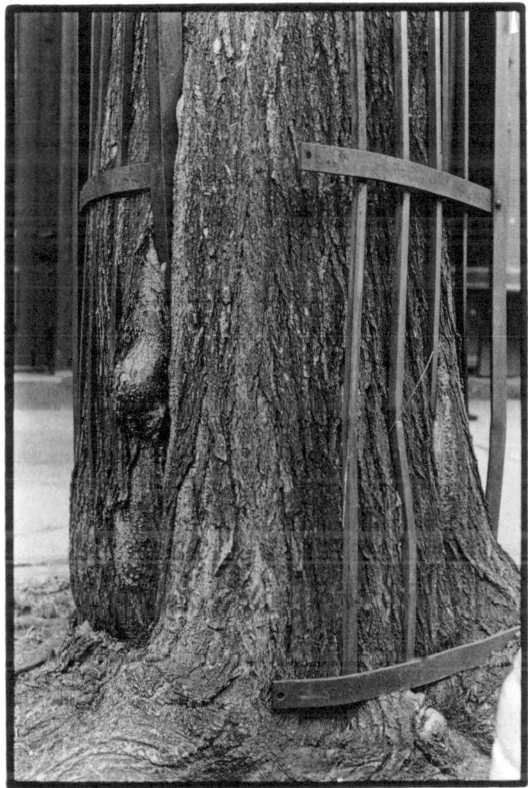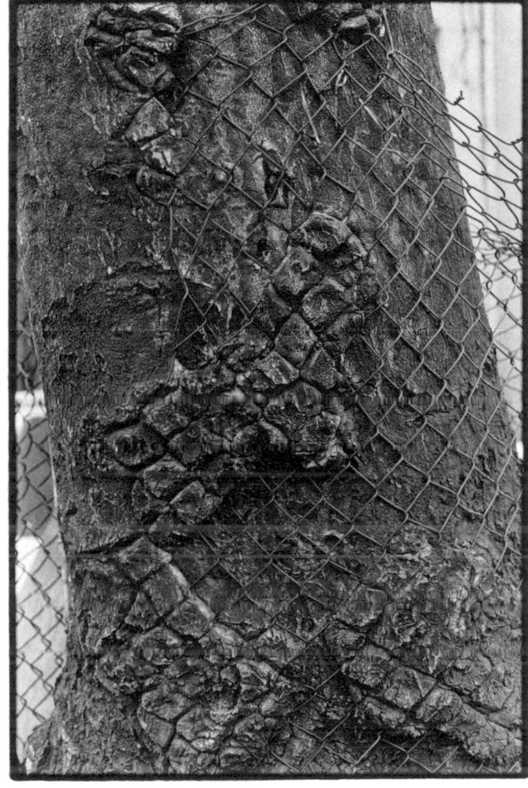

Zoe Leonard, both works are titled *Detail (Tree + Fence)*, 1998/1999. Gelatin silver print, 11 7/8″ × 8 ½″ © Zoe Leonard. Courtesy of the artist, Galerie Gisela Capitain, Cologne and Hauser & Wirth.

While Leonard was starting out as an artist in the 1980s
and early '90s, she was also engaged with queer and feminist
activism and grassroots organizing around the HIV/AIDS
crisis in New York. She was involved with ACT UP (the AIDS
Coalition to Unleash Power), participated in die-ins, and set up
needle exchanges, which at the time were illegal.[3] She was also
part of the direct-action feminist organization WAC (Women's
Action Coalition), the ACT UP-affiliated artist collective
Gang, and the lesbian artist and activist group Fierce Pussy.

During these years, as Leonard has recalled, she sometimes
felt ambivalent about her work as a solo artist. She was close
friends with David Wojnarowicz—an activist and artist
who died of AIDS-related illnesses, at the age of 37, in 1992.
She has recalled confiding in him about her concern that
in the midst of "the harshness of the reality of the crisis," she
was just "photographing clouds."[4] Wojnarowicz's response,
as Leonard remembers it, was to say, "Zoe, these [photographs
of clouds] are so beautiful, and that's what we're fighting for.
We're being angry and complaining because we have to,
but where we want to go is back to beauty. If you let go of that,
we don't have anywhere to go."[5]

Leonard's internal conflict about photographing nature during
the height of the AIDS crisis recalls how, for Brecht, speaking
of trees amid the rise of German fascism could feel like
criminal neglect. It also brings to mind a likely apocryphal
remark attributed to Henri Cartier-Bresson in the 1930s:
"The world is going to pieces and people like Ansel Adams
and Edward Weston are photographing rocks!"[6] In each of these
cases, engagement with the natural landscape is shadowed
by the guilt of political detachment and aesthetic indulgence.
Clouds, trees, and rocks are charged as props of willful oblivion—
or as mere vehicles for lubricating withdrawal from the ongoing
brutalities of history. Totalizing power constrains social life with
its insistence that everything—including resistance—must
address itself, at all times, to the dominant order. Such power
exerts a formative pressure on the moral imagination, not only
through acts of direct prohibition but also by regulating
what's considered to be socially irrelevant, frivolous, or "less real"
in relation to the hard reality of its violence.

3
Zoe Leonard Interview,
January 13, 2010,
*ACT UP Oral History
Project* #106, accessed
January 18, 2022,
https://actuporalhistory.
org/numerical-interviews/
106-zoe-leonard.

4
Cynthia Carr, *Fire in the
Belly: The Life and Times
of David Wojnarowicz*
(New York: Bloomsbury
USA, 2013).

5
Ibid.

6
See Ellen Macfarlane,
"Group f.64, Rocks,
and the Limits of the
Political Photograph"
in *American Art* (vol. 30,
no. 3, Fall 2016), 26–53.

Rather than being determined by feelings of guilt about
the perceived irrelevance of trees and clouds, Leonard's
work pushed against what she has described as "this curious
perception of a divide between nature and culture."[7]
This division comes undone in the *Tree+Fence* series,
as organic growth breaks into and out of the infrastructures
that were designed to enclose it. These images might be
distinguished from other works of Leonard's that present more
directly as activist interventions, such as her 1992 poem
"I want a president." But direct and indirect modes of address
can work alongside each other: at the artist's major survey
show at the Whitney Museum in 2018, "I want a president"
was installed next to the *Tree+Fence* series—each,
in different ways, affirming the force of impure abundance.

Leonard started taking the *Tree+Fence* photographs when
she had returned to NYC after several extended stays in
the Alaskan wilderness in the mid-'90s. During one eighteen-
month stint, she had lived alone in a small village on the
Yukon River, where she hauled her own water and firewood
while growing, gathering, and hunting for most of her
own food. Speaking to *Artforum* in 1999, Leonard recalled
that living off the grid in this way had "both expanded and
clarified" her politics.[8] Where previously she had experienced
a disconnect between social and environmental issues,
she began to sense how the struggles that had shaped
her life in the city (including "healthcare, gay rights, women's
rights, AIDS") and the local issues in Alaska (such as
"hunting regulations, oil, Native American rights, mining,
land allocations") were in fact "different parts of the same
beast."[9] Far from marking a withdrawal from her political
engagements, the artist's life away from the city made
her increasingly attuned to "the connections between social
issues in New York and land-use issues in Alaska."[10]
A vision of monolithic Nature as a space of retreat
no longer held up, as Leonard began to think more closely
about the complex interrelations of cosmopolitan life
and the ostensibly pure wilderness, including, for example,
the "economic link between the Alaska oil pipeline and
the urban consumer."[11]

7
Beth Dungan,
"An Interview with
Zoe Leonard" in
Discourse (vol. 24, no. 2,
Spring 2002), 76.

8
Zoe Leonard,
"Interviews: 1000 Words:
Zoe Leonard," *Artforum*
(January 1999), accessed
January 18, 2022,
https://www.artforum.
com/print/199901/1000-
words-zoe-leonard-32387.

9
Beth Dungan,
"An Interview with
Zoe Leonard,"
Op. Cit. 76.

10
Zoe Leonard,
"Interviews: 1000 Words:
Zoe Leonard," Op. Cit.

11
Ibid.

When she returned to Manhattan, Leonard found that
the city's trees attracted her attention in an entirely new way.
In addition to her *Tree+Fence* project, she also took a series
of photographs outside a building on Avenue A, where she had
started to notice some trees that often ended up with plastic
bags caught in them. The trees were positioned within a wind
tunnel, and the windier it was, the more stray bags would
gather on their branches. In Leonard's pictures, the trees
look cheerfully decorated while also serving as disgraced
depositories for floating garbage. There is no attempt at direct
messaging (as in, "pollution is bad"); rather, the trees arrive
in Leonard's pictures as decidedly impure, composite bodies.
She directs the eye toward branches that are tangled up with
the detritus of urban capitalism, but she also shows the trees
continuing to fulfill one of their most ancient functions,
as shelters for social life—with people sitting underneath their
branches, eating lunch, chatting, and hanging out.[12]

*

In photographing trees that have a touch of the city in them,
Leonard refuses to reproduce the clean antithesis between
nature and human sociality that was imposed by settler
colonialism and later reinforced by the white environmentalist
imagination. In canonical histories of North American landscape
photography, this manufactured opposition is emphatically
upheld. Take, for example, the work of Ansel Adams.
In his iconic black–and–white pictures of the American West,
you never see any footprints. His aesthetic continually evacuates
human traces; historical time is systematically expelled from
the scene, so that his images can give way to the spectacle
of static magnificence.

Adams's landscapes epitomize the twentieth–century
conservationist gaze, whose optics rendered American
landscapes as sublime but also as increasingly in need of
paternalistic protection. He was a lifetime member and served
as the director of the Sierra Club, the world's first large–scale
environmental organization, which campaigned to convert
large tracts of land into national parks. While it was presented
as a moral act of safeguarding what was precious to all,

12
See, for example,
the image published on
page 74 of Beth Dungan,
"An interview with
Zoe Leonard" Op. Cit.

establishing these ecological reserves became a way to lay claim to indigenous land by means other than direct warfare or coercive treaties. "Nature" was created as a recreational destination and spectacle as places that had been inhabited for more than ten thousand years were repackaged with foreign names and put under the management of the state's armed forces.

The whitewashing of history that was carried out under the auspices of environmentalism can be traced throughout Adams's 1959 monograph *Yosemite Valley*. The Ahwahnechee people who had lived in this area for thousands of years called the valley by another name: *Ahwahnee* or "gaping mouth." Adams's grandiose images of Ahwahnee Valley are captioned with idyllic descriptions of "the delicacy of the forest" and "the power of the waterfalls."[13] Lakes appear as mirror-still objects of reflection, rather than as sites that are open to immersion and permeated by practices of subsistence. The monumental sequoia and redwood trees are made to appear under the sign of Nature's abundance, but only through the erasure of human labor; in actuality, their extraordinary growth was made possible by practices of controlled burning, which indigenous people had practiced long before white environmentalists set out to establish themselves as the principled guardians of the forest.[14]

During the years when Adams was trekking through the Sierras with his huge camera, some Paiute and Miwuk peoples had managed to continue living within the boundaries of the national park, working as housekeeping staff or performing in the human exhibitions of the onsite museum, which was established for the white demographic that the Sierra Club welcomed onto stolen land. With mountains, waters, and animals enclosed under federal authority, native peoples living in "Yosemite" were subject to surveillance and terrorizing physical abuse by the National Park Service. Around the time that Adams was shooting some of his most iconic photographs, including *Moon and Half Dome* (1960), the state service evicted the remaining indigenous people and burnt down the cabins of native employees.[15] Despite returning to Yosemite Park every year of his life—

13
Ansel Adams, *Yosemite Valley* (San Francisco: 5 Associates, 1959), image #2.

14
The racist naturalist John Muir, who became the first president of the Sierra Club in 1892, successfully campaigned for fire suppression in Yosemite, as a means of "protecting" the Sierra forests. A 2010 study found that a century of bans on controlled burning practices had resulted in drastic declines in biodiversity, while increasing the region's vulnerability to catastrophic fires. See Andrew Scholl and Alan H. Taylor, "Fire Regimes, Forest Change, and Self-Organization in an Old-growth Mixed-Conifer Forest, Yosemite National Park, USA" in *Ecological Applications* 20, no. 2 (March 2010): 362–380. See also Douglas Deur and Rochelle Bloom, "Fire, Native Ecological Knowledge, and the Enduring Anthropogenic Landscapes of Yosemite Valley" in *The Routledge Handbook of Indigenous Environmental Knowledge* (New York: Routledge, 2021), 299–313.

15
See Mark David Spence, *Dispossessing the Wilderness: Indian Removal and the Making of the National Parks* (Oxford: Oxford University Press, 2000). Stephen Corry, "The Colonial Origins of Conservation: The Disturbing History Behind US National Parks," *Truthout*, August 25, 2018, accessed January 18, 2022, https://truthout.org/articles/the-colonial-origins-of-conservation-the-disturbing-history-behind-us-national-parks/.

Amelia Groom & M. Ty

beginning in 1916 when he was just fourteen years old—
Adams's images of this region hardly show even the faintest
ripple of this continuing history of state violence.

Adams's personal correspondence often swells with the pride
of being the first to arrive at a site with a camera, or being
the only one who could pull off the physical conquest that
allowed him to get the prized shot. In 1928, while on
a trip to New Mexico, he wrote to his wife Virginia: "there
is no one here, nor has there been anyone, who has had
the least luck with pictorial photography on a large scale.
I am amazed at the fresh prospects that no one has touched."[16]
This fetishization of places where, as Adams puts it, "nothing
has been done," resounds with settler-colonial logics
of "discovery"—and the creation of value through erasure—
on which America's identity was founded.[17] Many continue to
revere Adams for his attention to nature, but the significance
of his work lies elsewhere—namely, in the power of his
aesthetic to transfigure the psychosis of the colonial gaze into
something that could be circulated for universal appreciation.

*

In her video *Untouched Landscape* (2007), the artist
Laura Aguilar stands naked in front of a large brown body
of rock in Joshua Tree National Park. In a low and
characteristically unaffected voice that borders at times on
a mumble, she improvises a monologue in which she redefines
"untouched landscape" in terms of her own body—with all
of its valleys, mounds, rolls, and precipices. Her hand moves
along her belly as she narrates its landforms. If the trope of
feminized, virgin nature was recruited to inspire white settlers
to misrecognize their westward expansion as an entitlement
to which they were destined, Aguilar dramatically scales
down the idea and re-situates it in relation to her embodied
experience. In an unexpected way, "untouched" is diffracted
from its grandiose nationalist signification and inflected
otherwise, so as to name the scarcity of physical touch that
had become a lived reality for Aguilar, as someone whose
body deviated from hetero-normative standards of size
and beauty—and was often ambivalently read as Mexican

16
Ansel Adams, "Letter to
Virginia Adams, November
1928" in *The Grand
Canyon and the Southwest*
(New York: Little, Brown
& Company), 91.

17
Ibid.

or Native American, depending on what part of the country she
happened to be in. "I don't get a lot of touch in my life,"
she says. Reflecting on the pictures that she makes of herself,
naked in the outdoors, she realizes that "being nude,
out in nature" allows her to be "touched by the warmth of
the sunlight."

In an interview, her mentor Sybil Venegas mentions that Aguilar
had descended from "a lineage of women who collected rocks."[18]
Aguilar's San Gabriel Valley garden was populated with stones
that her grandmother had singled out and brought home.
When asked about a particular stone, Aguilar would often be
able to recall not only which of the rocks her grandmother
had collected, but also what her grandmother had thought they
resembled: this one, she'd point out, looks like a human form.
In this way, Aguilar's domestic rock collection grounded
a material and trans-generational practice of memory.
In contrast with mineral collections held by institutions of
natural history, her informal gathering did not extract portions
of the environment, submit them to the logic of the specimen,
and seek to resolve their identity with a fixed designation.
The rocks were not an occasion to answer the question
what are they? but rather, *what are they like?* In addition
to the specific memories with which they were attached,
the collected stones also transmitted a way of seeing:
a practice of attention, a form of play and perception that
lights up the material world with its ability to see something
in something else.

This principle of oblique resemblance animates Aguilar's series
Nature Self-Portraits, which she began shortly after her
best friend since high-school, the gay Chicano poet and author
Gil Cuadros, passed away from AIDS-related illnesses in
1996, at the age of 34. In *Nature Self-Portrait #5 (1996)*,
for instance, Aguilar's arms ramify the trunk of the tree
on which her feet take root. Branches stretch skyward in
a proliferation of the artist's hands. The shadows cast by
the limbs of the tree limn their shape onto the bends of her
folded trunk. And her trunk, in turn, gives a little more
body to the fallen tree, lending a variable inflection to its
visual rhythm.

18
Interview with Laura
Aguilar in *Artbound:
No Trespassing: A Survey
of Environmental Art*
(Season 9, Episode 6,
2018), KCET, directed
by Matt Glass & Jordan
Wayne Long, video
accessed January 20,
2022, https://youtu.be/
8gFB2lpYYwQ.

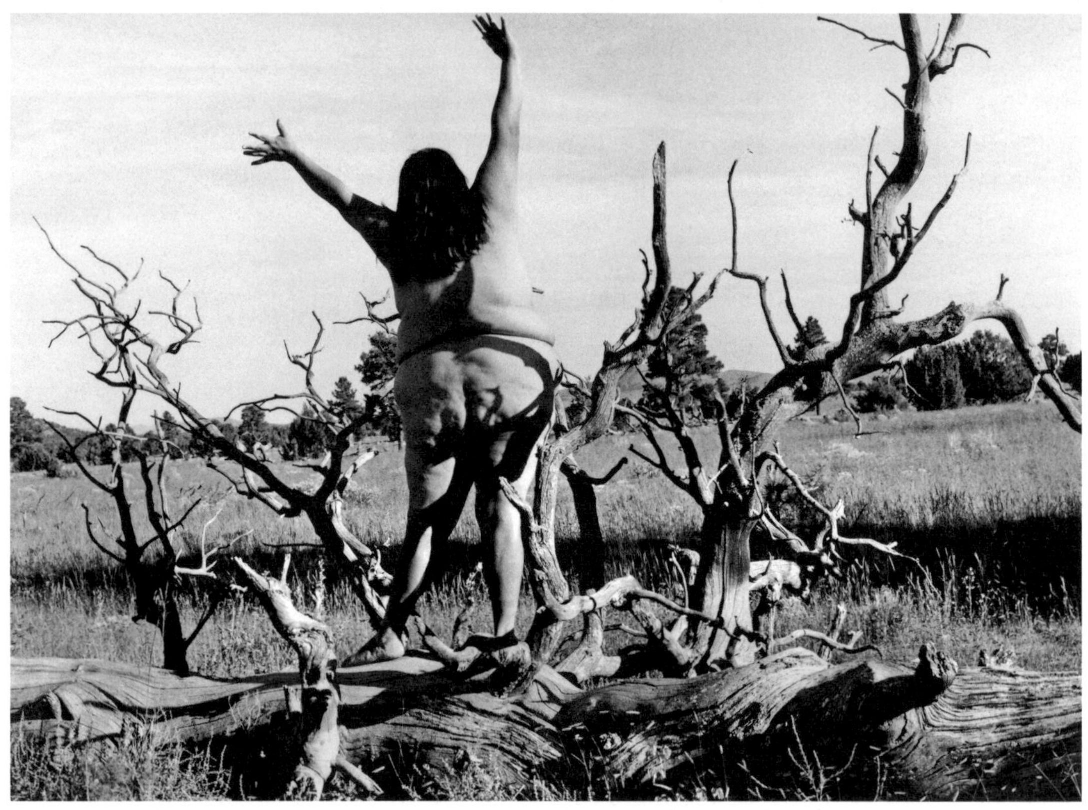

Laura Aguilar, *Nature Self-Portrait #5*, 1996. Gelatin silver print, 16″ × 20″. © Laura Aguilar Trust of 2016.

Throughout this series, Aguilar denies the portrait the face.
In turning away from the gaze that would otherwise settle on
her, she diffuses attention from the part of the body that
is conventionally privileged as the threshold of recognition,
or else profiled as a marker of racial identity. She redirects
the genre of the self-portrait away from a humanist
project of individuation, so that her body does not formally
pronounce itself, over and against a natural backdrop. Instead,
she transliterates her environment. She lets her body parts
be drawn into the course of a line that extends beyond her.
She partakes in the landscape's articulations without assuming
them as her own, and without throwing her voice onto
the land, as if it were some untouched stretch of *terra nullius*.

While she situated her work in some of the very same national
parks through which Ansel Adams had traveled—such as
Joshua Tree—Aguilar experienced them in a very different
way. She entered environmental reserves without the
entitlement of belonging there. She visited as a Chicana artist

in a white space of leisure; as a large body in a zone dedicated
to fitness and physical adventuring; and as a single lesbian
in a desert of family recreation. In an interview for a TV show
that aired shortly before her death in 2018, Aguilar mentions
that when she was working on her outdoor nude photographs,
she was always accompanied by one or two people, "so that
they could act as lookouts for me." In national parks, she says,
"You don't want to get arrested."[19] A good part of her work
involved avoiding being seen by the wrong kind of person.

Aguilar traveled through the deserts of the American West,
including the Mojave desert in California, as well as the
Malpais Monument and the Gila Mountains of New Mexico—
sites where, historically, the image of expansive Nature
was consolidated through the forced removal of Indigenous
presence from the pictorial frame. For decolonial sociologist
Macarena Gómez–Barris, Aguilar's practice of embedding her
mestiza body within sites of Indigenous dispossession
"visually counteract[s]" Frederick Turner's frontier thesis,
which defined the West as empty land, free for appropriation.[20]
Aguilar's distinctively queer embodiment, in Gómez–Barris's
account, obstructs the pristine vision of American expansion
and ruptures the cultivated amnesia surrounding white projects
of settlement by force.

But Aguilar does not directly negate the racist proposition that
non–whites are outside of the cultural field and are instead
a part of the nonhuman environment. Rather, she queers this
identification, to the effect that the regulative opposition
between Nature and Human crumples. Her earlier projects
documenting queers of East LA took up the genre of
portraiture in a more straightforward way. Her *Latina Lesbians*
series (1986—1990) and the photographs she took at a local
watering hole called Plush Pony both worked to bring queers
of color into a space of representation from which they were
routinely denied. Aguilar's later portraits experiment with a more
oblique position vis-á-vis the axis of inclusion and exclusion.
It's not simply that she inserts herself as a presence
where there was formerly an absence, thereby contravening
the historical interdiction of queer and brown bodies.
She also finds a way to be seen while withdrawing from

19
Interview with Laura
Aguilar in *Artbound:
No Trespassing: A Survey
of Environmental Art*
(Season 9, Episode 6,
2018), KCET, directed
by Matt Glass & Jordan
Wayne Long, video
accessed January 20,
2022, https://youtu.be/
8yΓB2lpYYwQ.

20
Macarena Gómez–Barris,
"Mestiza Cultural Memory:
The Self-Ecologies of
Laura Aguilar" in *Laura
Aguilar: Show and Tell*
(Los Angeles: Vincent
Price Museum, 2017), 82.

frontal identification and, at the same time, to bring into
the world a portrait, at the very point at which the eye passes
into landscape. This wayward entry into the representational
field disorders normative logics of invisibility, along with
the values of social recognition that they relay.

Aguilar's *Nature Self-Portraits* are partly documents of
momentary release from the imperative to conform to
the restrictive ideal of being white, thin, straight, and able
to speak without an audible disability. More than just being
the subject matter of her photographs, the environment was,
for Aguilar, a source of reprieve from being a spectacle
of marginalization. In a conversation with Carolina Miranda,
Aguilar mentions that she didn't like England at all when
she first visited. "Why not?" Miranda asks. Aguilar replies:
"'Cause people stared at me. Like they've never seen
someone of color and nor did they see someone large before
[....] I didn't like being stared at by adults and stuff and even
little kids."[21] Aguilar took refuge in treescapes and fields
of rock. In Joshua Tree National Park, she gravitated toward
a sense of scale in which her body did not immediately
pronounce itself as being out of place. "I have one area that
I prefer because the rocks are big," she notes. "I feel like
that's where my body fits in, because most places, my body's
bigger than the rocks."[22] An optic calibrated to normative,
fatphobic measurements of the human body would register
her physical embodiment as imposing. But outside city limits,
Aguilar was able to find her way toward places where she felt
in proportion with her surrounds.

It's funny to hear Aguilar cite Ansel Adams as one of her early
influences. Not long after graduating from high school,
she attended a lecture he gave for the Los Angeles Department
of Water and Power. At that point, Adams belonged to
a coterie of Bay Area photographers who called themselves
Group f.64. They were united by their commitment to
"the qualities of clearness and definition." Without any sense
of irony, they expressed their determination to produce
"pure" or "straight" photography. Adams had made a cult of
his own technical mastery. He codified his method into
the "zone system," which sought to maximize tonal range,

21
Laura Aguilar, Interview
with Carolina Miranda,
May 14 and 15, 2018,
Los Angeles, California,
*CSRC Oral Histories
Series*, no. 17
(Los Angeles: UCLA
Chicano Studies Research
Center Press, 2018),
104 accessed January
10, 2022, https://
www.chicano.ucla.
edu/publications/oral-
histories/laura–aguilar.

22
Interview with Laura Aguilar
in *Artbound:
No Trespassing: A Survey
of Environmental Art*,
Op. Cit.

partly by eliminating any appearance of pure black. This meant
that nothing in the frame would be permitted full obscurity.
No matter how distant or dark things were, Nature was to appear
in high definition, clean of any blur or grain.

In a 2014 oral history interview, Aguilar was asked about her
encounter with the master photographer. You'll hear;
it's striking—Aguilar's total disinterest in Adams's technical
virtuosity, and her laughter in the face of the reverence
that typically surrounds his "system":

CM So tell me about the Ansel Adams talk. What was that like?
LA Boring. [*laughs*] But the pictures, the photographs,
    were beautiful. [...] And then I learned about his system,
    which I didn't ever find interesting.
CM You didn't?
LA Oh, I found it boring as hell.
CM Why?
LA Because it's a lot of testing. [*laughs*] A lot of keeping track
    of things and stuff like that. [...] I just found it more
    mathematical than visually entertaining, you know.
    I mean he was the expert. I mean, I loved him until I saw
    Eliot Porter, then I sort of like dumped him. [*laughs*]
CM Really? Now what did you love about his work when you
    first saw it? [...]
LA Oh, just nature. Yosemite, stuff like that. I just found that's
    what I liked about it. [...] And then as the years went by,
    I just learned that it was more technically particular.
    And I mean it was beautiful [...] but [...] I thought that
    the technical stuff sort of takes the creativity away.[23]

Liking Adams while knowing he was totally boring; remaking
his black–and–white aesthetics of purity into a sexually
and racially marked photographic practice, one that invites
landscape and portrait to contaminate each other playfully—
in these ways, Aguilar saw a possibility of vision that did
not fall into the devastating alternative of accomplished
assimilation or sheer refusal. In many ways, the gaze that
Adams heroically canonized represented all the forces
that edged Aguilar to the margins of public life: contempt
for the non-normative body, ableism, tediously emphatic

23
Laura Aguilar, Interview
with Carolina Miranda,
Op. Cit. 22–23.

hetero–normativity, white entitlement. And yet, she nevertheless
retrieved some part of his work that she could reactivate—
queerly—disrupting the homogenous beauty of Adams's mono-
racial visual poetics. She could see through the sheen
of mastery, and still sense how the rocks and trees might offer
some improbable refuge.

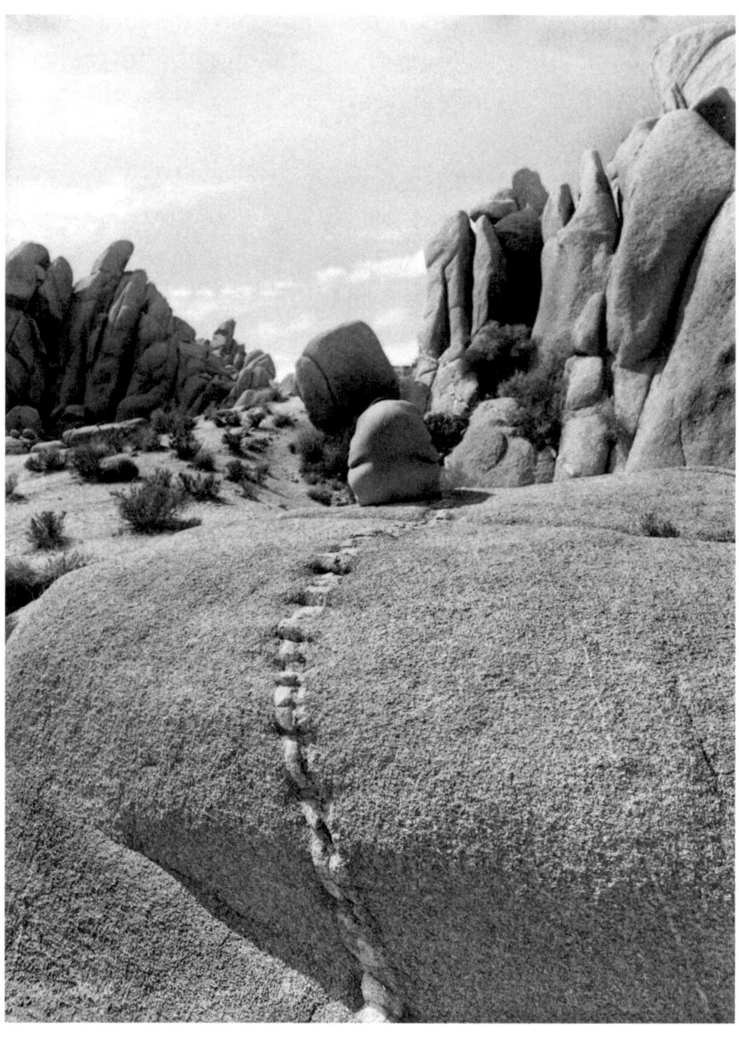

Laura Aguilar, *Grounded # 106*,
2006/7. Inkjet print, 22″ × 17″.
© Laura Aguilar Trust of 2016.

*

In 1991, Adrienne Rich responded to Brecht's address to
the "Nachgeborenen" with a poem whose title—"What Kind
of Times are These"—reprises his line, more than half
a century later. Her updated version begins in the mode of
pastoral poetry: "There's a place between two stands of trees

where the grass grows uphill."[24] However, any promise
of idyllic retreat quickly dissipates, as the place of this poem
turns out to be imbued with its history. It's a place that is
"ghost-ridden," as Rich puts it in the third stanza. If tree-talk
was, for Brecht, the telltale sign of escapist withdrawal,
Rich's trees form part of a landscape that is inescapably
haunted by its past. In her poem "North American Time"
(1983), Rich writes that "Poetry never stood a chance /
of standing outside history."[25] In "What Kind of Times are
These," it's not just poetry but also the natural landscape
in contemporary America that has never stood a chance of
standing outside history.

Rich's writing often returned to her dissatisfaction with standard
definitions of the political, which was too often "reduced
to government, to contests between the empowered,
or to petty in-group squabbles."[26] During the same year that she
wrote the poem "What Kind of Times Are These," she had
also started to write a letter to her friend Arturo Islas,
a gay Chicano novelist and poet who, at the time, was living
with AIDS. Before Rich had the chance to finish the letter,
Islas passed away. She had wanted to write to him about
the inseparability of poetry and politics. "Arturo—would you
agree?" she wrote, "we're unable to write love, as we
so much wish to do, without writing politics."[27] Gay poets
did not have the option to write love apolitically, and yet,
Rich observed, conventional definitions of the word "politics"
exclude the private and domestic spheres—"the places
where we lie down with our unsanctioned lovers."[28]
A decade earlier, in her famous 1980 essay "Compulsory
Heterosexuality and Lesbian Existence," Rich insisted that
in order to study the histories of resistance to hetero-patriarchy
that have been overlooked for so long, it is necessary to
attend to the radical rebelliousness that has been practiced
"in all the situations male ideologies have not perceived
as revolutionary."[29]

For Rich, the revolutionary artist is "the relayer of possibility."[30]
Rather than seeking to convince or instruct directly, they are
someone who works in opposition to society's "hatred of
multiformity, hatred of the natural world, hatred of the body,

24
Adrienne Rich, "What Kind
of Times are These"
in *Later Poems: Selected
and New 1971–2012*
(New York: W.W. Norton,
2012), 247.

25
Adrienne Rich, "North
American Time" in *Later
Poems: Selected and New
1971–2012*, 132–136.

26
Adrienne Rich, "Dearest
Arturo" in *What is Found
There: Notebooks on
Poetry and Politics* (New
York and London: W. W.
Norton & Company, 1993),
22–27; 24.

27
Ibid., 23.

28
Ibid., 24.

29
Adrienne Rich, "Compulsory
Heterosexuality
and Lesbian Existence"
in *The Lesbian and Gay
Studies Reader* (New York:
Routledge, 2012), 241.

30
Adrienne Rich, "What If?"
in *What Is Found There:
Notebooks on Poetry
and Politics*, 250.

hatred of darkness and women, hatred of disobedience"—
someone, she adds, who "loves people, rivers, other creatures,
stones, trees inseparably from art."[31] In her re–voicing of
the question "what kind of times are these?" Rich meets Brecht's
diagnosis with a reversal, which resounds today all the more:

> [...] so why do I tell you
> anything? Because you still listen, because in times like these
> to have you listen at all, it's necessary
> to talk about trees.

[31]
Adrienne Rich, "What If?"
in *What Is Found There:
Notebooks on Poetry
and Politics*, 250.

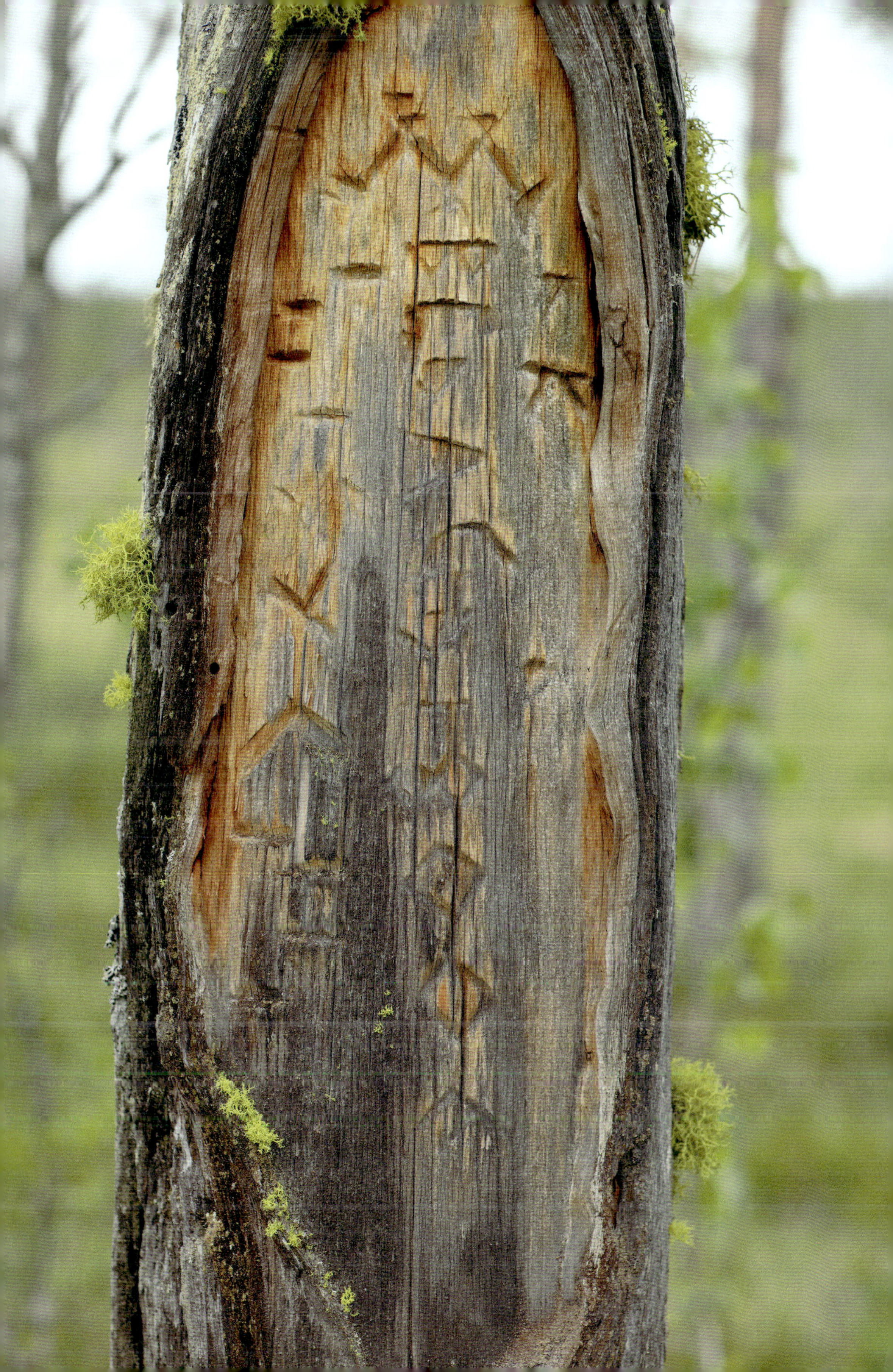

july

the cloudberries are almost ripe
we go to places we haven't been before

i make casts of three trees
the silicon smears into the text   it hardens easily

i gently pull off the mirrored imprint

i have learned to recognize some lichens and mosses

wolf lichen is rare and only grows where there is an old forest
neon green and poisonous

i guess the ages of the trees

we continue for five days   we are by ourselves now
sometimes we get lost   it's hot and we sweat

we are hungry and usually have too little to eat
it's tiring to walk in the boots

we hear a cuckoo   we don't see a bear   we see several moose
the cloudberries have started to color but are still hard

mamma säger

och man funderade vem som hade gjort dem
hur det var och sådär

att det var vackert

de hade en liten sten sägs det   som de slog mot yxans järn

för å precisera
få det snyggt   för å få till det

jag minns inte att det var några kalaverkningar då

det kom nog lite senare

de här kala   averkningarna

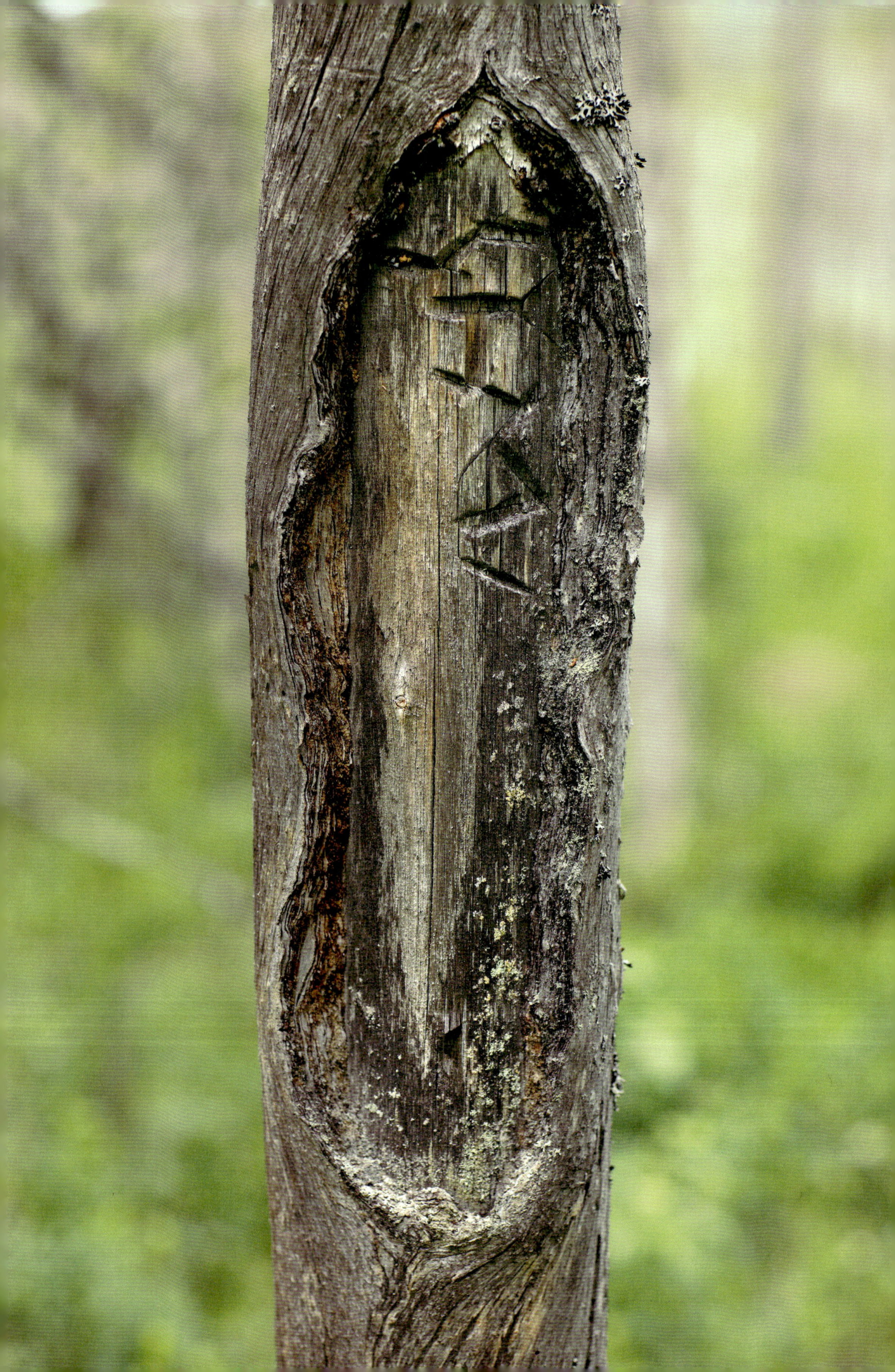

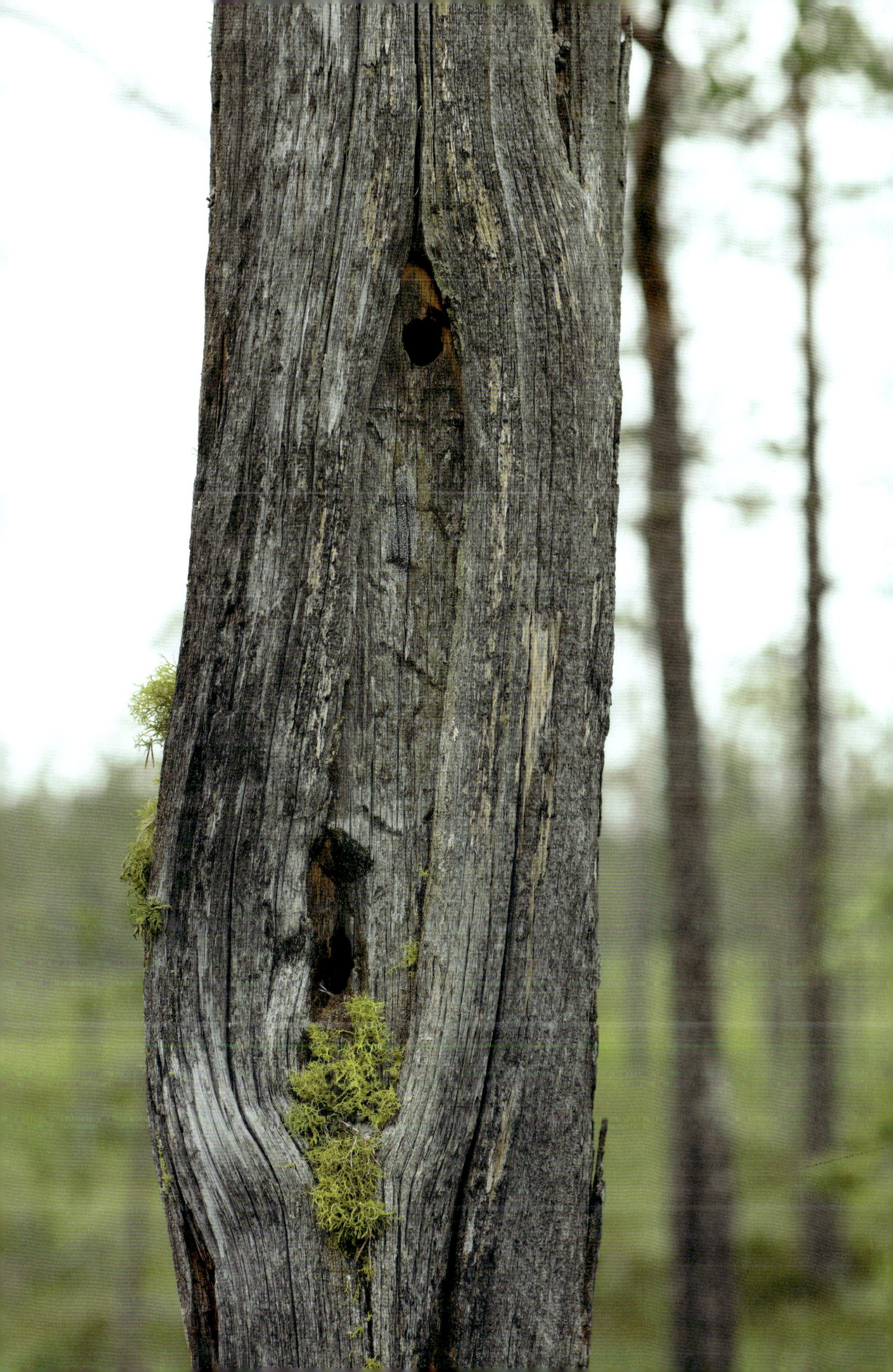

we drive back and forth along the road between dalfors and bingsjö
for another week

often the rivers are too deep to cross and we have to go back
to the car and drive around, to come from a different direction

we visit OBJEKT 2, OBJEKT 3, OBJEKT 6A, 6B, 6D,
and OBJEKT 8

XIII   AED
BED BED   AOD
W778   I DALEN
IIA AED KED   1776 I SÖKBODA

you saw
forest
forest
forest
forest
forest
forest
forest

dåggor uta ändö

the hospitals
the schools
the highways
the cities
wood welfare

two hundred
years after SY BGD AED XXXXXX

never churn butter when there is thunder

IIII
S

cows that bring
extra fat milk

resource

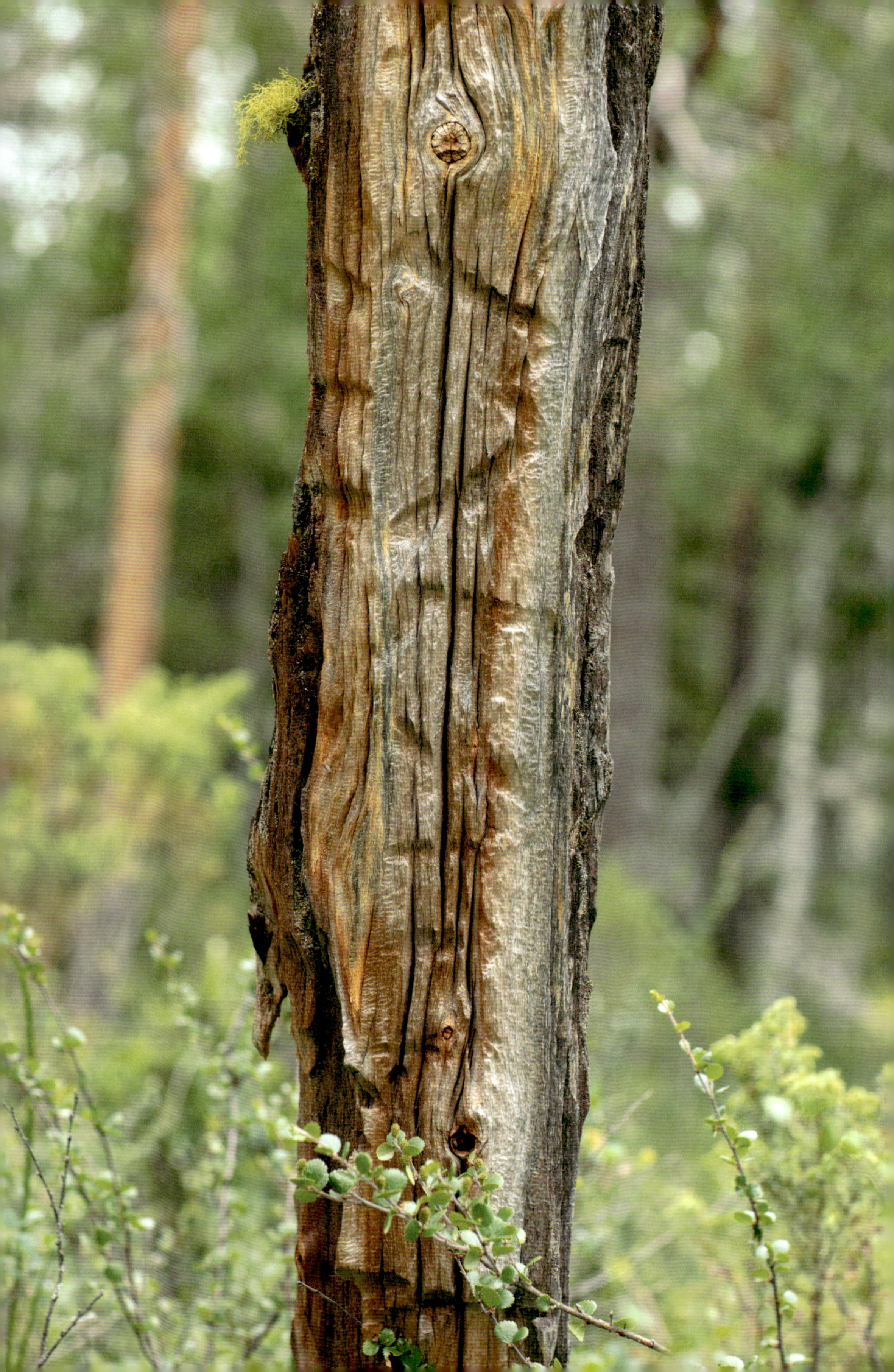

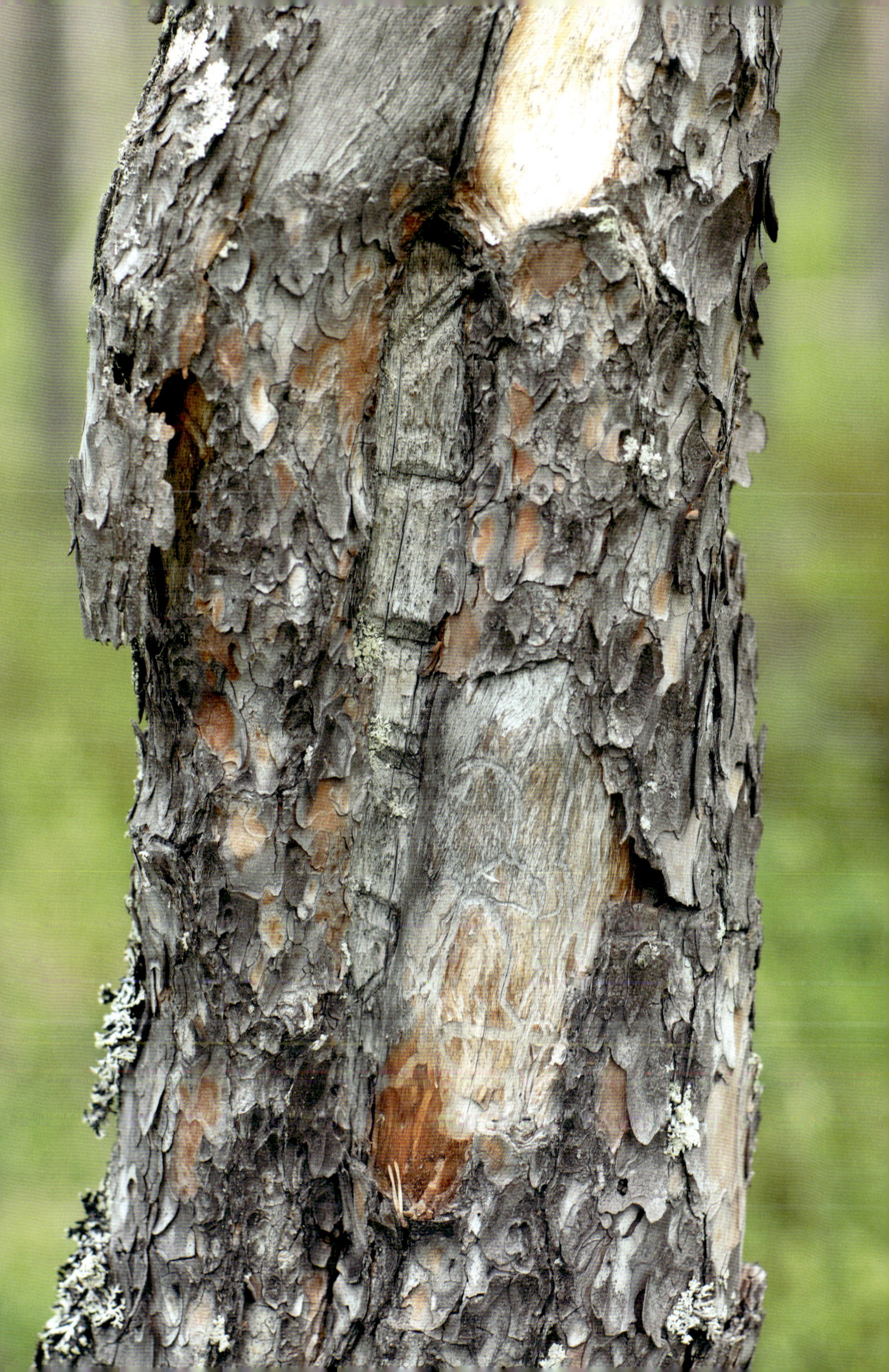

WE HAVE FUN

at three o'clock, i imagine anna luring the cow
it's time to go home
help me fjällros, she says to the cow   let's go home

anna starts to walk determinedly, and fjällros follows
anna calls out and fjällros replies

soon the other heifers follow

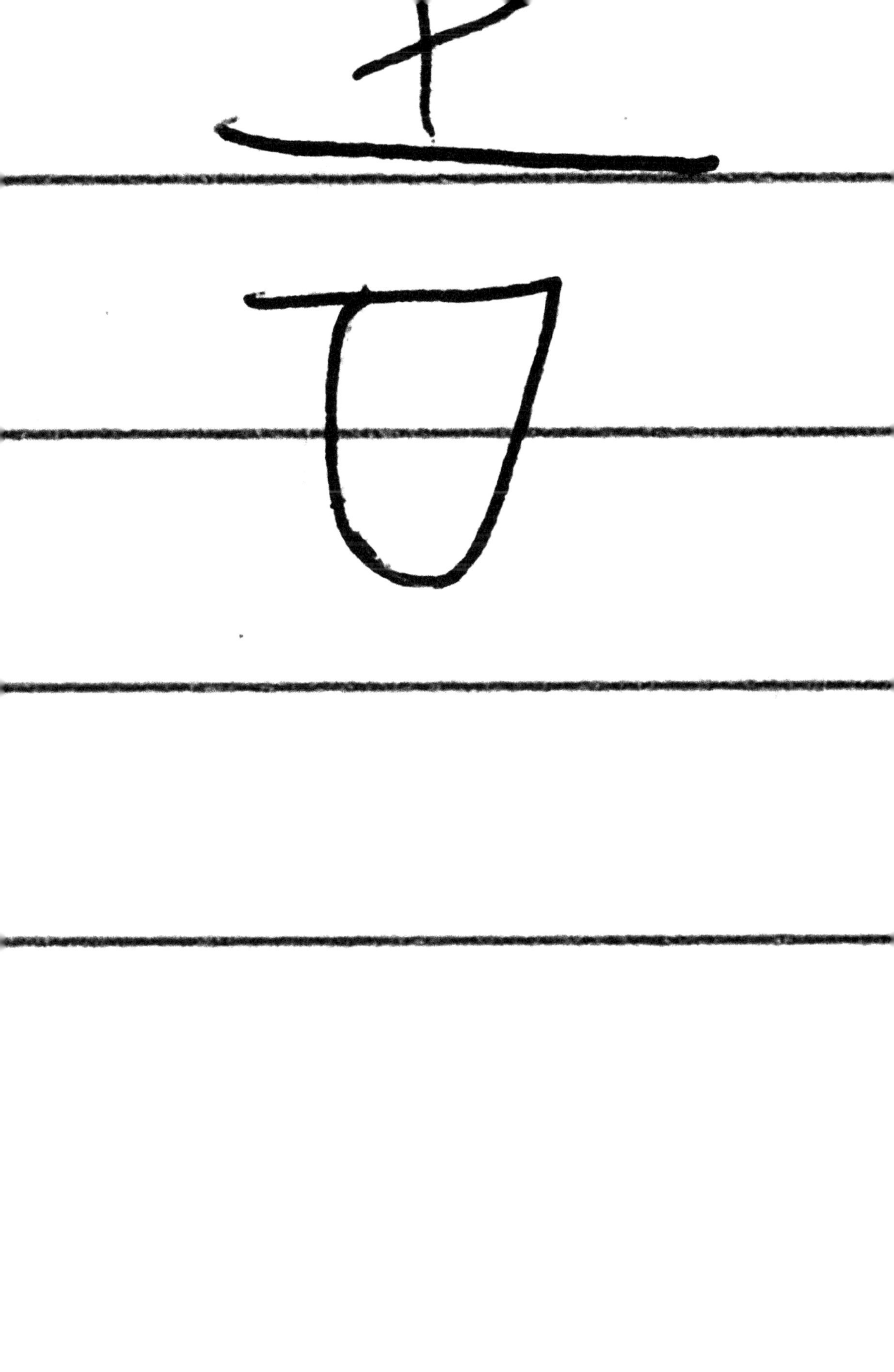

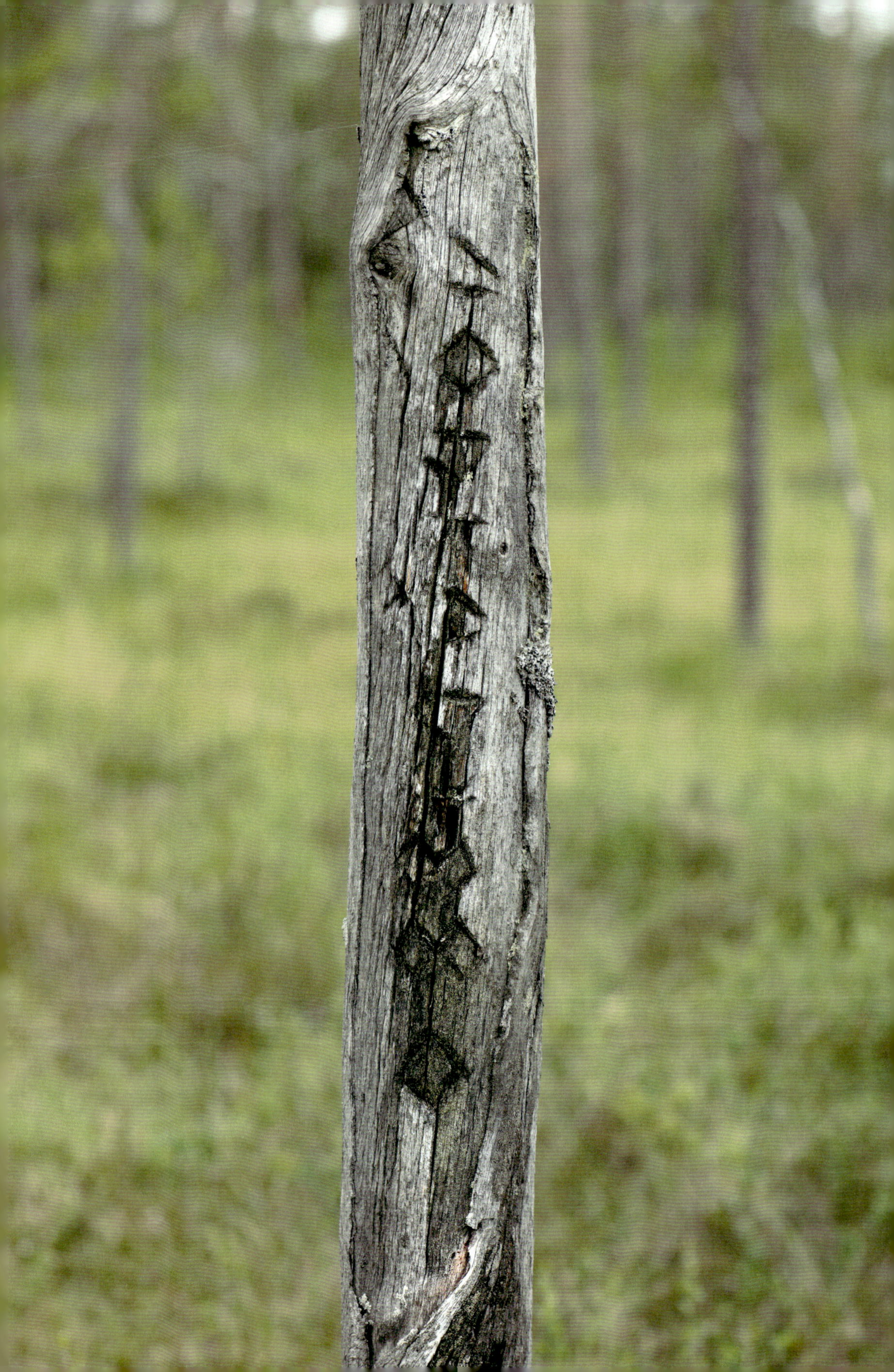

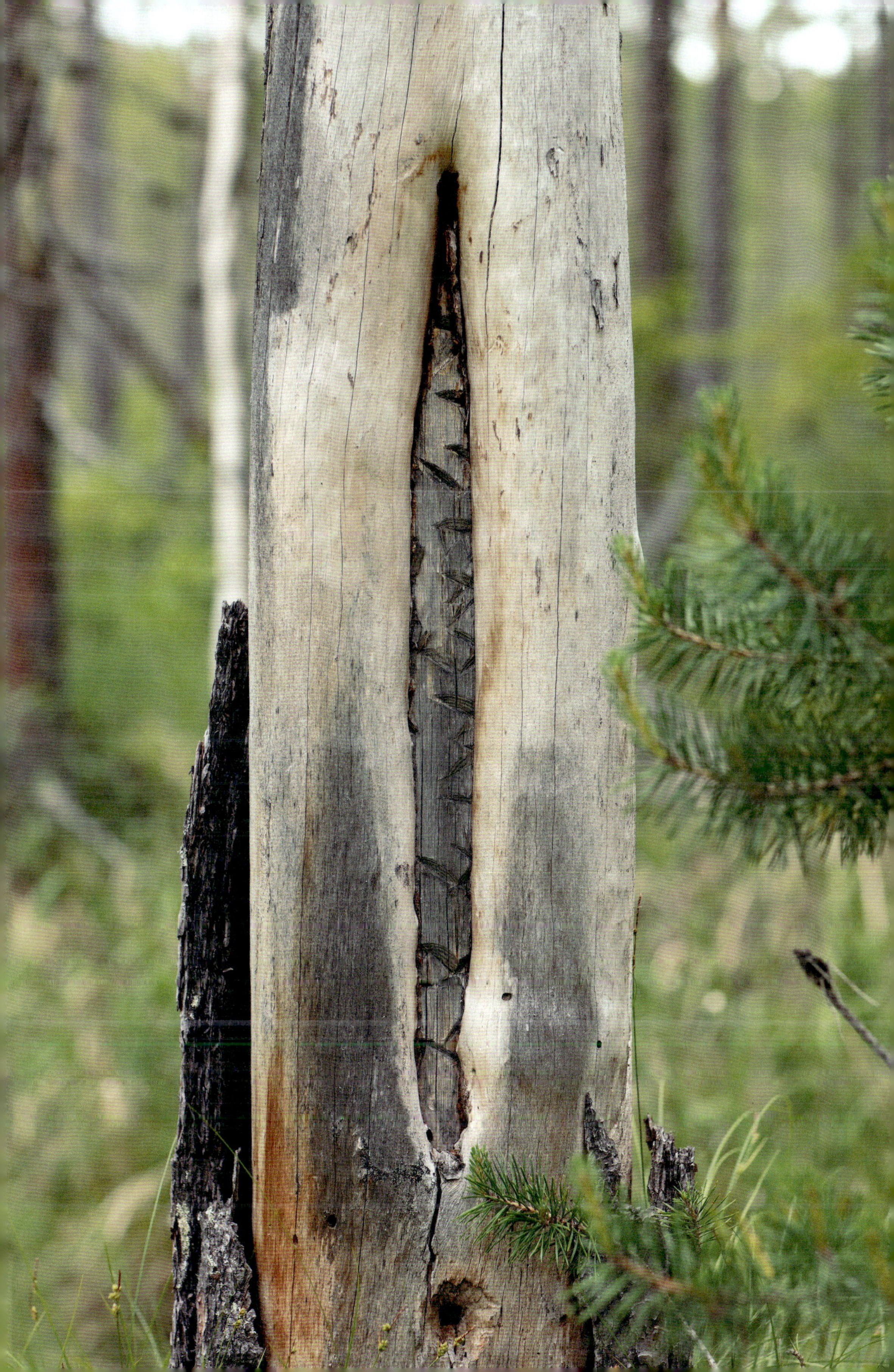

a cut–off thumb

counting time

putting a stick in a goat's mouth

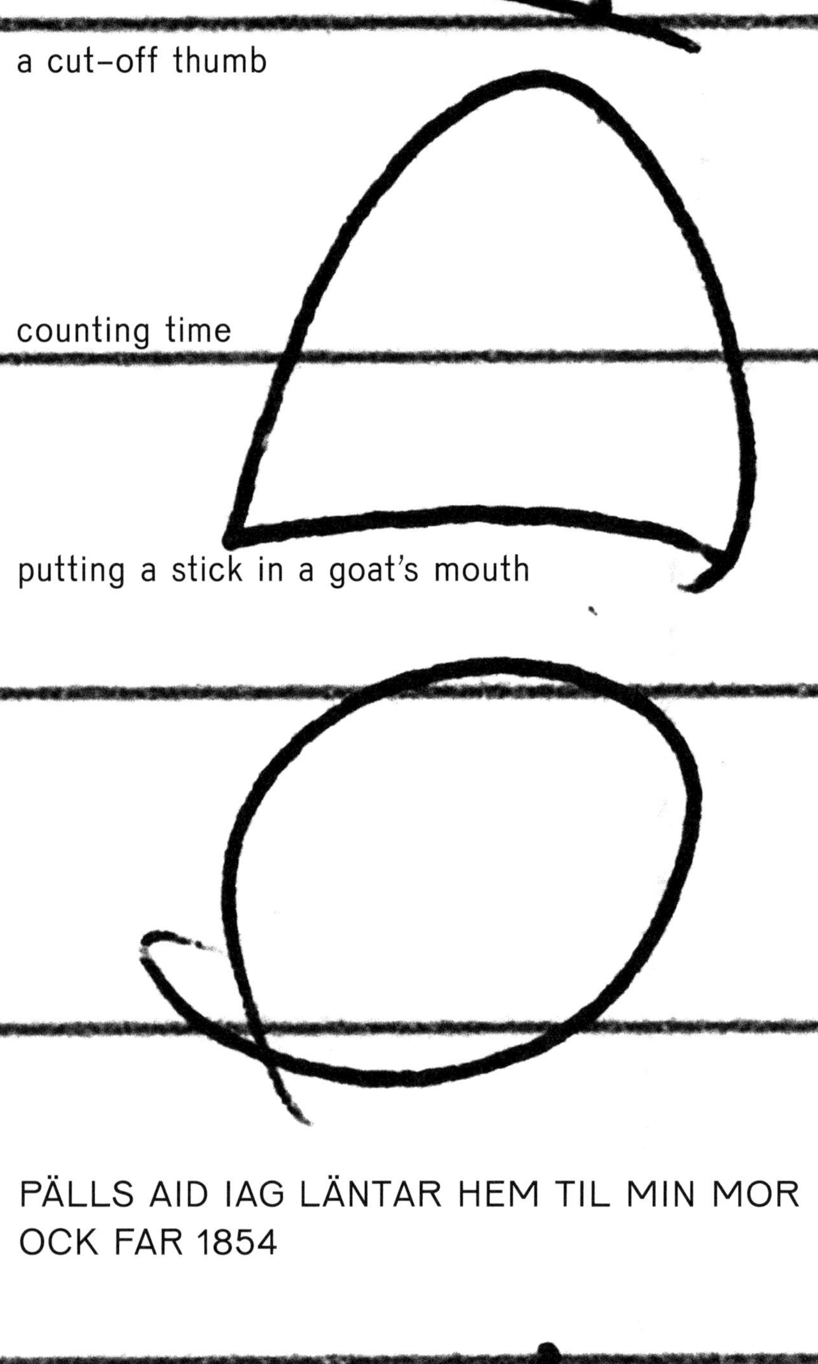

PÄLLS AID IAG LÄNTAR HEM TIL MIN MOR
OCK FAR 1854

SI A SED BPD ET   PAR   GO DA   KAMRATER WI MÅR
BRA TWÅ SOM ÄR BANKO DEM WIL OA SIG EN LITEN
STVND OM DAGGEN LIOT SKRIWA   1842

peeing in a bush and looking at a bird

kul, kih, geä

sole ä e öga
oppå nöd
går löche

one day   two days   three days   four hours

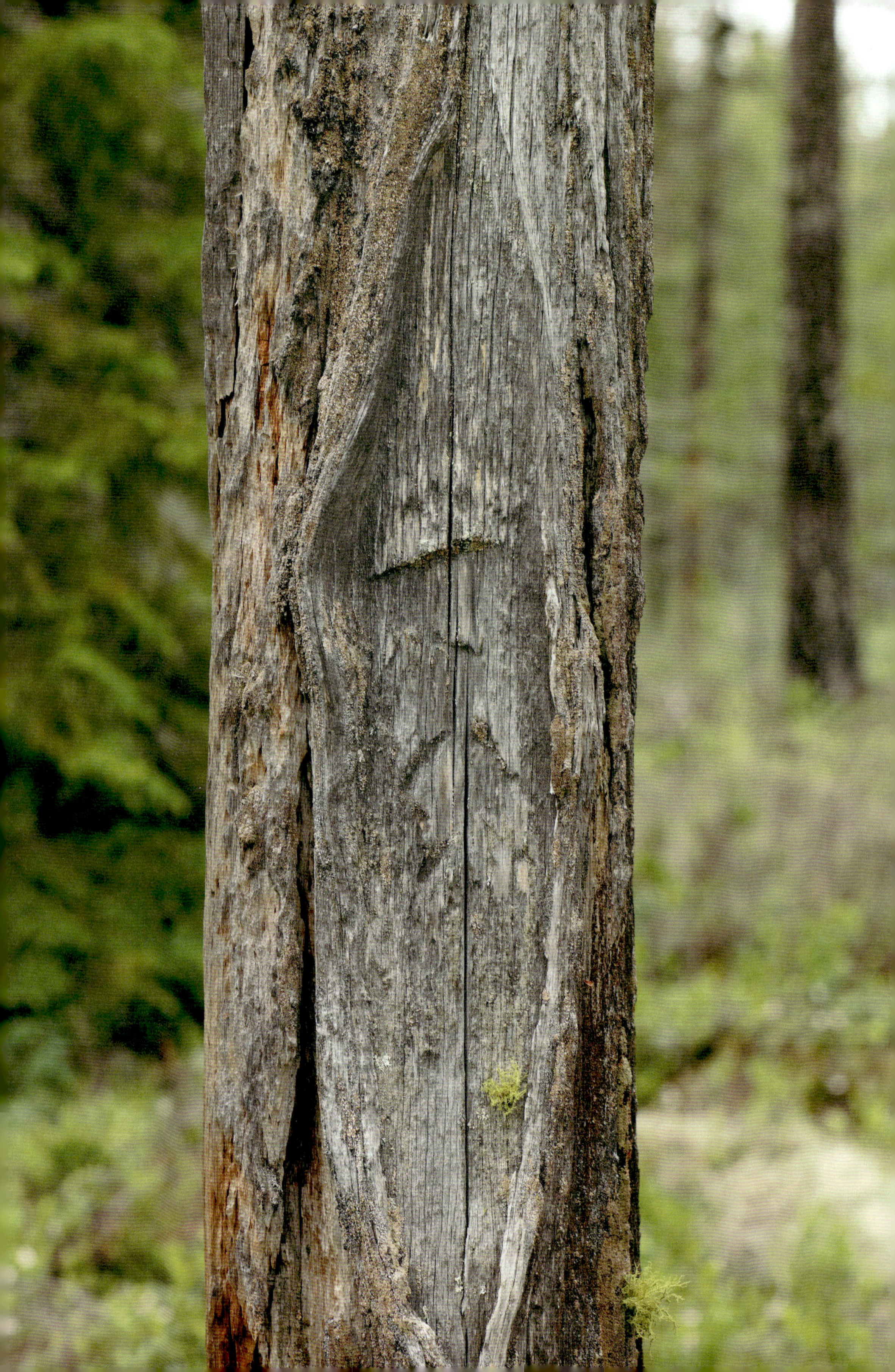

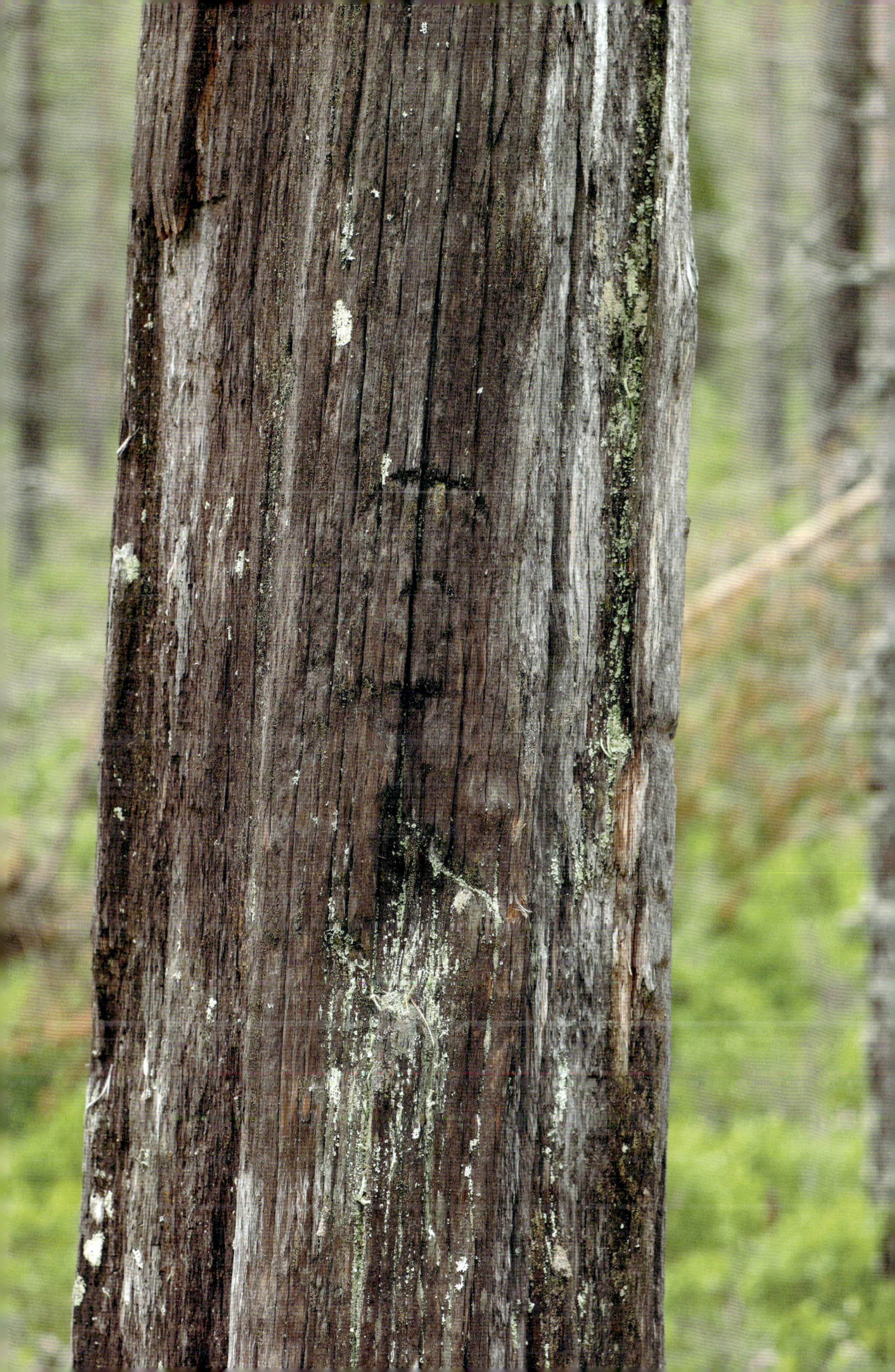

ta reda på allt

MAGGVS AAD DAHLFORS·AHD XXX 1883 BRA
DET ÄR EJ ROLIGT   AT HEP WA A ÄLSKA EN WÄN
SOM MAN ALDRIG KAN FÅ MEN   BRA ÄNDÅ

stone knocking against iron·

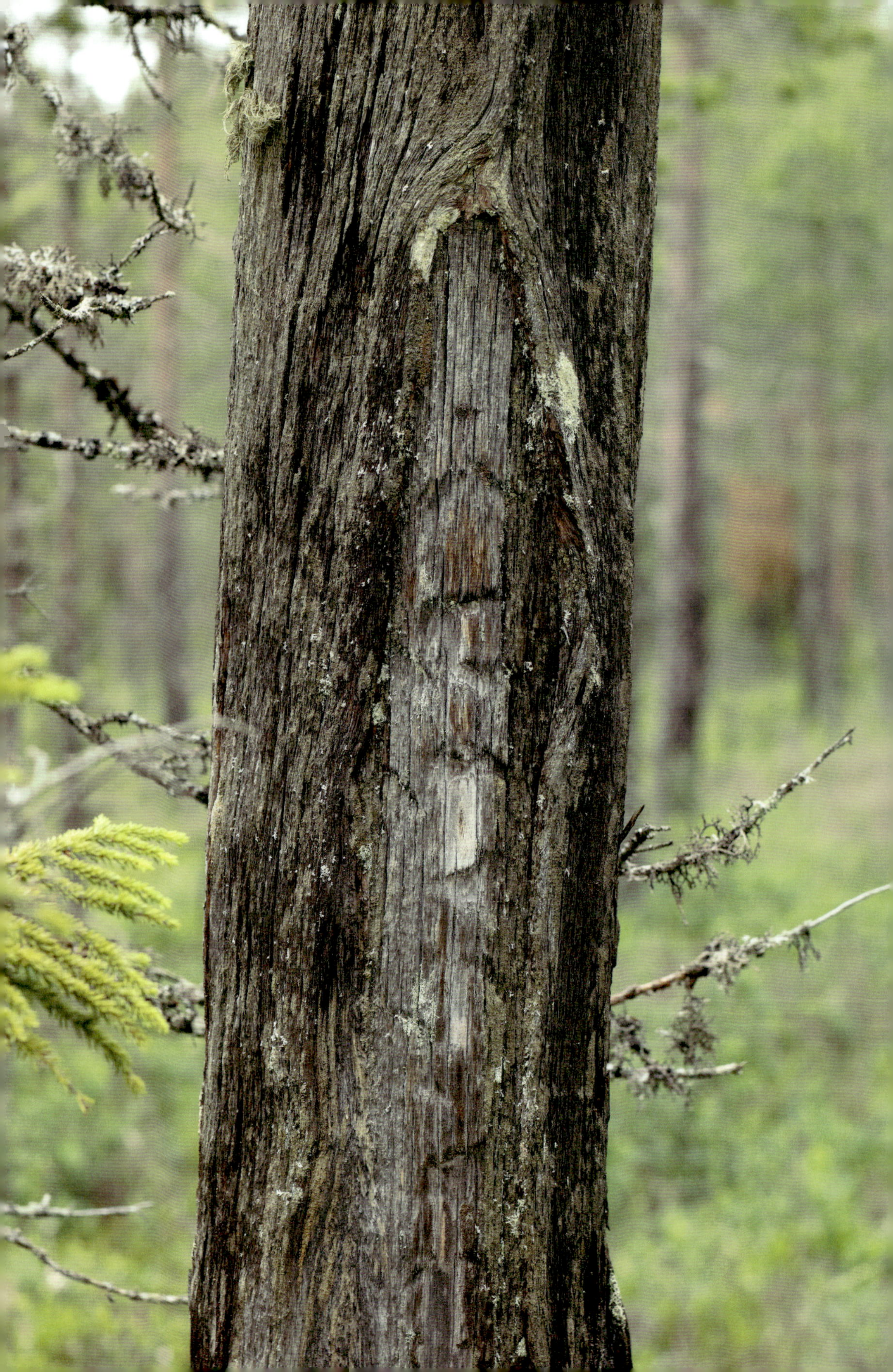

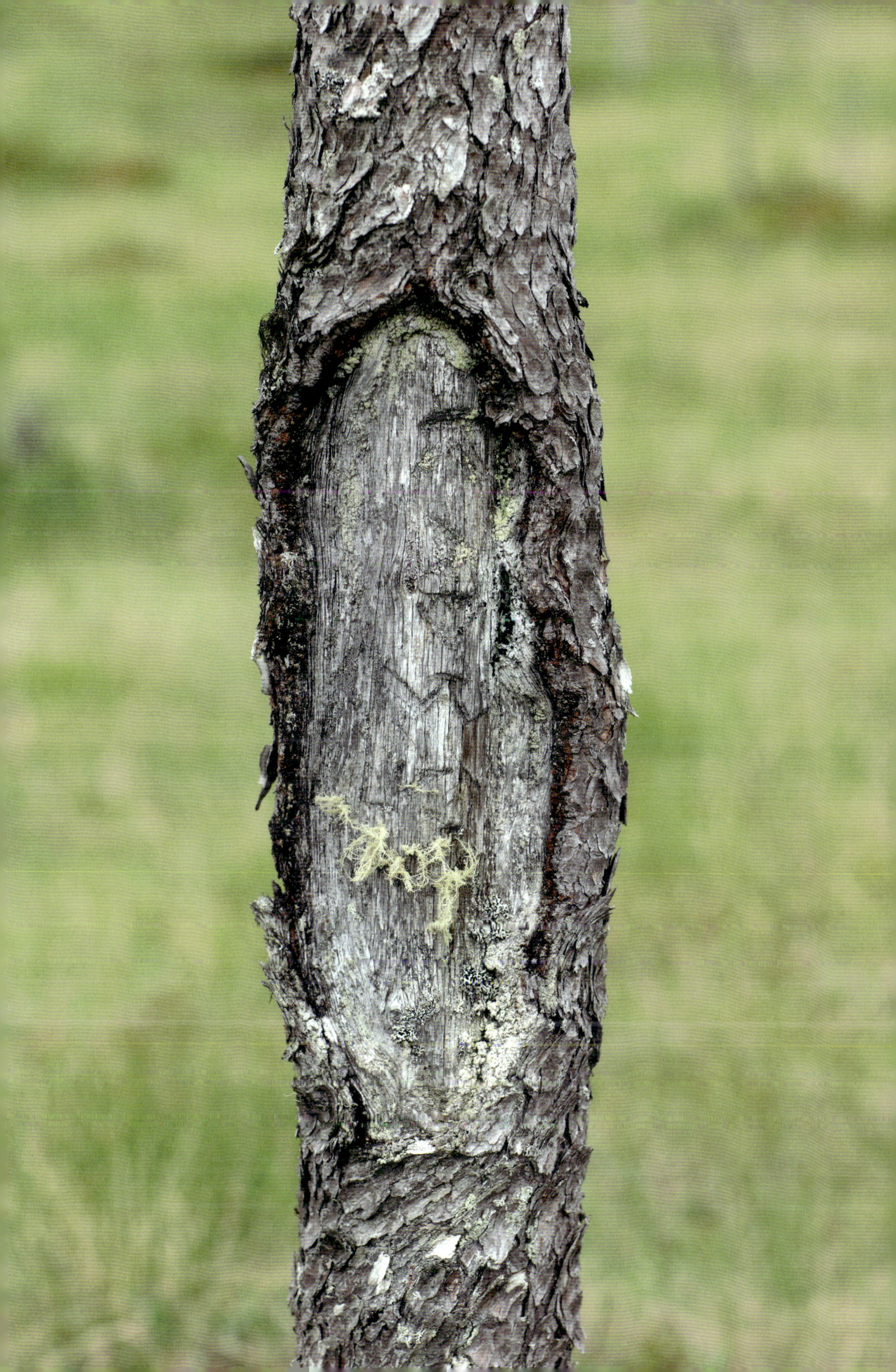

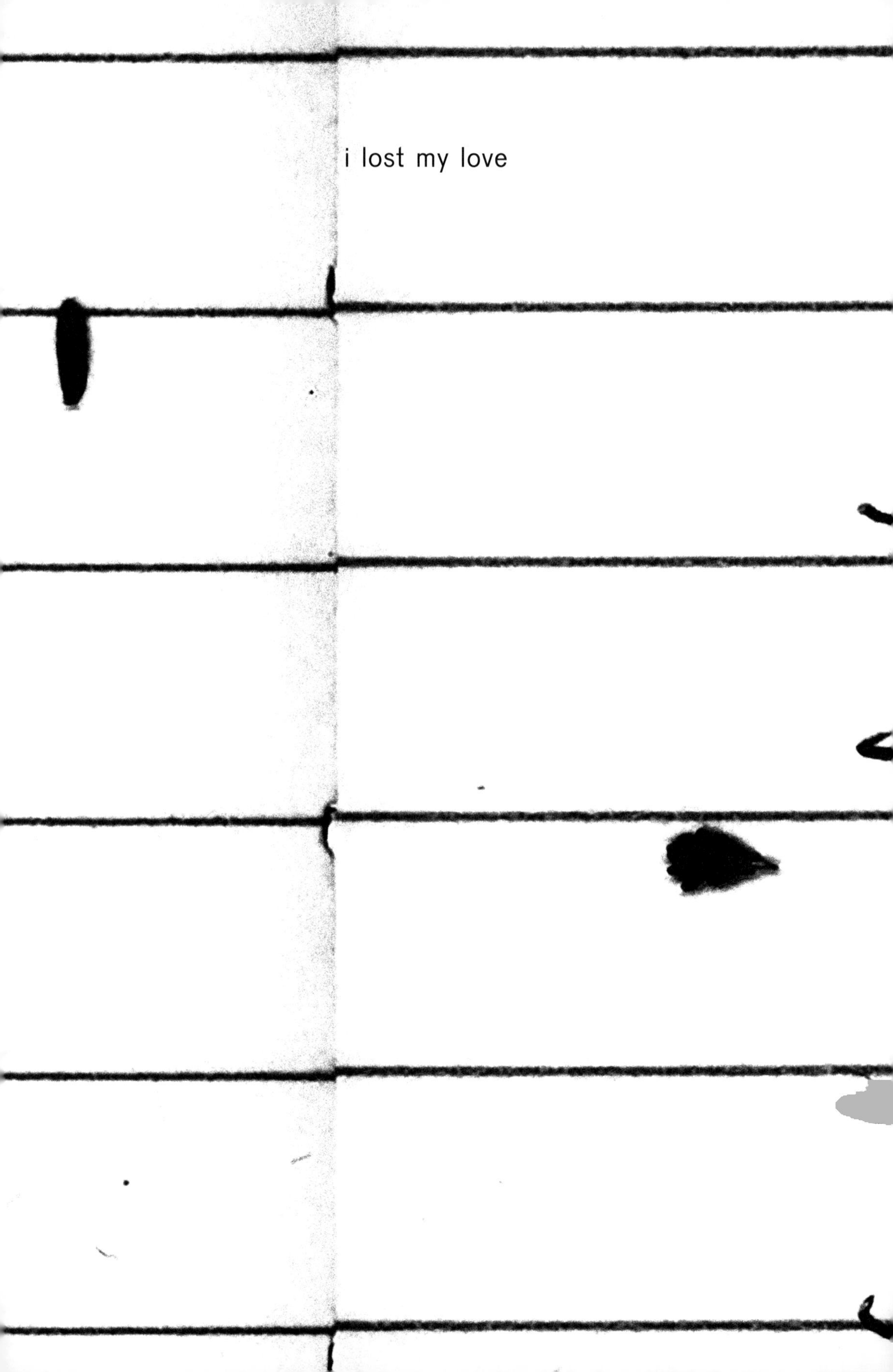
i lost my love

X (x3)
I (x6)
A (x19)
E (x10)
D (x20)
B (x5)
O (x2)
L
K (x2)
S (x3)
R
H
Ö
X (x3)

ka ärä for stjöllna

ljug o allt sant

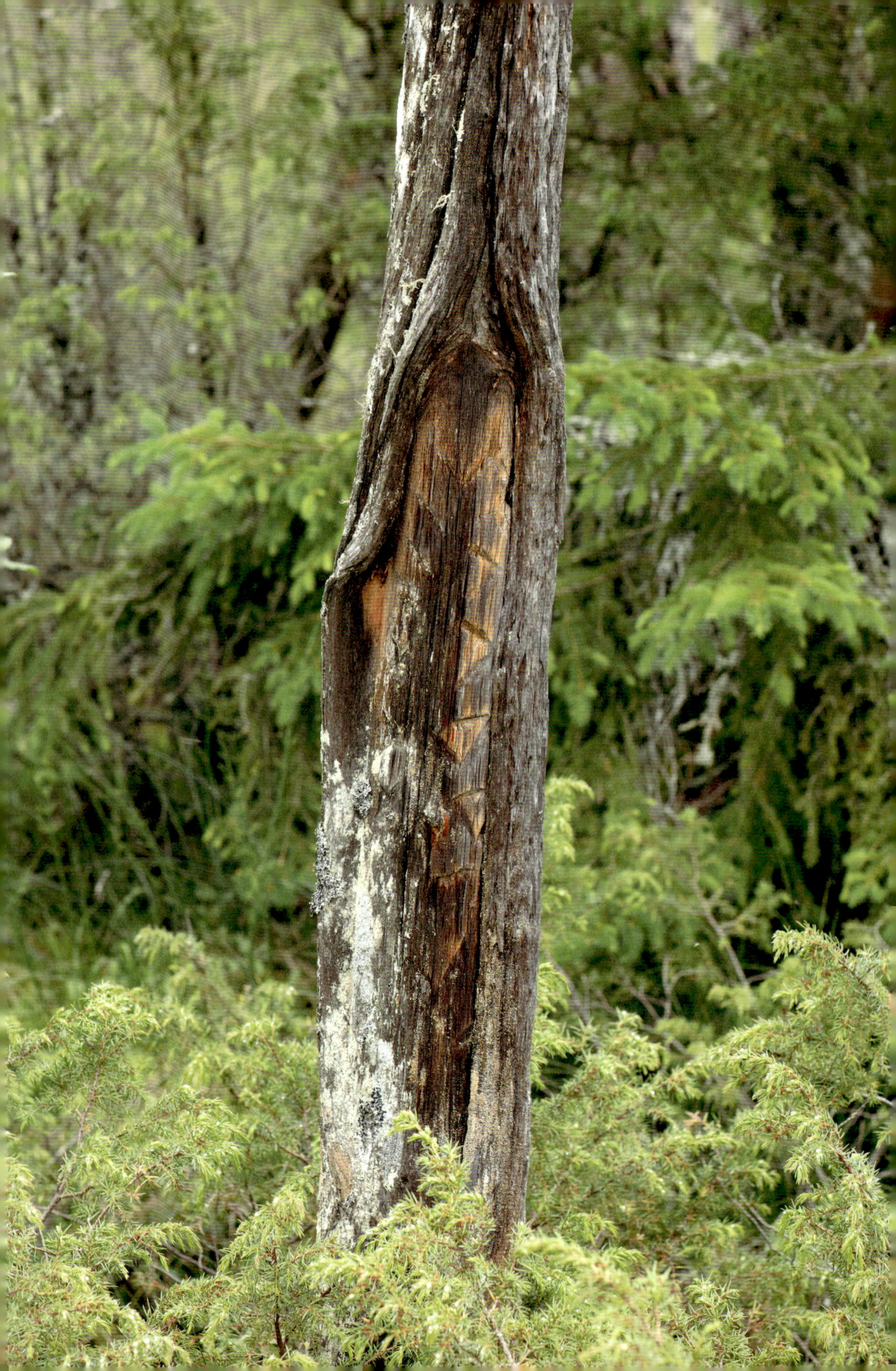

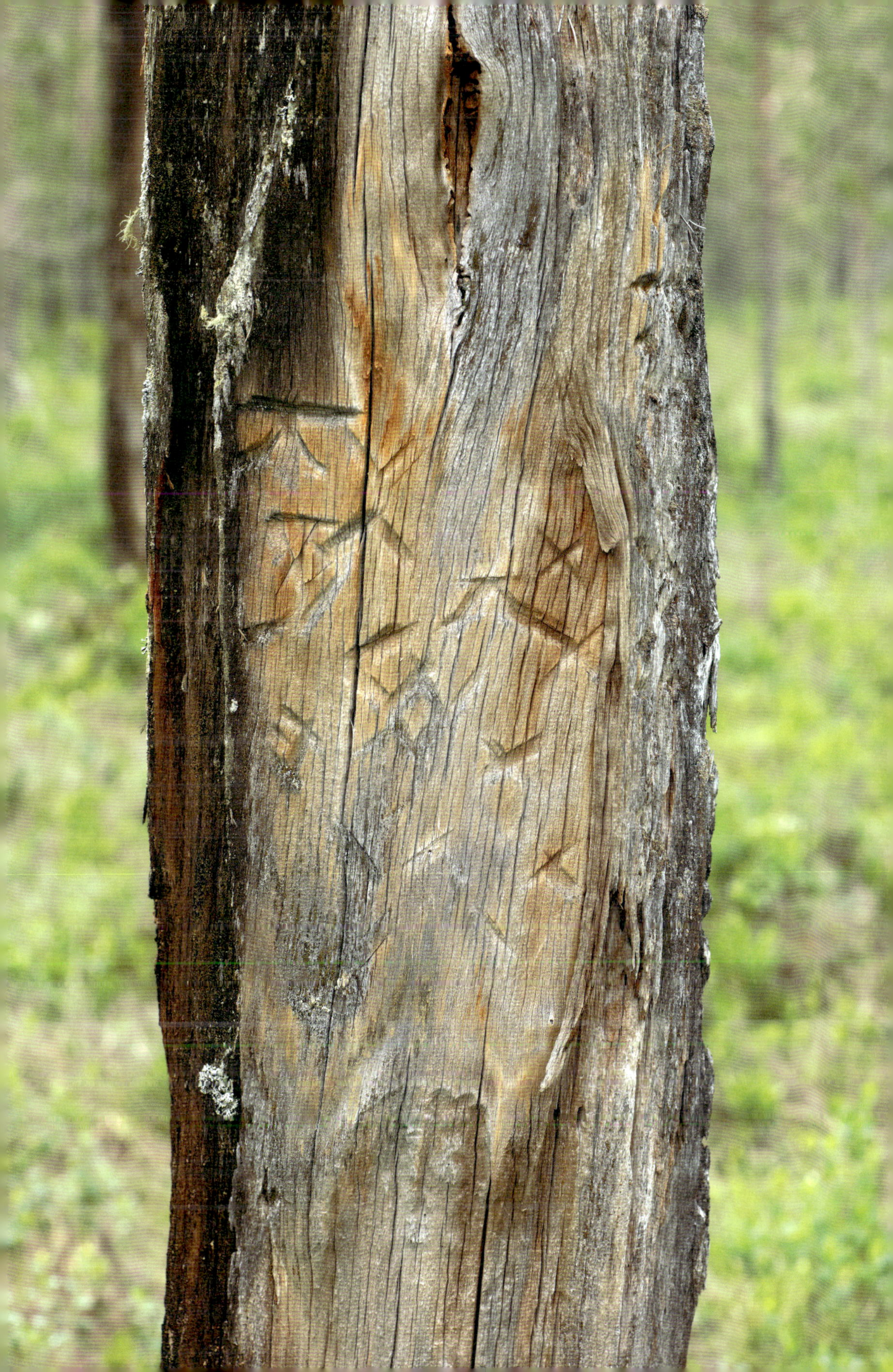

the trees are bright   without the lush green that usually surrounds
them, their trunks look bare

we have brought a lunch box but can't stay in the forest for long
because the cold is getting to us

i try to make a cast of a tree but the silicon won't harden
it is too cold

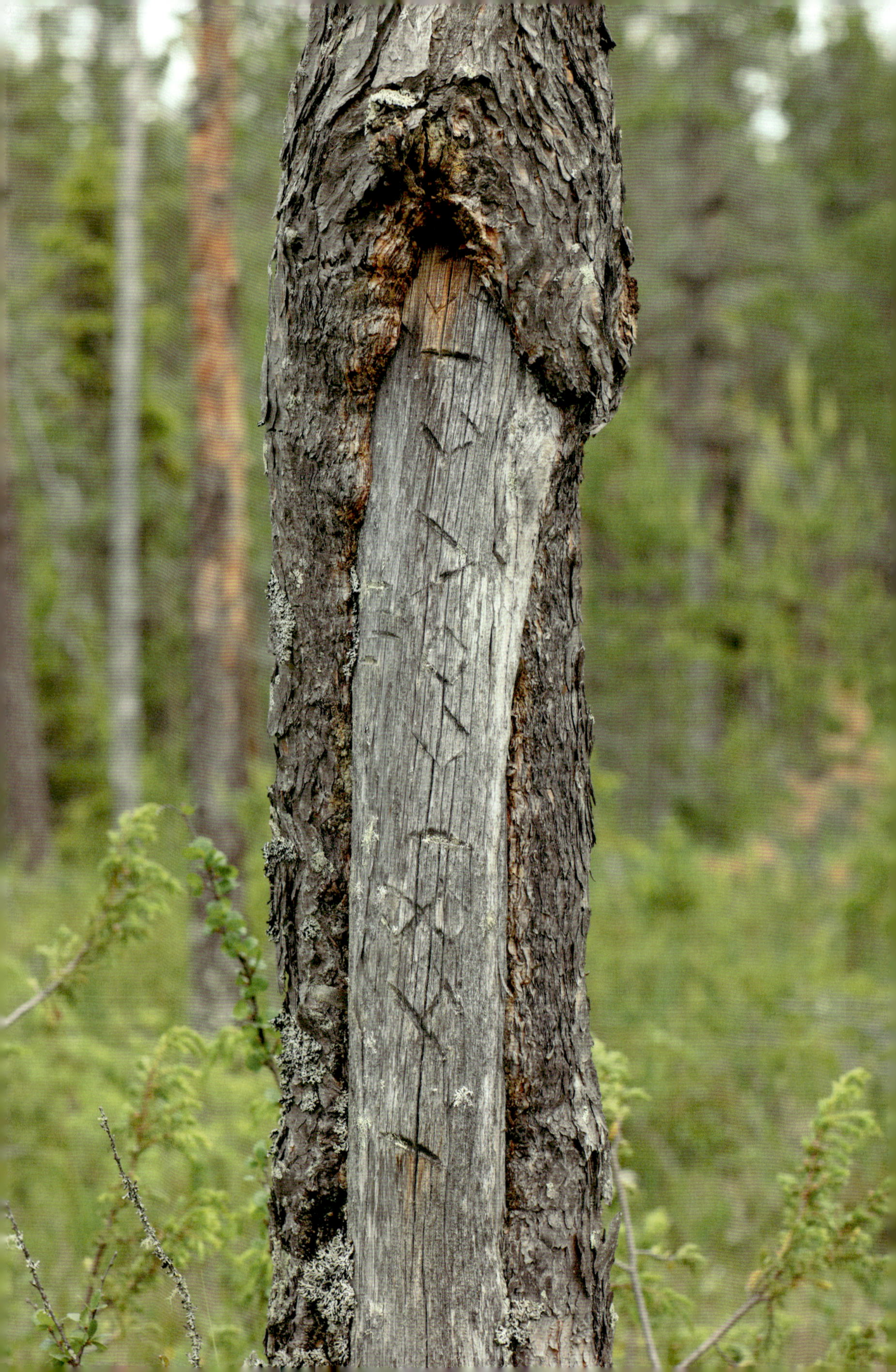

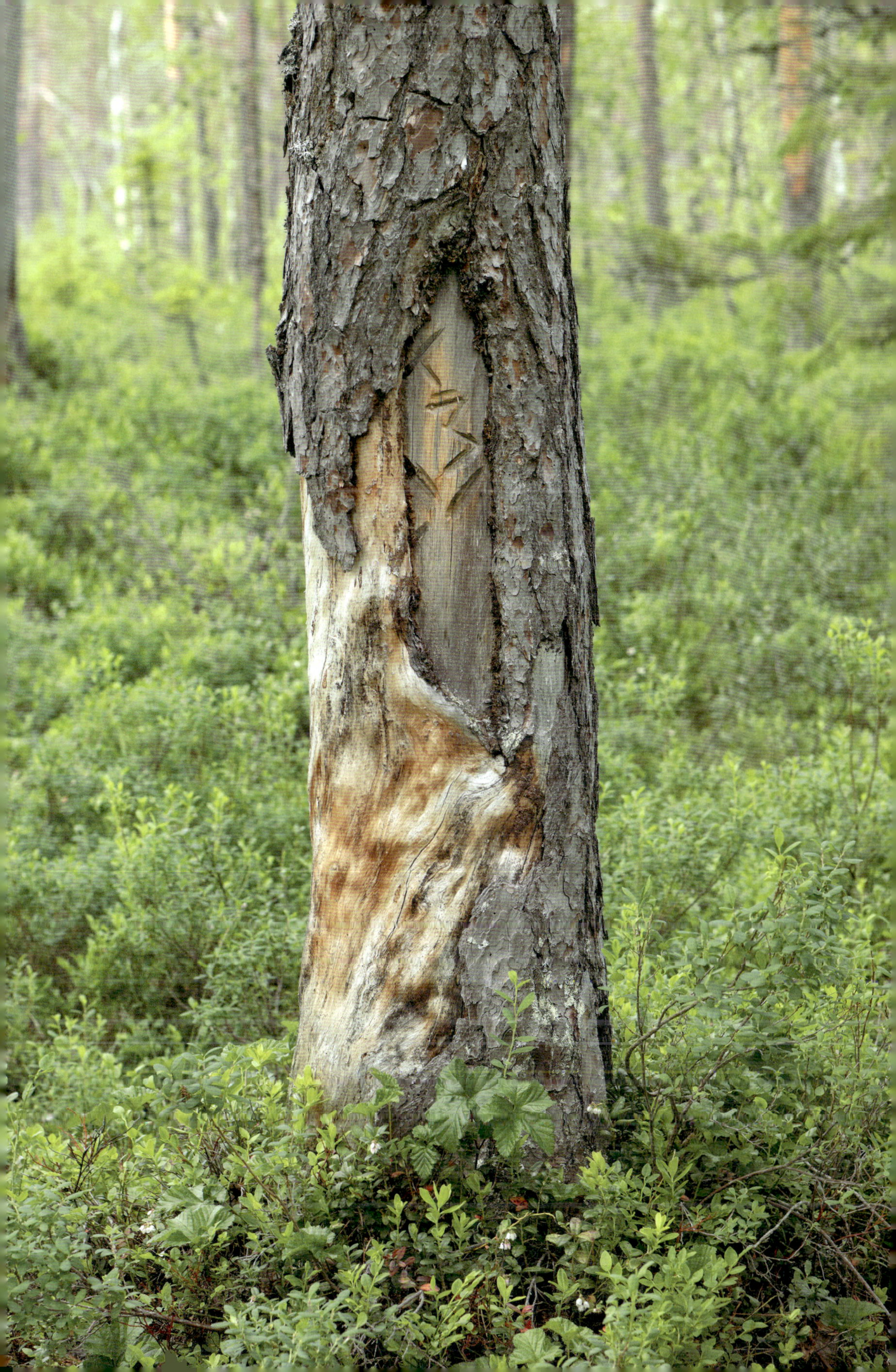

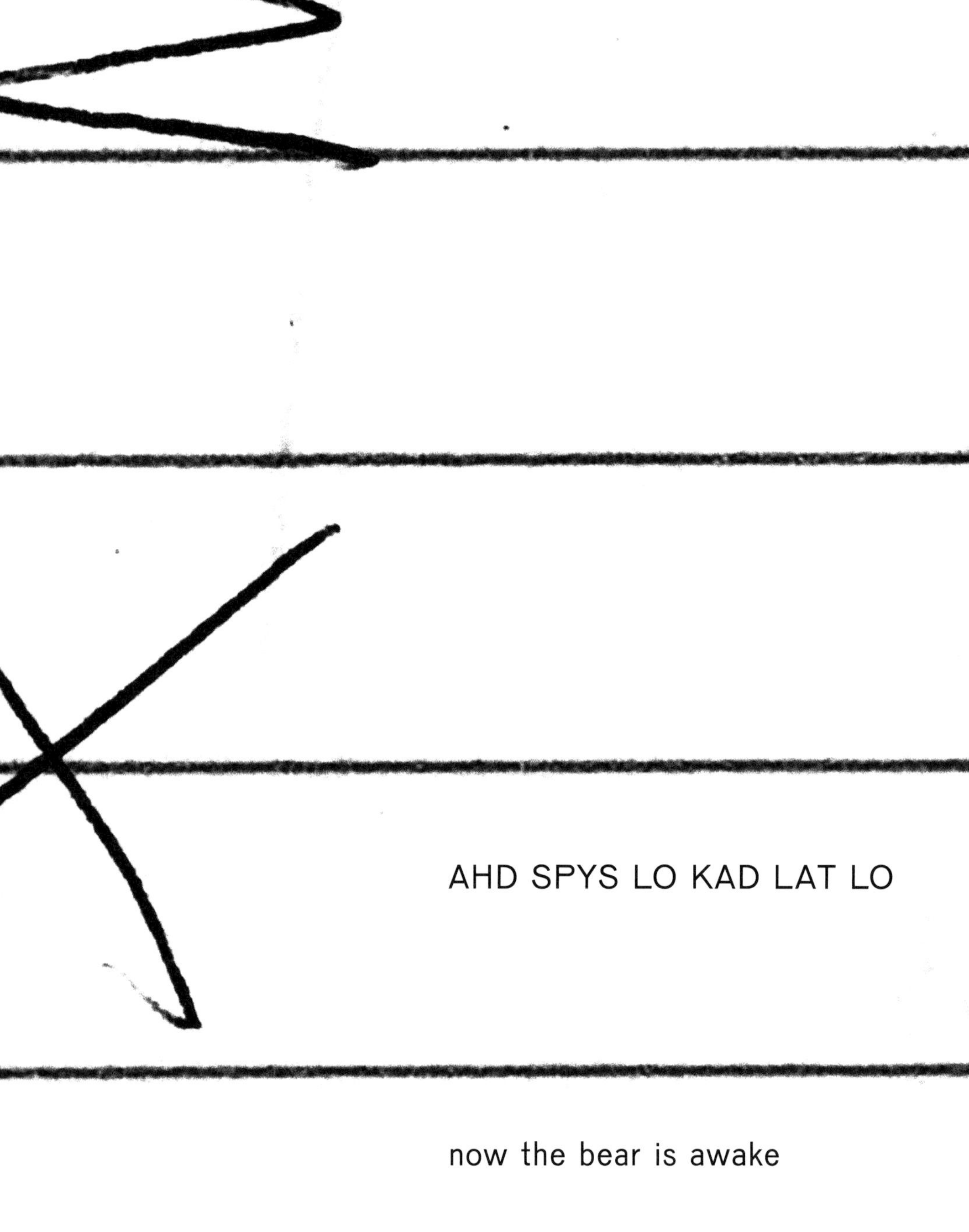

AHD SPYS LO KAD LAT LO

now the bear is awake

i write my name with joy

AED 1844

she puts the milk vessel in the river to make it swell
and become tight

kön bir je

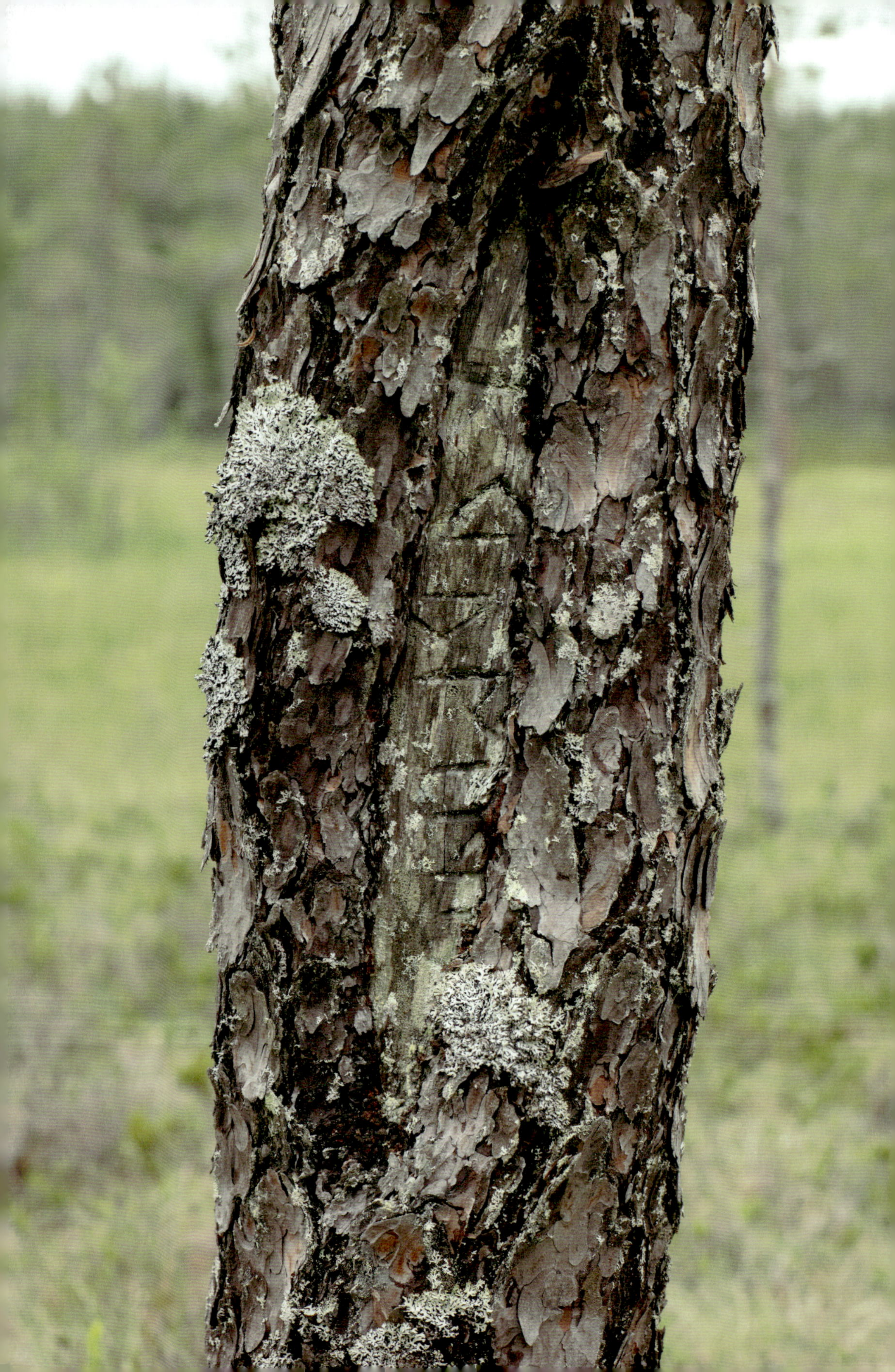

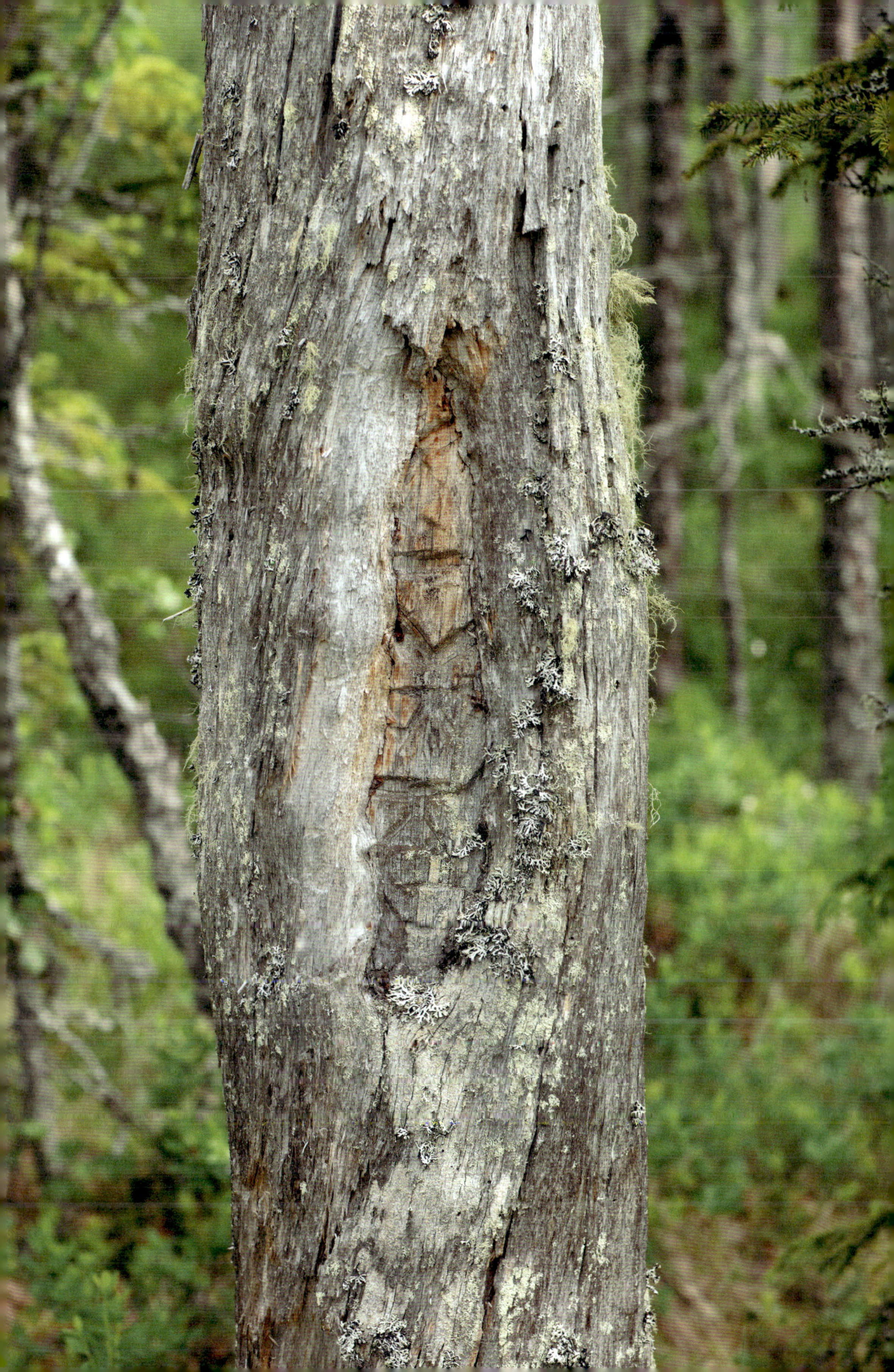

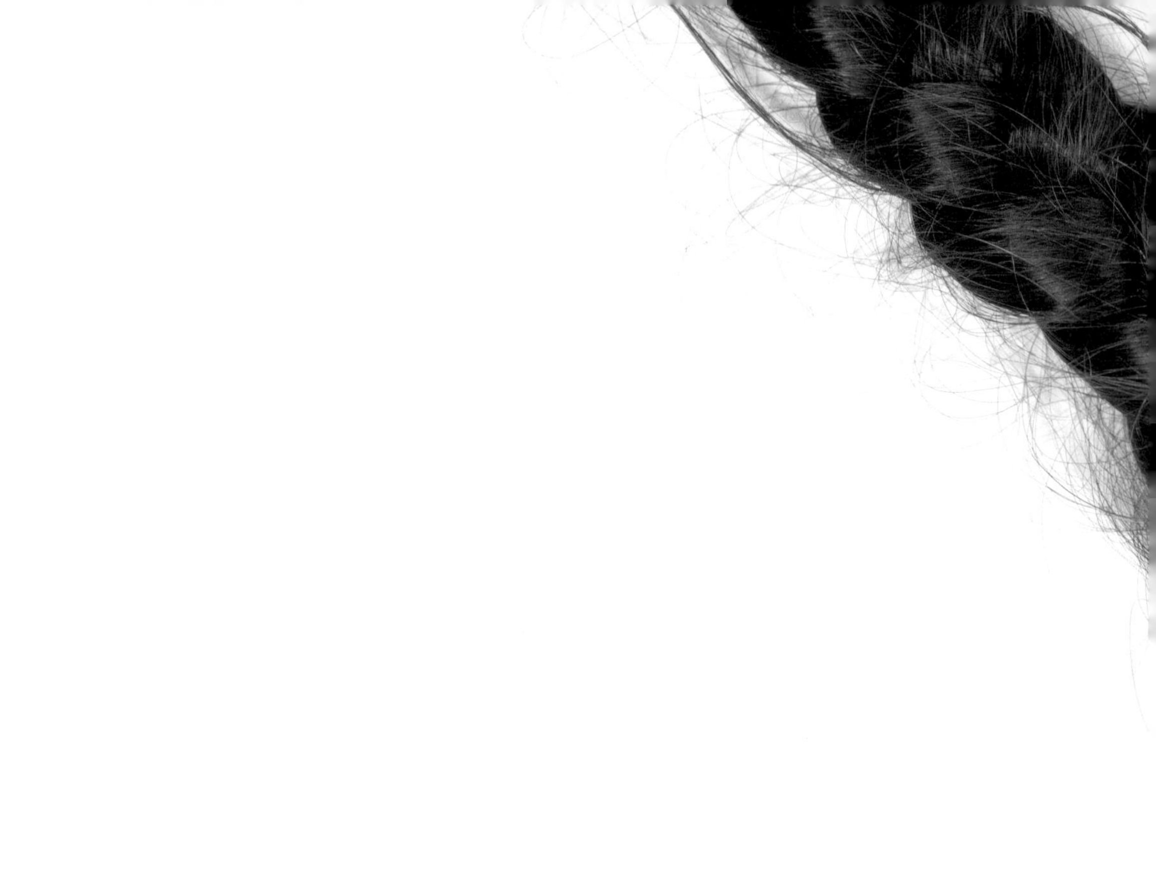

late july

the cloudberry has ripened   we take long breaks in the woods
we spread out, i sit and write, we eat eggs
laslo suns himself in the glade

i am thinking that the bear's cubs are small now

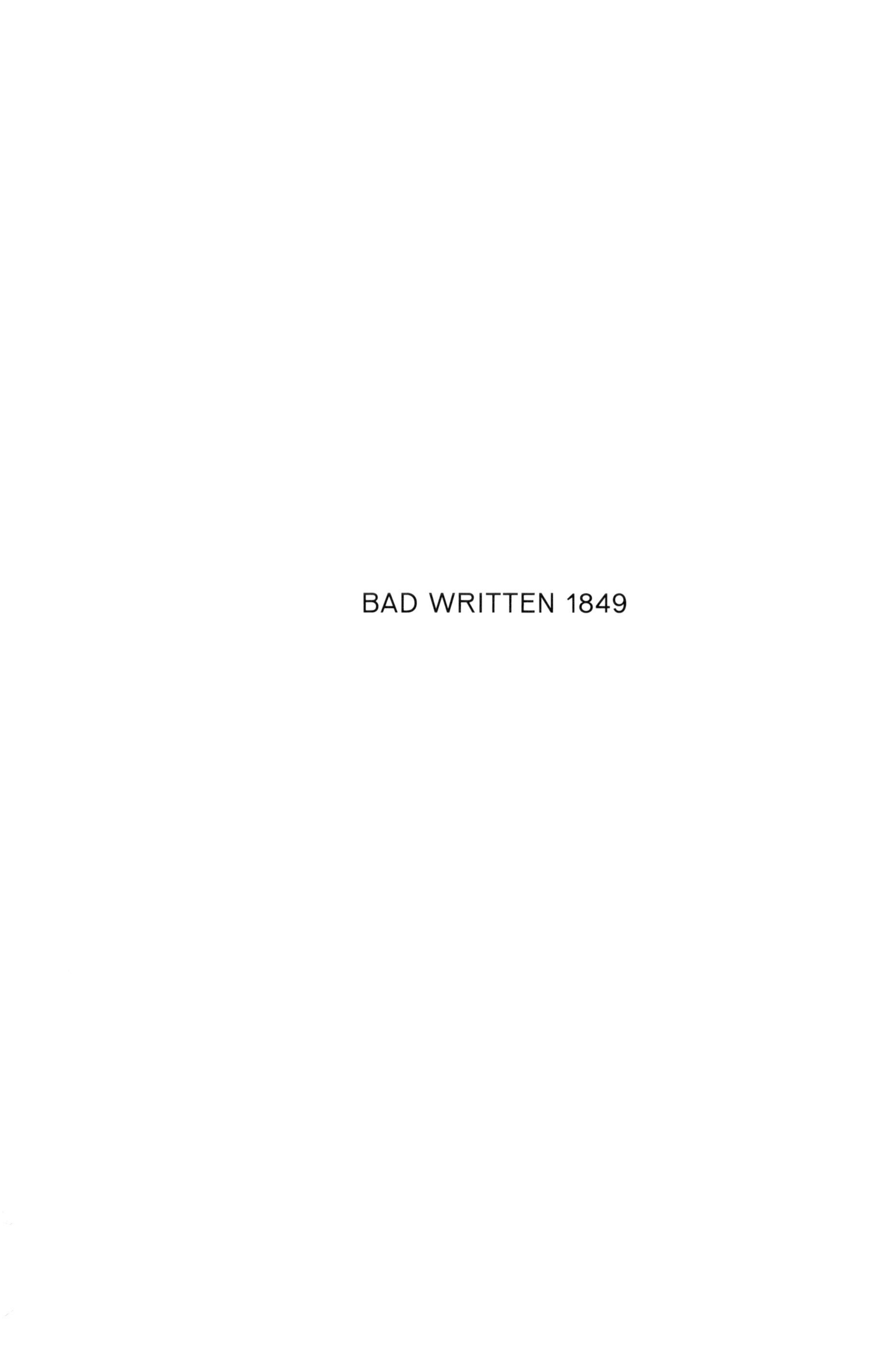
BAD WRITTEN 1849

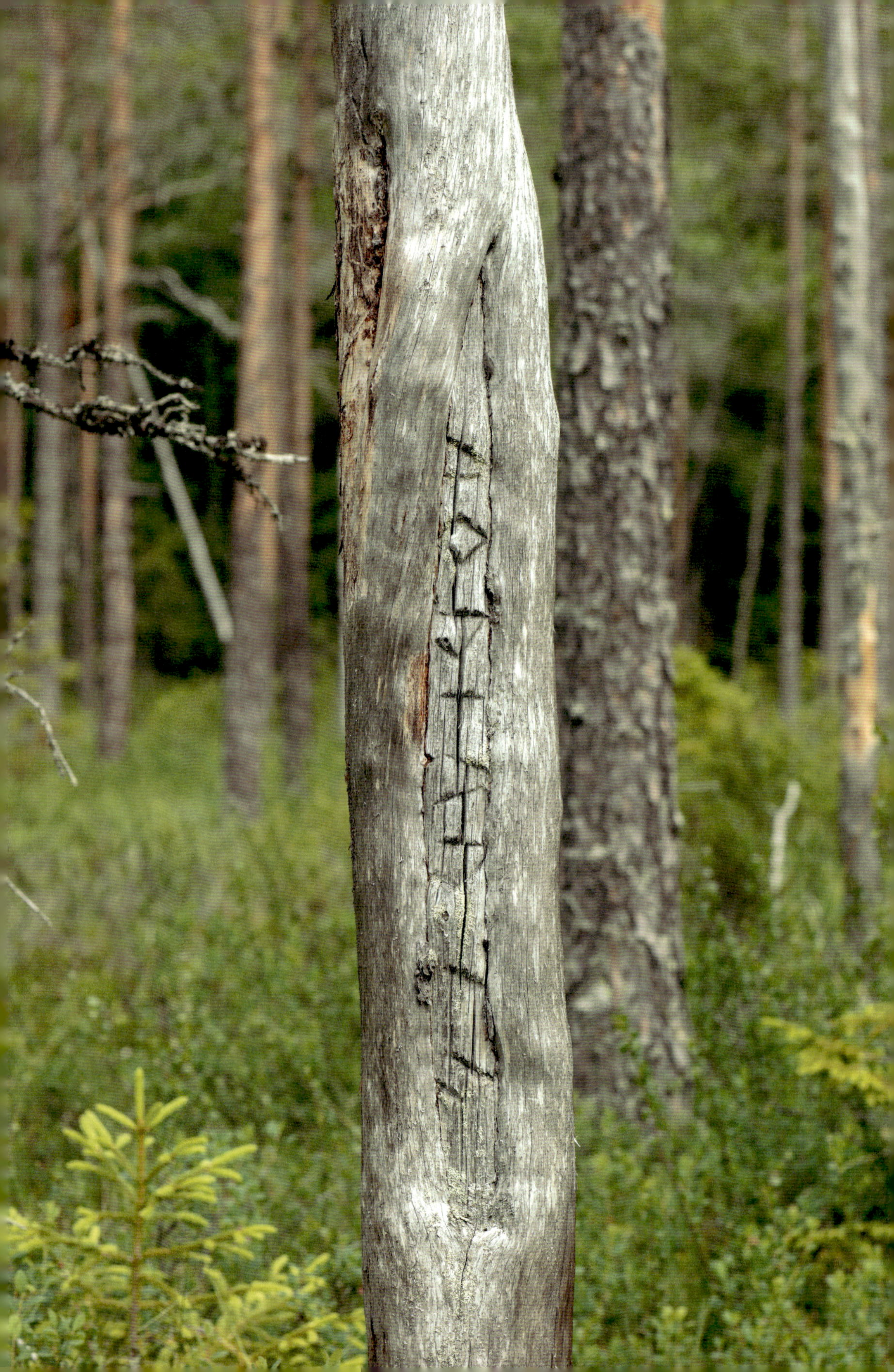

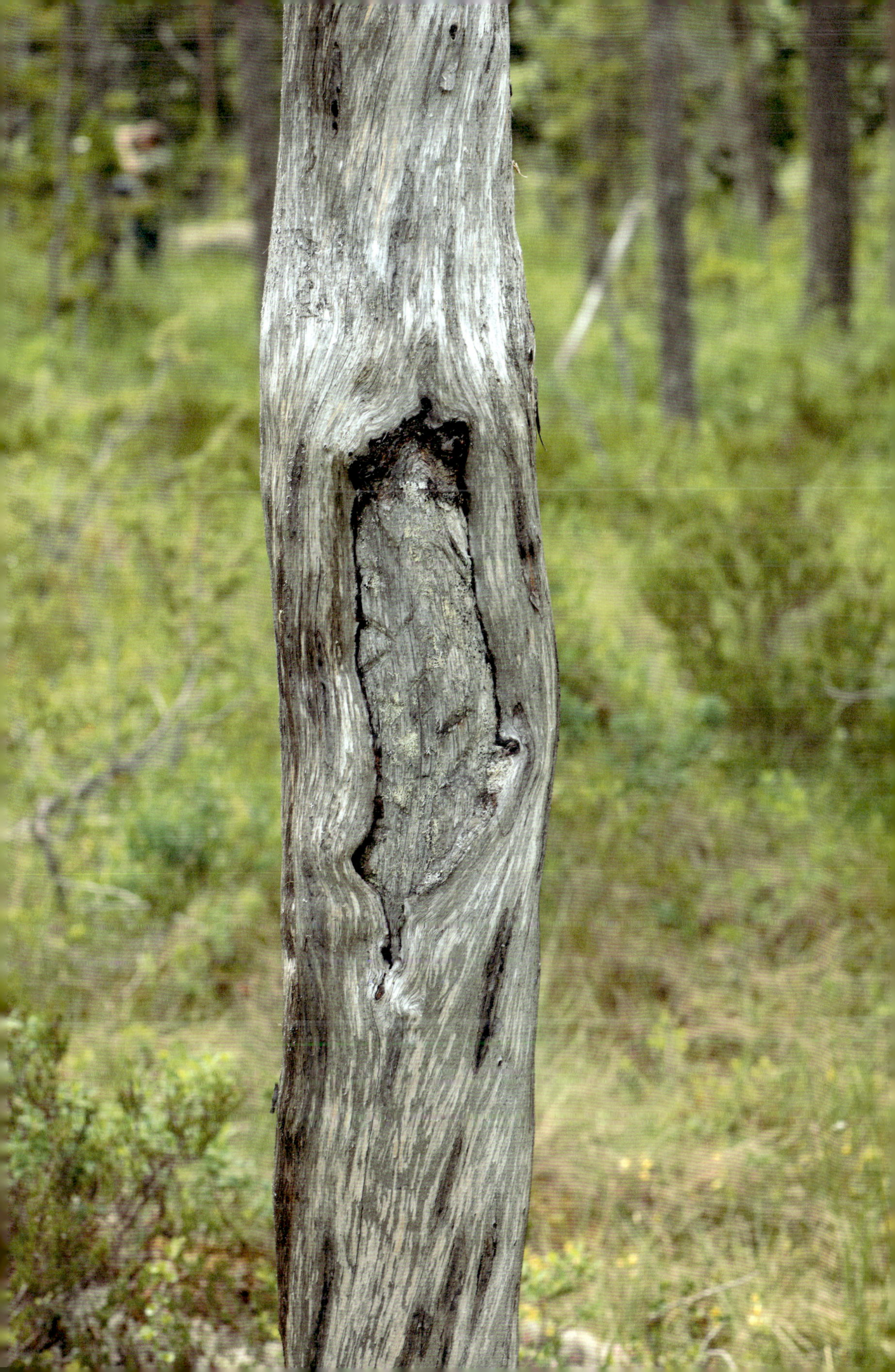

hi, how are you?

i'm good

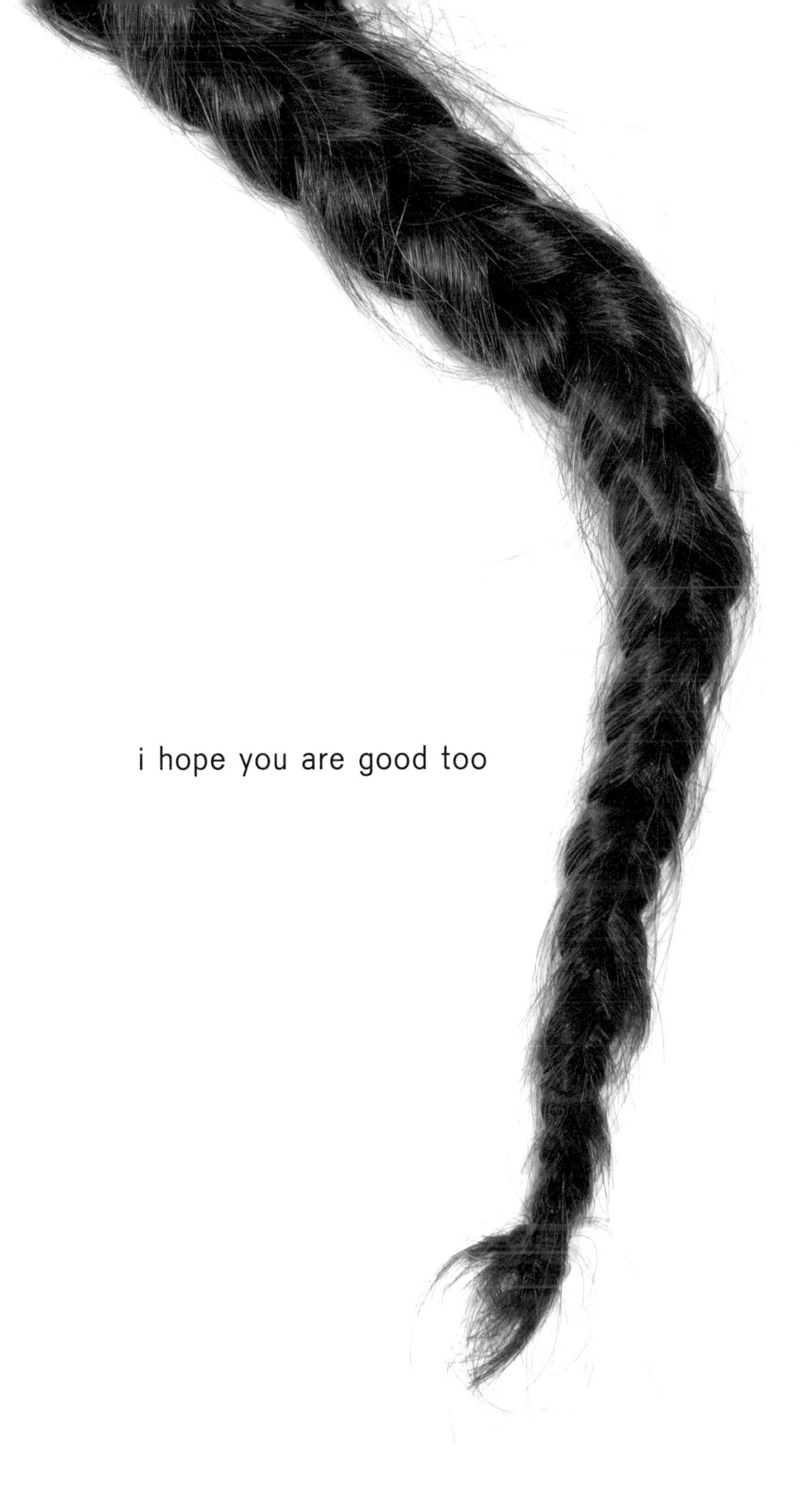
i hope you are good too

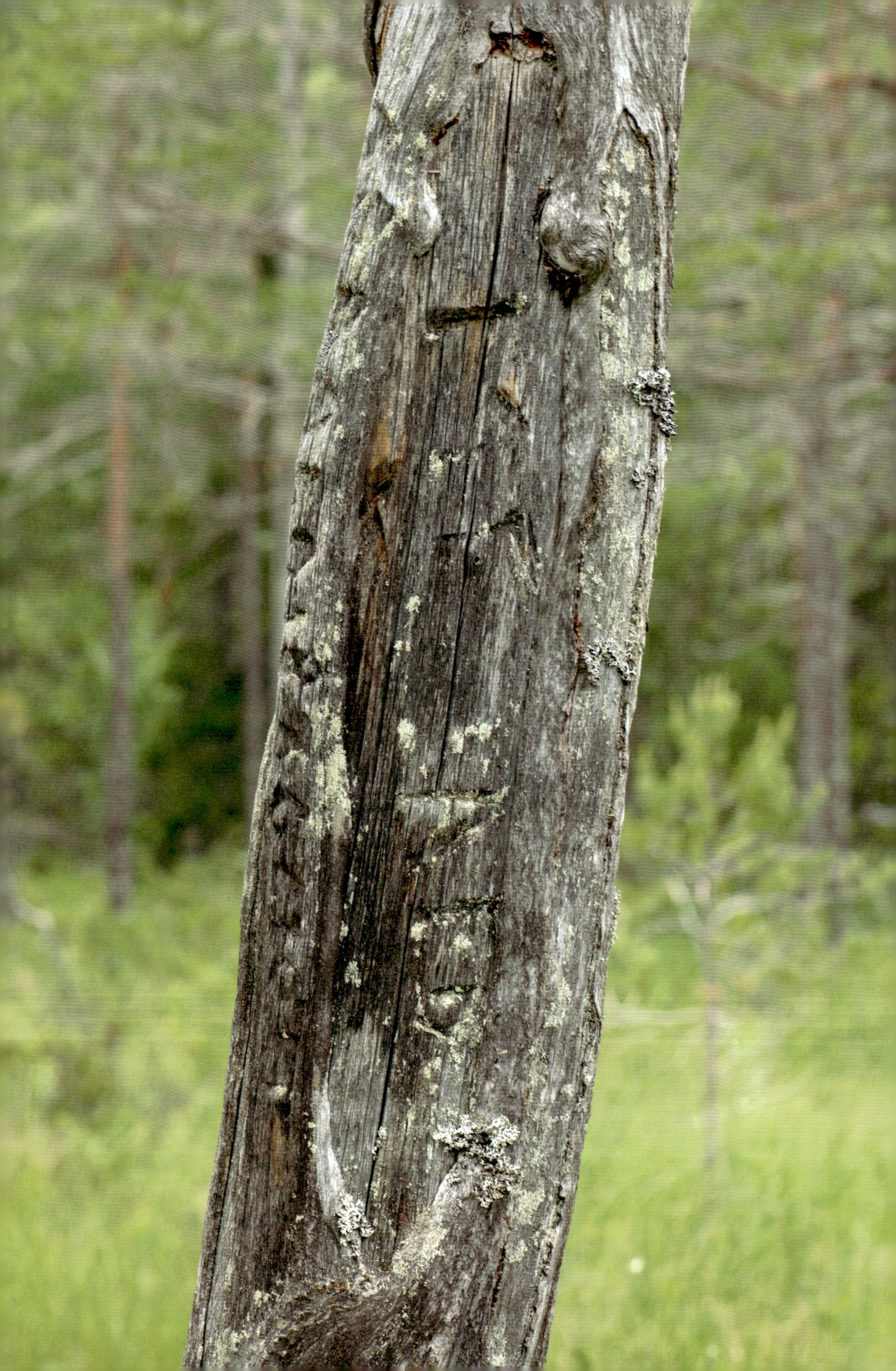

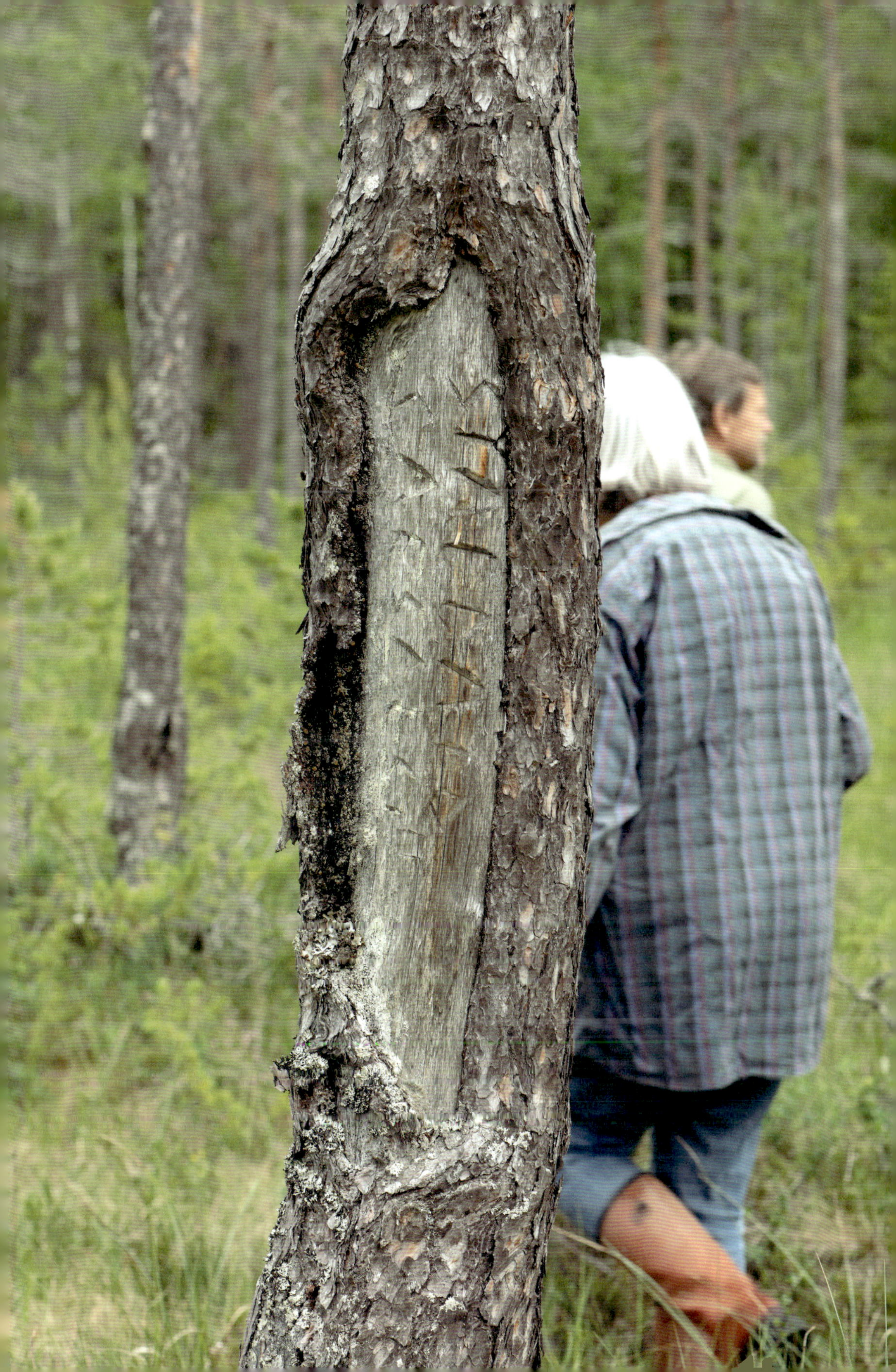

SOM EN SATÄ
GUD FÖRLÅT MIN SYND

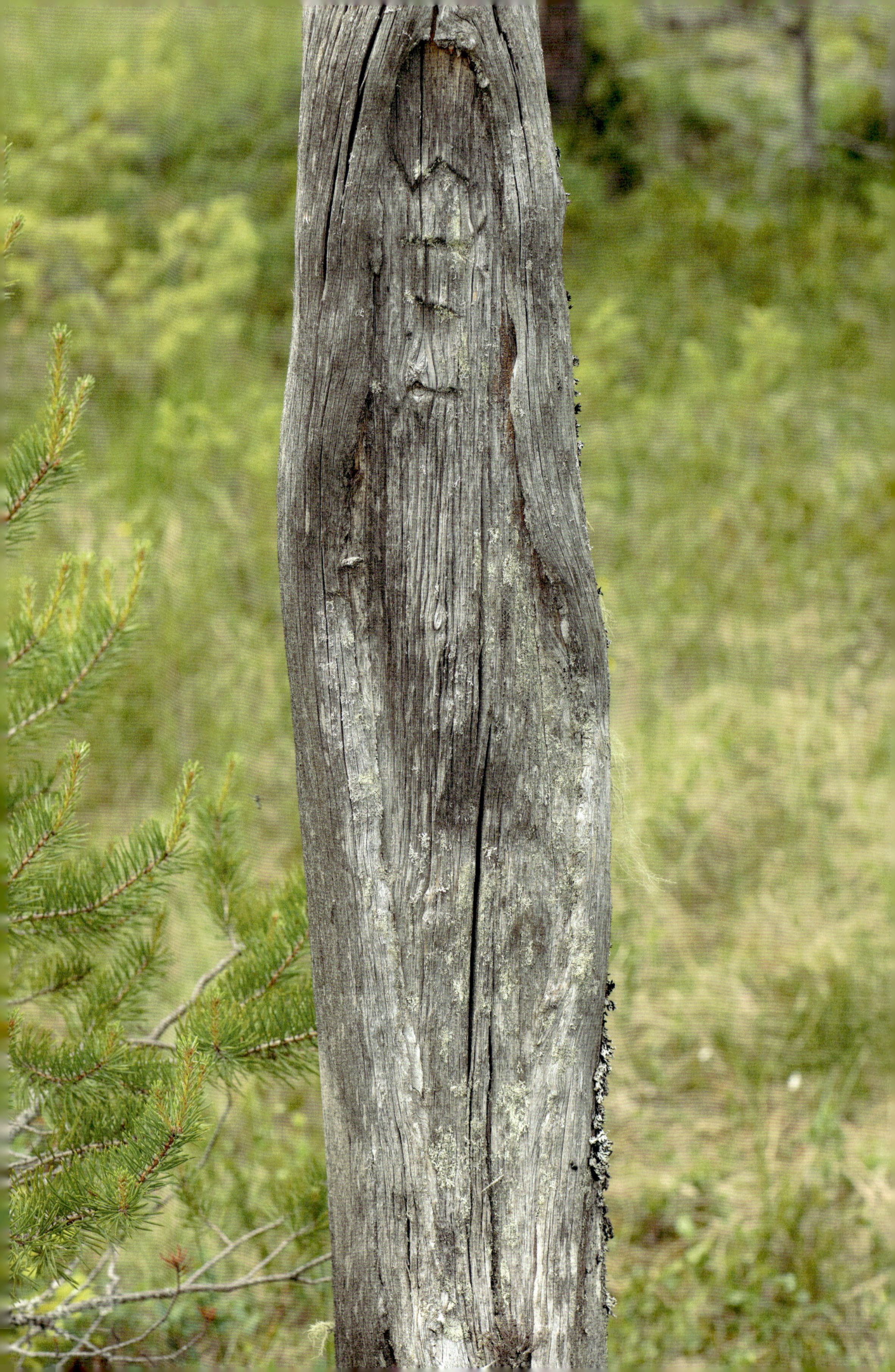

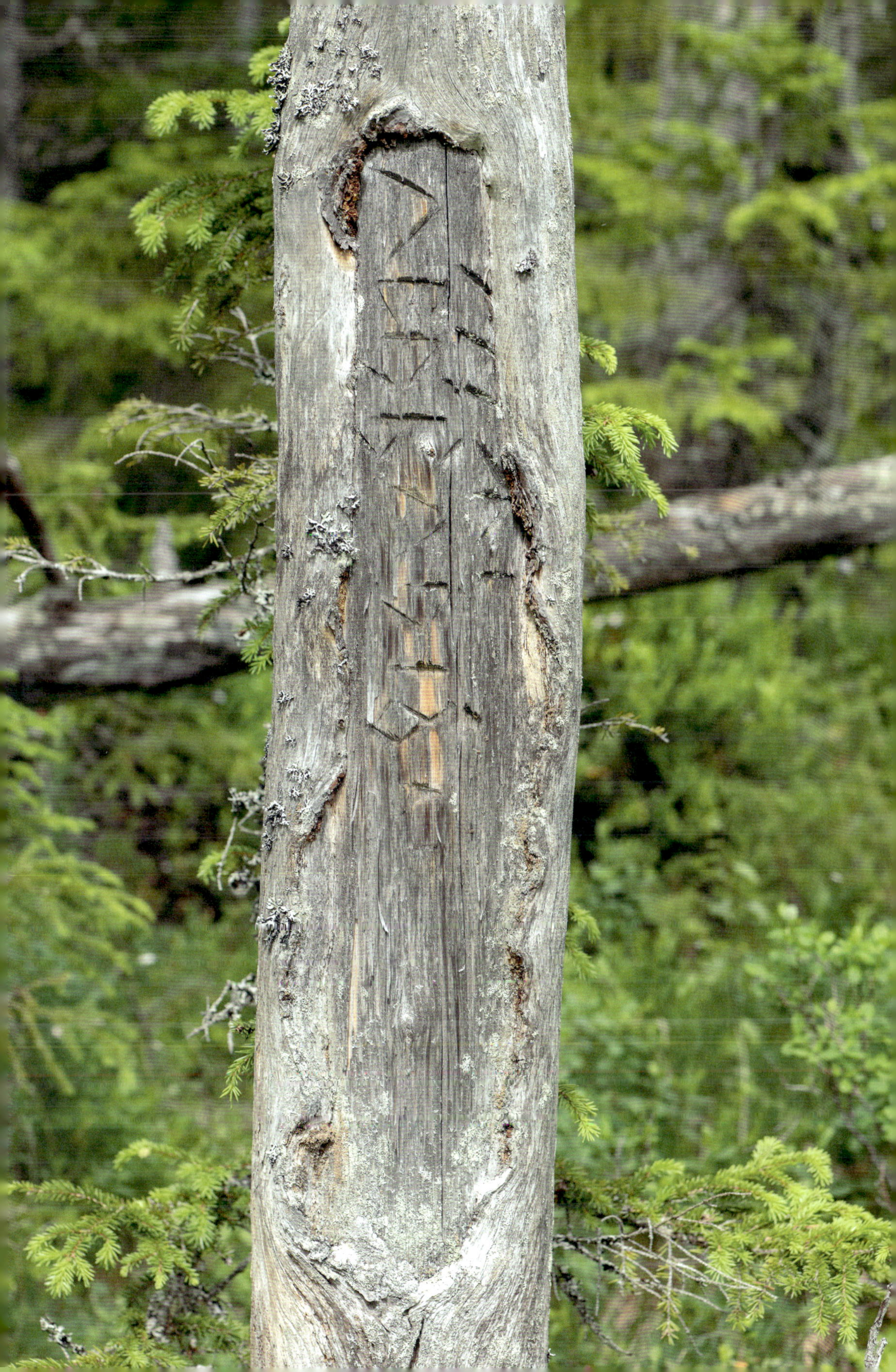

MPD APD KAD THE FIRST SUMMER WE HERD

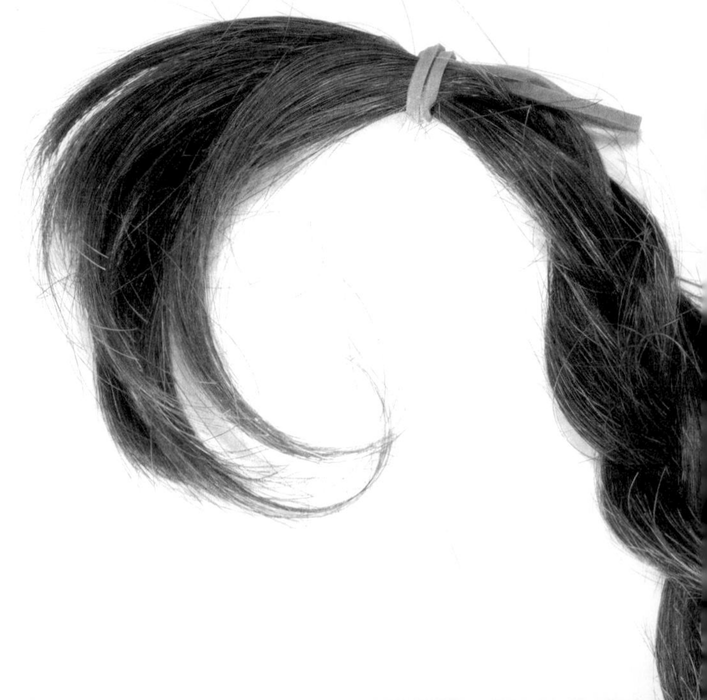

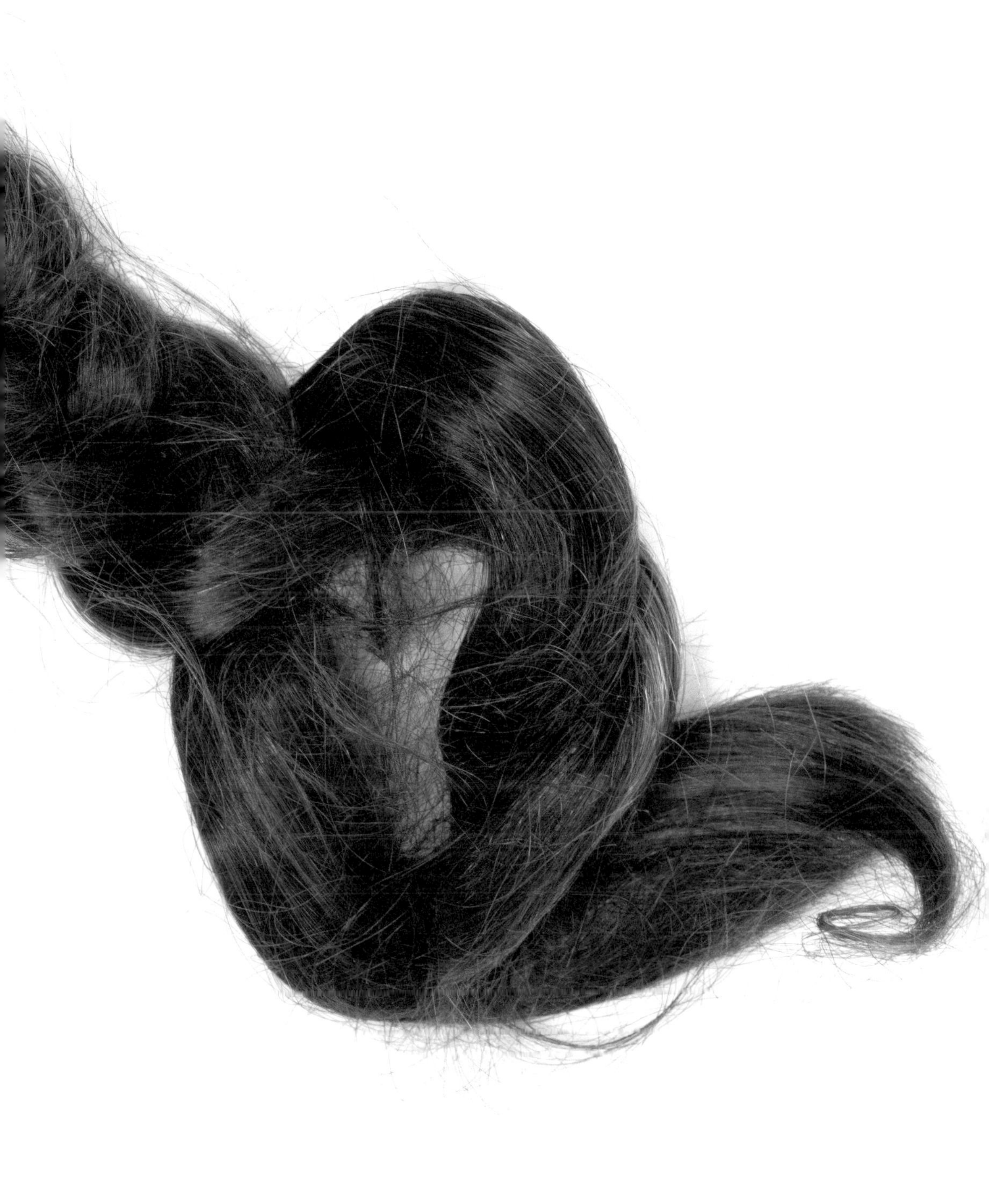

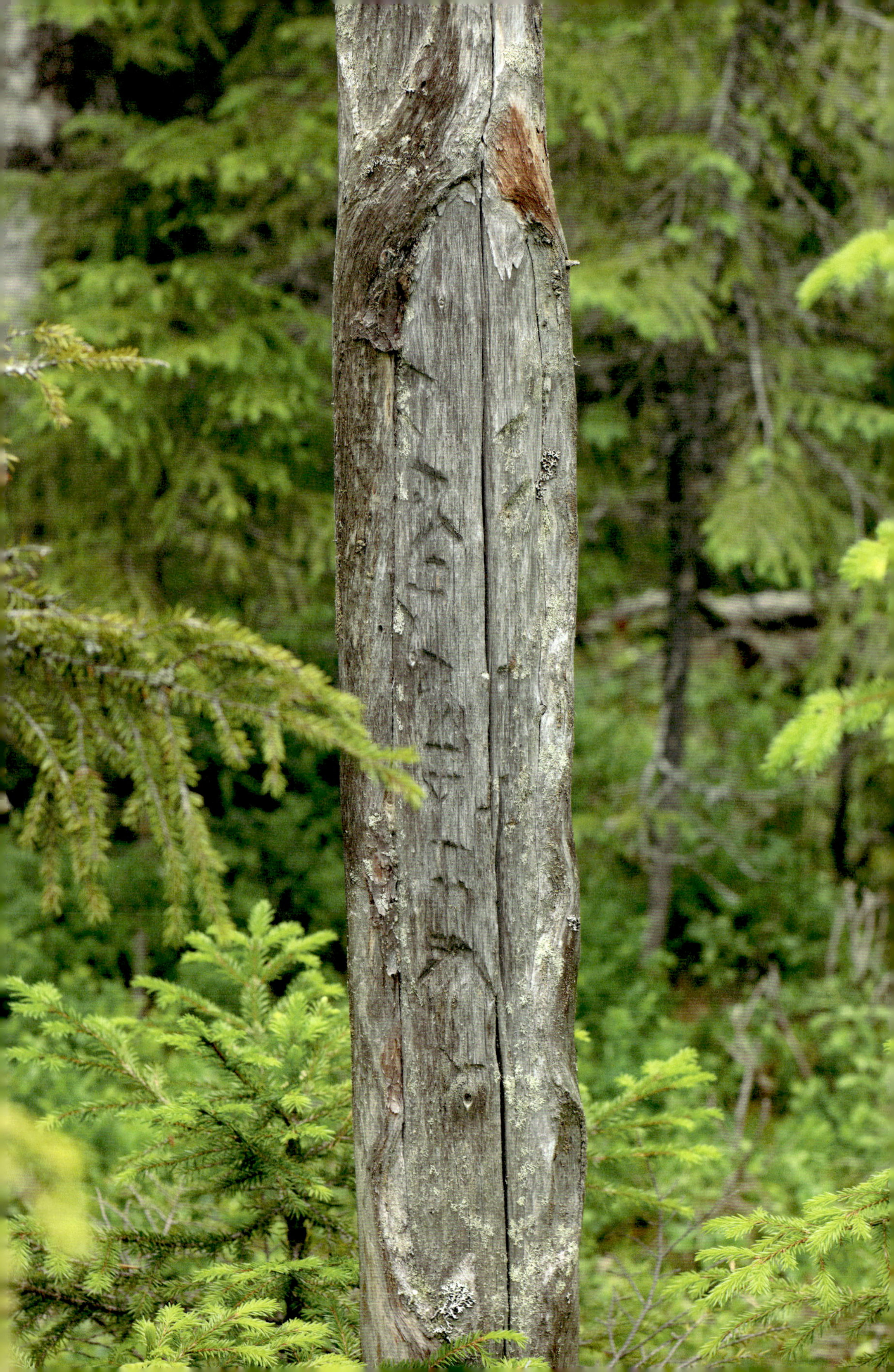

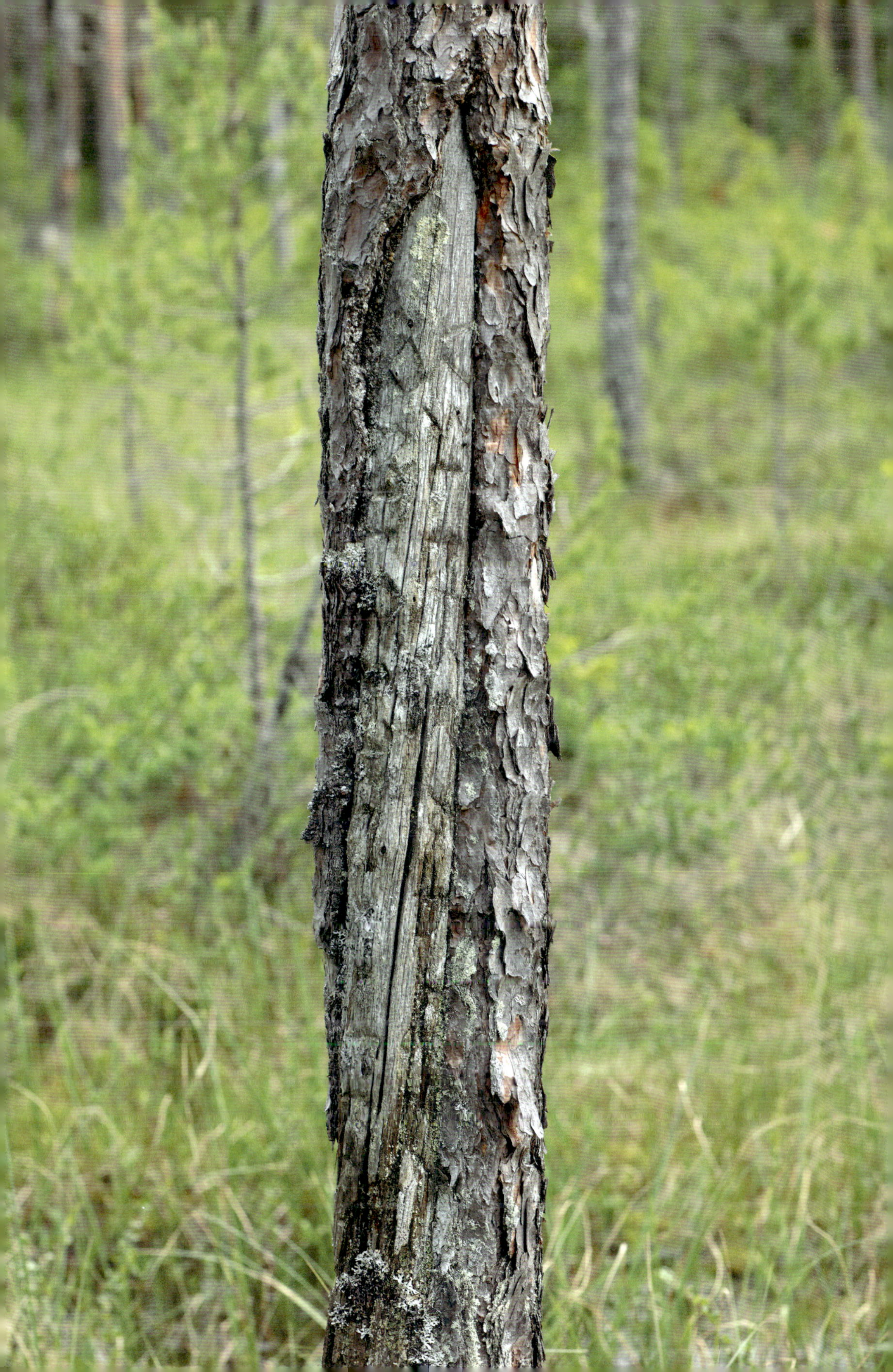

july 8

i make a 3d scan of a tree   scanning it requires 100 images
of the trunk, taken from different angles

we empty the memory cards in the evenings
my computer is getting slower and slower

mirrored K

april

i'm at my mom's house to help her clean out the attic
    in a plastic bag, i find my grandmother's cut braids
      they are brown and thick and long   i find it hard to believe
they're hers   she must have cut them off long before i was born

in her wedding photo, she has curly short hair

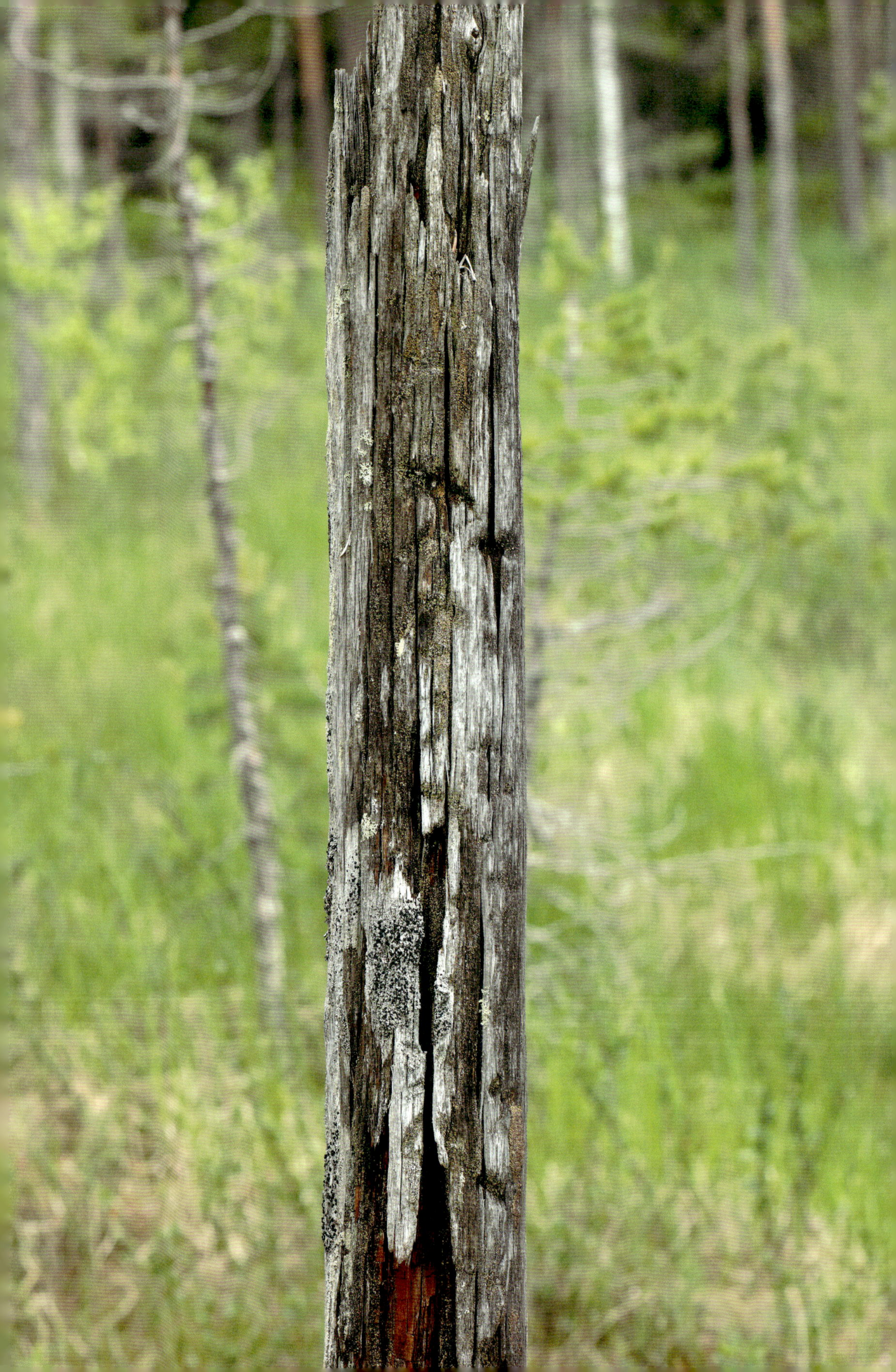

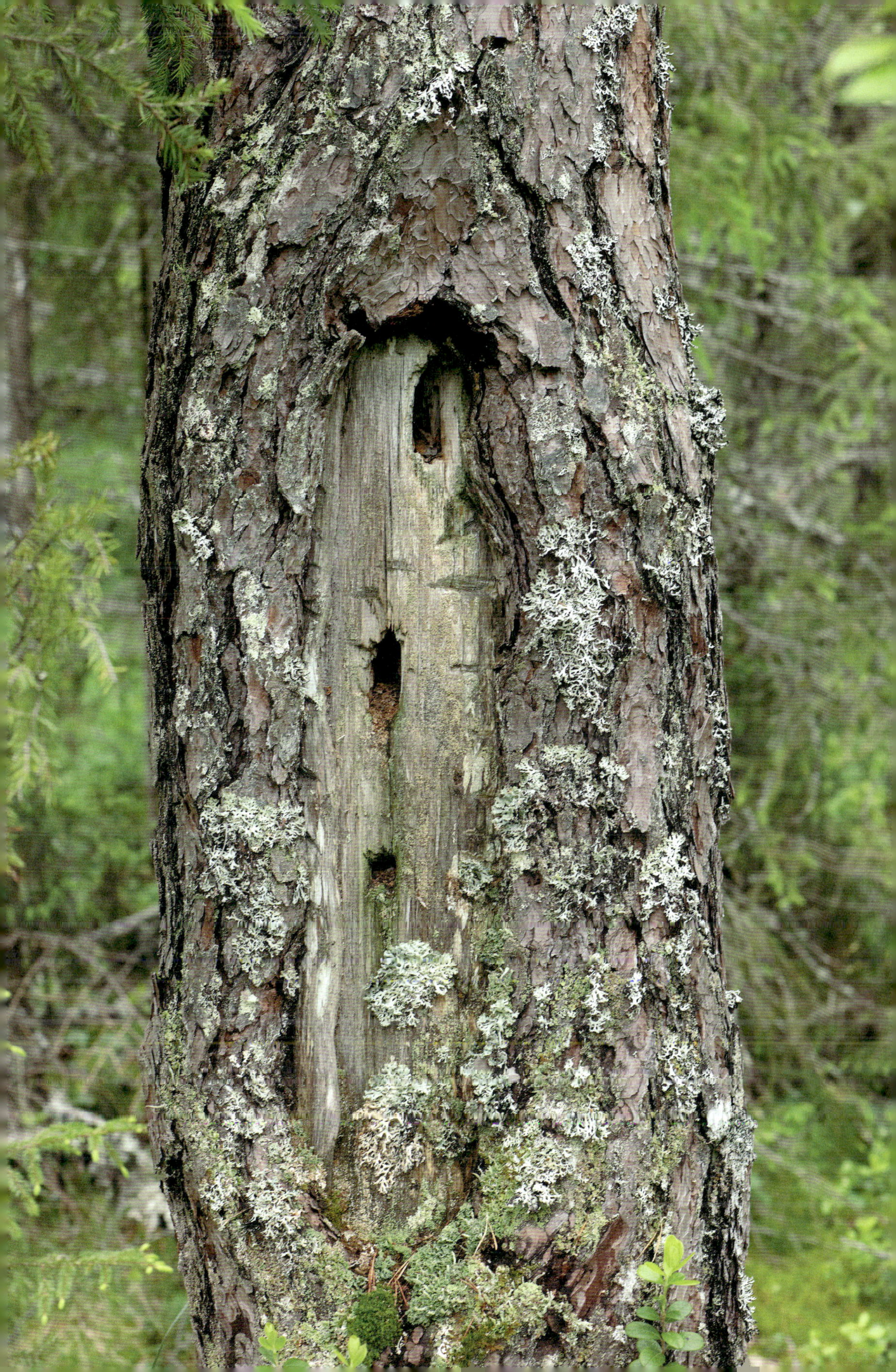

em
o
äxa
myschi

kärnmjölk
halvgräs
skummjölk
blodrot
grädde
mossa
gräs
täte

en ög ma pappir

october 17

the cloudberries are overripe

i see bear shit that looks like lingonberry jam

KID AOD WIRVS TILHOP

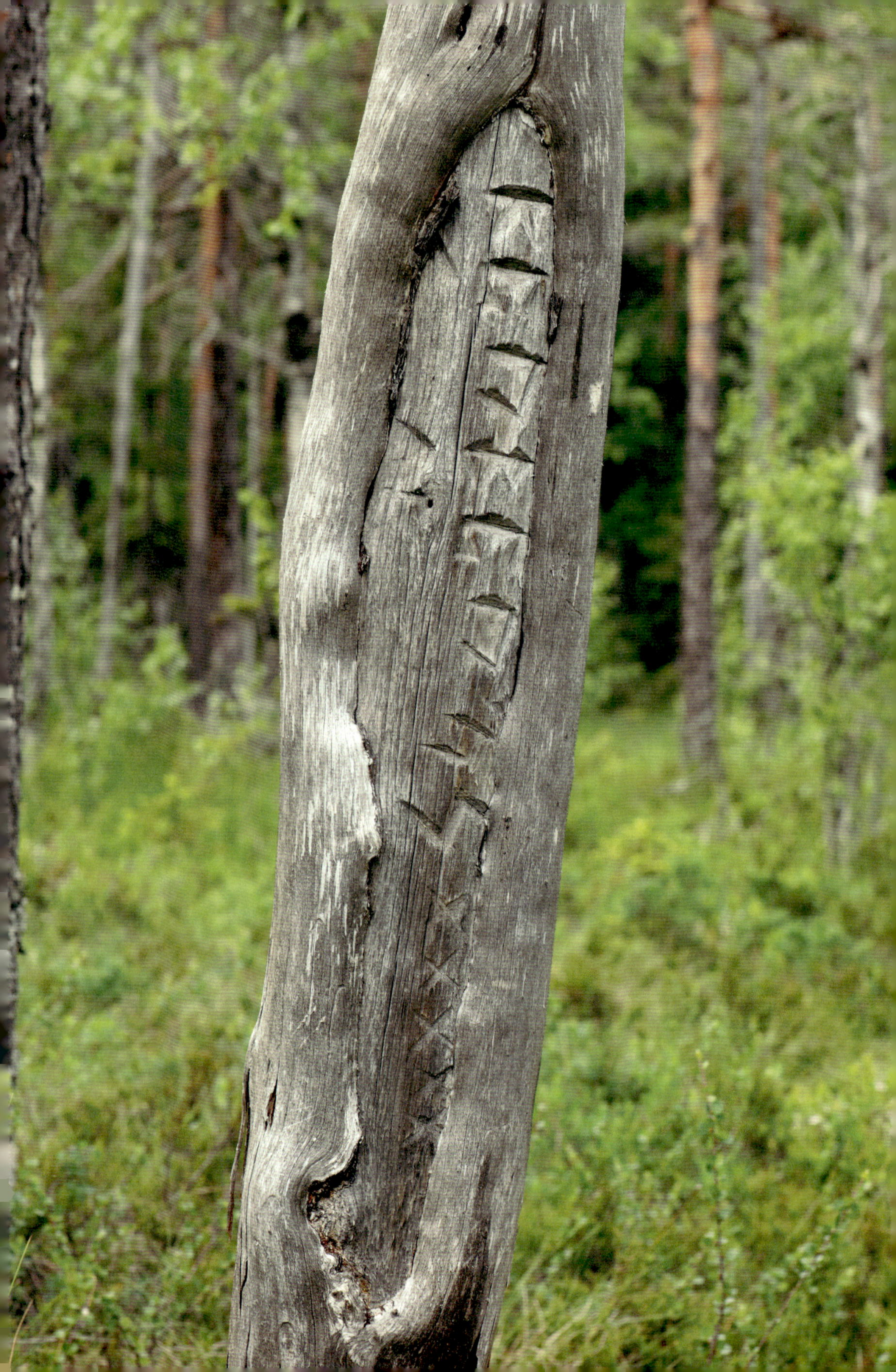

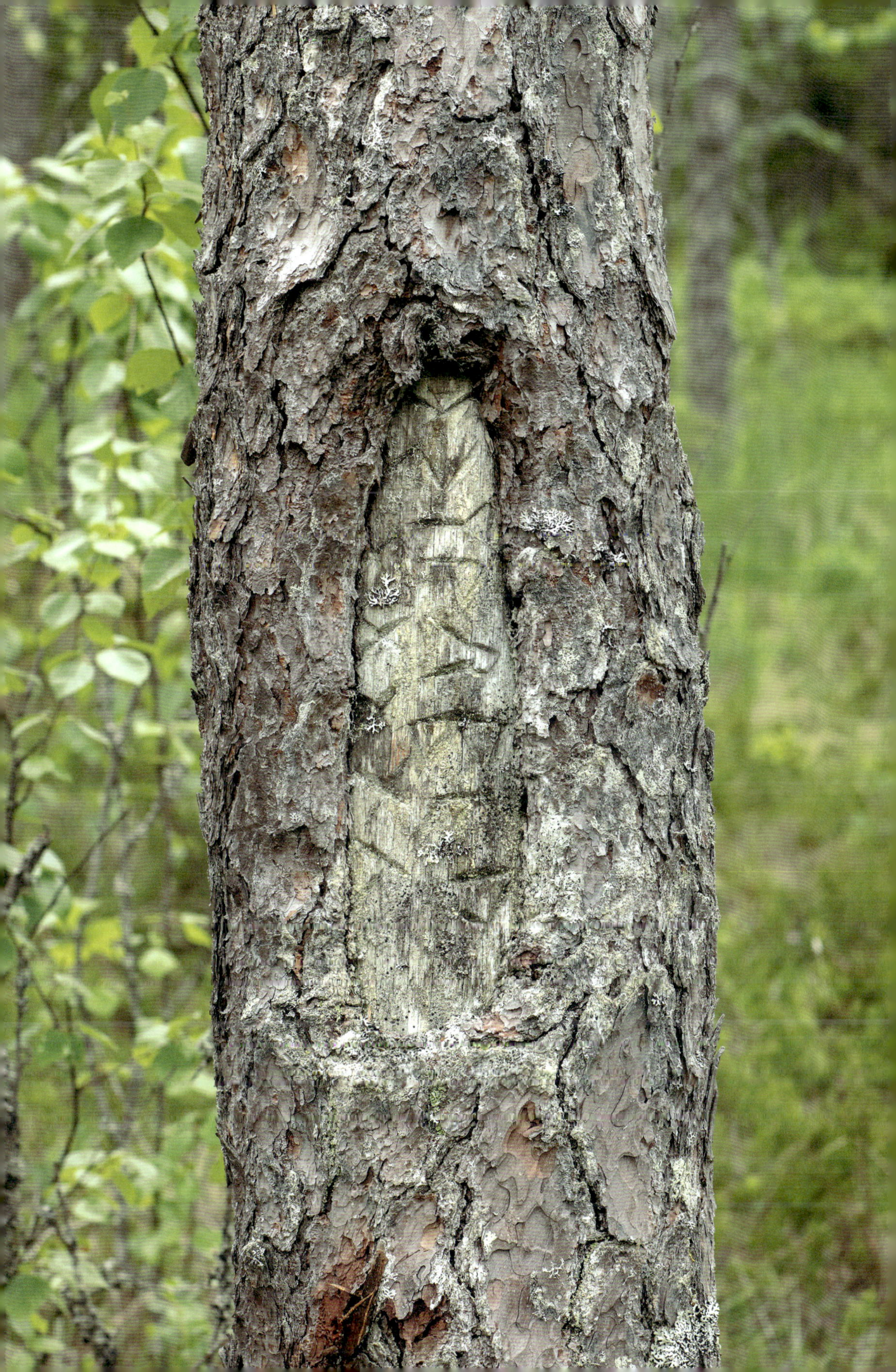

you wait for your friend

6,619 characters

mostly D

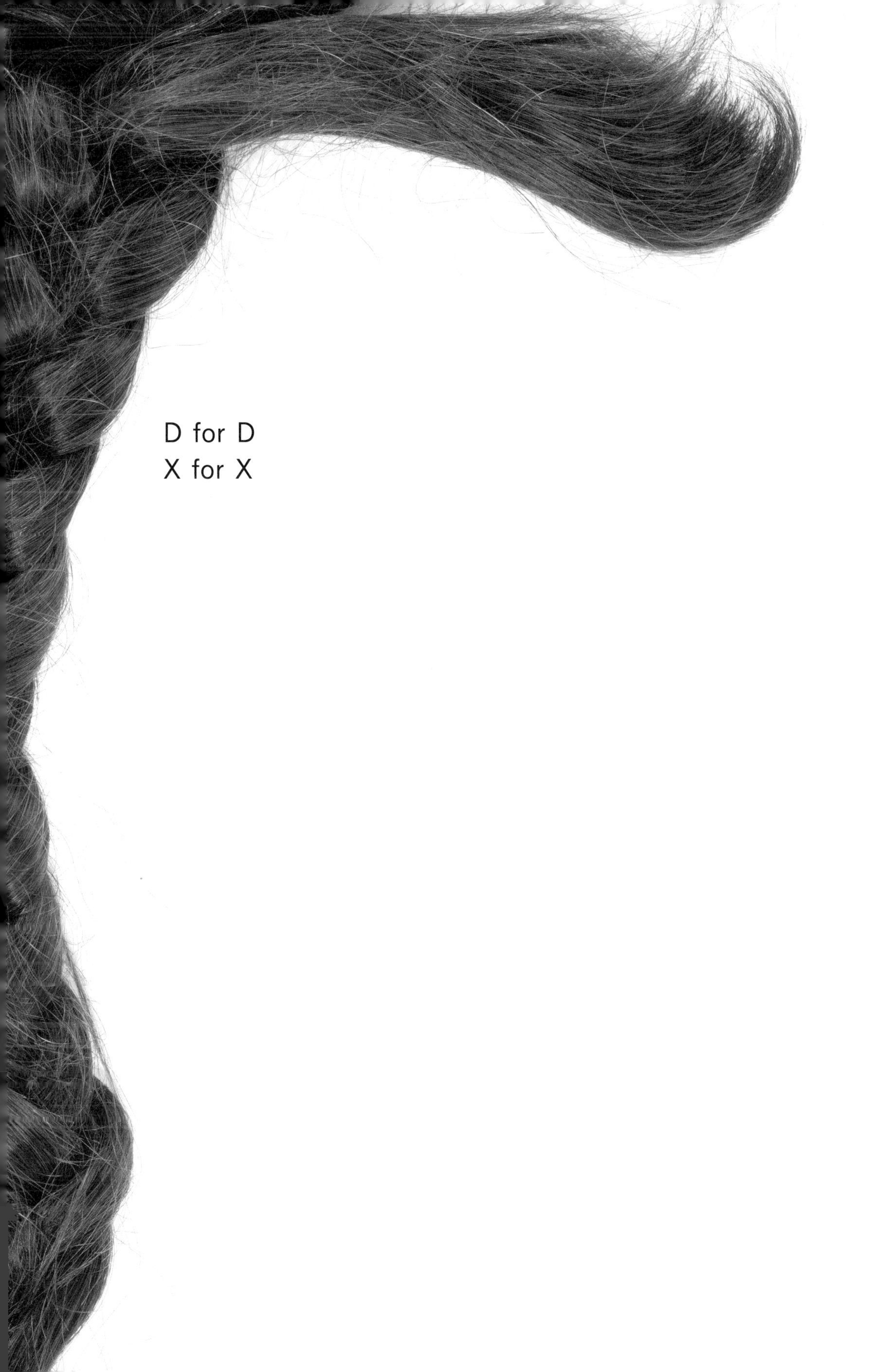

D for D
X for X

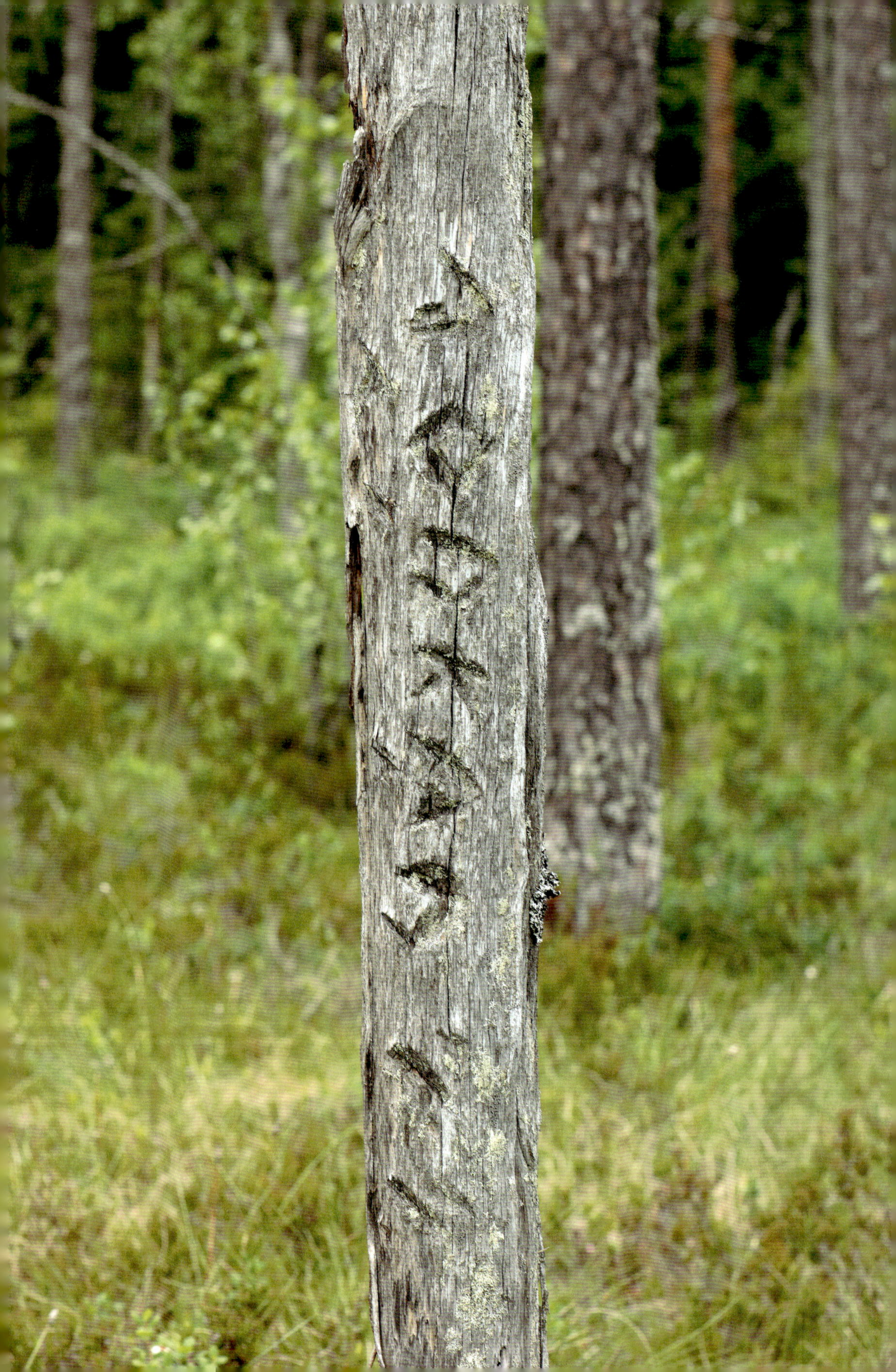

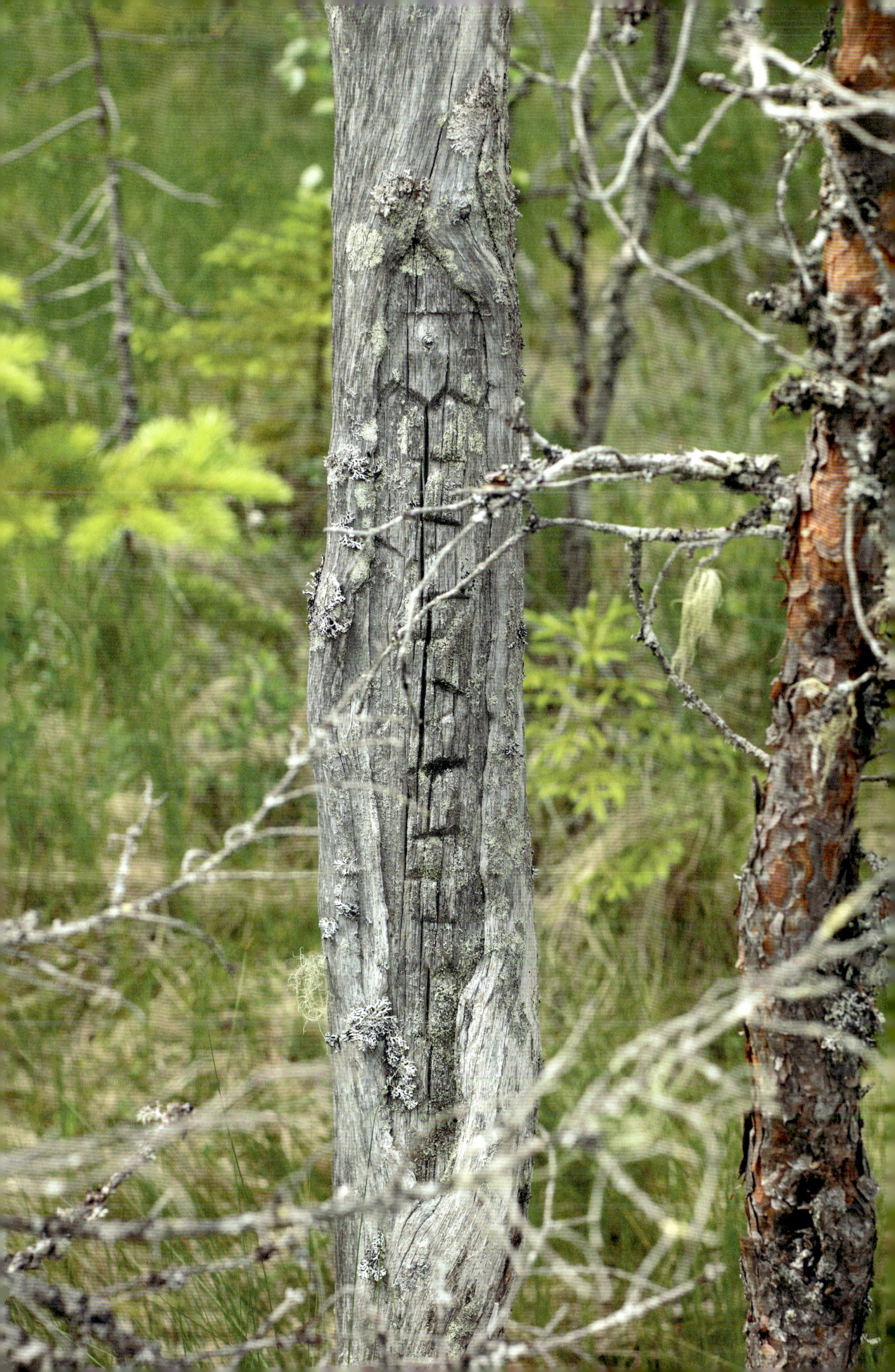

i put thin rice paper against the trunks
and trace them with charcoal

i have to take off my gloves to get a good grip on the charcoal bit

my fingers turn red and soon
i lose sensation

we photograph the trunks   you pull the trigger
we use an 85 mm lens   we need to go far away to fit
the whole tree in the picture

nåldyna
lissust
kunt
vindfånge
dagstuga
knivar
mjölkstugu
klövjestigar
fähus
varglav
koskälla
på bilden
ler hon
mot kameran
och stickar
samtidigt
en vante
mjölka
ysta
räkna
e rakt sträck i mittn
kärna
bära

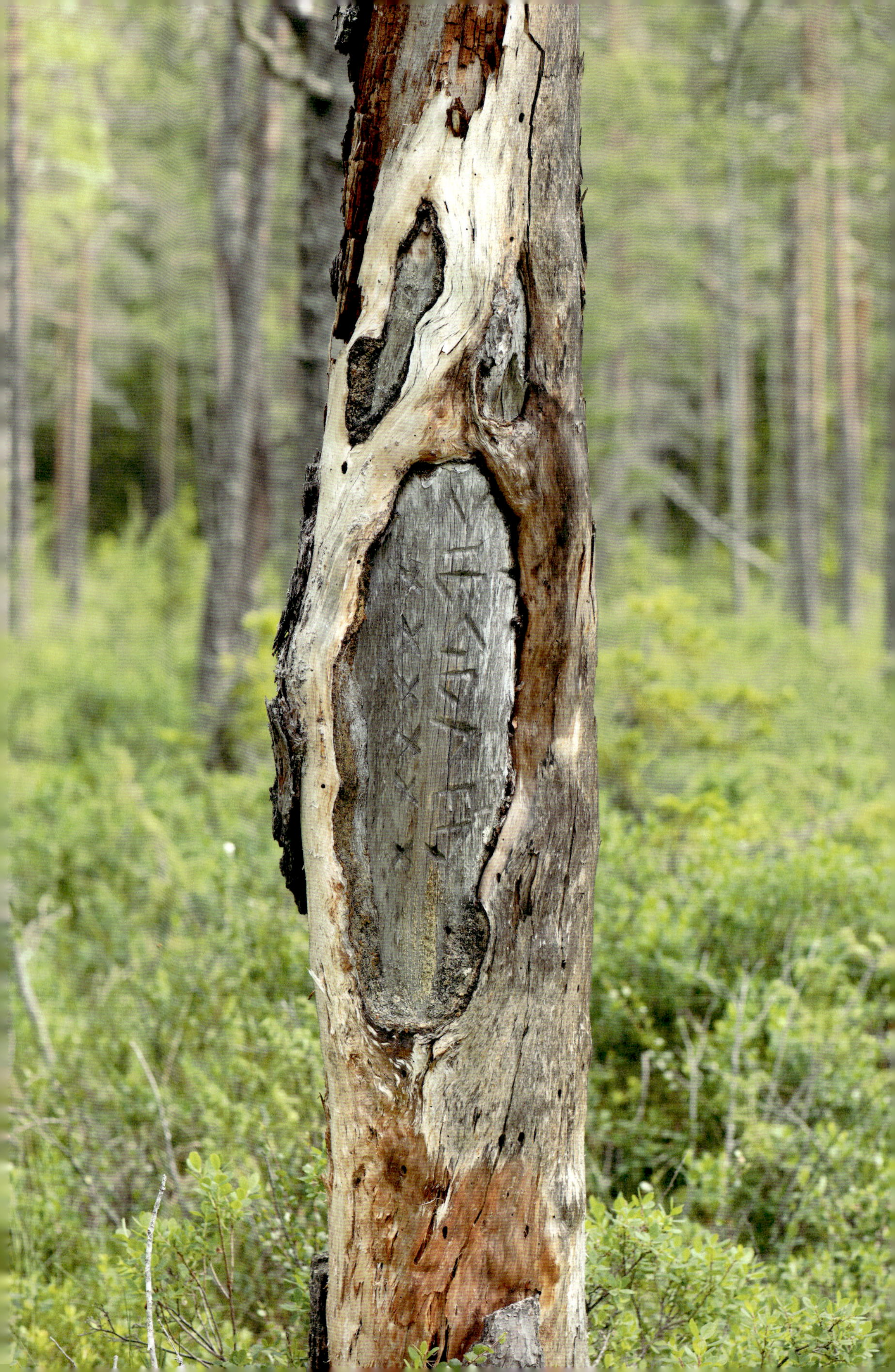

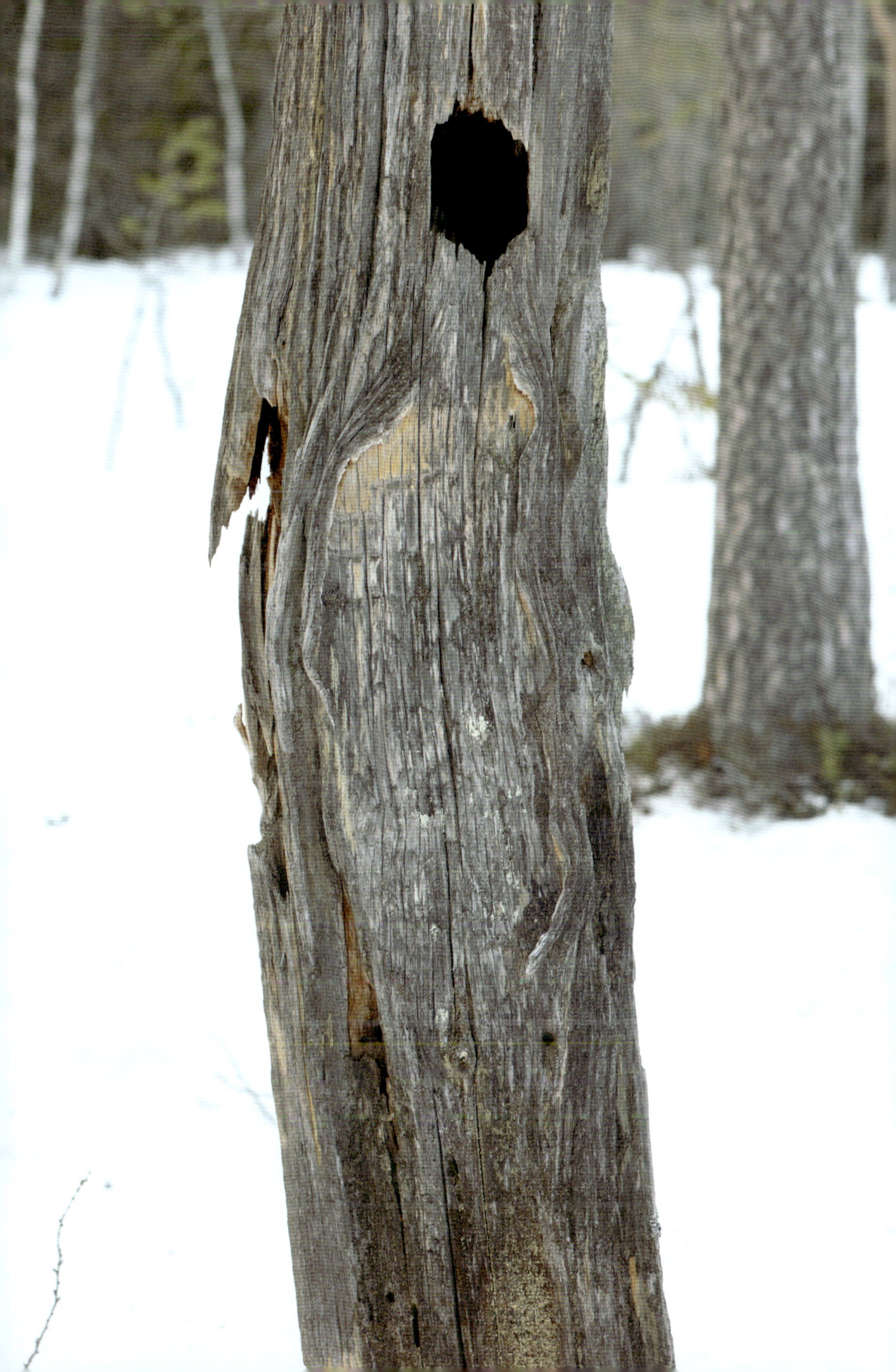

sila
mata
lösa
sopa
handen full
hämta vatten
plocka blommor

männistja
and

+   ' '
X   ' ' ' ' '
LAD ' ' ' '

– – – – – – – – – – – –

ALD ' ' ' '
     '” ' '
     ' ' ' '
     ' ' ' '
     ' ' ' '

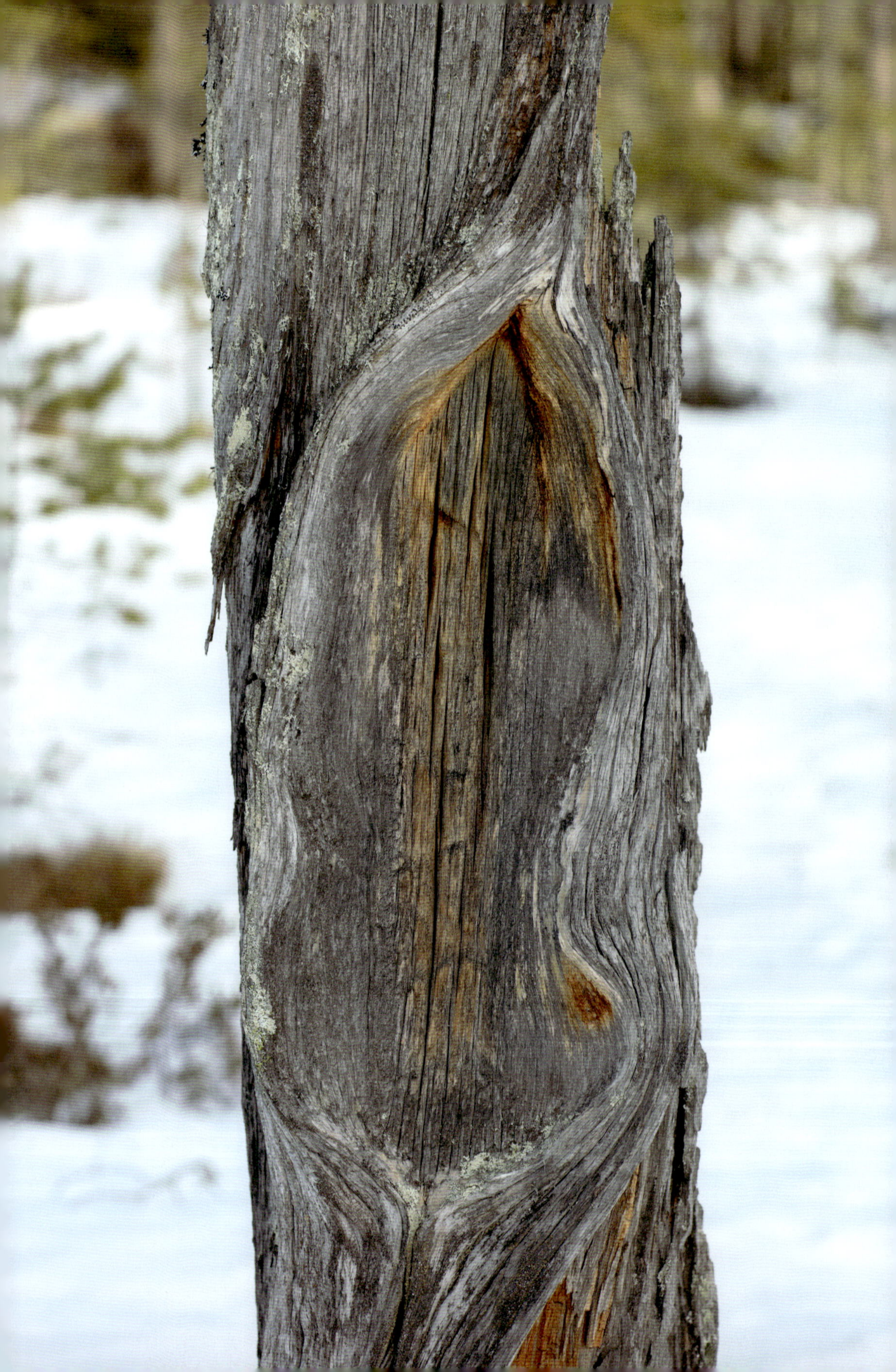

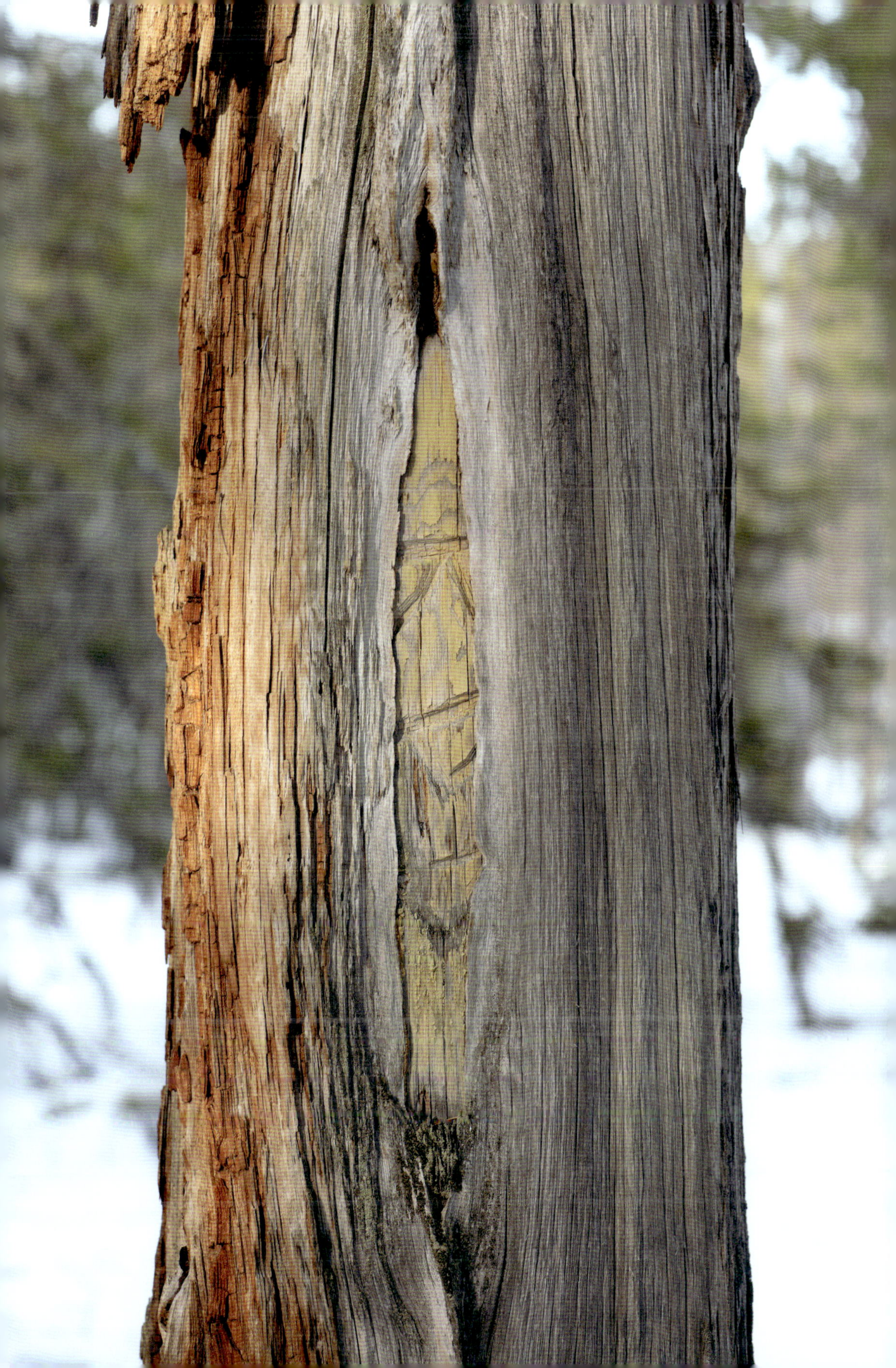

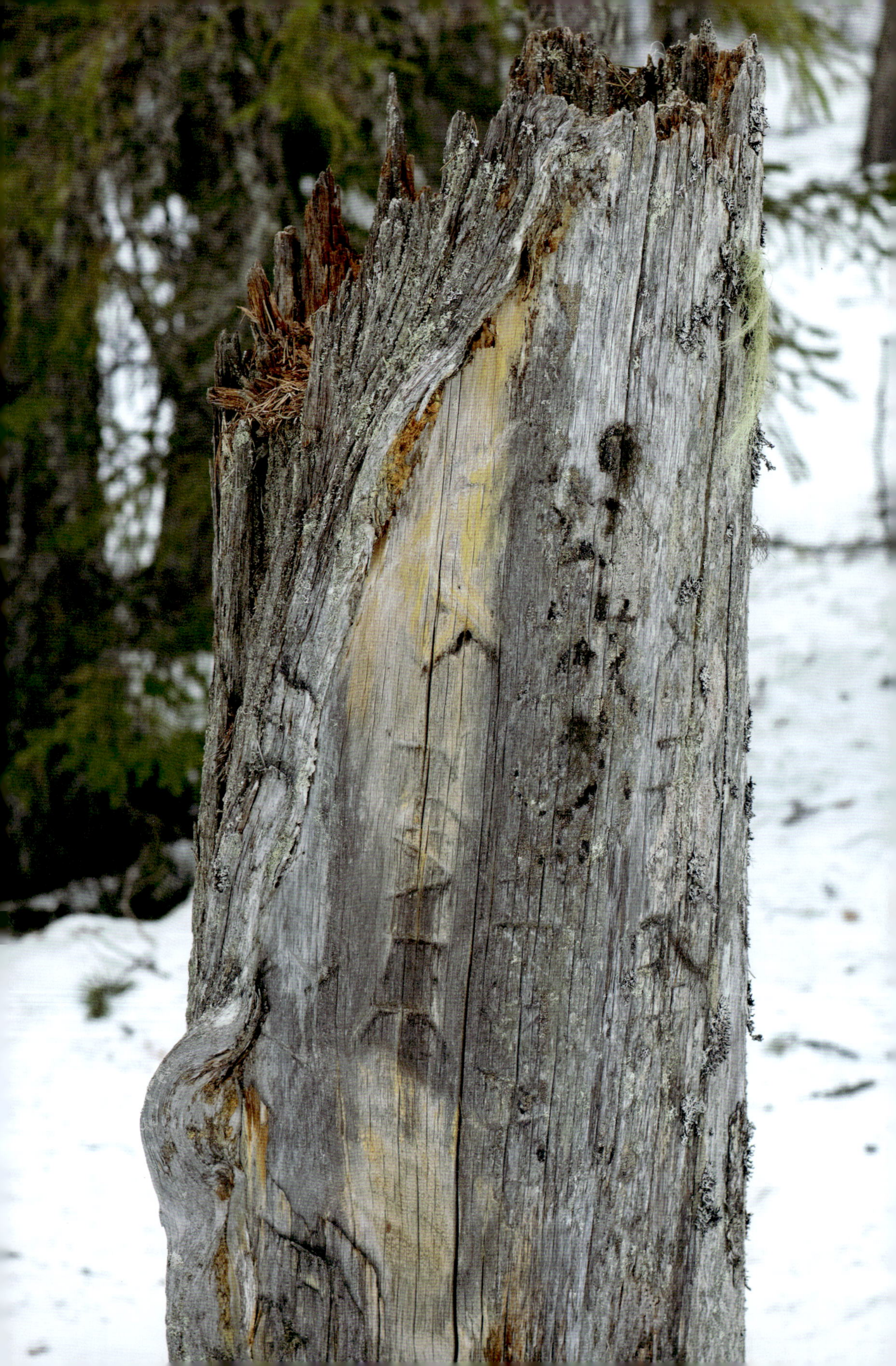

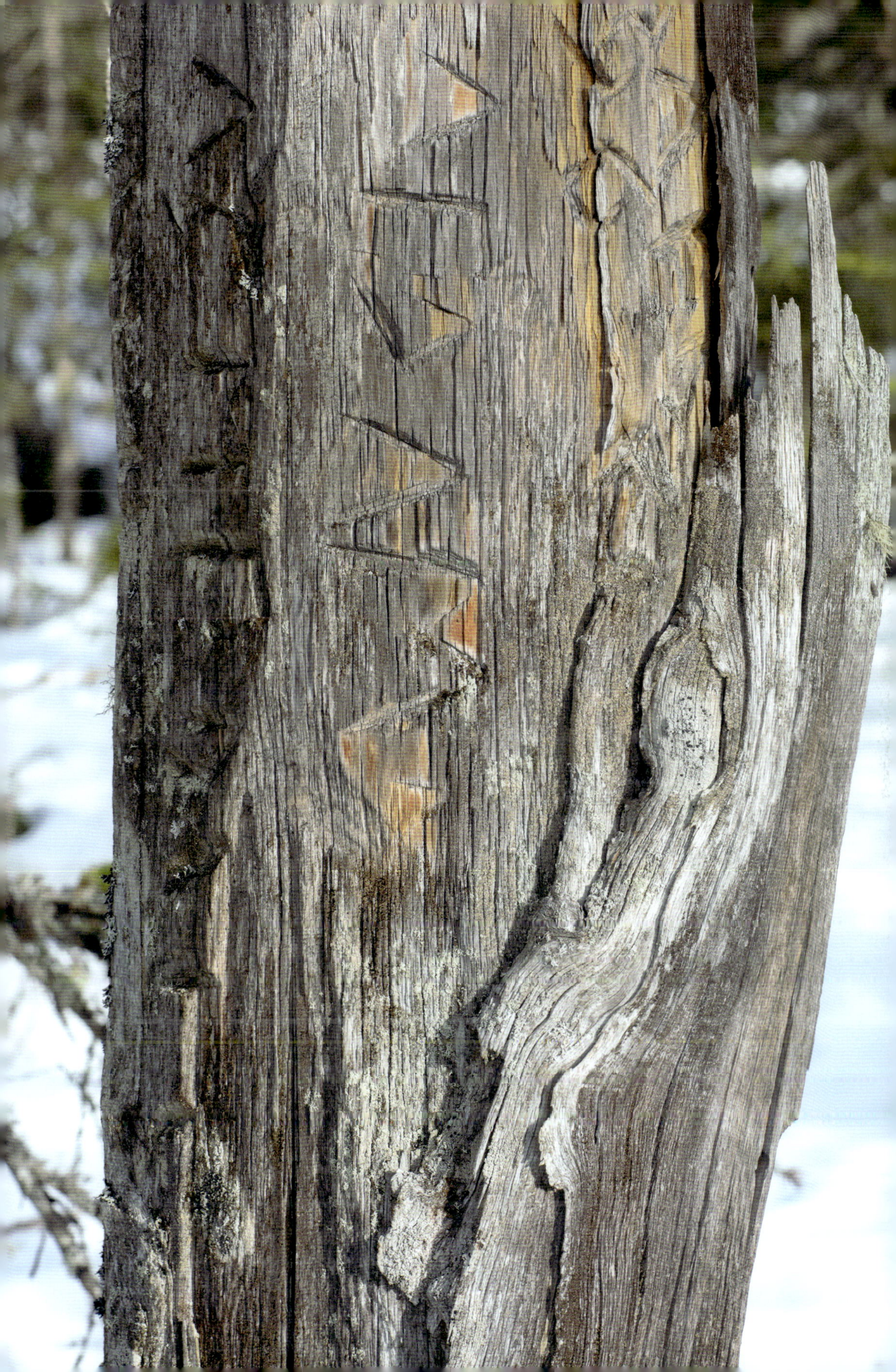

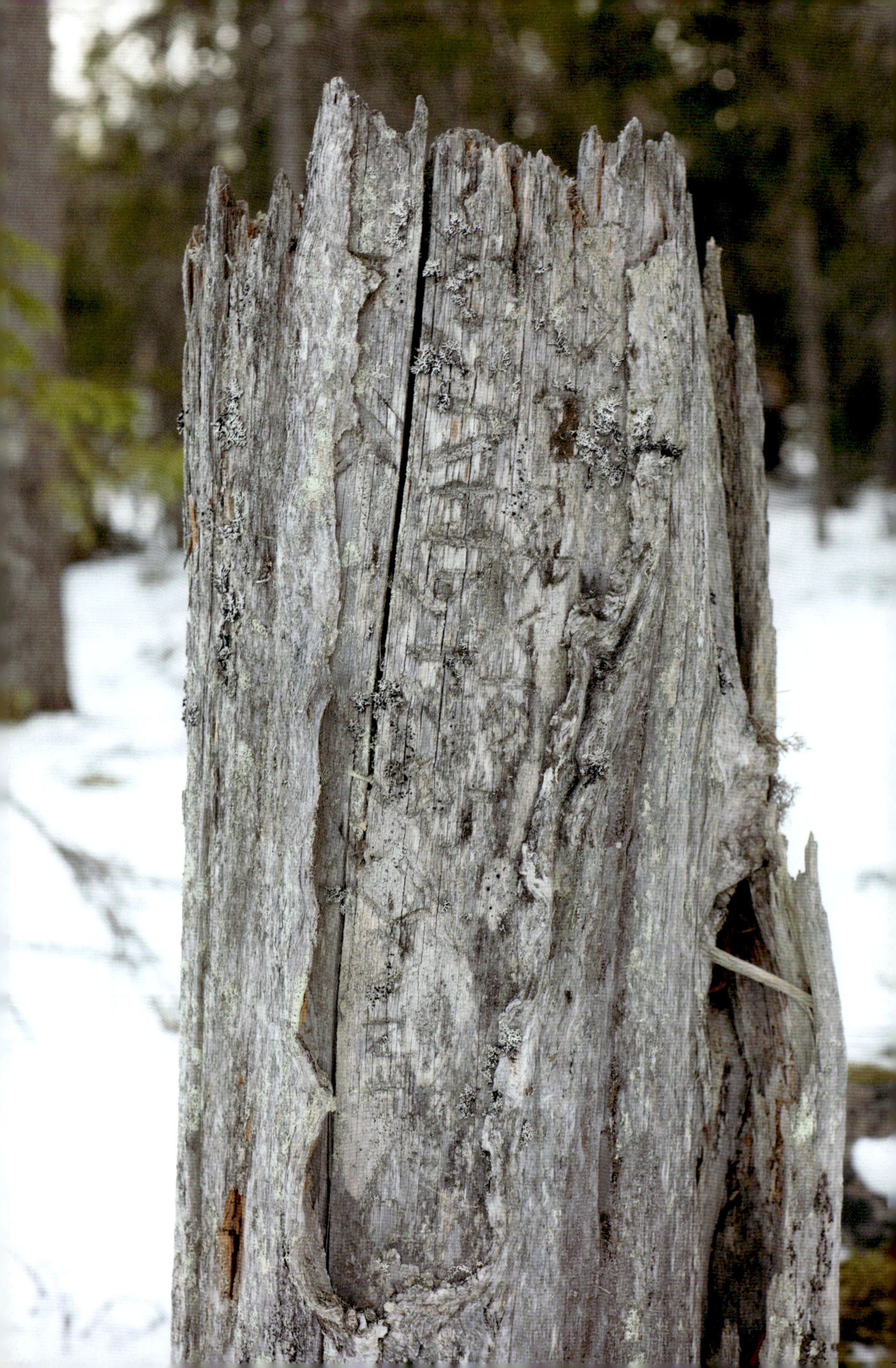

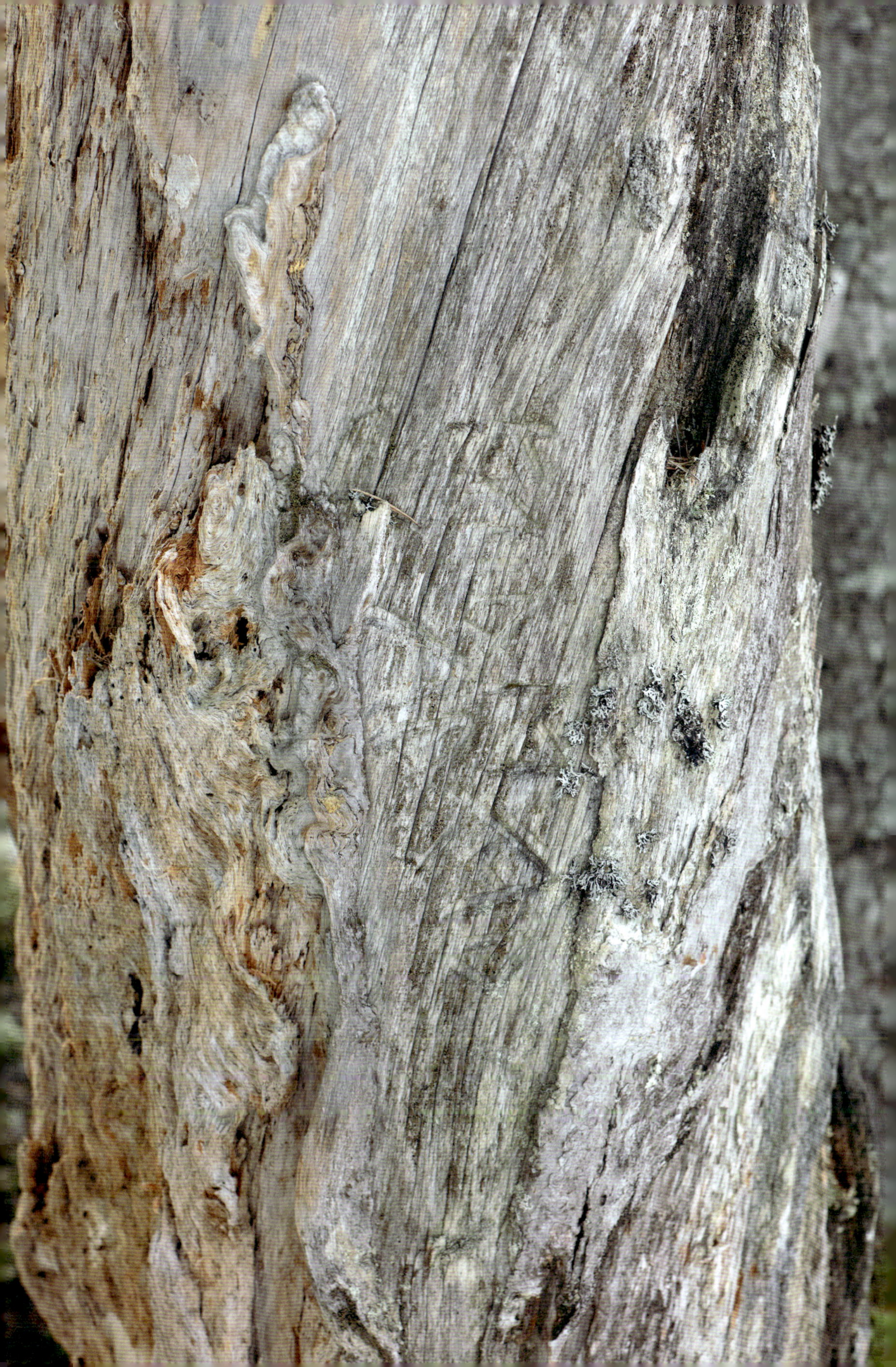

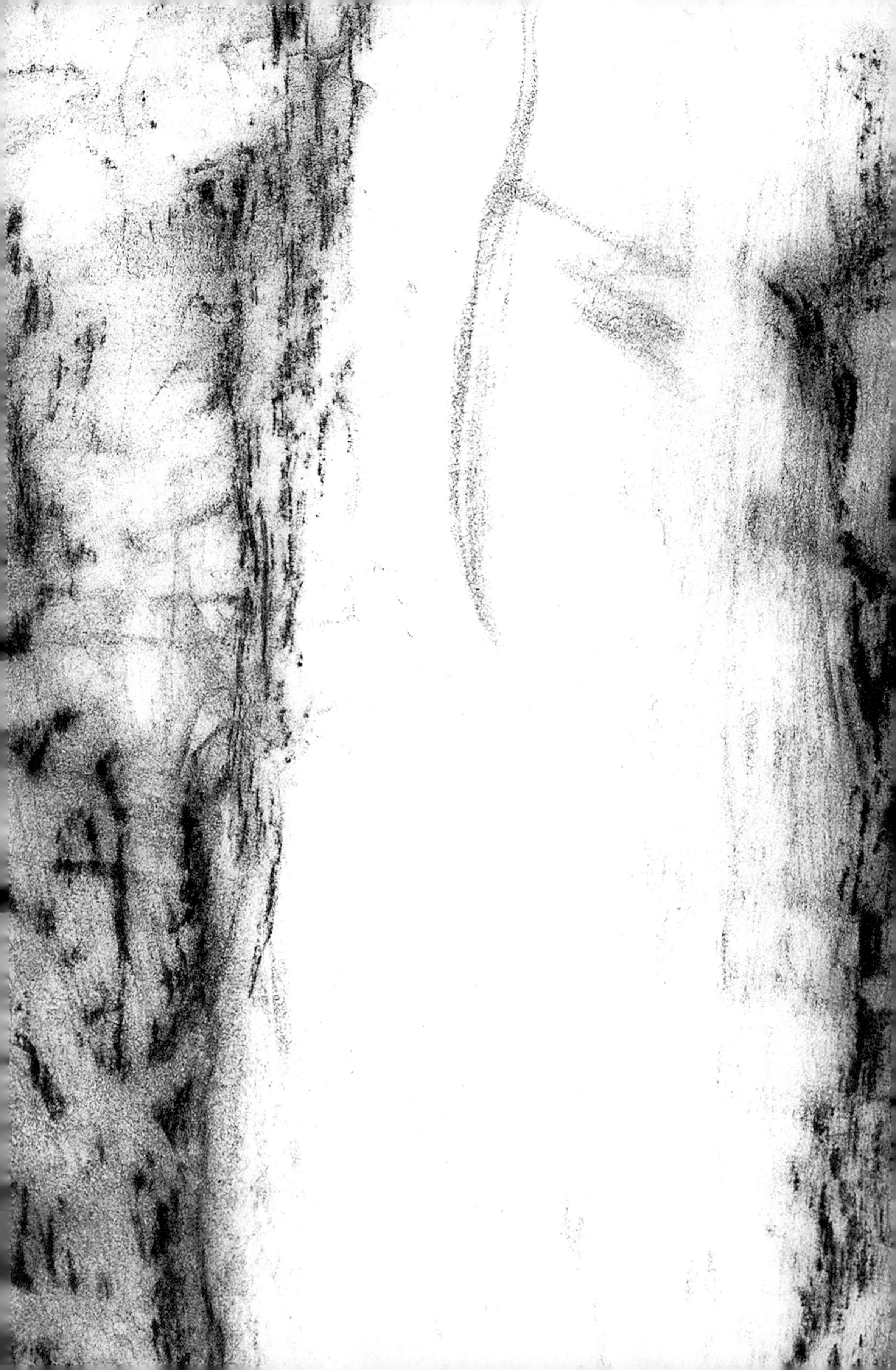

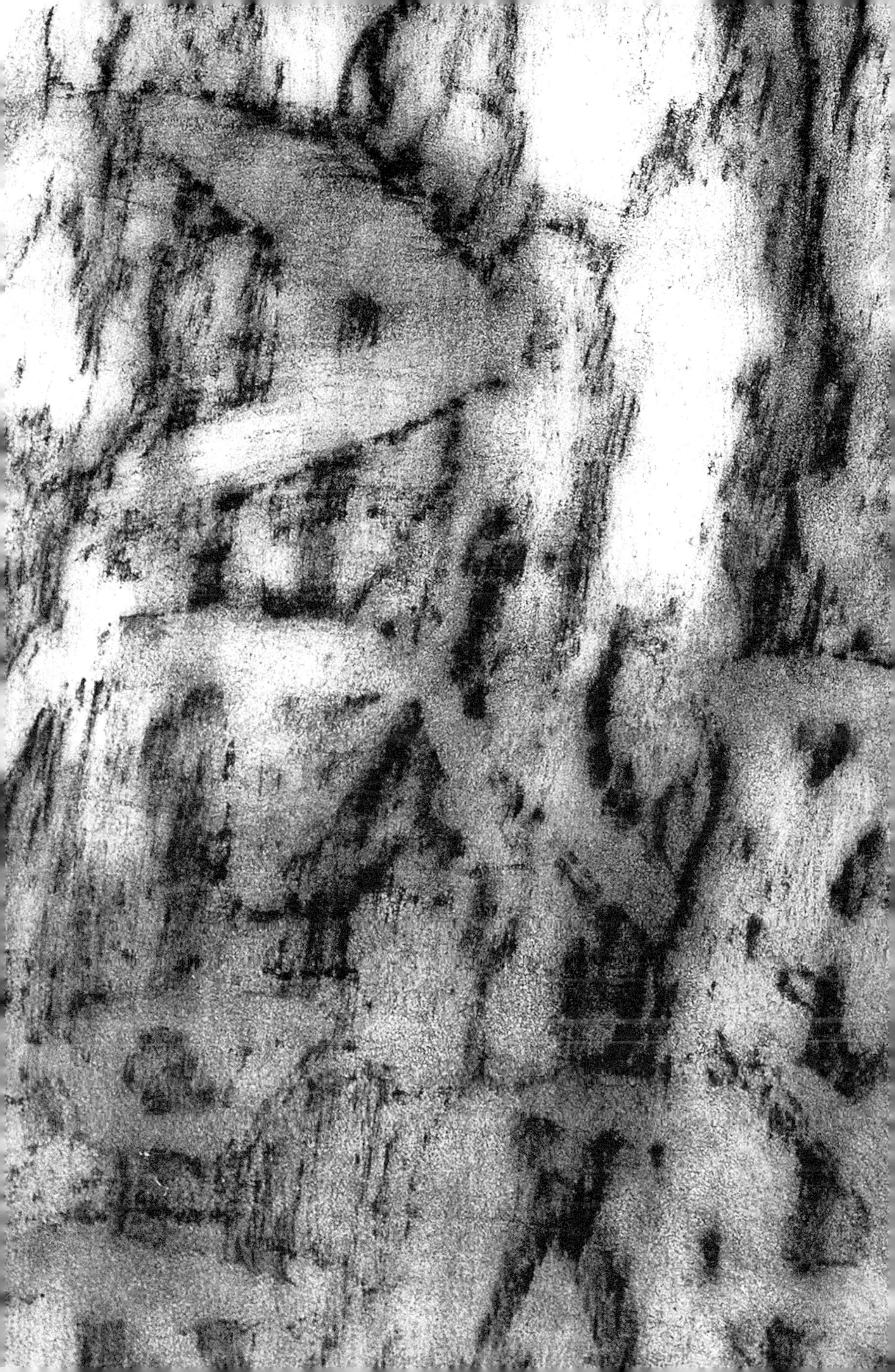

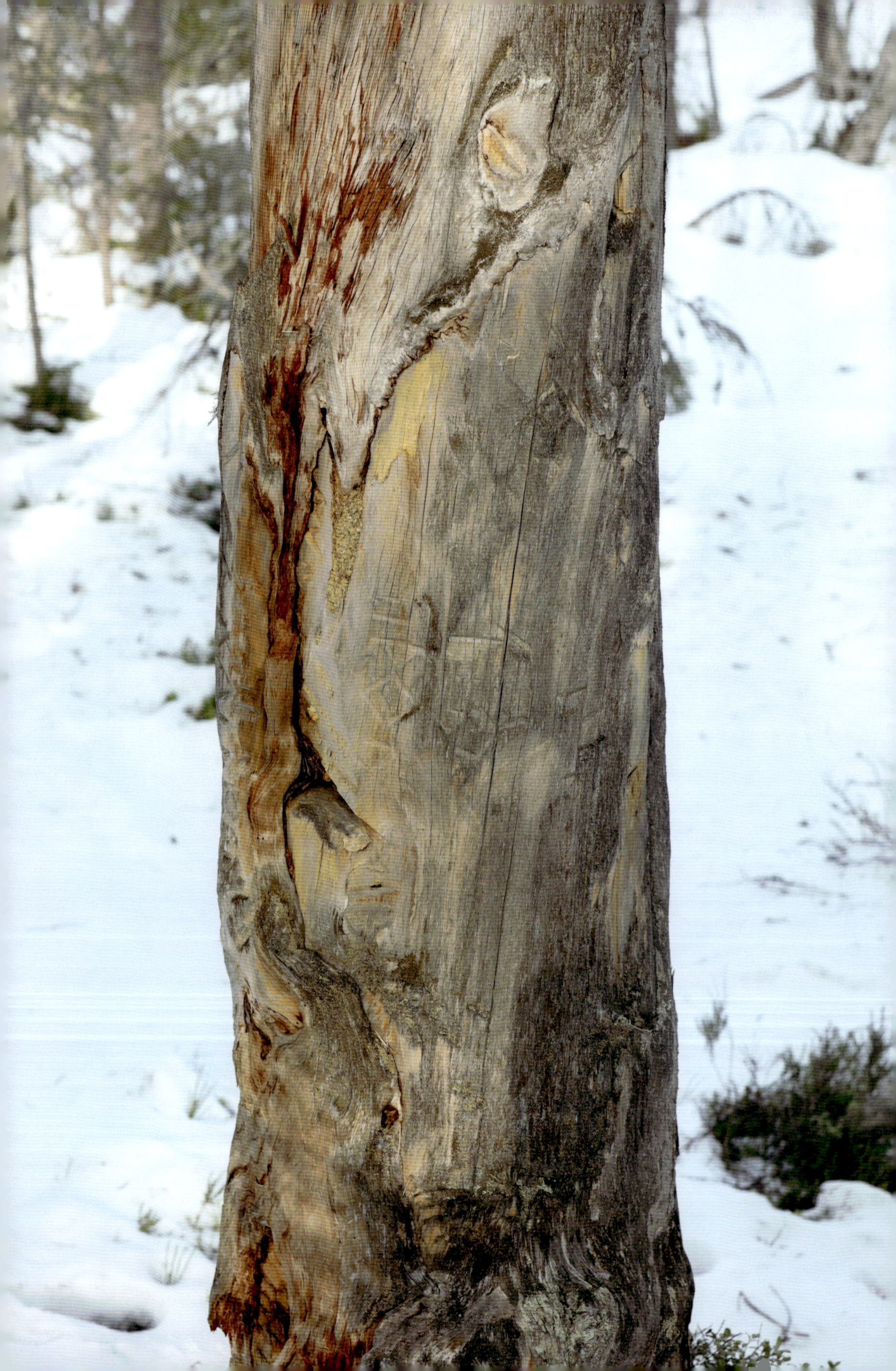

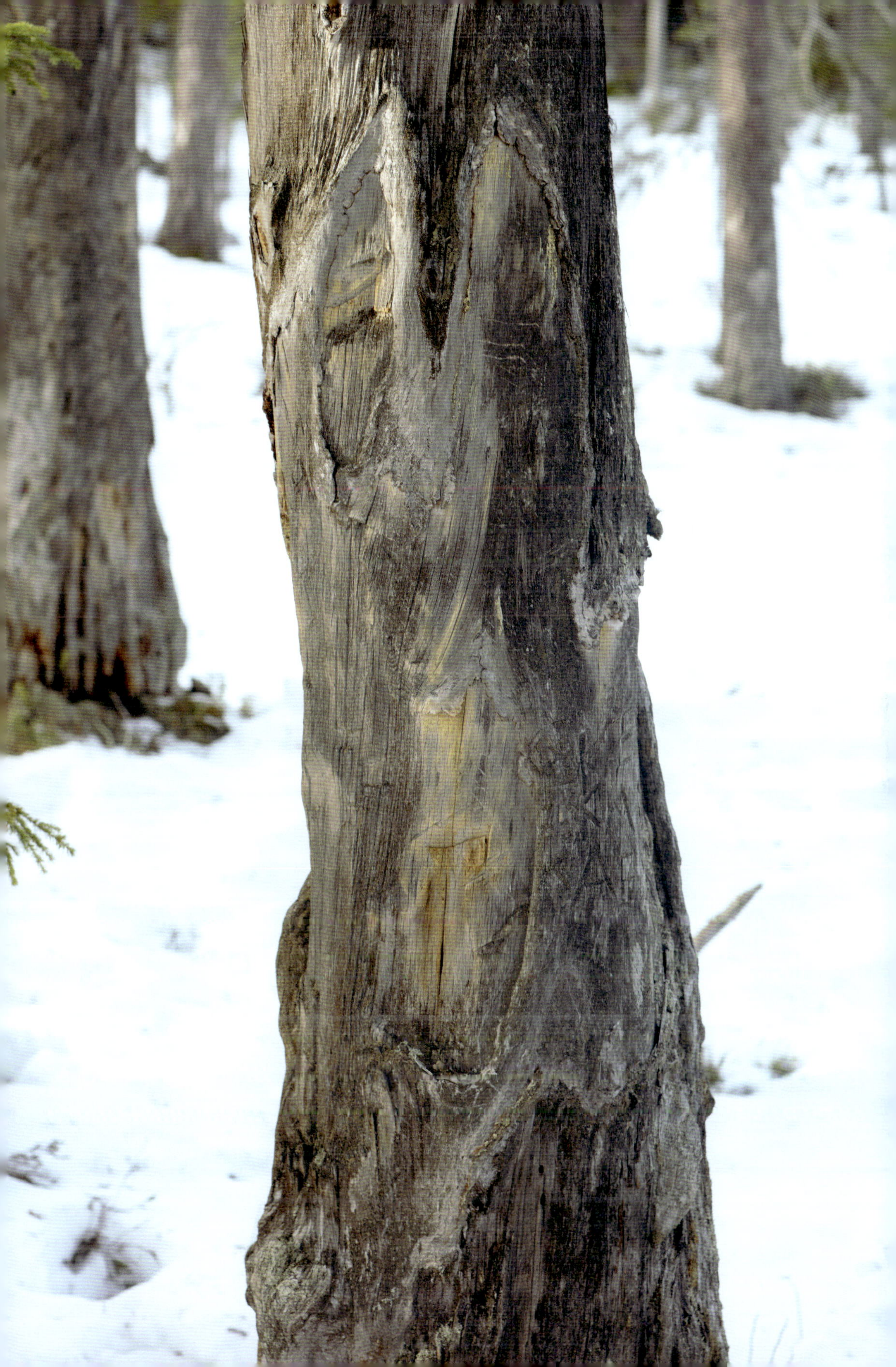

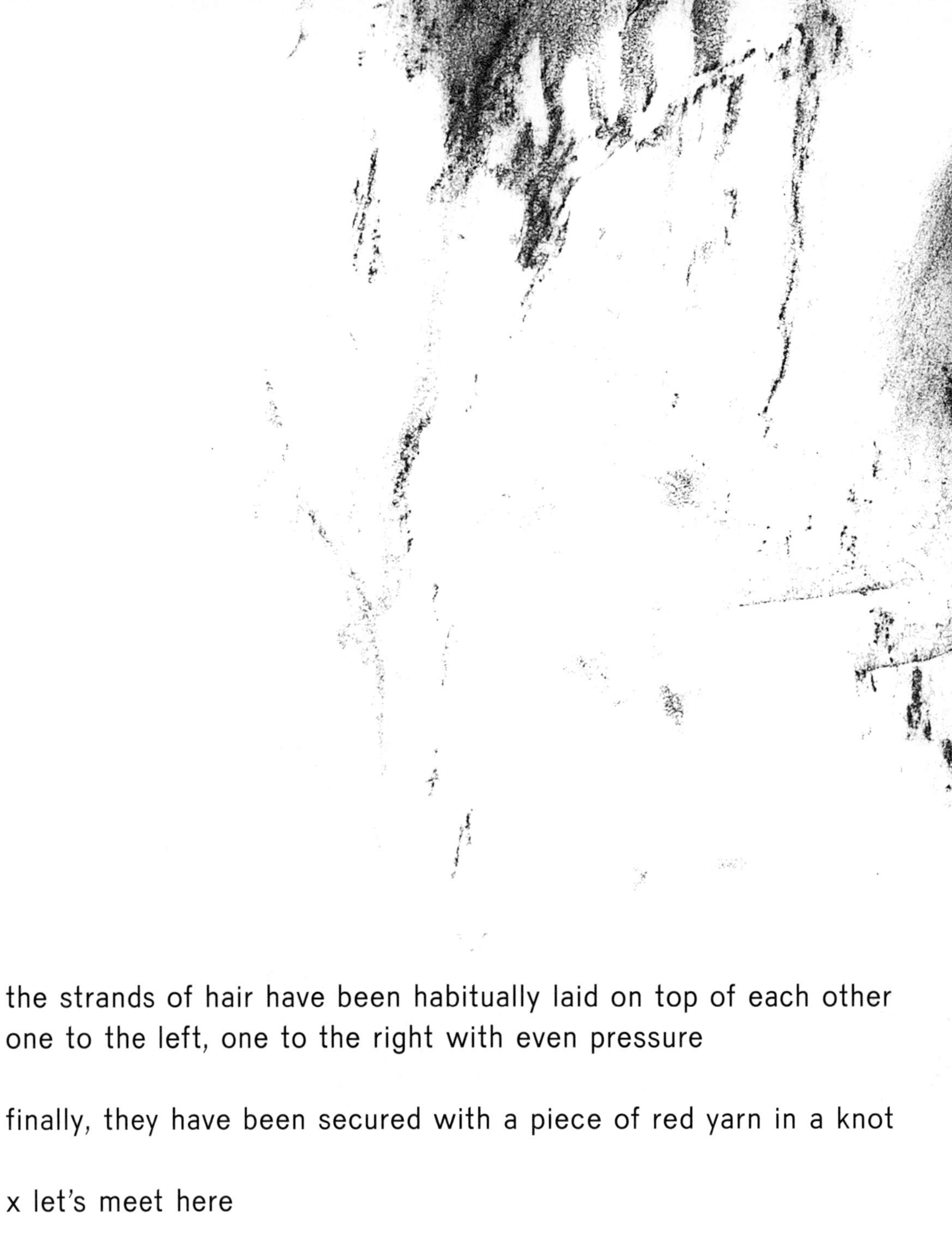

the strands of hair have been habitually laid on top of each other
one to the left, one to the right with even pressure

finally, they have been secured with a piece of red yarn in a knot

x let's meet here

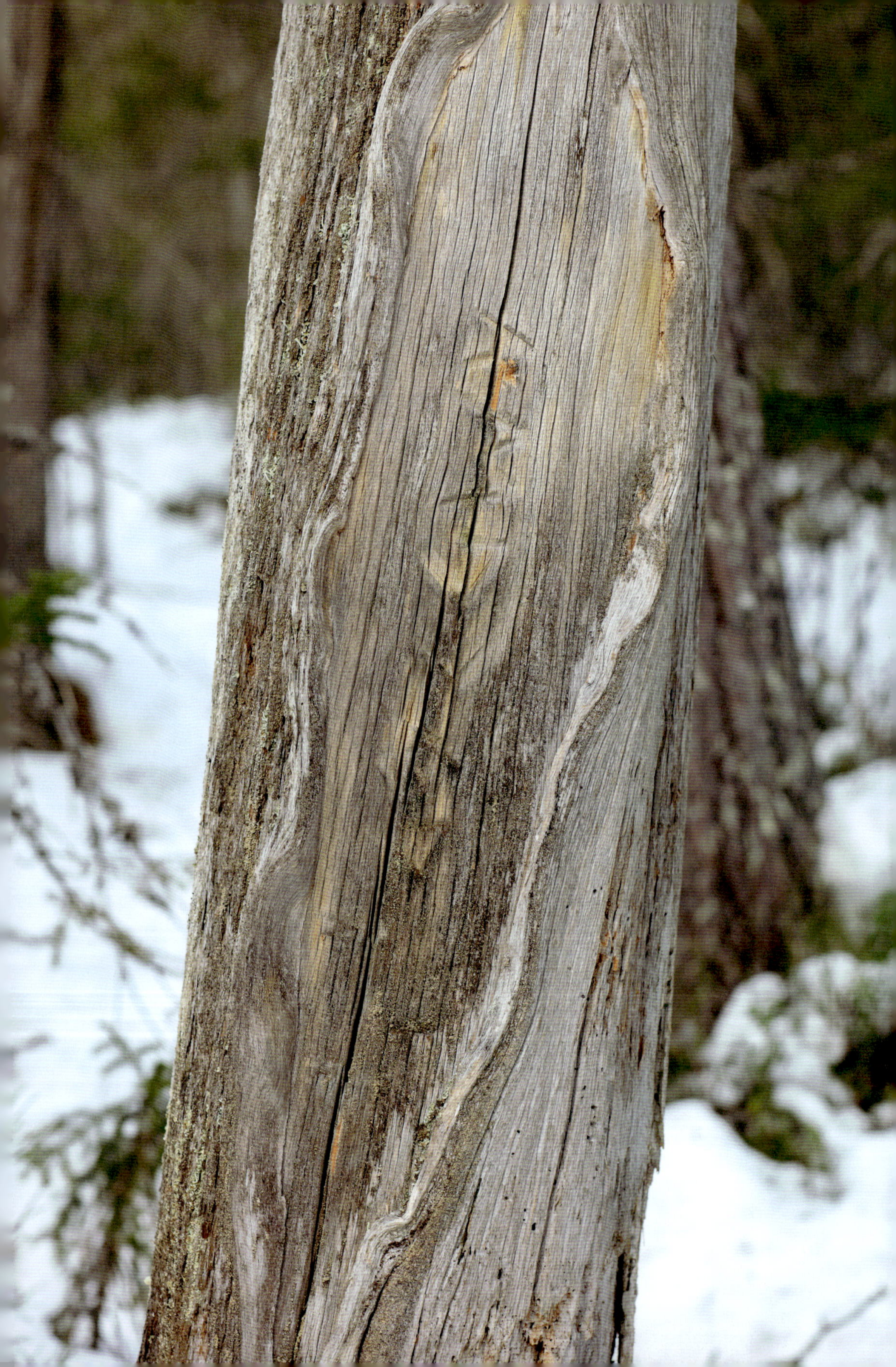

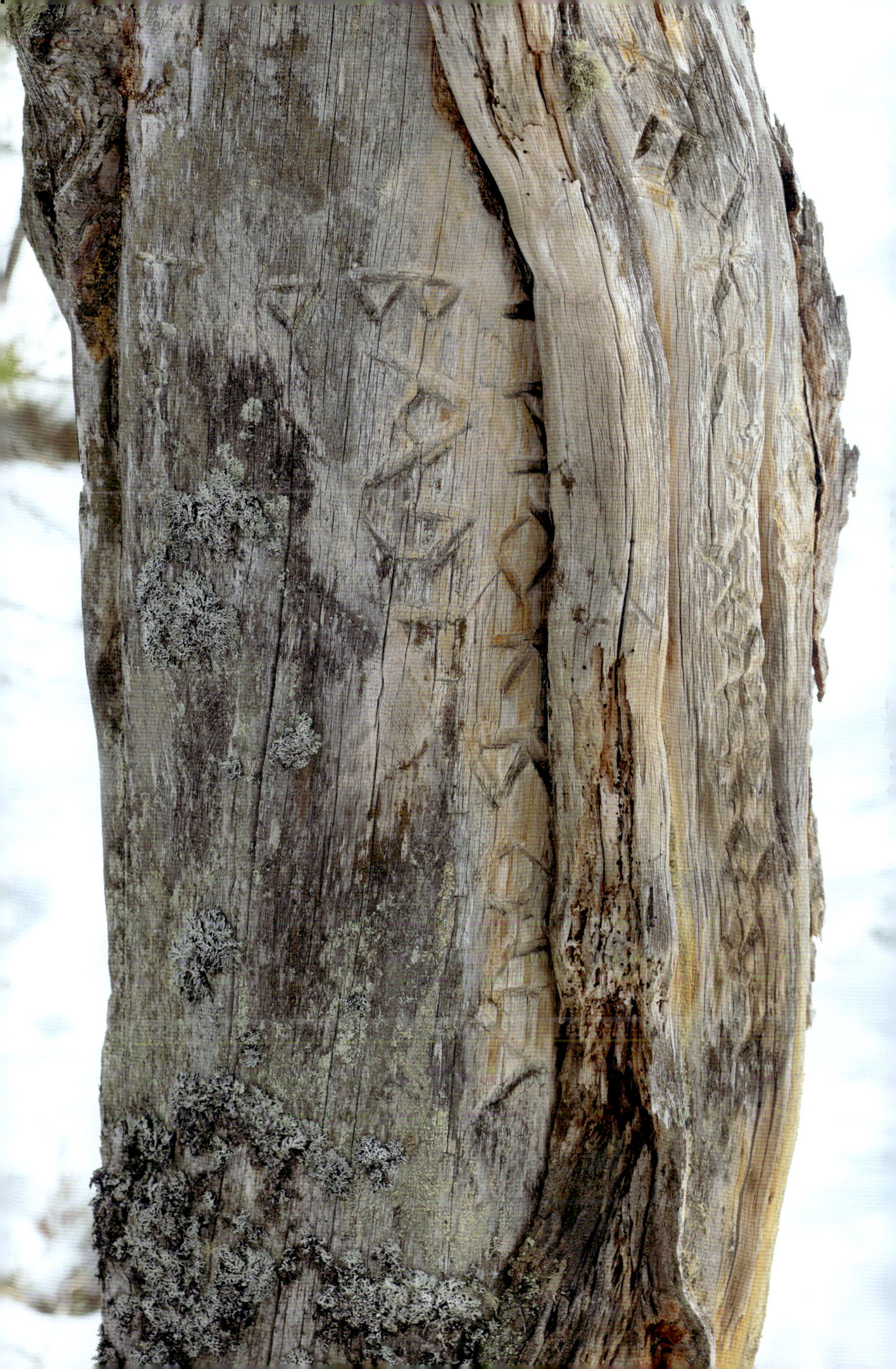

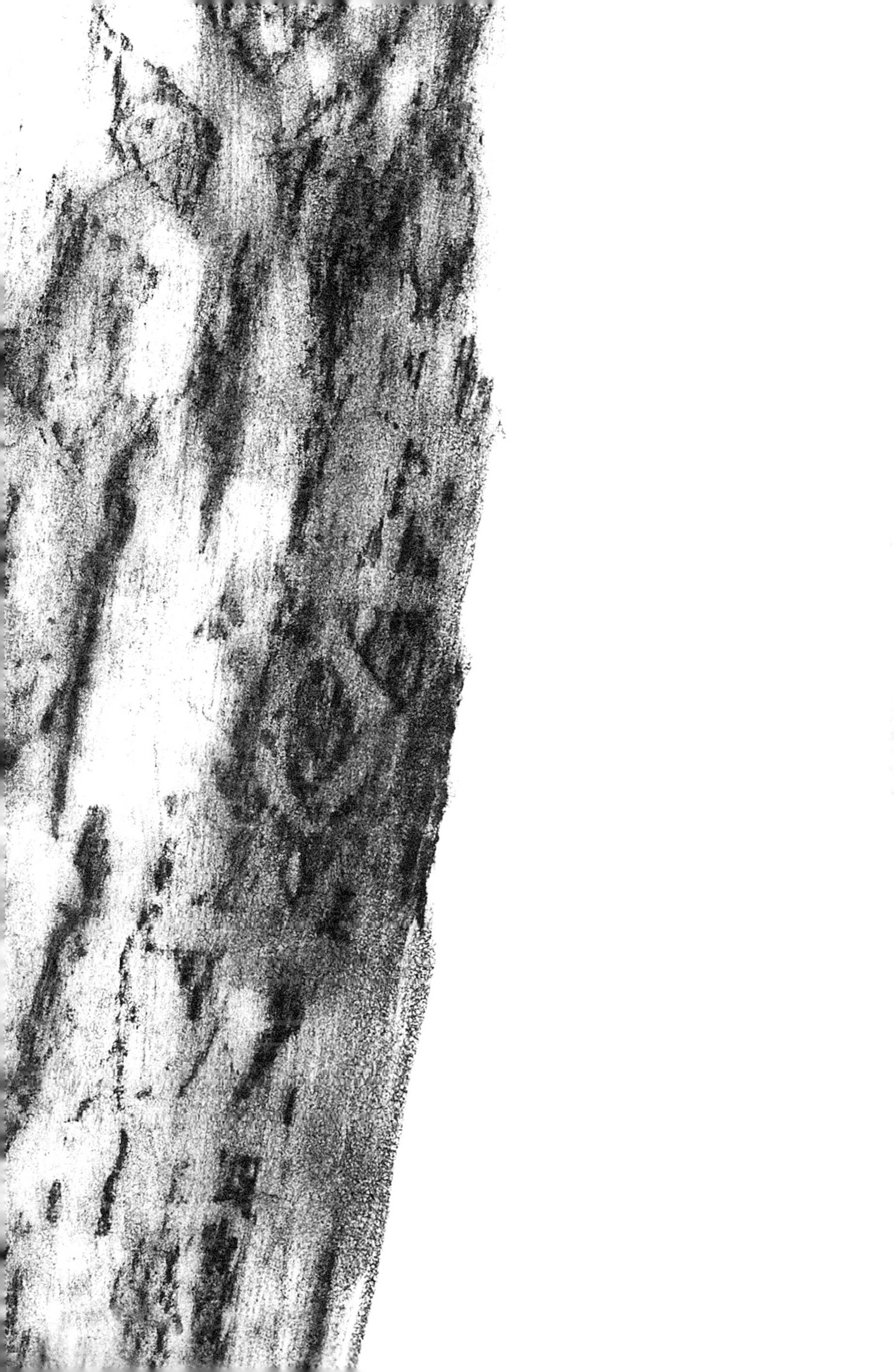

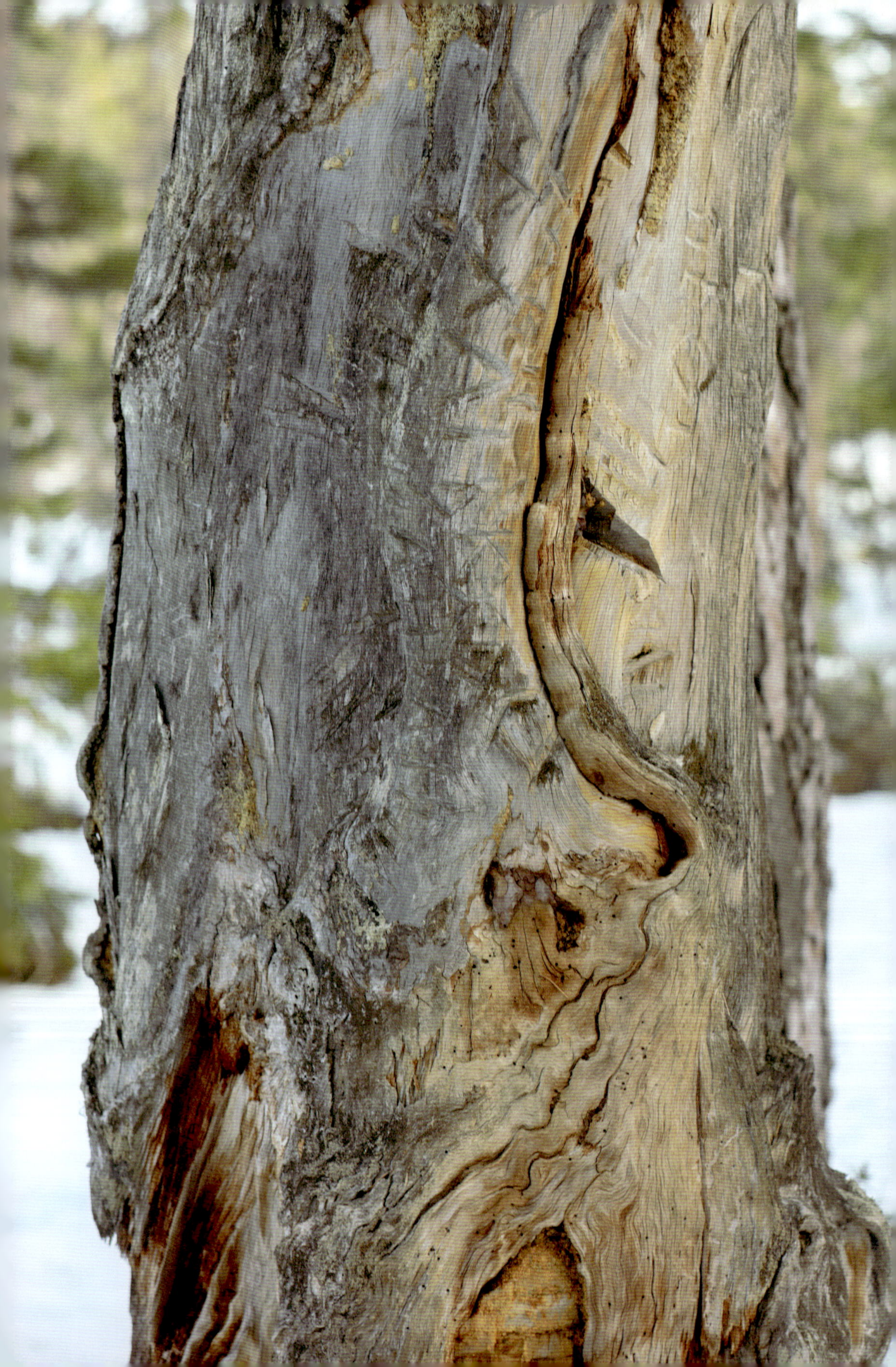

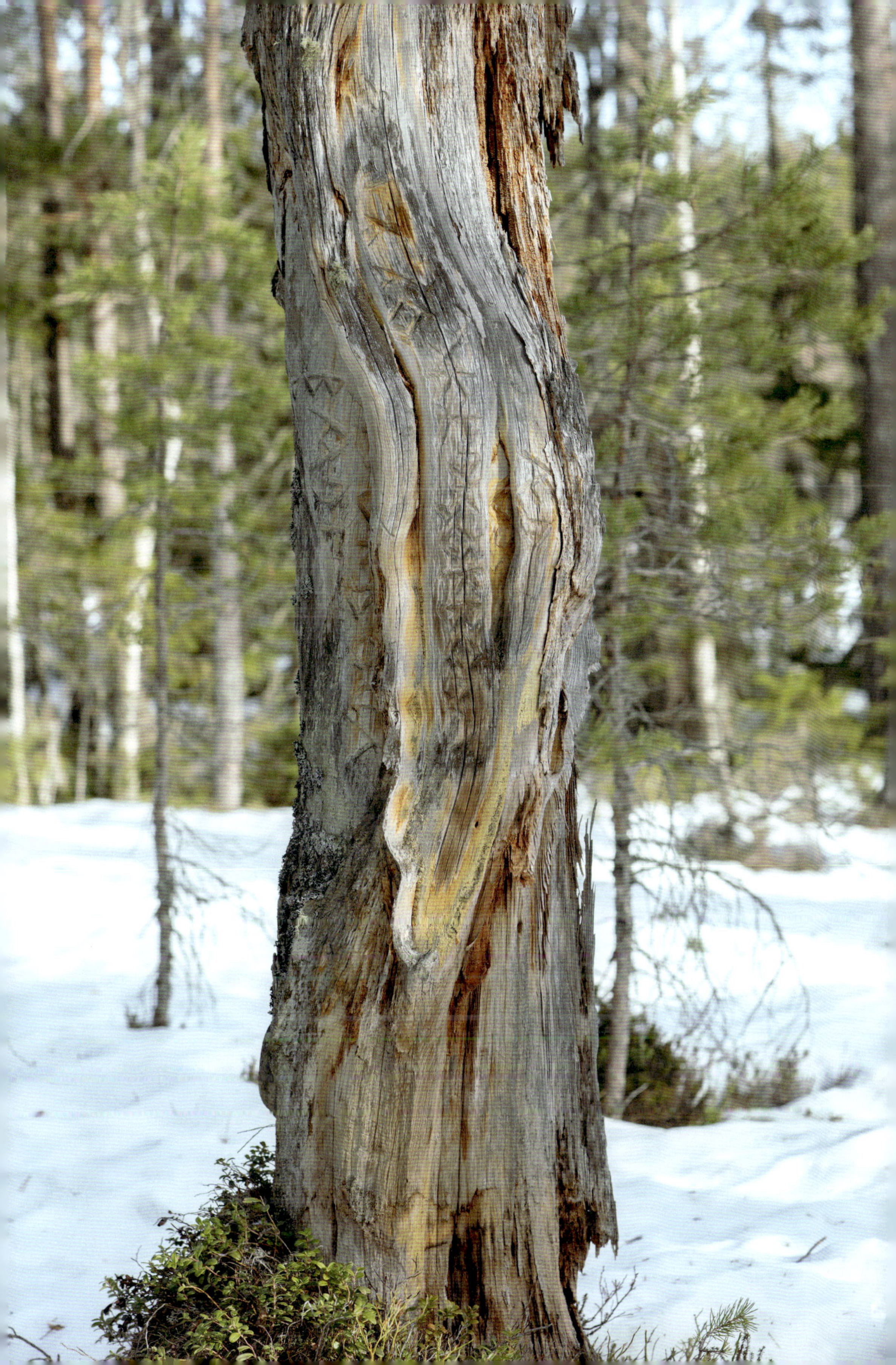

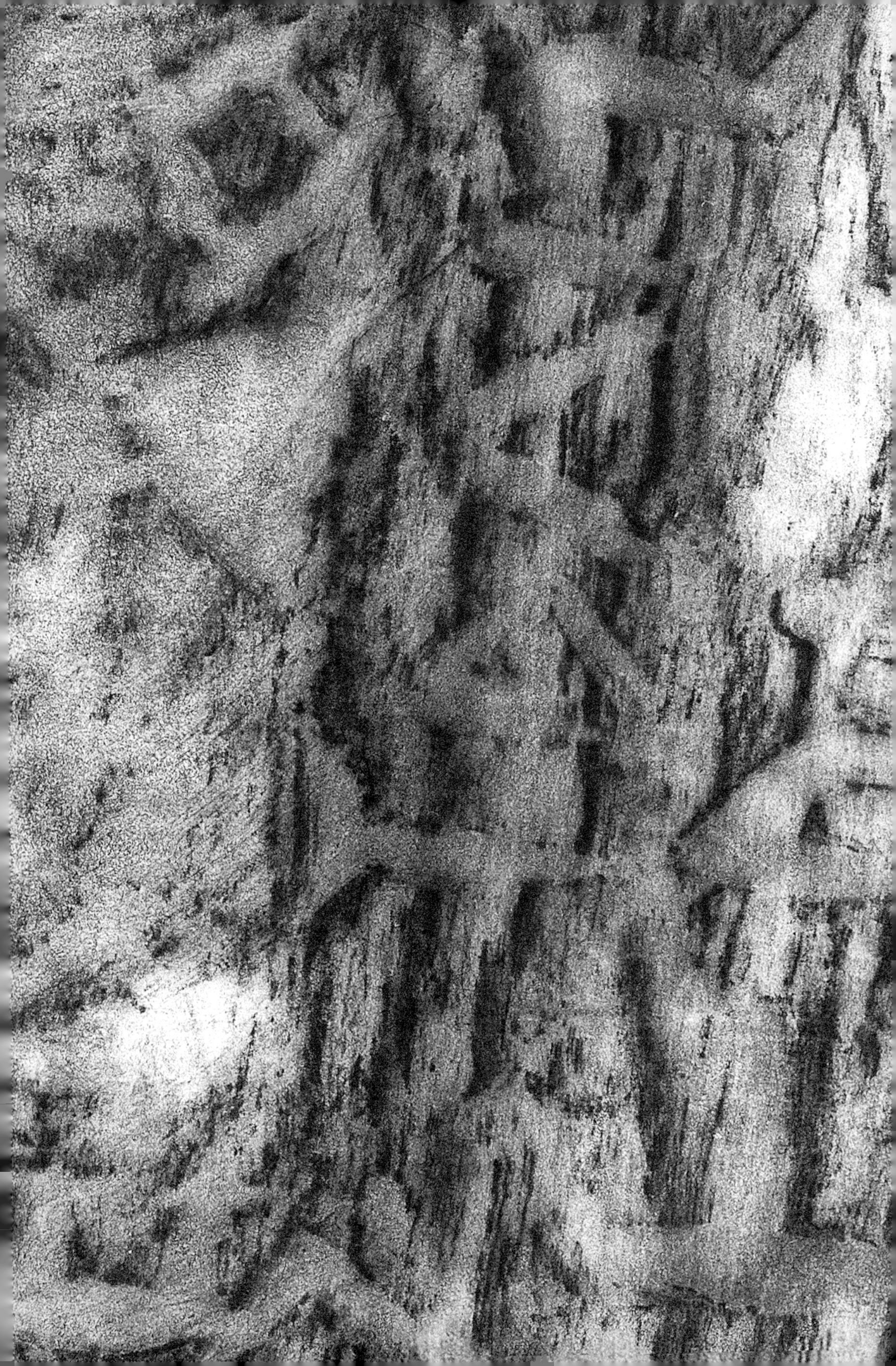

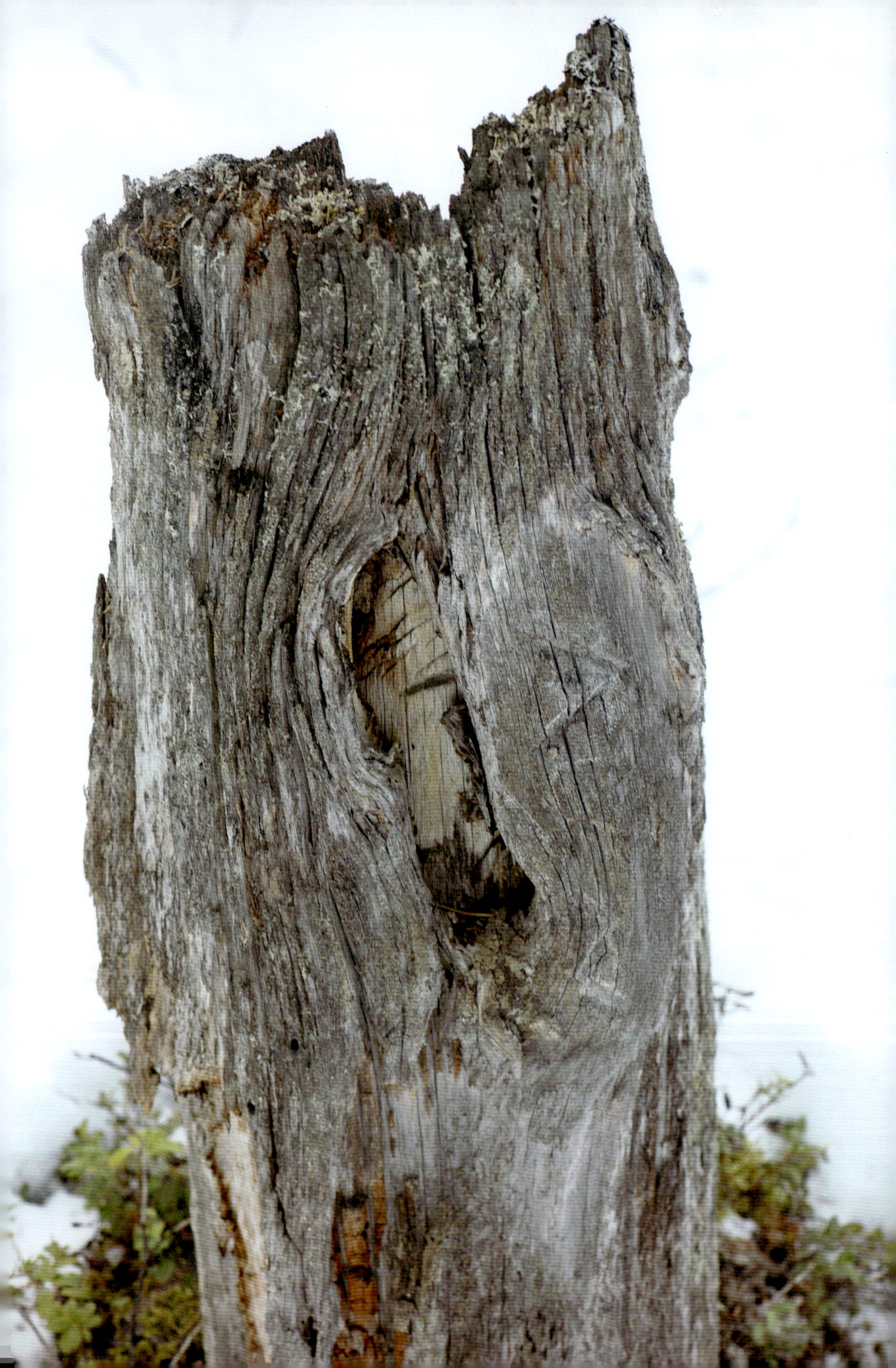

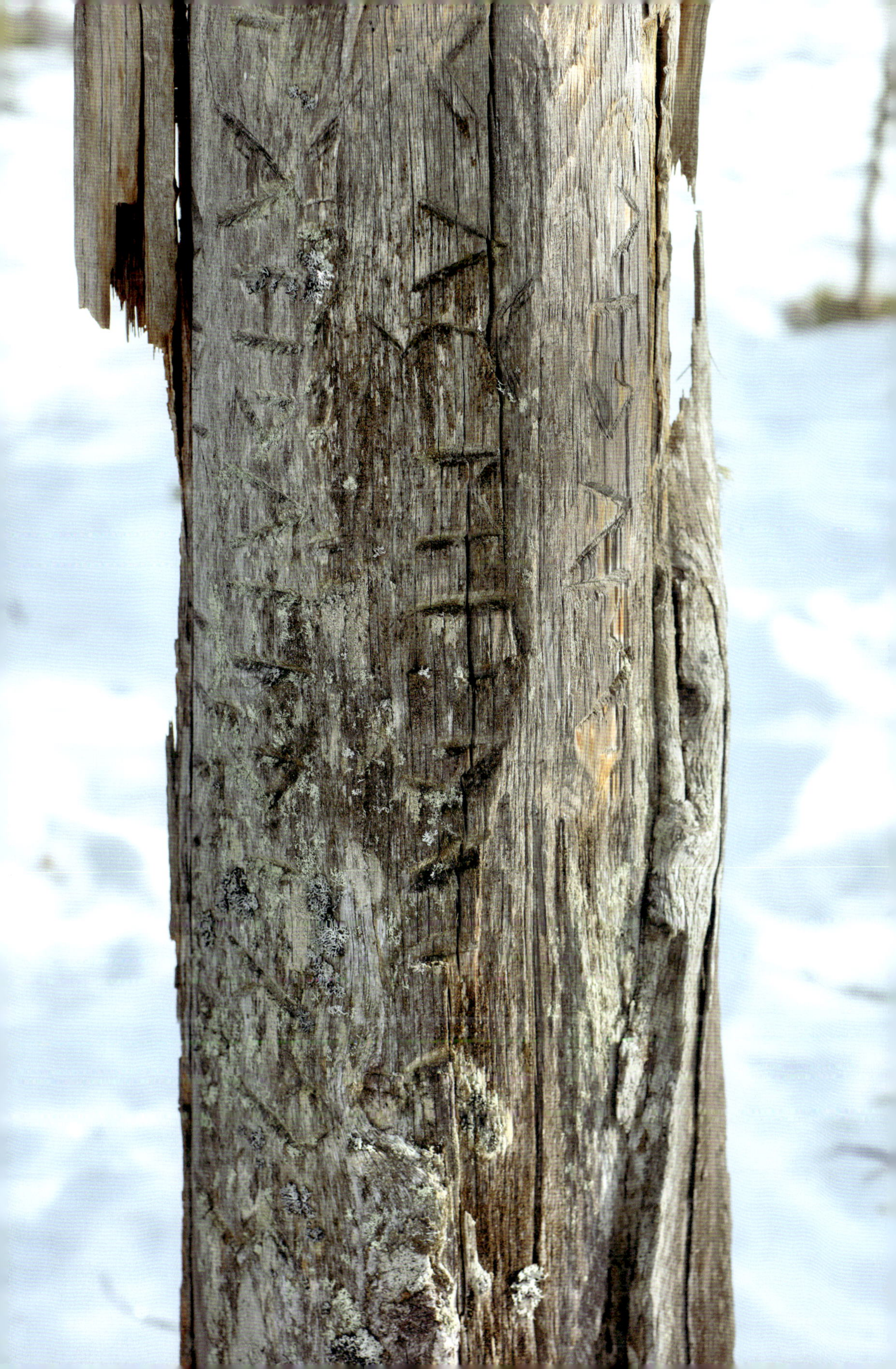

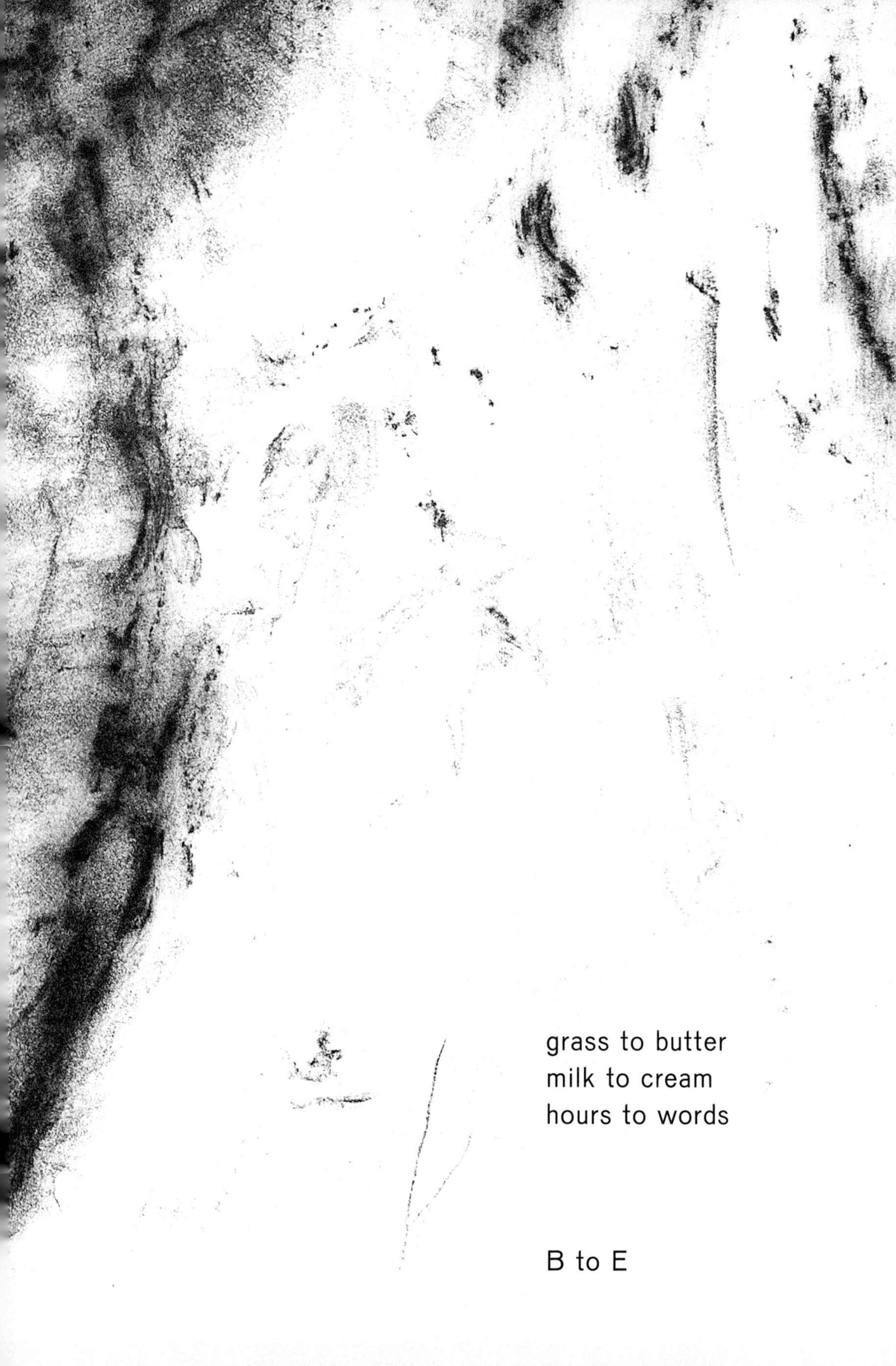

grass to butter
milk to cream
hours to words

B to E

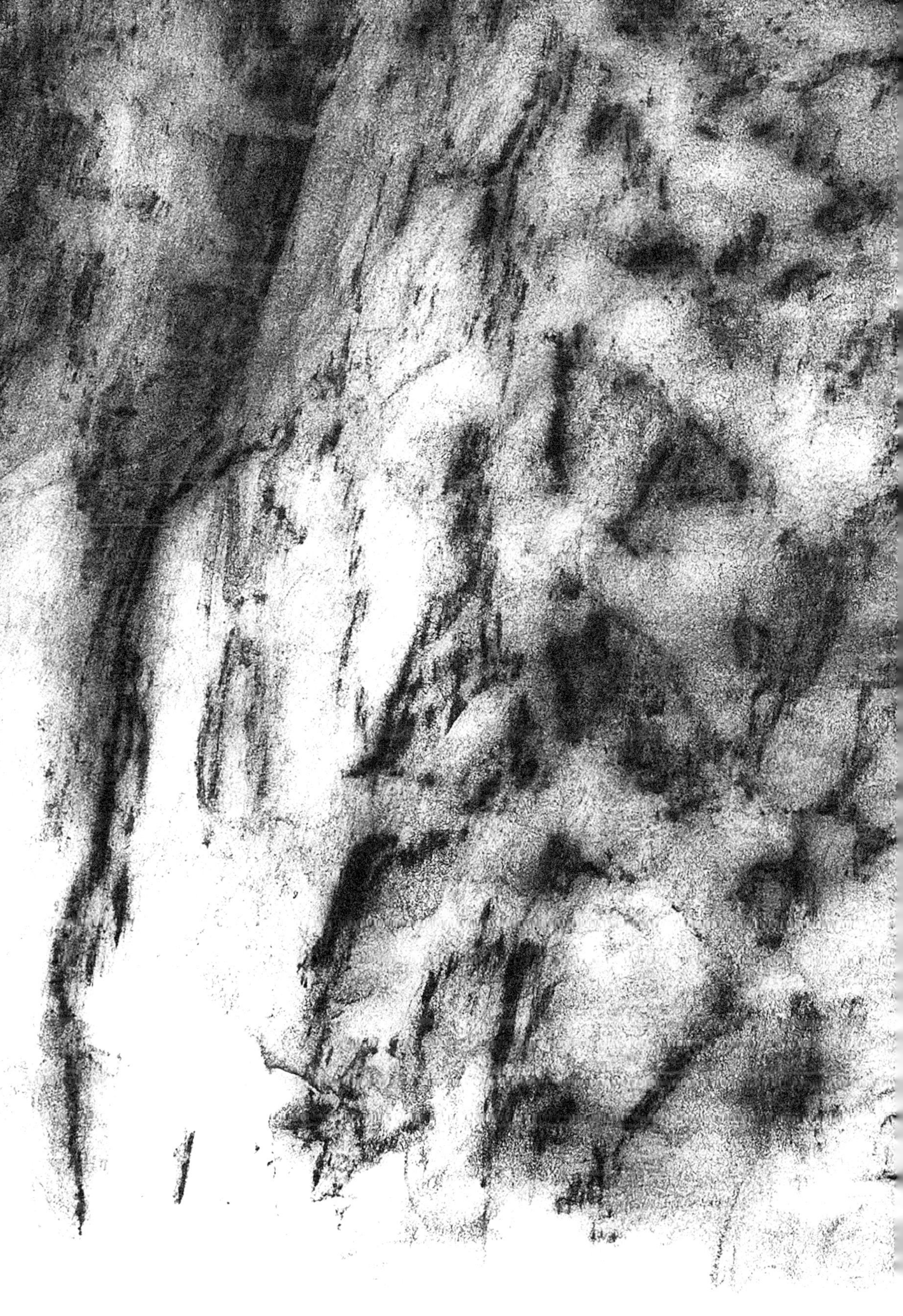

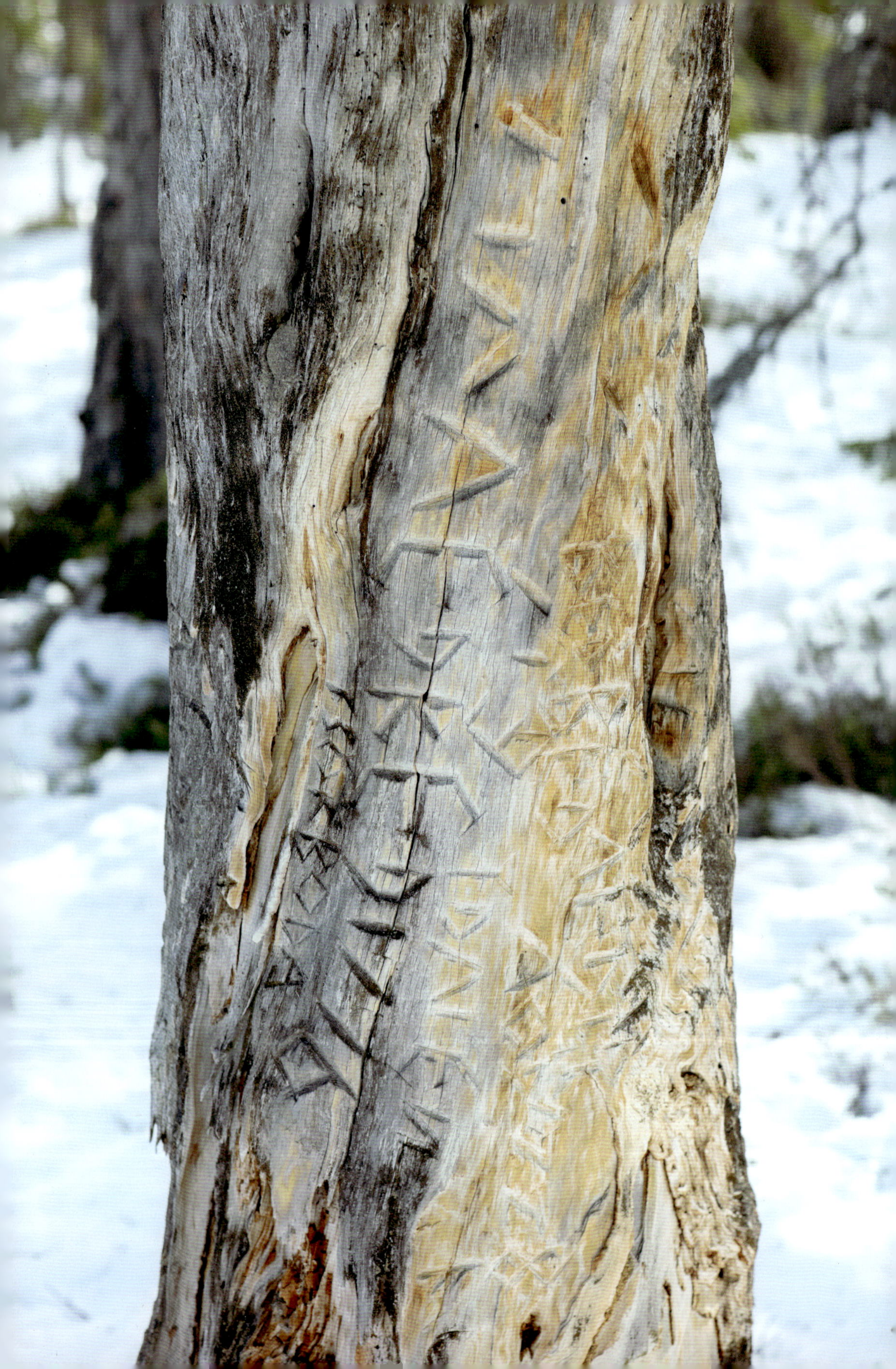